INSIGHT GUIDES
EGYPT

Discovery
CHANNEL

APA PUBLICATIONS
L
Part of the Langenscheidt Publishing Group

INSIGHT GUIDE
EGYPT

Editorial
Project Editor
Dorothy Stannard
Picture Manager
Steven Lawrence

Distribution

United States
Langenscheidt Publishers, Inc.
36–36 33rd Street 4th Floor
Long Island City, NY 11106
Fax: 1 (718) 784 0640

UK & Ireland
GeoCenter International Ltd
Meridian House, Churchill Way West
Basingstoke, Hampshire RG21 6YR
Fax: (44) 1256 817988

Australia
Universal Publishers
1 Waterloo Road
Macquarie Park, NSW 2113
Fax: (61) 2 9888 9074

New Zealand
Hema Maps New Zealand Ltd (HNZ)
Unit 2, 10 Cryers Road
East Tamaki, Auckland 2013
Tel: (64) 9 273 6459
Fax: (64) 9 273 6479

Worldwide
**Apa Publications GmbH & Co.
Verlag KG (Singapore branch)**
38 Joo Koon Road, Singapore 628990
Tel: (65) 6865 1600. Fax: (65) 6861 6438

Printing

Insight Print Services (Pte) Ltd
38 Joo Koon Road, Singapore 628990
Tel: (65) 6865 1600. Fax: (65) 6861 6438

©2009 Apa Publications GmbH & Co.
Verlag KG (Singapore branch)
All Rights Reserved

First Edition 1987
Sixth Edition 2009

ABOUT THIS BOOK

The first Insight Guide pioneered the use of creative full-colour photography in travel guides in 1970. Since then, we have expanded our range to cater for our readers' need not only for reliable information about their chosen des-tination but also for a real under-standing of the culture and workings of that destination. Now, when the internet can supply inexhaustible (but not always reliable) facts, our books marry text and pictures to provide those much more elusive qualities: knowledge and discern-ment. To achieve this, they rely heavily on the authority of locally based writers and photographers.

How to use this book

This book is carefully structured to convey an understanding of Egypt's people and culture, and guides read-ers through its ancient sites, mod-ern resorts and intense capital.

◆ The **Best of Egypt** section at the front of the guide helps you to pri-oritise what you want to do.

◆ The **Features** section, indicated by a pink bar at the top of each page, covers the natural and cultural history of Egypt and includes illumi-nating essays on food and coffee houses, markets and bazaars and popular culture.

◆ The main **Places** section, indi-cated by a blue bar, is a complete guide to all the sights and areas worth visiting. Places of special interest are coordinated by number with the maps.

◆ The **Travel Tips** listings section, with a yellow bar, provides full infor-mation on transport, accommoda-tion, shopping, activities, an A–Z section of essential practical infor-

LEFT: view o[...] Cairo from the Citadel

mation, and handy Arabic phrases. An easy-to-find contents list for Travel Tips is printed on the back flap, which also serves as a bookmark.

◆ The **Photographs** are chosen not only to illustrate the beauty of Egypt's landscape and ancient monuments, but also to convey its cultural diversity.

The contributors

This new edition was commissioned and edited by **Dorothy Stannard**, Insight Guides' Executive Editor and commissioning editor for North Africa and the Middle East.

Like other guides in the series, its production involved a team of expert writers, researchers and photographers, including several long-term residents of Egypt.

Chief among these for this edition was **Sylvie Franquet**, an Arabic scholar who worked in Cairo as a model, translator and tour operator before starting to write on North Africa and the Middle East. As well as writing the essays on Egyptian cuisine and popular culture, Franquet expanded the Places chapters on Middle and Upper Egypt and updated the travel tips section of the guide.

Further updating was completed by **Chris Bradley**, a writer, lecturer and photographer who also specialises in North Africa and the Middle East. Bradley took many of the new images in this edition, and updated the Places chapters on Cairo, Giza, the Oases, Alexandria, Suez, Sinai and the Red Sea. In addition, he supplied new photo features on the Egyptian Museum, Islamic Cairo and the Pyramids.

Bradley has also contributed to Insight guides on Jordan and The Silk Road and written guides to Egypt in the Berlitz series, including *Cairo* and *Egypt's Red Sea Resorts*.

This new edition of *Insight Guide: Egypt* builds on the work of the first edition that was supervised by **John Rodenbeck** when he was the Professor of English and Comparative Literature at the American University in Cairo.

Among the contributors to that first edition whose work is still evident in this guide are **Hisham Youssef**, **Jill Kamil**, **Elizabeth Maynard**, **Max Rodenbeck**, **William Lyster**, **Carina Campobasso**, **Alice Brinton** and **Cassandra Vivian**.

The book was proofread by **Sylvia Suddes** and indexed by **Isobel McLean**.

Map Legend

▬▬ ▪▪	International Boundary
▬ ▬ ▬	Province Boundary
▬ ▪ ▬	National Park/Reserve
▬ ▬ ▬	Ferry Route
⊖	Border Crossing
✈ ✈	Airport: International/Regional
🚌	Bus Station
Ⓜ	Metro
❶	Tourist Information
✉	Post Office
† †	Church/Ruins
∴	Archaeological Site
☪	Mosque
✡	Synagogue
∩	Cave
🗿	Statue/Monument
★	Place of Interest

The main places of interest in the Places section are coordinated by number with a full-colour map (e.g. ❶), and a symbol at the top of every right-hand page tells you where to find the map.

Contents

LEFT: Nileside village,
Upper Egypt.

Travel Tips

LEFT: the Sphinx.
BELOW: a diver descends.

THE BEST OF EGYPT: TOP ATTRACTIONS

At a glance, everthing you can't afford to miss in Egypt, from the emblematic Pyramids to diving among the coral reefs of the Red Sea

△ **Aswan** in Upper Egypt is set on the picturesque First Cataract, where the Nile is scattered with islands such as Elephantine (above). It is a great place to relax, with a superb winter climate. *See page 226.*

▽ The necropolis of Thebes, on the west bank of the Nile at Luxor, is riddled with ancient royal tombs. Among the tombs open to the public in the **Valley of the Kings**, is the Tomb of Ramesses III *(see picture below)*. Also don't miss the wonderfully decorated **Tombs of the Nobles**. *See pages 216 and 219.*

△ The **Temple of Karnak** at Luxor was developed over many centuries. Its massive Hypostyle Hall, is the largest hall of any temple in the world. Its columns are carved with scenes of the pharaohs who built it. See *page 208.*

△ **Cairo's** historic mosques, madrasahs and bazaars nestle below the domes and minarets of the Citadel. *See pages 139–151.*

◁ The **Pyramids of Giza** on the edge of the desert plain west of Cairo are one of the original Seven Wonders of the World. *See page 163.*

△ Egypt's **Red Sea** coral reefs offer some of the best diving and snorkelling in the world. If you don't dive, you can unwind on white sand beaches. *See page 291.*

△ The Temple of Isis at Philae is one of the finest **Ptolemaic temples**. Spectacularly set on Agilqiyyah island, it is approached by boat from Aswan. *See page 241.*

△ There are many ways of enjoying the Nile, but it is hard to beat a **cruise**, either on a modern cruise boat, a dahabeeyah, or a simple felucca. *See page 223.*

◁ The **Temple of Abu Simbel** on the shores of Lake Nasser is one of Egypt's most impressive temples. *See page 246.*

The **Egyptian Museum** in Cairo is ▷ crammed with pharaonic treasures, statues, papyrus, mummies and tomb goods. If you want to learn more about ancient Egypt a visit is highly recommended. *See page 128.*

THE BEST OF EGYPT: EDITOR'S CHOICE

**Setting priorities, unique attractions, top beaches...
here, at a glance, are our recommendations, plus some tips and tricks
even the locals won't always know**

PHARAONIC HIGHLIGHTS

● The Pyramids of Giza
One of the Seven Wonders of the Ancient World, the Pyramids are on the edge of Cairo. Also here are the Sphinx and the Solar Boat Museum. *See page163.*

● Saqqarah
A day-trip from Cairo, Saqqarah is well worth visiting. Its Step Pyramid is the earliest of all the pyramids, and its tombs are among the most finely decorated. *See page 169.*

● Thebes necropolis
Comprising the **Valley of the Kings**, the **Valley of the Queens** and the **Valley of the Nobles**, as well as the various mortuary temples, this vast necropolis on the west coast of the Nile has the greatest concentration of ancient sites in Egypt. Highlights include the **Tomb of Tutankhamun**, the beautifully decorated **Tomb of Nefertari**, and the highly decorated **Tomb of Ramose** in the Valley of the Nobles. *See page 213.*

● Karnak
The splendid Temple of Amun-Ra at Karnak, Luxor, was one of the most important religious and intellectual centres for over 13 centuries. *See page 208.*

● Abu Simbel
The Temple of Ramesses II on Lake Nasser, south of Aswan, is all the more awe-inspiring for being cut into the cliff face. Nearby is the Temple of Queen Nefertari. *See page 246.*

● Edfu
This Ptolemaic temple south of Luxor is dedicated to the falcon god Horus and is one of the best preserved temples. *See page 223.*

● Kom Ombo
This temple dedicated to Sobek the crocodile god and Horus the falcon god is set on a sweeping bend in the Nile 40 km (25 miles) north of Aswan. *See page 224.*

● Philae
Set on the island of Aqliqiyyah, this Ptolemaic temple was moved here stone by stone to escape the waters of Lake Nasser after the creation of the Aswan Dam. *See page 241.*

TOP LEFT: temple pillar in Kom Ombo.
ABOVE: painting in the tomb of Ramesses VI, Valley of the Kings, Thebes.
LEFT: galloping past the Pyramids of Giza.

IMPORTANT CHRISTIAN SIGHTS

● **The churches of Misr al Qadima**
Confusingly called "Old Cairo", this area contains the remains of Roman and early Christian Cairo, including several churches dating from the 4th century. *See pages 135.*

● **The Coptic Museum**
This museum in Old Cairo contains items from early churches all over Egypt. *See page 137.*

● **St Catherine's Monastery**
This fortress monastery in the Sinai was constructed on the orders of the Roman emperor Justinian and contains 6th-century mosaics, silver chests inlaid with precious stones and ancient icons. *See page 286.*

● **The Monasteries of Wadi Natrun**
This handful of ancient monasteries in the Western Desert once numbered 50. *See page 267.*

BEST VIEWS

● **The Pyramids**
Nothing quite matches the view of the Pyramids, even though Cairo's suburbs are near. *See page 163.*

● **The Nile at Aswan**
The views across the First Cataract at Aswan are among the loveliest in Egypt, especially when a felucca or two is floating past. *See page 226.*

● **Gabal Sirbal**
Offers far-reaching views of the Sinai Desert that haven't changed since biblical times. *See page 286.*

● **View from Cairo's Citadel**
Great views of Cairo can be had from the Citadel. Darb al-Ahmar, leading north from the Citadel, offers evocative views of the city's medieval archi-tecture. *See page 144.*

ABOVE: view over the First Cataract from the Old Cataract Hotel, Aswan.
BELOW: the Mosque of Muhammad Ali dominates Cairo's eastern skyline.

MOSQUES AND MADRASAHS

● **Mosque of Ibn Tulun, Cairo**
This mosque dates from 905 and is built in the imperial style of the Abbasid court in Samarra in Iraq. *See page 140.*

● **Sultan Hasan's Madrasah, Cairo**
This 14th-century madrasah is the greatest of the Bahri monuments. Its neighbour, the **Rifa'i Mosque**, is also worth seeing. *See pages 142–3.*

● **Muhammad Ali Mosque, Cairo**
Built in the Ottoman style, this mosque with its slender minarets and dome forms an evocative silhouette on the city's eastern skyline. *See page 145.*

● **Madrasah of Qansuh al Ghuri, Cairo**
The beautiful madrasah and mausoleum of one of the last Mamluk sultans. *See page 149.*

● **Mosque of Amir Aqsunqur, Cairo**
This 17th-century mosque adorned with Damascene tiles is often known as the Blue Mosque. *See page 147.*

● **Mosque of Al-Azhar**
The Al-Azhar was one of the first universities in the world. *See page 149.*

BEST MUSEUMS

● **The Egyptian Museum, Cairo**
This huge collection of Egyptian artifacts is one of Egypt's must-see attractions. Among the many highlights are the Mummy Room and the Treasures of Tutankhamun. *See page 128.*

● **Islamic Art Museum, Cairo**
One of the world's finest collections of Islamic applied arts. *See page 148.*

● **The Coptic Museum, Cairo**
Treasures and relics from churches all over Europe, including the Nag Hammadi Codices, a leather-bound 1,200-page collection of 4th-century Christian texts on papyrus. *See page 137.*

● **The National Museum of Alexandria**
State-of-the-art setting for a superb collection of pharaonic and Greco-Roman artefacts. *See page 258.*

● **Luxor Museum**
Contains a small but high quality collection that is well displayed. *See page 212.*

● **Solar Boat Museum, Giza**
This intriguing museum near the Great Pyramid contains the reconstructed cedar-wood funerary boat of Khufu, excavated in 1954. *See page 166.*

BELOW: papyrus figure of Anubis, the Egyptian Museum.
RIGHT: one of the Treasures of Tutankhamun, the Egyptian Museum, Cairo.

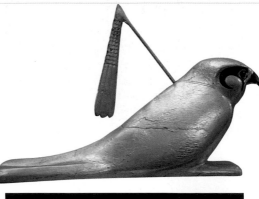

REST AND RELAXATION

● **The Red Sea**
The coral reefs of the Red Sea are among the world's top diving sites. **Sharm al-Shaykh** on the coast of Sinai and **Hurghadah** on the coast of the Eastern Desert are the best known resorts. *See pages 288, and 294.*

● **Aswan**
Built on the banks of the First Cataract, Aswan enjoys one of the loveliest settings in Egypt. Experience it from the terrace of the Old Cataract Hotel or take a felucca cruise to Kitchener's island. *See page 226.*

● **Luxor**
With its wealth of pharaonic tombs and temples, Luxor offers most for active, culture-loving visitors. But it also has a lovely setting, good hotels and a superb winter climate and is a great spot for bird-watching. *See page 205.*

● **Nile Cruise**
Sit on the sun-deck and watch the specacle of Egypt slide past. Also consider a cruise on a *dahabeeyah*, a 19th-century sailing boat equipped with mod-cons which offers a more intimate and romantic experience than the floating hotels. *See page 310.*

ABOVE: exploring the colourful coral reefs of the Red Sea.

BEST ATMOSPHERE

- **Cairo's Coffee Houses**
Café culture is especially vibrant in Cairo. Among the more atmospheric venues try Cafe Riche on Tala'at Harb where Gamal abdel Nasser plotted the revolution. *See page 157.*
- **Historic hotels**
The Old Cataract in Aswan and the Winter Palace in Luxor have bags of character. Even if you don't stay in them, visit their terraces for afternoon tea – perhaps travelling along the corniche by caleche, a horse-drawn carriage.

- **Sound and Light Shows**
These take place in Luxor, Philae, Abu Simbel and The Pyramids. In spite of the hammy actorial voices, dramatic use of music and lighting do bring the monuments to life in a unique way.
- **Felucca trips**
A late afternoon felucca cruise in Luxor or Aswan is one of the best ways of experiencing the magic of the Nile. Lean back on the cushions, enjoy the breeze and sip a glass of mint tea brewed by the captain's mate. *See page 311.*

BEST SUQS AND BEST BUYS

- **Khan al Khalili Bazaar, Cairo**
This labyrinthine bazaar remains the best place to buy copperware, silver, gold and amber jewellery, and other souvenirs.
See page 150.
- **Shari' al-Muski**
To get away from tourist-oriented goods and to immerse yourself in local commerce join the throng along this street near the Khan al Khalili. Early evening is one of the best times to come. *See page 149.*
- **Pharaonic replicas**
Alabaster statuettes, sphinxes, cats, etc abound, but for top quality visit the shop in the Egyptian Museum, Cairo. *See page 128.*
- **Papyrus**
You will find hand-painted papyrus, often replicating tomb paintings, in any souvenir shop, but the best quality and choice is found at Dr Ragab's Papyrus Institute. *See page 154.*

- **Cotton**
Egypt is renowned for its high quality cotton, but much of it is exported. For good quality *galabiyas* and kaftans, visit the more upmarket shops of Cairo, Luxor and the Red Sea resorts.
- **Tapestries and carpets**
For brightly coloured cushion covers, bedspreads and wall-hangings visit the Silk Merchants' Bazaar in Cairo *(page 145).* For attractive rugs and wall-hangings visit the Wissa Wassef tapestry workshops in the weaving village of Harraniyyah near the Pyramids.
See page 168.

LEFT: an evening *felucca* cruise.
BELOW: lamp in the Kahn al Khalili Bazaar, Cairo.

TRAVELERS' TIPS

- **Visas** One-month tourist visas are issued on the spot upon arrival in Cairo or Luxor. These are cheaper than visas issued from an Egyptian consulate abroad and don't usually involve too much hassle.
- **City Transport** Taxis are very cheap and readily available and are usually the best way to get around. However, the taxis that congregate outside hotels tend to charge more, so it is best to walk a few blocks and hire one on the street.
- **Sleepers between Cairo and Upper Egypt** The first-class deluxe sleeper is the best bet, but it should be booked in advance, preferably by a few days and even longer if you are travelling on a national holiday. Go in person to the railway station on Maydan Ramesses in Cairo.

- **Evening visiting** Some monuments, especially in Upper Egypt, are open until quite late in the evening, when temperatures are cooler and the sites are much quieter.

THE SPELL OF EGYPT

Egypt is the Nile, and the Nile is Egypt, or so
the saying goes. But there is much more to
this ancient land than that ...

The Land of the Nile has long exercised a potent spell over ordinary people. Egypt – or someone's idea of it – has inspired poetry and literature, and styles in everything from Western architecture to paper packaging.

Egypt has even influenced Western ways in matters of life and death, often grotesquely so. Interest in mummified flesh, for example, arose when word spread in medieval times about the therapeutic value of powdered *mumia* in the treatment of ailments. By the 16th century, mummies so fascinated visitors to Egypt that an active trade in their desiccated flesh began. Ancient burial grounds were dug up, mummies were stripped of their coverings and sent piecemeal to the apothecaries of Europe.

The search for antiquities

Descriptive accounts and attractive sketches of Egypt made in the 18th century joined with a trickle of small objects – scarabs, amulets, and a multitude of fakes – excited interest in Egypt as a source of the "primitive", a search for which was one of the century's preoccupations. Napoleon's expedition to Egypt, with assorted savants, who recorded the various antiquities along the Nile, took place largely in response to this new fashion.

One event that particularly captured English imagination in 1821 was the opening of the Egyptian Hall in London as a museum of "natural curiosities". On display were the latest finds, casts and sketches by the Italian Giovanni Belzoni, who had cleared the Temple of Abu Simbel and shipped tonnes of treasures back to England.

The event that attracted world attention, however, was Howard Carter's discovery of Tutankhamun's tomb in 1922. The 5,000 works of art discovered in the tomb were widely publicised. Thousands of sightseers flocked to Egypt and made their way to the Valley of the Kings. When the treasures toured the world in the 1960s and '70s, the number of people wanting to visit Egypt skyrocketed. Tour companies began devising affordable package tours and Nile cruises were no longer the preserve of the rich and cultured. ❏

PRECEDING PAGES: the Ptolemaic Temple of Edfu, Upper Egypt; life in the Sinai desert; festival tent, Cairo. **LEFT:** the Nile at Aswan.
FROM TOP: view from the Citadel; image on a lantern; statue of Ramesses II.

THE EGYPTIANS

Egyptians are said to be humble, pious, mischievous and extremely hospitable but the people of every region have their own defining characteristics. They mostly bear poverty with good grace, while hoping for better things

When God created the nations, so Arab wisdom has it, he endowed each with two counterbalanced qualities: to the intelligence of the Syrians he thus added fatuousness; to Iraq he gave pride, but tempered it with hypocrisy; while for the desert Arabs he compensated hardship with good health. And Egypt he blessed with abundance at the cost of humility.

It does not require a deep understanding of the past to feel that, as far as Egypt is concerned, God has withdrawn the first half of his covenant – or that, at any rate, he has made a new deal with the desert dwellers. As any Egyptian will explain, it is not many generations since Egyptian donations fed the poor of the holy cities of Mecca and Medina, in what is now Saudi Arabia. To the desert Arabs, however, God has given abundance, in the form of oil, while Egypt, formerly the land of plenty, has suffered unaccustomed hardship, in the forms of war and overpopulation.

Egyptian humility takes many forms. One is a tragic sense of life, arising from a tragic view of history. While the West embraces the idea of progress as a solution to all man's ills, the Egyp-

Naguib Mahfouz encapsulated the Egyptians' tragic sense of life when he wrote:"Life is wise to deceive us, for had it told us from the start what it had in store for us, we would refuse to be born."

tians have an impulse to turn towards a utopian past, perhaps to a time when Muhammad's successors, the four Rightly Guided Caliphs, brought justice, prosperity and true belief to the land.

LEFT: looking out over the mother of the world.
RIGHT: city barber.

The humiliating defeat suffered by Egypt in the 1967 war would have brought on a revolution in another country. Yet when President Nasser, in an emotional speech, offered to resign, the response was dramatic: millions of Egyptians poured into the streets demanding that he stay. His willingness to share their humiliation brought forth instant sympathy from the masses, who saw it as more important that his intentions had been morally right than that he had failed to realise them.

Islam and popular piety

Any visitor to Egypt will be struck by the piety of its people. Humility is inherent in the very word Islam, the religion of nine-tenths of Egyptians. Islam (from the Arabic roots *salima*, to be safe;

aslama, to surrender and *salaam*, peace) means "submission", whether it be to God, fate or the social system framed by the Qur'an.

Many Muslims do not go to the mosque or pray five times a day, but the majority believe in a supreme deity and the imminence of the Day of Judgement. The dawn-to-dusk fast during Ramadan is officially observed by the entire country, a sign of Islam's pervasiveness. And many Egyptian tastes, habits, and preferences are referred directly back to the Qur'an.

The Coptic Christians, too, conscious of being members of one of the earliest Christian sects, maintain a degree of devoutness that often bewilders Westerners. Religious expressions of a kind that have almost vanished from European speech proliferate in everyday language. "God willing", "By God's permission", "Praise God" and "Our Lord prevails" are as common as the word "Goodbye" is in English. The proper response to the greeting *Salam aleikum* (Peace be upon you) is *Aleikum as-salam wa rahmat Allah wa barakatu* (Upon you be peace and the mercy of God and his blessings).

Apart from piety, however, this exchange also reflects a point of etiquette – any greeting must be followed by a response that outdoes the other in politeness. Religiosity, though abundant, is not always heartfelt.

THE POWER OF THE WORD

Many Westerners find perplexing the continuing dominance of Islam in what purports to be an age of reason. The important thing to recognise is that Muslims believe the Qur'an – literally, a "recitation" – is the word of God as directly transmitted by the Prophet Muhammad. The power of the Word thus has a strength in Islam that is unmatched by the literature of any other "revealed" religion; and the beauty of the Qur'an, which is by definition "inimitable", is cited as a miracle in its own right. For this reason translations of the Qur'an are considered vastly inferior and all Muslims are urged to read the Qur'an in Arabic. For non-Arabic speakers, a 2008 translation by Tarif Khalidi (Penguin) is considered to be one of the best.

Jests, gibes and practical jokes

Egyptian piety is balanced by a deep love of mischief. If anything can compete in public esteem with holiness, it is wit; Egyptian humour holds nothing sacred. Political jokes are particularly sharp and irreverent, but the smallest incident can provoke laughter. In a café or bar, wisecracks are fired back and forth with increasing hilarity until the whole company falls off its chair.

Some intellectuals have remarked that, while the condition that formulates much of Western behaviour is a sense of guilt, arising from an individual "conscience", in the East it is shame, arising from a sense of public disapproval or contempt. Egyptian children, raised with the idea that whatever you can get away with socially is morally permissible,

For many, belief in the supernatural extends beyond orthodoxy to a world of genies and spirits of the dead. Fertility rites are still held in Upper Egyptian temples, and magicians, witches and fortune-tellers do a brisk trade in spells and potions.

than hard labour and careful planning. It is a habit of mind that even President Mubarak castigates in his fellow citizens. Although much of it can be attributed to overcrowding and a faulty educational system, the degree of cheating in Egyptian schools and universities is scandalous.

must rank among the world's naughtiest. Historically, Egyptian mischievousness has its roots in the legacy of centuries of repressive government. Numerous are the stories that celebrate the victory, through a mix of cunning and trickery, of the poor *fellah* (peasant) over pashas or foreigners.

Coercion and conformity

Egyptians are generally not trustful of one another, believing that only by overt pressure can people be prevented from overstepping the bounds of morality. This explains, more than political exigencies, the heavy police presence in the country. Belief in the need for coercion and forced restraint

This love of trickery has its drawbacks, as the 15th-century Egyptian historian Al Maqrizi noted in an unflattering portrayal of his countrymen: "That which dominates in the character of the Egyptians is the love of pleasure... They are extremely inclined to cunning and deceit."

Maqrizi notes, among other things, that the Egyptians of his time showed a distinct disdain for study. This indifference, it must be said, is very pronounced to this day, and most evident in a tendency to attempt to achieve goals by means other

LEFT: man with a prayer bruise, a conspicuous sign of piety. **LEFT:** a Christian in Coptic Cairo displays penance with chains for self-flagellation. **ABOVE:** a smiling bride.

is strengthened by religious attitudes. It is commonly presumed that without the just guidance of Islam, society would fall apart.

Attitudes to sex are framed by the same phenomenon. It is believed that men – and women – cannot resist the temptations of sex. Sex is not only openly discussed by both men and women, but also lurks on the edges of ordinary conversation. Since the Arabic language itself is full of sexual innuendoes, its richness lends a wonderful bawdiness to Egyptian talk.

The mazes of matrimony

Marriage, however, is deemed an absolute prerequisite for sex, as well as for full adulthood and respectability. Among women, whose freedom is still very much limited by rigid social norms, finding and keeping the right husband is the major focus of life. Since the 1920s substantial progress towards equality of the sexes has been made, but it is still the rule for a girl to remain in the care of her father until the day she is passed into the care of her husband.

Respect for parents and elders is so strongly ingrained that it is uncommon for even a male child to leave home before marriage. Things are gradually changing in Cairo, but few urban males can afford to marry much before the age of 30. Despite Islam's flexibility on the subject – easy divorce and polygamy are both sanc-

tioned – marriage is regarded as a binding agreement, made more absolute by economics. For this reason, couples are expected to work out every detail of their future life together before signing the contract.

"Money and children," the Qur'an says, "are the embellishments of life." Egyptians adore children, and large families are the norm. The family is more important than the individual as a social unit, extending not only over several generations but also to distant cousins. The fierce vendettas that still rage in Upper Egypt, often claiming dozens of lives over many decades, illustrate this point. Family honour and prestige are serious mat-

ters. The crime columns regularly tell of adultery-related murders: a woman's honour, it is said, "is like a matchstick: it can only be used once".

In the cities, political and business alliances are often reinforced through marriage. Because numerous children enlarge a family's potential for wealth and influence, and also because it is considered healthier for children to grow up with lots of siblings, the family planners have had a hard time bringing down the birth rates.

Egyptian mothers are notoriously soft on their children. Centuries of high infant mortality, sexual roles that give housebound wives complete responsibility for children, and lingering belief in the power of the evil eye mean that mothers are inclined to cater to their child's every whim for fear that some harm may befall him or her. This is particularly true in the case of boys. It is not uncommon, in fact, for a woman's strongest emotional tie to be with her eldest son rather than her husband. As infants, children are swaddled and doted upon. By the time they can walk, however, they are often left to spend time as they wish. This unorthodox combination of coddling and freedom is often cited as a reason for the self-confidence and even obstinacy of the Egyptian character.

Life-support systems

Beyond the family, Egyptians have a strong attachment to their immediate community. Village solidarity – when not torn apart by blood feuds – is very strong. In the big towns the *hara* (alley) is the main unit of social bonding. The main function of *hara* solidarity is to defend the interests of the community. Gangs of toughs, whose mandate varied from protection of neighbourhood women to simple extortion rackets, formed part of the urban landscape until quite recently.

Regional loyalties persist strongly, too. Each major town and province has its acknowledged characteristic, from Alexandria in the north to Aswan in the south. Alexandrians are known chiefly for their toughness and willingness to fight, but also noted for their cosmopolitan outlook and business acumen. The farmers of Lower Egypt and the Delta are regarded as hardworking, thrifty and serious. Rashidis, from Rosetta, are supposed to be kind-hearted, while Dumyatis, from Damietta at the Nile's eastern mouth, are said to be untrustworthy.

Cairenes, like New Yorkers or cockneys, are seen as slick, fast-talking and immoral. Simply being from the capital allows them to sneer at less sophisticated compatriots, a Cairene habit that their country cousins dislike.

The Saidi people of Upper Egypt are considered to be simple-minded and impulsive and will even joke about these traits themselves. On the positive side, Saidis are noted for their generosity, their courage, virility and sense of honour.

The dark-skinned Nubians of the far south, an ancient people with their own languages, are considered to be the most gentle and peaceful of Egyptians. Long isolated by the cataracts that

LEFT: everything stops for prayer on a busy Cairo street. **ABOVE RIGHT:** the tombs of holy men, or sheikhs, are popular places of pilgrimage.

> *Some reputations are universal: the tough, cosmopolitan character of Alexandrians is one that is attributed to the inhabitants of most port cities.*

made the Nile above Aswan impassable, Nubian life, relaxed and carefree, had a unique charm. Nubian villages are spotlessly clean, the spacious mud-brick houses always freshly painted, and both men and women are apt to be more enterprising than their Egyptian neighbours.

The desert Bedu have not given up their ancient

occupation of smuggling, and fierce tribal loyalty is still maintained. The Bedu are feared, scorned and envied for their aristocratic wilfulness. The old rivalry between these free-wheeling bandits of the desert and the hardworking peasants of the valley has all but died out, but their pure Arab blood and the beauty of their women are still admired.

Pride and prejudice

This catalogue of accepted regional differences obscures an essential homogeneity of attitudes and feelings, however. Despite differences and despite the bitter legacy of imperialism – of defeat, occupation and dependence – pride in Egypt and "the Egyptian way" is fervent. The purpose of all allegiances, from the family to the neighbourhood to the region to the nation and even beyond, is to prevent being pushed around.

It is characteristic of the Egyptians that they prefer compromise to conflict. By inclination, habit and training, Egyptians are tactful and diplomatic, sometimes to the point of obsequiousness. Forms of address are complex and varied, as befits a highly stratified society. A taxi driver may be addressed as "O Chief Engineer" or "O Foreman". (Note that, when sitting in a taxi, one is a temporary guest, not merely a fare, so it is insulting for a lone male passenger to sit in the back seat by himself.) A person of high social standing should be addressed as "Your

> *An old Arab adage serves to illustrate the pride in Egypt and all things Egyptian: "I and my brothers against my cousins, I and my cousins against my tribe, and I and my tribe against the world."*

millionaires, and for a time in the late 1970s poverty-stricken Egypt was importing more Mercedes cars than any other country in the world. On Cairo's streets today the contrast between the elegance of imported luxury and the rolling slum of a packed bus is particularly shocking.

Presence", while a person of respectable but indeterminate standing is "O President" or "O Professor". An older person is "O Teacher" or "O Pilgrim", the latter referring of course to someone who has made the pilgrimage to Mecca. Even Turkish titles – bey, pasha, *hanem* – survive, though they have no legal standing, and are used for courtesy's sake.

This diversity underlines the cohesiveness of the society rather than its disparateness: Egyptians see all men as equals, but allots to each a specific status and with it a role.

Making do

As in many other developing countries, sharp disparities of wealth exist. There are some 50,000

After years of economic restructuring, urban Egyptians generally are poorer than they were in 1958, and although life for rural people has improved they, too, are poorer today than in the early 1980s. In 2005 it was estimated that 29 percent of the population was illiterate.

Open doors, closed options

Materialist ostentation became rife after the mid-1970s, when President Sadat reversed 20 years of socialist legislation with his Open Door policy. Before him, Nasser had worked to redistribute the country's wealth, parcelling out the great feudal estates, seizing the property of the richest families and reinvesting it in new state industries. Nasser's policies brought dignity to the majority at the expense of the few, but also frightened off private initiative. Not many landlords bothered even to paint their houses, for fear of attracting the tax man. With the Open Door policy, the lid was abruptly removed; and luxury imports boomed as money came out of Swiss banks or from under the floorboards.

Allowing people who were underpaid at home to work profitably abroad, the Open Door policy brought improved living standards in the form of more cars, better clothing and a richer diet. It also inflated expectations and undermined social cohesiveness, something that President Mubarak's economic reforms, stressing private initiative, have exacerbated. Neither the poor nor the old elites approve of today's nouveaux riches.

A country without dreams is a depressing place. The primary condition of Egypt – too many people – doesn't help.The population pyramid looms menacingly on the horizon – it was estimated at just under 82 million in 2008, of which 26 million were under 14 years of age. Schools in Cairo already operate three shifts.

The products of a school system that stifles curiosity and promotes learning by rote, more and more young Egyptians feel a sense of frustration regarding the future. Among men, those who do not go on to university or manage to obtain an exemption must face three years of military service, often under conditions of extreme hardship. In the bigger cities, many younger women find jobs before marriage, but the majority stay at home and hope for the best. Better prospects await the one in 10 young Egyptians of both sexes who attend university, but the country's dozen institutions of higher learning are appallingly overcrowded, understaffed and disorganised.

New anxieties

Low pay and a general loathing for the bureaucracy has meant that government jobs have lost most of their prestige. Increasingly one finds university graduates working as taxi drivers, plumbers, mechanics and the like. The money is better and tradesmen stand a likelier chance of saving in order to get married, though with inflation and the limited availability of decent apartments, many are obliged to scrimp for years before they can establish a household.

Universally aspired to in Egypt, marriage pro-

vides no passport to a life of ease. The average lifespan is 74 for women and 69 for men, but many Egyptians appear to die of worry or grief before they reach the stage when they require medical care. Money, in particular, causes endless anxieties; feeding, educating and underwriting the marriages of children is not cheap, especially when respectability must be maintained. While families and neighbourhoods provide a degree of support unimaginable in the West, they also eliminate privacy; and even the smallest problems become everybody's business.

The housing shortage means that too many people are often cooped up in the same house, and

LEFT: newly finished chairs get an airing.
ABOVE RIGHT: there is no such thing as precarious.

A LITTLE LIGHT WORK

Until relatively recently, the government followed a policy of providing guaranteed employment for every university graduate. The result of this policy is that the Egyptian bureaucracy and the public-sector industry, which together employ half of the country's non-agricultural workforce, is catastrophically overstaffed. Astonishingly, studies have shown that an average government employee actually only works for between six and 30 minutes a day. Low salaries and lenient employment policies have encouraged apathy and abuse at every level – with obstruction, absenteeism and corruption rampant, and matched by intolerable rudeness to the taxpayer who ultimately foots the bill.

there are some districts of Cairo where the average density is three to a room. With more than 25,000 people per square kilometre, Cairo is one of the most densely populated urban agglomerations in the world. Cairo has a similar population to Paris, but on a surface area nine times smaller.

Compensations

An atmosphere of melancholy pervades life but, strangely enough, the salient characteristic of the Egyptians is their cheerfulness. They are past masters at coping. All problems and situations are so endlessly discussed and analysed that they end by becoming mere topics of amusement. The tales of intrigue, frustrated love, good fortune or catastrophe that even the simplest people in this country relate in connection with their own personal lives retain a quality of wonder reminiscent of *One Thousand and One Nights*. Everyone has a story.

The protective structure of society, based on the strength of family ties, allows Egyptian men and women to give free rein to their emotions. Families, neighbours and countrymen at large can all be relied on for compassion, commiseration or help. This solidarity makes Egypt one of the safest countries in the world. When someone shouts "Thief!" on the street, every shop empties

FOOTBALL FEVER

Cairo is the home of the two biggest football teams in Egypt, al-Ahly and Zamalek, whose success or failure is passionately followed throughout the autumn and winter season. Ahly (www.ahlyclub.com) is one of the biggest teams in Africa.

Originally formed by Englishman Mitchell Ince in 1907, they soon became an Egyptian club for Egyptians and have won the Egyptian League more than any other team. Their name means "national" and the team is supported by the majority of fans in Egypt. In 1984 they were managed by former England manager Don Revie. The are nicknamed the Reds.

Ahly's great rival is their fellow Cairo club, Zamalek

(www.zamalek-sc.com), founded by a Belgian lawyer in 1911 and originally called Kasr el-Nil. After the 1952 Revolution they took the name Zamalek Sporting Club and were briefly managed in the mid 1980s by Dave Mackay, a former player with the north London club Tottenham Hotspur. They are nicknamed the White Knights.

Both clubs have been Champions of Africa five times and league matches between these two giants are great occasions which are often so heated that foreign referees have to be brought in to ensure neutrality. After the match, the city's streets are crowded with flag-waving jubilant fans hanging out of car windows and blowing their horns.

as all and sundry help to chase the culprit, who is almost invariably caught and hauled off to the nearest police station by a gesticulating mob. Following the horrifying attack by Islamic fundamentalists on tourists at the Temple of Hatshepsut in Luxor in 1997, the murderers were pursued across the hill (and caught and killed) by outraged locals. Throughout Egypt fewer murders are committed in a year than take place annually in any typical large city in America – a comparison reflecting the fact that Egyptian society allows fewer people to be marginalised. Every person has his recognised place in the scheme of things.

> The most important mouled is that of Sayyidna Husayn, the martyred nephew of the Prophet. Up to 2 million rural people flock to Cairo for the occasion.

Muslim fundamentalist groups, which claim they are un-Islamic.

DVDs, video tapes, television, with its melodramatic soap operas and trashy foreign serials, now provide the entertainment of the majority. These appurtenances of modern life have a powerful effect in a traditional society. Glorifying the bour-

Taking time out

Egypt's true carnivals, in the form of *mouled* or saints' days, offer a glimpse of this street energy in concentrated form. Push-carts hawking everything from plastic guns to chickpeas sprout overnight, vying for space with the tents and sleeping bodies of country pilgrims. On the Big Night, while dervishes dance to exhaustion to the *dhikr* rhythms (chanting in remembrance of God), local children try out the swings, shooting galleries and assorted tests of strength. However, *mouleds* have attracted considerably fewer believers in recent years, under pressure from

LEFT: fans of the "Reds". **ABOVE:** school trip to the Step Pyramid at Saqqarah.

geois and "liberal" attitudes of the city and thus homogenising Egyptian life, television has also deprived it of much of its vitality. Visiting shopping malls is also a popular pastime, particularly for the young, who find them a convivial arena in which to meet the opposite sex. Mobile phones and Bluetooth have given them much more freedom than their parents ever had.

In spite of the many changes, it will be a long time yet before the Egyptian people lose their special appeal. Sensitivity and kindness still abound. Solicitous for the welfare of their fellows, Egyptians are invariably helpful, friendly and hospitable. The warmth of human relations brings a soft sweetness, even extended to visitors, that has always been the best part of Egypt's charm. ❏

DECISIVE DATES

tion by Theban rulers; powerful central government. Pyramids at Dahshur and Hawarah built by Amenemhet III (1842–1797). Pyramids at Al-Lisht, Mazghunah and south Saqqarah built.

SECOND INTERMEDIATE PERIOD
1782–1570 BC
13th–17th dynasties. Country divided again. Asiatics ("Hyksos") rule in Delta.

EARLY DYNASTIC PERIOD
3150–2686 BC
First and Second dynasties: Memphis founded as the capital of Egypt. The rulers are buried in tombs at Saqqarah, where the first pyramids were built.

OLD KINGDOM
(2686–2181 BC)
2686–2613 BC
Third Dynasty. Zoser complex at Saqqarah built.

2613–2498 BC
Fourth Dynasty. Centralised government; pyramids at Dahshur, Giza and Abu Ruwash built.

2498–2181 BC
Fifth and Sixth dynasties. Pyramids and sun temples at Abu Sir and Saqqarah built. Tomb reliefs at Saqqarah and Giza, and Pyramid texts executed.

FIRST INTERMEDIATE PERIOD
2181–2040 BC
Seventh–Tenth dynasties. Country divided among local rulers; famine and poverty.

MIDDLE KINGDOM
2040–1782 BC
11th–12th dynasties. Reunifica-

NEW KINGDOM
(1570–1070 BC)
1570–1293 BC
18th Dynasty. Reunification under Theban kings; expulsion of Asiatics in north and annexation of Nubia. Period of greatest prosperity, with Thebes (Luxor) as main royal residence. Pharaohs include Akhenaten (1349–1334) and Tutankhamun (1334–1325).

1293–1185 BC
19th Dynasty. Ramesses II (1278–1212) embodies ideal kingship and builds many monuments.

1185–1070 BC
20th Dynasty. Invasions by Libyans and "Sea Peoples". Weak kings rule from the Delta.

THIRD INTERMEDIATE PERIOD
1069–525 BC
21st–26th dynasties. Tanis, in the northeastern Delta, is capital, but is displaced as Egypt is divided among several rulers.

712–656 BC
25th Dynasty from Kush (Sudan) unites country. Assyrian invasions in 667 and 663.

664–525 BC
26th Dynasty rules from Sais in western Delta. First settlement of Greeks at Memphis.

LATE PERIOD (525–332 BC)
525–404 BC
27th Dynasty (Persian). A canal linking the Nile with the Red Sea is completed under Darius I. A fortress called "Perhapemon" (Babylon in Greek) is built at the Nile end of the canal on future site of Cairo.

404–342
28th–30th dynasties. Slow decline.

342–330
31st Dynasty (Persian).

658–750
The Umayyad caliphs rule from Damascus.

750–878
The Abbasid caliphs rule from Baghdad. Al-Askar built. First Turkish governor appointed, 856.

TULUNID EMPIRE
AD 878–905
Ahmad Ibn Tulun, the Turkish governor, declares independence, founds Al-Qatai, and builds the great mosque that carries his name, 876–9.

ABBASID INTERIM
905–935
Rule from Baghdad reasserted.

FATIMID EMPIRE (969–1171)
Golden age.

969
Al-Qahirah, royal enclosure, founded.

970–72
Al-Azhar built.

996–1021
Reign of Al-Hakim, known as "The Mad Caliph".

PTOLEMAIC EMPIRE (332–30 BC)
332–30 BC
Alexander the Great conquers Egypt and founds Alexandria. Ptolemy I rules as governor after Alexander's death in 323 BC, then after 304 BC as first king of dynasty.

ROMAN PERIOD
30 BC–AD 324
Rule from Rome. Fortress rebuilt at Babylon in AD 116 under Trajan (98–117). Visits to Egypt by Vespasian, Trajan, Hadrian (twice), Septimus Severus and Caracalla. High taxes, poverty and revolt. Spread of Christianity, despite persecution from AD 251.

BYZANTINE PERIOD
AD 324–642
Rule from Constantinople (Byzantium).

324–619
Christianity made state religion in 379. Coptic Church separates from Catholic Church in 451. Last pagan temple (Philae) converted into church in 527.

619–29
Third Persian occupation.

629–39
Re-establishment of Byzantine rule.

639–42
Arab conquest under Amr ibn al-As, who founds new capital, Fustat, next to Babylon.

ARAB EMPIRE
AD 642–868
Rule by governors on behalf of caliph.

642–58
The Rashidun ("Orthodox") caliphs.

FAR LEFT TOP: the Old Kingdom Pyramids. **LEFT BOTTOM**: Ramesses II. **LEFT TOP**: Darius I, who built a canal linking the Nile and the Red Sea. **TOP**: the Temple of Philae, engraving by David Roberts. **ABOVE**: Emperor Trajan. **RIGHT**: part of Luxor Temple is topped by a mosque.

1085–92
Mosque of al-Guyushi, walls of Al-Qahirah, Bab al-Futuh, Bab an-Nasr and Bab Zuwaylah built.

1168
Frankish invasion; Fustat destroyed.

AYYUBID EMPIRE (1171–1250)
Saladin (Salah ad-Din) and his successors conduct campaigns against Franks and other invaders.

1174
Crusader invasion repelled. Jerusalem and most of Palestine retaken 1187–92.

1219–21
Frankish invasion by sea; occupation of Damietta. Advance on Cairo ends in Muslim victory at Mansura ("The Victorious") in the Delta.

1249
Frankish invasion under St Louis culminates in second Muslim victory at Mansura.

BAHRI MAMLUK EMPIRE (1250–1382)
Era of expansion and prosperity.

1260–79
Reign of Baybars al-Bunduqdari. Defeat of the Mongols, reduction of Frankish states to vassalage, extension of empire.

1279–90
Reign of Qalawun.

1293–1340
Three reigns of An-Nasir Muhammad ibn Qalawun. Period of architectural splendour in Cairo.

1340–82
Reign of the descendants of An-Nasir Muhammad.

BURGI (CIRCASSIAN) MAMLUK EMPIRE (1382–1517)
Continuation of building works under the rule of 23 sultans.

OTTOMAN PERIOD (1517–1914)
1517–1798
Ottoman rule through 106 governors. Cultural decline, commercial prosperity.

1798–1805
French invasion and occupation.

1805–48
Muhammad Ali Pasha. Massive programme of modernisation and creation of new empire.

1848
Ibrahim Pasha is viceregent for just 11 months and predeceases his father.

1849–54
Abbas Pasha expels French advisors, grants railway concession to the British. He is murdered by two bodyguards.

1854–63
Said Pasha rules. Suez Canal concession granted. Cairo–Alexandria rail link and Nile steamship service begins.

1863–79
Ismail the Magnificent reigns. Programme of modernisation. Chamber of Deputies established (1866), principle of primogeniture accepted by sultan. Title of "Khedive" (sovereign) granted (1867). Suez Canal opens (1869).

1879–92
Khedive Tawfik. British Occupation begins (1882).

1892–1914
Khedive Abbas Hilmi II.

POST-1914: PROTECTORATE–REPUBLIC
1914–17
Sultan Husayn Kamel. British Protectorate declared, martial law instituted.

1917–22
Sultan Fuad. Revolution of 1919.

1922–36
King Fuad I rules. Monarchy established.

1936–52
King Faruq. Saad Wafd party formed. During World War II Egypt is neutral, but is reoccupied by Britain, which installs its own candidate as prime minister. Rioting and fires of Black Saturday (1952) lead to a bloodless military coup, engineered by Nasser.

1952–53
The July Revolution deposes King Faruq in favour of his infant son, Ahmad Fuad, then declares Egypt a republic. Gamal Abdel Nasser becomes leader and negotiates a new Anglo-Egyptian treaty.

1956
Suez Canal nationalised. Tripartite attack on Egypt by Britain, France and Israel. US and USSR force the aggressors' withdrawal. Egypt, Syria and Yemen form the United Arab Republic.

1967
The Six-Day War against Israel.

1970
Nasser is succeeded by Anwar Sadat. He expels Soviet teachers and advisors.

1973
The October War against Israel.

1974–77
Open Door Policy, political liberalisation. Sadat visits Israel (1977) and addresses the Knesset.

1979
Camp David accords lead to peace treaty with Israel. Egypt is then boycotted by the rest of the Arab World, which denounces the accords as treachery.

1981
President Anwar Sadat assassinated. Vice-president Hosni Mubarak succeeds him. He at first tries to promote a more democratic government but gradually becomes more repressive.

1996–7
Spate of terrorist attacks on tourists. Perpetrators are executed.

2000
Egyptian government proclaims the Islamists completely crushed after a campaign of mass arrests.

2004
Bomb at the Taba Hilton in Sinai kills 34 people.

2005
Bombs in Sharm al-Shaykh on the Red Sea kill 88 people. Mubarak asks his parliament to amend the constitution to permit the first free presidential elections, but restrictions on serious opposition candidates result in a landslide victory for Mubarak that sees his term extended to 2011. A new party, Kifaya ("Enough" in Arabic), and the Muslim Brotherhood demand change.

2008
In April, riots in protest at the soaring cost of food and low wages culminate in a general strike. ❑

FAR LEFT TOP: the Fatimid Bab Zuwaylah. LEFT: Muhammad Ali watching the massacre of Mamluk rebels in the Citadel. TOP: the Suez Canal, the main link between Europe and Asia before air travel. ABOVE: King Faruq. RIGHT: Hosni Mubarak, Egypt's current president.

ANCIENT EGYPT

Egypt's ancient civilisation saw the rise of the great pharaohs but also witnessed their fall, which opened the floodgates to centuries of foreign rule

Egypt produced one of the earliest and most magnificent civilisations the world has ever witnessed. Five thousand years ago, when Mesopotamia was still the scene of petty squabbling between city states and while Europe, America and most of western Asia were inhabited by Stone-Age hunters, the ancient Egyptians had learned how to make bread, brew beer and mix paint. They could smelt and cast copper, drill beads, mix mineral compounds for cosmetics, and glaze stone and pottery surfaces. They had invented the hoe, the most ancient of agricultural implements, and had carried out experiments in plant and animal breeding.

Egypt is a land of unusual geographic isolation, with well-defined boundaries. To the east and west are vast deserts. To the north is the Mediterranean Sea. To the south there was, before the construction of the High Dam at Aswan, a formidable barrier of igneous rock, beyond which lay the barren land of Nubia. Within these recognisable boundaries, however, was a land divided; Upper Egypt extended from Aswan to a point just south of

> Were it not for the Nile, Egypt would not exist. It would be one of the most barren places on earth. This becomes obvious when seen from the air today: a green strip borders the river; the rest is desert.

modern Cairo and was largely barren, apart from a narrow strip of land flanking the river; the Delta, or Lower Egypt, spread from the point where the

LEFT: the Sphinx and the Pyramids. **RIGHT:** the Narmer Palette depicts King Narmer striking a foe. Some archaeologists have suggested that it represents Narmer's conquest of Lower Egypt.

Nile fanned into a fertile triangle some 200 km (125 miles) before reaching the Mediterranean Sea. Linking Upper and Lower Egypt was the vital artery, the River Nile.

Before the Nile was harnessed by technology, the annual flood, a result of the monsoon rains on the Ethiopian tableland, spilled into the flood plain, leaving a thick layer of alluvial soil. Since rainfall in Egypt is almost nil, the people depended on the river for their crops; and it was ultimately on the fertility of the soil that ancient Egyptian civilisation was based.

The earliest human inhabitants of the Nile Valley were hunters who tracked game across northern Africa and the eastern Sudan, later joined by nomadic tribes of Asiatic origin who filtered into

Egypt in sporadic migrations across the Sinai peninsula and the Red Sea.

Late Paleolithic settlements (*c*.12000– 8000 BC) reveal that both these newcomers and the indigenous inhabitants had a hunting and gathering economy. As time went by, their lives became

It is probable that Paleolithic people had no means – or no concept – of preserving the rich bounty that nature offered them. They may have dried meat in the heat of the sun and smoked fish over fires, although we have no evidence of this.

from April to June, game scattered, food became scarce, and hunting was pursued once more.

Despite their diverse origins, therefore, there was a natural tendency for the people to group together during the "season of abundance" when there was plenty of food to eat and then to split up into smaller groups or communities during the low-flood season or during periods of drought.

Religion and agriculture

As a certain rhythm formed in their lives, people observed that the gifts of their naturally irrigated valley depended on a dual force: the sun and the river, both of which had creative and destructive

bound to the ebb and flow of the annual flood. As the water rose each year in July, the inhabitants were obliged to draw back from the banks. By August, when the waters swept across the lowlands, they took to the highlands and pursued hunting activities, tracking antelope, hartebeest, wild ass and gazelle, with lances, bows and arrows. In the first half of October the river attained its highest level, and thereafter began to subside, leaving lagoons and streams that became natural reservoirs for fish.

A variety of plants grew in the fertile, uniform deposit of silt. During this season of plenty, hunting activity was at a minimum. From January to March seasonal pools dried out and fishing was limited, but in the swampy areas near the river there were turtles, rodents and clams. At low Nile,

RESURRECTION MYTH

Some form of resurrection myth has been central to the beliefs and customs of most societies throughout the ancient world. Universally, this myth was connected to the reappearance in spring of foliage on trees and plants that had seemed withered and dead and, as in Egypt, to the nightly death and daily rebirth of the life-giving sun (represented in Egyptian tomb paintings by the goddess Nut; stretched over the earth, she was thought to swallow the setting sun and give birth to it each morning). Among the people of the Nile Valley this belief would have been intensified by the annual flooding of the river, and the bounty that this unfailingly brought in its wake.

powers. The life-giving rays of the sun that caused a crop to grow could also cause it to shrivel and die. And the river that invigorated the soil with its mineral-rich deposits could destroy whatever lay in its path or, if it failed to rise sufficiently, bring famine. These two phenomena, moreover, shared in the pattern of death and rebirth that left a profound impression: the sun that "died" in the western horizon each evening was "reborn" in the eastern sky the following morning; and the river was responsible for the germination or "rebirth" of the crops after the "death" of the land each year.

Agriculture was introduced into the Nile Valley about 5000 BC. Once grain (a variety of domesti-

Slowly, assimilation took place. Some villages may have merged as their boundaries expanded; or small groups of people may have gravitated towards larger ones and started to trade and barter with them. The affairs of the various communities became tied to major settlements, which undoubtedly represented the richest and most powerful. This tendency towards political unity occurred in both Upper and Lower Egypt. In Upper Egypt, the chief settlement was Nekhen, where the leader wore a conical White Crown and took the sedge plant as his emblem. In the Delta or Lower Egypt, the capital was Buto; the leader wore the characteristic Red Crown and adopted the bee as his symbol.

cated barley from Asia) could be cultivated and stored, the people could be assured of a regular food supply, an important factor in the movement away from primitive society towards civilisation. Agriculture made possible a surplus of time and economic resources, which resulted in population increase and craft specialisation. Polished stone axes, well-made knives, and a variety of pottery vessels were produced, as well as ivory combs and slate palettes, on which paint for body decoration was prepared.

FAR LEFT: the gods Anubis and Horus being presented with *ankhs*, the ancient Egyptian symbol of life.
LEFT: tomb painting of hunting and agriculture.
ABOVE: tomb painting of the Pyramid builders.

When life became less of a struggle for day-to-day survival, craft work flourished and items of adornment as well as domestic tools were produced.

The Old Kingdom

Unification of Upper and Lower Egypts has been ascribed to Narmer (Menes), around 3100 BC. He set up his capital at Memphis, at the apex of the Delta, and was the first king to be portrayed wearing both the White and Red Crown. He stands at the beginning of Egypt's ancient history, which was divided by Manetho, an Egyptian historian (*c*.280 BC), into 30 royal dynasties starting at Menes and ending with Alexander the Great.

The dynasties were subsequently combined and grouped into three main periods: the Old Kingdom or Pyramid Age, the Middle Kingdom and the New Kingdom. Although further divided by modern historians, these periods remain the basis of ancient Egyptian chronology.

The Old Kingdom, from the Third to Sixth Dynasties (2686–2181 BC), is considered by many historians as the high-water mark of achievement. A series of vigorous and able monarchs established a highly organised, centralised government. The Great Pyramids of Giza, on the western bank of the Nile southwest of Cairo, have secured undying fame for Khufu (Cheops), Khafre (Chephren) and Menkaure (Mycerinus).

These kings ruled during a period of great refinement, an aristocratic era, which saw rising productivity in all fields. Cattle and raw materials, including gold and copper, were taken in donkey caravans from the Sudan and Nubia. Sinai was exploited for mineral wealth and a fleet of ships sailed to Byblos (on the coast of Lebanon) to import cedar wood. The "Great House", *peraha*, from which the word pharaoh is derived, controlled all trade routes throughout the land, as well as all the markets.

A LOVE OF BEAUTY

Most of the buildings of ancient Egypt, including the royal palaces, were built of perishable materials such as brick, wood and bundles of reeds, while tombs were built of stone, designed to last for eternity. This distinction gives the erroneous impression that the ancient Egyptians were preoccupied with thoughts of death, but evidence to the contrary is abundant.

Wishing to ensure bounty in the afterlife similar to that enjoyed on earth, the ancients decorated their tombs with a wide variety of farming scenes and manufacturing processes as well as leisure activities such as hunting parties and musical gatherings, along with scenes from their own personal lives.

The Old Kingdom tombs at Saqqarah, south of Giza, are adorned with painted relics of the deceased, his wife and children, overseers of his estates, supervisors of his factories, scribes, artisans and peasants. The graphic portrayals of everyday life are clear evidence that the ancient Egyptians took great pride in beautiful possessions: chairs and beds (which often had leather or rope-weave seats or mattresses fastened to the frame with leather thongs) had legs carved in the form of the powerful hind limbs of an ox or lion; the handle of a spoon was fashioned to resemble a lotus blossom. The Egyptians may have been very aware of death, but they were concerned to surround themselves with things of beauty while they were alive.

The end of the Old Kingdom

In the Old Kingdom the power of the pharaoh was supreme and he took an active part in all affairs of state, which ranged from determining the height of the Nile during the annual inundation, to recruiting a labour force from the provinces, to leading mining and exploratory expeditions. Naturally, such responsibility was too much for one person and he therefore delegated power to the provincial lords, who were often members of the royal family. The provincial nobility became wealthier, began to exert power, and the result was an inevitable weakening of centralised authority. At the end of the Sixth Dynasty some of the provinc-

A powerful family of provincial lords from Herakleopolis Magna (Middle Egypt) achieved prominence in the Ninth and 10th dynasties and restored order. In Upper Egypt, meanwhile, in the Theban area (near Luxor), a confederation had gathered around the strong Intef and Mentuhotep family, who extended their authority northwards until there was a clash with the family from Herakleopolis. A civil war resulted in triumph for the Thebans.

The Middle Kingdom

The Middle Kingdom covers the 11th and 12th dynasties (c.2040–1782 BC). Amenemhet I, whose rule heralded a revival in architecture and the arts,

es shook themselves free from the central government and established independence. The monarchy collapsed. The Old Kingdom came to an end.

The era known as the First Intermediate Period, between the Seventh and 10th dynasties, saw anarchy, bloodshed and a restructuring of society. The provincial lords who had gained power and prestige under the great monarchs began to reflect on the traditional beliefs of their forefathers. It was a time of soul-searching; and great contempt was voiced for the law and order of the past.

LEFT: *View of the Sphinx and the Great Pyramid*, painted by Nicolas Jacques Conté in the 18th century.
ABOVE: ibex depicted in the mastaba of Kagemni, a Sixth Dynasty official, at Saqqarah.

as well as a breakthrough in literature, established the 12th Dynasty, one of the most peaceful and prosperous eras known to Egypt. Political stability was soon reflected in material prosperity. Building operations were undertaken throughout the whole country. Amenemhet III constructed his tomb at Hawarah (in the Fayyum) with a funerary monument later described by classical writers as "The Labyrinth" and declared by Herodotus to be more wonderful than the Pyramids of Giza. Goldsmiths, jewellers and sculptors perfected their skills, as Egyptian political and cultural influence extended to Nubia and Kush in the south, around the Eastern Mediterranean to Libya, Palestine, Syria and even to Crete, the Aegean Islands and the mainland of Greece.

The Osiris legend

According to legend, Osiris was a just and much-loved ruler who taught his people how to make farm implements, rotate crops and control the waters of the Nile. He also showed them how to adapt to a wheat diet and make bread, wine and beer. Isis, his devoted wife, was also popular. She taught the people how to grind wheat and weave linen with a loom.

Osiris had a brother, Seth, who was jealous of his popularity. He tricked Osiris into climbing into a chest, had it sealed, then cast it into the Nile. Broken-hearted, Isis went in search of the body of her husband, eventually found it, and hid it.

But Seth discovered the body and tore it into 14 pieces, which he scattered over the land. Isis again went in search of Osiris, collected the pieces, bound them together with bandages and breathed life back into the body. Isis then descended on her husband in the form of a winged bird, received his seed, and brought forth an heir, Horus. She raised her son in the marshes of the Delta until he grew strong enough to avenge his father's death by slaying Seth. Horus then took over the earthly throne and the resurrected Osiris became king of the underworld.

The cult of Osiris captured the popular imagination. It became desirable to have a stele erected

In the Middle Kingdom an increasingly wealthy middle class led the ordinary man to aspire to what only members of the aristocracy had had before: elaborate funerary equipment to ensure a comfortable afterlife.

To pay homage to their legendary ancestor, Osiris, thousands of pilgrims from all walks of life made their way to the holy city of Abydos each year, leaving so many offerings in pottery vessels that two low mounds developed consisting entirely of broken votive pots, and the site acquired the name of Umm al-Gaab, meaning "Mother of Potsherds".

Abydos continued to be a place of pilgrimage right up to the end of the pharaonic period.

at Abydos, so the spirit of the deceased could join in the annual dramatisation of his resurrection, enacted by the temple priests. During the New Kingdom, when Thebes became capital, deceased noblemen were borne to Abydos and placed in the temple precinct before being interred at Thebes. If for some reason this posthumous pilgrimage could not be made, it was done symbolically, their tombs decorated with handsome reliefs of boats bearing their mummified bodies to Abydos.

End of the Middle Kingdom

At the end of the 12th Dynasty the provincial rulers once again rose against the crown. During this period of instability the Hyksos, who are believed to have come from the direction of Syria, challenged Egyptian authority. With the assistance of horses and chariots (which were hitherto unknown in Egypt, and must have had a devastating effect), they swept across the northern Sinai, fortified a stronghold at Tel ad-Deba, south of Tanis in the northeastern Delta, then

Hyksos is a Manethonian term corrupted from Hekakhasut, which means simply "rulers of foreign countries" – perhaps an appropriate name for those who challenged Egyptian authority.

The humiliation of foreign occupation came to an end when Ahmose, father of the New Kingdom (18th–20th dynasties, 1570–1070 BC) started a war of liberation and finally expelled the hated invaders from the land.

This first unhappy exposure to foreign domination left a lasting mark on the Egyptian character. The seemingly inviolable land of Egypt had proved vulnerable, and now had to be protected from invasion. To do so meant not only to rid the country of enemies, but to pursue them into western Asia. Out of the desire for national security was born the spirit of military expansion characteristic of the New Kingdom.

moved towards the apex of the Delta, from where they surged southwards.

The damage done to Egypt's great cities can only be guessed at. Pharaohs of later times inscribed self-aggrandising declarations that they "restored what was ruined" and "raised what had gone to pieces", but the almost total absence of contemporary documents during the Hyksos occupation leaves scant evidence of what actually took place.

LEFT: the invasion of the Hyksos at the end of the 12th Dynasty led to foreign occupation.
ABOVE: as this carving of Hittite prisoners of war at Abu Simel shows, Egypt's fortunes revived during the New Kingdom, especially under Ramesses II.

The New Kingdom

The New Kingdom (1570–1070 BC) was the period of empire. The military conquests of Thutmosis III, in no fewer than 17 campaigns, resulted in the establishment of Egyptian power throughout Syria and northern Mesopotamia, as well as in Nubia and Libya. Great wealth from conquered nations and vassal states poured into Thebes (Luxor). The caravans were laden with gold, silver, ivory, spices and rare flora and fauna.

The greater part of the wealth was bestowed upon the god Amun who, with the aid of an influential priesthood, was established as Amun-Ra, "King of Gods". Thebes flourished, and some of Egypt's most extravagant monuments were built during this period.

The 18th Dynasty was a period of transition. Old values were passing and new ones emerging. The spirit of the age was based on wealth and power. But grave discontent, especially among the upper classes, was apparent in criticism of the national god Amun and the materialism of the priests who promoted his cult.

Akhenaten's revolution

It was in this atmosphere that Amenhotep IV (Akhenaten) grew up. He was the pharaoh who would revolt against the priests and order temple reliefs to be defaced, shrines to be destroyed, and the image of the god Amun to be erased. Akhen-aten transferred the royal residence to Al-Amarnah, in Middle Egypt *(see page 195)*, and promoted the worship of one god, the Aten, the life-giving sun. The city was called Akhetaten ("The Horizon of the Aten").

Unfortunately, the ideal needs of a religious community and the practical requirements of governing an extensive empire were to prove incompatible demands. After the deaths of Akhenaten and his half-brother Smenkare, the boy-king Tutankhamun (famous today as one of the few pharaohs whose remains escaped the early tomb-robbers) came to the throne. Tutankhamun abandoned Al-Amarnah and returned to Memphis and

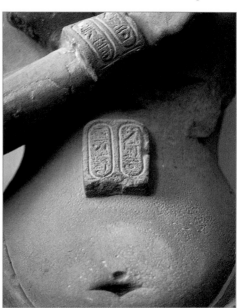

A REVOLUTION IN ART

Certain innovations had already begun to transform the character of Egyptian art in the early years of Akhenaten's reign. By the time of his move from Thebes to Al-Amarnah, these slight innovations had become radical reforms. For many centuries portrayals of the pharaohs had been highly stylised; they were always depicted as being strong and powerful, and artists were not permitted to divert from this image in any way.

Now, with the consent, it seems, of Akhenaten, figures in a variety of movements and postures were sculptured in exquisite low relief. Akhenaten himself wished to exaggerate his physical imperfections in order to create the impression of a pharaoh who was mortal – a stark contrast with

the representations of earlier pharaohs, which had portrayed them as physically perfect god-kings.

Artistic representations of Akhenaten make him look quite strange, with an unusually long, prominent chin, a protruding belly, and hips that are unnaturally wide for a man. Some scholars have suggested that he suffered from a disease that was responsible for these attributes, but it is more likely that the depictions were some form of religious symbolism. His mummy has never been discovered so it is impossible to know if the sculpted representations were realistic.

It should be noted, however, that his wife, Nefertiti, was always represented as extremely beautiful.

Thebes. The priests of Amun were able to make a spectacular return to power.

Empire-builders

Horemheb, the general who seized the throne at the end of the 18th Dynasty, was an excellent administrator. He re-established a strong government and started a programme of restoration, which continued into the 19th Dynasty, when the pharaohs channelled their boundless energies into reorganising Akhenaten's rule. Seti I, builder of a famous mortuary temple at Abydos, fought battles against the Libyans, Syrians and Hittites; Ramesses II, hero of a war against the Hittites,

cence of their architectural and artistic endeavours, especially in the great Temple of Amun at Karnak. It became a temple within a temple, shrine within shrine, where almost all the pharaohs wished to record their names and deeds for posterity.

As new pylons, colonnades and shrines were built, valuable blocks of inscribed stone from earlier periods were often used. The sun temples of Akhenaten suffered this fate: thousands of their distinctly uniform, decorated sandstone blocks, known as *talatat*, were buried in various places in Karnak, such as beneath the flagstones of the great Hypostyle Hall.

with whom he signed a famous peace treaty, was also celebrated as a builder of great monuments, including the famous temples at Abu Simbel; and Ramesses III not only conquered the Libyans, but successfully protected his country from the "People of the Sea".

All these warrior kings of the 19th Dynasty raised magnificent temples in honour of Amun. It was considered both a duty and a privilege to serve the state god, who granted them military success; and successive pharaohs systematically tried to outdo their predecessors in the magnifi-

FAR LEFT: mosaic of Akhenaten, Al-Amarnah.
LEFT: statue of Akhenaten showing a swollen belly.
ABOVE: the *Temple of Ramesses II*, by David Roberts.

KARNAK'S GLORY

The Hypostyle Hall at Karnak is the largest single chamber of any temple in the world, covering an area of 4,983 sq. metres (53,318 sq ft), with the roof supported by 134 columns, arranged in 16 rows. According to Napoleon's savants, who examined the hall in 1798, the whole of Notre Dame cathedral would fit within its walls. Seti I was responsible for the northern half of the hall and Ramesses II for the southern portion, but other 19th-Dynasty pharaohs also recorded their names there, honouring Amun.

Ramesses III

Ramesses III (1182–1151 BC) was the last of the great pharaohs. His ever-weakening successors fell more and more under the yoke of the priests of Amun who controlled enormous wealth. According to a text known as the Harris Papyrus, written in the reign of Ramesses III, they possessed more than 5,000 divine statues, more than 81,000 slaves, vassals and servants, well over 421,000 cattle, 433 gardens, 690,000 acres (279,000 hectares) of land, 83 ships, 46 building yards and 65 cities.

Naturally, such a priesthood wielded enormous power and gradually the priests came to regard themselves as the ruling power of the state. At the

end of the 20th Dynasty, around 1085 BC, the high priests of Amun overthrew the dynasty. In theory, the country was still united, but in fact, the government became synonymous with corruption. Anarchy flourished and occupation by successive foreign military powers ensued.

Centuries of foreign rule

In 945 BC, Sheshonk, who was from a family of Libyan descent, but had become completely Egyptianised, took over the leadership. His Libyan followers were probably descendants of mercenary troops who had earlier been granted land in return for military service. The Libyan monarchs proceeded to conduct themselves as pharaohs and their rule lasted for two centuries.

In 748 BC a military leader, Piankhi, from the region of Kush (northern Sudan), marched northward. Because his people had absorbed Egyptian culture during a long period of Egyptian rule he did not view himself as a conqueror, but as a champion freeing Egypt from the barbarism that had engulfed it.

The Egyptians did not regard Piankhi and the Kushites as liberators and it was only after a military clash at Memphis, when the foreign invaders surged over the ramparts, that they surrendered. Like the Libyans before them, the Kushites established themselves as pharaohs, restored ancient temples and were sympathetic to local customs.

The Assyrians, who were reputedly the most ruthless of ancient peoples, conquered Egypt in 667 and 663 BC. With a disciplined, well-trained army they moved southward from province to province, assuring the local population of a speedy liberation from oppressive rule.

During these centuries of foreign rule Egypt had one short respite. This was the Saite Period, which ensued after an Egyptian named Psamtik liberated the country from Assyrian occupation. He immediately turned his attention to reuniting Egypt, establishing order and promoting tradition.

The unflagging efforts of this great leader, and the Saite rulers who followed him, to restore former greatness led them to pattern their government and society on the Old Kingdom, a model 2,000 years old. Instead of channelling their energies into creating new forms, they fell back on the traditions of the past.

Egypt's revival came to an end when the Persian King Cambyses occupied the land in 525 BC and turned it into a Persian province. The new rulers, like the Libyans and the Kushites before them, at first showed respect for the religion and customs of the country in an effort to gain support. But the Egyptians were not deceived and as soon as an opportunity arose they routed their invaders. Unfortunately, they were able to maintain independence for only about 60 years before another Persian army invaded.

When Alexander the Great marched on Egypt in 332 BC, he and his army were welcomed by the Egyptians as liberators. ❏

LEFT: image of Ramesses III in the tomb of his son, Amun-Khopshef, the Valley of the Kings, Thebes.
RIGHT: hieroglyphs combined alphabetical signs, pictures (ideograms) and symbols representing sounds (phonograms).

A PARADE OF THE MORE IMPORTANT GODS

The ancient Egyptians explained the mysteries of nature and the world through myths concerning the origins and powers of their gods

The movement of the sun was one of the most significant forces in the ancients' world and, according to his myth, the sun-god Ra created himself from the primeval waters where everything was dark and chaotic. His eyes became the moon and the sun and, mating with his own shadow, he created Shu, god of the air, and Tefnut, goddess of mist. At this point, Ra wept and his tears fell as men and women. Shu and Tefnut then gave birth to Geb, god of the earth, and Nut, goddess of the sky, which completed the creation of the universe. Isis and Osiris, Seth and his sister-wife Nephtys were created through the union of Geb and Nut.

Rise and fall of the gods

Through the centuries, different gods gained importance as the capital moved from city to city. In Memphis, Ptah was considered the supreme god and creator of the universe. He was usually depicted as a bald man with a mummiform body and false beard. His consort Sekhmet, a woman with a lion's head, was goddess of war and represented the harmful powers of the sun. Imhotep, architect of the step pyramid at Saqqarah, was later deified as their son and the god of medicine (and equated with Asklepios by the Greeks). Amun was the supreme god of Thebes, depicted as a ram with curved horns.

The life-bringing Nile was also personified as the god Hapi, while fertility was represented by Min, depicted with an erect phallus and celebrated in the important Feast of Min.

LEFT: Amun-Ra, a composite god of Ra, sun god of Heliopolis, and Amun, god of the wind, became a national deity during the Middle Kingdom.

LEFT: an early Egyptian Earth Mother, depicted as a cow, or as a woman with cow's ears or horns, Hathor was the goddess of beauty, love and music (identified by the Greeks with Aphrodite). Her image is often found in Ptolemaic temples, sometimes on capitals.

LEFT: one of the most important gods, falcon-headed god Horus was a sun-god (he often has a sun disk on his head), god of the sky, a protector of kings and a guide to the dead in the underworld. Every pharaoh was considered an incarnation of Horus.

THE MURDER OF OSIRIS

The myth of the murder of Osiris and his sister-wife's hunt for his body clearly illustrates the Egyptian belief in the afterlife.

Osiris was born a god but grew up as a man who became the king of Egypt. His brother Seth was so jealous of his popularity and success that he locked him in a coffin, which he threw into the Nile. Isis, mourning her husband's death, went looking for the coffin and eventually found it near Byblos (modern Lebanon) where it had been surrounded by a tree.

Having recovered the body, Isis took the form of a bird (symbol of the spirit) to revive Osiris, but only managed to stir him long enough to impregnate herself with a son, Horus the Younger. While Isis was giving birth to her son, Seth was cutting Osiris's body into 14 pieces, which he scattered across Egypt. Isis later recovered all of them except his penis, which had been eaten by Nile fish. She reassembled the parts and made a mould of the missing organ, while Horus, having fought a battle with Seth, brought the eye of his father's murderer and placed it in Osiris's mouth, ensuring his eternal life.

The image above depicts Isis on the canopic shrine of Tutankhamun.

TOP: represented as an ibis or a baboon, Thoth was the god of wisdom, science and medicine. He invented hieroglyphics and the art of writing and became the scribe in the Hall of Judgement.

ABOVE: depicted as a jackal, or a man with a jackal head, Anubis greeted the dead in the underworld and protected their bodies from decay.

LEFT: Osiris, depicted as a mummified king, with a false beard and carrying the royal crook and flail, was the god of the underworld and of resurrection

THE PTOLEMAIC PERIOD

Under Ptolemaic rule, Egypt became the seat of a powerful empire and Alexandria, its capital, a centre of learning. But internal rivalry, during the reign of Cleopatra, reduced the country to a province of the Roman Empire

When Alexander the Great marched on Egypt, the Egyptians had no reason to fear that this would mark the end of their status as an independent nation. He first made his way to thickly populated Memphis, the ancient capital, where he made an offering at the Temple of Ptah, then lost no time in travelling to Siwah Oasis to consult the famous oracle of Amun-Ra *(see page 184)*. When he emerged from the sanctuary he announced that the sacred statue had recognised him, and the priests of Amun greeted him as the son of the god.

Governing Egypt

Before he left Egypt, Alexander laid down the basic plans for its government. In the important provinces (*nomes* in Greek), he appointed local governors from among Egyptian nobles; he made provision for the collection of taxes and he laid out the plans for his great city and seaport, Alexandria, so situated as to facilitate the flow of Egypt's surplus resources to Greece and to intercept all trade with Africa and Asia.

The finest Ptolemaic temples can be seen in Upper Egypt, at Denderah north of Luxor, between Luxor and Aswan (Esna, Edfu and Kom Ombo) and Philae just south of Aswan.

When Alexander died from a fever at Babylon, his conquests fell to lesser heirs. Egypt was held by a general named Ptolemy, who took over leadership as King Ptolemy I. During the three centuries

LEFT: a 19th-century engraving of the Ptolemaic Temple of Philae showing traces of the original colours.
RIGHT: Sixth-century mosaic showing Alexandria.

of Ptolemaic rule that followed, Egypt became the seat of a brilliant empire once more.

The first of the Ptolemies

Ptolemy did not continue Alexander's practice of founding independent cities. With the exception of Ptolemais, on the western bank of the Nile in Middle Egypt, and the old Greek city of Naucratis in the Delta, only Alexandria represented a traditional Greek city-state. Ptolemy chose instead to settle his troops (Greeks, Macedonians, Persians and Hellenised Asiatics) among the Egyptian population in towns near the capitals of the provinces into which Egypt was divided. Many settlers married Egyptians and by the second and third generations their children bore both Greek and Egyptian names.

In Alexandria Greeks formed the bulk of the population, followed in number by the Jews. But there was also a large Egyptian population, which lived west of the city, in the old quarter of Rhacotis. Alexandria occupied the strip of sandy soil between Lake Mareotis and the sea, where the island of Pharos stood, surmounted by its famous lighthouse, one of the Seven Wonders of the World *(see page 261)*.

Alexandria, seat of learning

Alexandria became capital in place of Memphis and was soon to become the major seat of learning in the Mediterranean world, replacing Athens as the centre of culture. Ptolemy II commissioned Egyptians to translate their literature into Greek; and a priest, Manetho, wrote the history of his country. Research was also fostered; and distinguished astronomers, mathematicians, geographers, historians, poets and philosophers gravitated to the *Mouseion* or Museum attached to the Library in Alexandria, which was a research institution.

Alexandrian astronomers revised the Egyptian calendar, then, some two centuries later, the Roman one, creating the Julian calendar that was used throughout Europe until the end of the Renaissance. Literary critics and scholars edited classical texts, giving them the editions we now know.

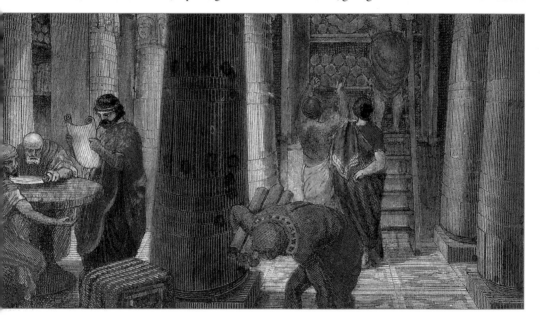

THE APIS BULL

Ptolemy I introduced a cult designed to provide a link between his Greek and Egyptian subjects. He observed that the Apis bull was worshipped at Memphis and assumed that the cult was popular and widespread, although this was not the case. The deceased Apis was known as Osiris-Apis or "Oserapis", from which the name Serapis was derived. Ptolemy supplied Serapis with anthropomorphic features and declared him to be a national god.

To slot the new deity deftly into the path of his own career, Ptolemy announced that he had had a dream in which a colossal statue was revealed to him. No sooner had he communicated his revelation to the people than a statue of Serapis, closely resembling his vision, was put on view.

The cult of Serapis was to have some success throughout Greece and Asia Minor, in Sicily, and especially in Rome where, as the patron god of the Ptolemaic Empire, its presence enhanced the empire's prestige.

In Egypt Serapis was worshipped in every major town, but especially in Alexandria and in Memphis, where the Serapeum, the Temple of Serapis and the catacomb of the Apis bull, in the necropolis of Saqqarah *(see page 169)*, became a famous site.

Many living poets such as Theocritus, Callimachus and Apollonius Rhodius received generous financial support.

The Ptolemies regarded Egypt as their land and they consequently played a dual role in it, conducting themselves simultaneously as bearers of Greek culture and as guardians of Egyptian cul-

The resemblance between Biblical and Egyptian expression and imagery are not surprising in view of the centuries of contact between Egyptians and Jews in Egypt.

ture. Although they resided in Alexandria, as pharaohs they lavished revenues on local priesthoods for the upkeep of temples, or at least exempted them from taxes.

One aspect of the power of the pharaoh was his capacity to uphold religious order; and the Ptolemies thus continued an ancient tradition. Ptolemaic temples were built on traditional lines, often on the sites of more ancient temples. The

ABOVE LEFT: woodcut depicting the Mouseion Library of Alexandria founded by Ptolemy II. **LEFT:** Apis bull in Alexandria. **ABOVE:** statue of Herhor in the Graeco-Roman Museum, Alexandria.
ABOVE RIGHT: Sobek the crocodile god is revered at the Ptolemaic Temple of Horus, Kom Ombo.

walls were adorned with scenes depicting Ptolemaic kings in the manner of the ancient pharaohs. Like the ancient pharaohs, the kings fulfilled religious duties and made ceremonial journeys up the Nile, enjoying the public worship of political leadership that was a feature of life in Egypt.

The Greek language

Bilingual Egyptians realised long before the conquest by Alexander that if they transcribed their own language into the Greek alphabet, which was well known among the middle classes and was simpler to read, communication would be easier. Scribes started the translitera-

tion, adding seven extra letters from the Egyptian alphabet to accommodate sounds for which there were no Greek letters, and created a new script, now known as Coptic.

Greek also became the mother-tongue of the Jews in Egypt, who constituted the second-largest foreign community. Many had been imported as soldiers, even before the arrival of the Ptolemies. When Palestine fell under the control of Ptolemy I in 301 BC, he brought back Jewish mercenaries, who joined the established communities. Unable to speak Hebrew, which had already disappeared as a living language, the Egyptian Jews soon felt a need to translate their sacred books into Greek, which resulted in the version of the Old Testament known as the Septuagint.

The Ptolemies encouraged other foreigners to come to live in Egypt, including Syrians and Persians, as well as Greeks. There was a strong anti-Egyptian feeling among the sophisticated Greeks, who did not encourage Egyptians to become citizens of Alexandria and the Greek cities. Although they held Egyptian culture in reverence in many ways, they did not learn the Egyptian language or writing. Even the Greek masses, although they were fascinated by the "sacred mysteries" and "divine oracles" of the Land of Wonders, nevertheless held the Egyptians in contempt. There were reciprocal anti-Greek sentiments among the Egyptians, who had a strong sense of cultural superiority towards anyone who did not speak their language.

Although there is evidence that Egyptian priests and officials collaborated with the Ptolemies, there are also indications that they rebelled frequently, resentful of the fact that they were being treated as a conquered race. Prophetic writings were widely circulated among the Egyptian people, promising the expulsion of the foreigners.

The last of the Ptolemies

Towards the end of the 2nd century BC Egypt experienced economic problems and political unrest,

THE REAL CLEOPATRA

Cleopatra's contemporaries were entranced by her seductive voice and witty repartee. It seems she was an accomplished linguist, capable of conversing with Egyptians, Ethiopians, Hebrews, Arabs, Syrians, Medes and Parthians. We cannot really know what she looked like because her adversary, Octavian, destroyed most of the statues and portraits of her after her death. But, despite her reputation as a beauty, there has been plenty of uncomplimentary conjecture about the size of her nose. "All that we can feel certain about," wrote a Victorian historian, "is that she had not a short nose."

An exhibition devoted to Cleopatra at the British Museum in London brought to light 10 previously unrecognised Egyptian-style images of this endlessly fascinating queen. In depictions on coins and statues sculpted during her lifetime, she is shown with a very long neck and the sharp features of a bird of prey – more of a wicked witch than a seductive beauty. In the view of Plutarch, it was quite possible to gaze upon her without being bowled over, which suggests that, even then, her reputation for beauty exceeded the reality. But big noses are said to represent strength of character, and this is probably what the 17th-century French philospher Pascal had in mind when he wrote: "If Cleopatra's nose were shorter, the shape of the world would have been different."

along with a decline in foreign trade. Some territories outside Egypt were lost, and the prosperity of the kingdom waned. The court, rich in material wealth and lax in morals, became the scene of decadence and anarchy.

By the last century of Ptolemaic rule, the Egyptians had acquired a position that was somewhat closer in equality to the Greeks than they had endured under the earlier Ptolemies. This era saw the emergence of a landed, wealthy Egyptian population, who were ardently nationalistic and had little respect for the settlers. It was from their ranks that the great spiritual leaders of Coptic Christianity *(see page 59)* were to arise.

> When her son Caesarion was only four years old, Cleopatra made him her co-regent. As Ptolemy XV, he retained this role until he was assassinated, probably on the orders of Octavian, in 30 BC.

afterwards Cleopatra bore his only son, Caesarion.

A little over five years later, she met Mark Antony at Tarsus. Their legendary love affair brought her three more children, but succeeded in alienating Antony from his supporters in Rome. His purported will, stating his wishes to be buried

Famous queen

Cleopatra VII, the most famous of the Ptolemies, came to the throne at the age of about 18, as co-regent with her even younger brother Ptolemy XII. They were at that time under the guardianship of the Roman Senate and Romans interfered in the rivalry between them, which led Ptolemy to banish his 21-year-old sister from Egypt. Cleopatra sought refuge in Syria, with a view to raising an army and recovering the throne by force. When Julius Caesar arrived in Alexandria in 47 BC, he took the side of the banished queen and set her on the throne. Soon

FAR LEFT AND LEFT: contrasting images of Cleopatra VII.
ABOVE: *Cleopatra's Banquet* depicting Antony and Cleopatra, painted by Giovanni Battista in 1744.

at Alexandria, angered many Romans, and gave Octavian (later known as Emperor Augustus) the excuse he was looking for to declare war on Antony. Octavian marched against him, defeating him at Actium and capturing Alexandria. Antony committed suicide and Cleopatra is recorded as having caused her own death with the bite of an asp. Caesarion, who had been co-regent since 43 BC, was murdered, and Octavian became sole ruler in 30 BC.

Egypt thenceforth was a province of the Roman Empire, subject only to the rule of the emperor in Rome, and to viceroys or prefects nominated by the emperor, who followed the example of the Ptolemies and represented themselves as successors of the ancient pharaohs. ❑

Cuem Adbefptue.
adiutorui meii itede.

THE ROMAN PERIOD AND EARLY CHRISTIANITY

Early Christians were brutally persecuted under the Romans, until the conversion of Emperor Constantine. Once Christianity was established, dogmatic differences within the new religion led to fierce factional disputes

The Roman occupation of Egypt, ostensibly a mere extension of Ptolemaic rule, was, in fact, markedly different. While a mutual hostility towards the Persians and a long history of commercial relations bound Egyptians and Greeks together, no such affinity existed between Egyptians and Romans. Alexander the Great had entered Egypt without striking a blow; Roman troops fought battles with Egyptians almost immediately. The Ptolemaic kings had lived in Egypt; the Roman emperors governed from Rome and their prefects took over the position formerly held in the scheme of government by the kings.

To the Egyptians the prefect, not the emperor, was therefore the royal personage. And the prefect did not perform the ceremonial functions of divine kingship, which was by tradition highly personal. There was thus a drastic change in the climate of leadership throughout this period.

The seeds of strife

The Emperor Augustus made the mistake of arousing the ire of the Greeks when he abolished

The burning of the esteemed Mouseion Library in Alexandria resulted in the loss of some 490,000 rolls of papyrus.

the Greek Senate in Alexandria and took administrative powers from Greek officials. Further, in response to an appeal by Herod, king of Judaea, he not only agreed to restore to him the land that

LEFT: *The Flight into Egypt* from the Playfair Book of Hours, late 15th-century.
RIGHT: chapel on Mount Moses.

had been bestowed on Cleopatra during her short refuge in Syria, but also agreed to grant self-government to the Hellenised Jews of Alexandria.

All this caused great consternation among the Greeks. Fighting soon broke out, first between Greeks and Jews, then with the Romans when they tried to separate the two. The unrest that marks the beginning of the Christian era in Alexandria had already begun. Ships in the harbour were set on fire, the flames spread and the Mouseion Library was burned.

The Romans thenceforth stationed garrisons at Alexandria, which remained the capital; at Babylon (Old Cairo), which was the key to communications with Asia and with Lower Egypt; and at Syene (Aswan), which was Egypt's southern boundary. They controlled Egypt by force, and an enormous burden of taxation was placed on the people of the Nile Valley. A census was imposed on villages throughout the land and house-to-house registration of the number of residents was made, which might have been considered normal procedure in Rome, but was regarded as an infringement of privacy by Egyptians. Calculation of the wheat quota was based not on the productivity of the land, but on the number of men in a village.

Those Egyptians who had enjoyed certain privileges under the later Ptolemies and acquired considerable wealth received no special consideration by the Romans, but had their problems com-

number, then 60, then 100 from a single village. Some took refuge in remote areas of the desert, while others hid in caves and ancient tombs flanking the Nile Valley. When men fled or hid, their families suffered the penalties.

Strategic planning

The Romans made an overt show of respect for Egyptian priesthoods by constructing new temples or completing older ones built by the Ptolemies. The temple to the goddess Hathor at Denderah, for example, which was started under the later Ptolemies, was completed some 185 years later under the Emperor Tiberius; and temples in the

The Romans regarded Egypt, like other parts of North Africa, as no more than a granary, supplying wheat to Rome, and as a pleasure-ground for the Roman upper classes.

pounded when the Emperor Trajan declared that peasant farmers should be recruited for the Roman Army. Hadrian reduced rentals on imperial lands and exempted citizens of Greek cities and Greek settlers in the Fayyum from taxation, but the Egyptian rural population was assessed at a flat rate, without regard for income, age or capacity for work. Hardship followed. There are records of men having "fled leaving no property", 43 in

traditional style were completed at Esna, Kom Ombo and Philae. It is worth noting, however, that these sites were chosen for their strategic position as well as the sake of ancient tradition. Esna had been a centre for local commerce from earliest times; Kom Ombo, situated on a hill, commanded the trade routes to Nubia in the south; and Philae was situated on Egypt's southern border.

Temple lands elsewhere, however, were annexed and placed under the control of the Roman Government. Local priests were allotted only a small part of sacred property and their own material wealth was curbed. The produce of vineyards, palm groves and fig plantations owned by temples was collected by Roman officials and taxes were levied on sheep, oxen, horses and donkeys. A Roman official held the title of "High Priest of Alexandria and all Egypt".

Early Christianity

Such were the conditions in Egypt during the 1st century of the Christian era, when the apostle Mark preached in Alexandria. Remains from the period showing the diffusion of Christianity in Egypt are scant, but New Testament writings found in Bahnasa in Middle Egypt date from around AD 200, and a fragment of the gospel of St John, written in Coptic and found in Upper Egypt, can be dated even earlier. They testify to the spread of Christianity in Egypt within a century of St Mark's arrival.

writer who is considered as the greatest of the early Christian apologists. Like Clement, he was highly critical of the Gnostic movement (from the Greek *gnosis* or "knowledge").

Gnosticism

The origin of the Gnostic communities is obscure and until recently not much was known about them: the Gnostics were hounded into silence, in the name of orthodox Christianity, from the 4th century onward and their writings were burned. Fortunately, however, a collection of manuscripts was discovered in Nag Hammadi in Upper Egypt in 1945. These texts, which have raised some im-

The Catechetical School of Alexandria was the first important institution of religious learning in Christian antiquity. It was founded in 190 by Pantanaeus, a scholar who is believed to have come to Alexandria approximately 10 years earlier. Significantly, the emergence of the school coincides with the first direct attacks by the Romans on the Christians of Alexandria.

Clement (160–215), a convert from paganism who succeeded Pantanaeus, is regarded as an early apostle of Christian liberalism and taught in Alexandria for more than 20 years. He was succeeded by Origen (185–253), the theologian and

ABOVE: St Anthony's Monastery in the Eastern Desert was founded in the 4th century.

THE NAG HAMMADI CODICES

The 12 Nag Hammadi codices were collected by Egyptians and translated into Coptic, the Egyptian language of the time. They vary widely in content, presenting a spectrum of heritages that range from Egyptian folklore, Hermeticism, Greek philosophy and Persian mysticism to the Old and New Testaments. The codices include a "a gospel of Thomas", a compilation of sayings attributed to Jesus; extracts from Plato's *Republic*; and apocrypha ("secret books") related to Zoroastrianism and Manichaeism. With such diversity, it is perhaps little wonder that the Gnostics came under attack from orthodox Christians, who eventually destroyed the majority of their writings.

portant questions about the development of Christianity in Egypt, are copied from original writings that may date from the second half of the 1st century AD *(see box page 57)*.

Neoplatonism's Egyptian roots

A more formidable rival to Christianity in the long run came directly from pagan thought: Neoplatonism. Coalescing in Alexandria during the 3rd century, this philosophical school revived the metaphysical and mystical side of Platonic doctrine, explaining the universe as a hierarchy rising from matter to soul, soul to reason and reason to God, conceived as pure being without matter or

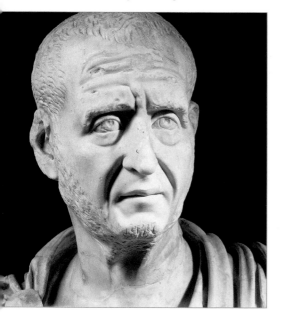

form. Neoplatonists understood reality as the spiritual world contemplated by reason and allowed the material world only a formal existence. Ascetic disciplines were part of their ethical code, which urged them to ascend from the bonds of matter to the spiritual world, in order to become ecstatically united with the divine.

The first Neoplatonist, Ammonius Saccas, had been the teacher of Origen and was a lapsed Christian, while his famous successors – Plotinus, Porphyry, Iamblichus, Hypatia and Proclus – were all pagans. Plotinus, born in Asyut, was the most influential, making many converts at the imperial court in Rome. Porphyry, who was his student, came to be regarded by the Christian bishops as their greatest enemy – they burned his books in public – and the last important work of the school was Proclus's defence of the pagan philosophical tradition against Christianity. More than one Christian was a student of Neoplatonism, nevertheless, and even Porphyry found Christian readers and translators, by whom Neoplatonic ideas were co-opted into the teachings of the early Church.

Religious persecution

The first systematic attempt to put an end to Christianity by depriving the Church of both its leaders and followers took place under the emperor Decius (249–251), who ordered Egyptians to participate in pagan worship in the presence of Roman officers and to submit certificates of sacrifice. Those who refused were declared to be self-avowed Christians and were tortured. Some Christians sent in false certificates; others managed to escape to the solitude of the desert. Many, however, were willing to die rather than

NEOPLATONIC LEGACY

Many major Neoplatonic works survived intact, and by the end of the Middle Ages a handful of Europeans could read them in the original. As knowledge of Greek began to extend outside the clergy, aristocratic study-groups sprang up, most notably in Florence, and Neoplatonism rapidly became first a fashion, then a movement. The 15th-century humanist philosopher, Marsilio Ficino, founder of the Florentine Academy, was particularly influential in spreading Neoplatonist ideals. Within a few years its influence had spread from northern Italy throughout Western Europe, largely creating that cultural consensus we call the Renaissance.

Thus a common element in the paintings of Botticelli

or Titian, the engravings of Dürer, the sculpture of Michelangelo, or the poetry of Shakespeare, which distinguishes them from earlier European art, is their rootedness in Neoplatonic images and ideas. For two centuries or so, while a 1,000-year-old Christian orthodoxy came increasingly into question, these images and ideas were to be the conceptual currency of every educated European, although they were not regarded as being in opposition to Christianity.

They were also modern man's first key to an understanding of the ancient pagan culture that the early Church, in Egypt and elsewhere, had consciously set out to destroy.

abjure their faith, and their martyrdom further accelerated the Christian movement.

Beginnings of Monasticism

St Paul the Theban, orphaned as a youth, and St Anthony, who came from a wealthy family of landowners, were two of Egypt's earliest and greatest spiritual leaders. Both lived lives of meditation and prayer at about this time; each, unknown to the other, had chosen a retreat in the Eastern Desert in a range of mountains near the Gulf of Suez. St Paul, older than St Anthony and with the gift of healing, is believed to have retired to the desert at the age of 16 to escape the perse-

Thousands of ascetics, whose original models may be traced to pre-Christian times in Egypt, were living either alone or in small groups during the 3rd and 4th centuries.

beyond the borders of the country in which they took root, contradictory beliefs as to the origins of Monasticism have emerged. St Jerome credits St Paul the Theban with being the first hermit. In both Coptic and Western tradition, however, St Anthony holds a more prominent position, and Copts regard him as the prototype of the Egyptian anchorite.

cutions of Decius. St Anthony, after visionary inspiration, sold his inheritance, gave his money to the poor, then retreated to the cliffs flanking the Nile Valley, later settling beneath a range of mountains known today as the South Qalala.

These two men became regarded as having special powers and a special relationship with the divine, attracting other eremites to draw near them looking for guidance and instruction in an atmosphere of security and spirituality.

As with most great movements that spread

LEFT: Emperor Decius (AD 249–251) tried to halt the march of Christianity. **ABOVE:** *The Thebaid* by Ucello Paolo (1397–1475) depicting the valley of the Nile under Roman domination

A turning point

In 284 the Roman army elected Diocletian emperor and his reforms mark a turning-point in the history of Christianity. The appalling social and economic conditions throughout the Roman Empire led him to reorganise it along military lines. He divided Egypt into three major provinces, separated civic and military powers, then imposed new methods of tax assessment based on units of productivity. Under these reforms Egyptians were forced into public service and, to facilitate control, Latin was introduced as the official language.

Unification of the Roman Empire was undoubtedly the reason for these reforms, but Egyptians had had enough. They rebelled so violently that Diocletian decided that if they could not be subjugated, they should be eliminated. They were dismissed from government service, their property was confiscated, and their houses levelled. Searches were made for Christian literature, and copies of the scriptures, when found, were burned. Though thousands of people died during the terrible persecutions of Diocletian, unknown numbers escaped to refuge in the deserts, taking their zeal for Christianity with them, to create new converts.

Early monastic reform

St Pachom (Pachomius in Latin, Anba Bakhum in Arabic), born about 285, first saw the benefits

of organising the widespread anchoritic communities, and became the founder of a form of monasticism that took his name. A native Egyptian who learned Greek only late in life in order to communicate with strangers, Pachom established a community near Akhmin, where the caves in the hills flanking the Nile floodplain were populated with large numbers of ascetics. Pachom drew them together and introduced a schedule of activities for every hour of the day and night, emphasising that a healthy body provided a healthy spirit, and stressing that there should be no excesses of any kind, even in spiritual meditation.

Pachom's aim was to establish a pious, enlightened and self-sufficient community that would set an example to others. An applicant for admission did not have to exhibit spectacular feats of mortification of the flesh – this would have contradicted Pachom's dislike of excess. Although there are numerous examples of physical self-torture in the lives of the Desert Fathers, a candidate for Pachomian monasticism merely had to undergo a period of probation, after which he was clothed in the habit of a monk and officially became part of the community.

Pachom's first monastery was so successful that he moved on to found a second similar institution and yet another, until he had established no fewer than 11 monasteries in Upper Egypt, including two convents for women, although not all the ascetic communities adopted St Pachom's rule.

Conversion and controversy

The famous revelation of the Emperor Constantine in 312, which resulted in his conversion to Christianity, was followed by the Edict of Milan, which established Christianity as the favoured religion throughout the Roman Empire. It was at last safe to admit to being a Christian in Egypt. Unfortunately, the theological disputes that had plagued the early Christian movement became even more fierce in the 4th and following centuries. The controversies centred on the attempt to define the Incarnation: if Jesus was both God and Man, had He two natures? If so, what was their relationship? Defining the nature of Jesus was of crucial importance to a new religion that attracted people from many backgrounds, with different traditions, concepts of godliness, and styles of worship. It concerned such definitions as "Father", "Son", "begotten" and "unbegotten".

The chief antagonists were the Arians, named after Arius, an elderly Alexandrian presbyter, and

ST PACHOM'S MONKS

Leading healthy, disciplined lives, St Pachom's monks brought productivity to the soil, revived crafts and, more importantly, were in communication with non-Christian neighbouring communities. There is much evidence in the surviving records of various monasteries that the monks aided the people economically by providing them with their crop surpluses and with products from their craft industries. They dispensed medication to the sick and even acted as mediators in grievances, whether between members of a family or in disputes over land or water rights between neighbours. Their monasteries were usually fairly close to settlements, which made communication easler.

All Christian monasticism stems from Pachomian monasticism: St Basil, organiser of monasticism in Asia Minor, visited Egypt around 357; St Jerome made it known to the West; and St Benedict used the model of St Pachom in a stricter form.

the Monophysites, led by Alexander, bishop of Alexandria. The former held that "a time there was when He was not", in other words that Jesus did not have the same nature as God the Father. The Monophysites regarded this doctrine as recognition of two gods and a reversion to polytheism.

quence, reasoning and persistence that the Nicene Creed, to the effect that Father and Son are of the same nature, was sanctioned and remains part of the Christian liturgy. Constantine formally accepted the decision of the bishops, and issued a decree of banishment against those who refused to subscribe to it.

The decline of Alexandria

Soon after the Council of Nicea, Constantine moved his capital to the ancient Greek town of Byzantium, which became Constantinople (Constantine's city), and gained much of the prestige that once belonged to Alexandria. The new me-

They believed that Father and Son were intrinsically of one nature, and that Jesus was therefore both divine and human.

The dispute was discussed in a highly charged atmosphere and reached such an impasse that Constantine felt impelled to define a dogma to unify Christian belief. The Council of Nicea, convened in Asia Minor in 325 for this purpose, was the earliest and most important church council, the first meeting between the Church and the State. Bishop Alexander officially led Egypt's delegation but his deacon, Athanasius, was his chief spokesman. It says a great deal for his elo-

tropolis was embellished with great monuments from many ancient cities, including an obelisk over 30 metres (100 ft) high shipped from Egypt. Known as "New Rome", Constantinople became a storehouse of Christian and pagan art and science. It rapidly usurped Alexandria's reputation as a seat of learning, held since Ptolemaic times.

Thus began an era when ecclesiastical dignitaries excommunicated one another in Egypt and mobs sacked churches of opposing factions. Athanasius was driven into exile five times and sought shelter with hermits in their isolated caves.

Under Theodosius I Christianity was formally declared the religion of the empire and the Arians were again declared heretics. The Monophysite bishops of Alexandria were reinstated but, as a

LEFT: mosaic depicting St Pachom, father of monasticism in Egypt. **ABOVE:** the Council of Nicea.

result of the partition of the empire between the emperor Honorius of Rome and the emperor Arcadius of Constantinople, their power was limited. Egypt fell under the jurisdiction of the latter and the so-called Byzantine rule of Egypt began.

Byzantine period

Theophilus was made patriarch of Alexandria and displayed tremendous zeal in destroying heathen temples. A wave of destruction swept over the land of Egypt. Tombs were ravaged, walls of ancient monuments scraped, and statues toppled. In Alexandria the famous statue of Serapis was burned and the Serapeum destroyed, along with its library, which had replaced the Mouseion as a centre of learning. It was a folly of fanaticism in the name of orthodoxy not, ironically, so different from that which had earlier opposed Christianity. In 415, under Theodosius II, Patriarch Cyril expelled the Jews of Alexandria from the city.

Despite the growth of the Christian movement, factional disputes continued, especially when the see of Alexandria officially lost precedence to the see of Constantinople at the Council of Constantinople in 381. There had been riots so violent that the Catechetical School, a central force in intel-

lectual life at Alexandria for nearly two centuries, had been destroyed.

The Coptic Orthodox Church

Convened in 451, the Council of Chalcedon showed Byzantine determination to exert authority throughout Egypt. A new statement of dogma declared that Christ had two natures "concurring" in one person. When the Egyptians refused to endorse this revisionist doctrine, their patriarch was excommunicated. In the struggle that followed, several Egyptian leaders were killed, and Alexandria was pillaged by imperial troops. From then on, Egypt generally had two patriarchs, one representing the orthodoxy of Constantinople, the other upholding the "one person" beliefs of the majority of Egyptian Christians, embodied in the Coptic Orthodox Church, the national Church of Egypt, which emerged as a separate entity.

The English word Copt, meaning "Egyptian Christian", is derived from the Arabic *qibt*, which is derived in turn from *Kyptaios*, the Coptic form of the Greek word *Aigyptios*. It also designates not only the last stages of the ancient Egyptian language and script, but also the distinctive art and architecture that developed everywhere in Egypt except Alexandria – which remained attached to cosmopolitan forms – during the country's Christian era. It is used, finally, to refer to most of modern Egypt's Christian minority, who officially consti-

The end of Byzantine rule

Under Justinian, the Copts were saved from persecution only by the interest of the Empress Theodora, his wife. After her death, however, Justinian sent Alexandria a patriarch-prefect determinedly armed with both civil and religious powers. Greeted by a mob, which stoned him when he attempted to speak in church, the new bishop retaliated with force by ordering the troops under his command to carry out a general slaughter. This act effectively quelled immediate resistance, but completed the alienation of the Copts, who henceforth simply ignored any ecclesiastical representatives sent from Constantinople.   ❏

tute about 9 percent of the population and who continue to be identified with the same intense patriotism that distinguished their forebears.

The Emperor Zeno's attempt in 482 to mend the breach between Churches was unsuccessful, but after strengthening his garrison and deporting the more obstreperous Copts to Constantinople, he let matters rest. There were no more significant disturbances involving the Christians until the reign of Justinian (528–565).

LEFT: drawbridge leading to the keep at the Monastery of St Baramus, Wadi Natrun, in the desert between Cairo and Alexandria. ABOVE LEFT: image from St Bishoi's Monastery. ABOVE RIGHT: Coptic painting showing Byzantine influences.

OLD FOR NEW PLACES OF WORSHIP

In the 4th and 5th centuries many ancient temples were converted into monastic centres – Deir al-Medinah and Deir al-Bahri, both in the Theban necropolis, are two well-known examples – or churches, as in the second court of the Mortuary Temple of Ramesses III at Medinat Habu and the Court of Amenhotep III in Luxor Temple. One of the earliest Christian buildings in Egypt was constructed between the Birth House and the Coronation House of the Temple of Hathor at Denderah, using some of the blocks from the Birth House. It is possible that this church was the famous Christian centre somewhere in the neighbourhood of Denderah that St Jerome alludes to as sheltering an assembly of 50,000 monks to celebrate Easter.

EGYPT UNDER ISLAM

The Fatimid caliphs claimed direct descent from the Prophet Muhammad and believed themselves the rightful rulers of the Arab world. After their overthrow in 1171, Egypt was ruled from Turkey until the mid-20th century.

In the early 7th century, while the great rival Byzantine and Sasanian empires were exhausting themselves in a futile and costly struggle for supremacy, the Arabs were being spiritually and politically united by the Prophet Muhammad. His call for the creation of a Muslim community (the Ummah) obedient to the commands of God, as revealed in the Holy Qur'an, cut across tribal conflicts and forged the Arabs into a single nation.

Under the leadership of his successors, the caliphs, the energy of the Arabs was directed outward against the contending empires of the north, who were too weak to resist an invasion from the heart of the Arabian Peninsula. Inspired by both the duty of waging jihad (Holy War) against non-believers and the promise of rich booty, the Muslim armies conquered all of Persia and half of the Byzantine Empire between 636 and 649.

Fall of the Byzantines

The Byzantine province of Egypt was invaded in 639 by 'Amr ibn al-'As, one of the ablest of the early Muslim generals, who had visited Alexandria in his youth and had never forgotten the

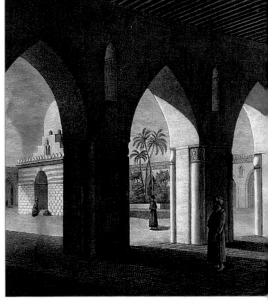

The Muslim general 'Amr ibn al-'As, justified his actions by saying that the people of Egypt were sheep, that its land was gold, and that it belonged to whoever was strong enough to take it.

Egyptian capital's obvious wealth. Acting on his own initiative, he was a master of hit-and-run tactics, and his horsemen easily defeated a Byzantine

LEFT: the minaret of the 9th-century mosque of Ibn Tulun. **RIGHT:** engraving of Ibn Tulun's Mosque from Napoleon's *Description de l'Egypte*.

army near the ancient ruins of Heliopolis in 640. He then set about besieging both the fortress of Babylon, at the head of the Delta, and Alexandria itself. Paralysed by internal problems and foreign wars, the Byzantines were unable to reinforce their army in Egypt. Babylon fell in 641 and the rest of the country was formally surrendered soon after.

Coptic allies

The Arabs were aided in their conquest by the indifference of the native Egyptians, the Copts, whose political and religious disputes with Constantinople had made them deeply hostile to Byzantine rule. Not yet interested in converting subject peoples to Islam, which they still viewed as a purely Arab religion, the Muslim conquerors favoured the Coptic

Church over the Byzantine establishment and allowed it autonomy, using it to assist them in collecting the poll tax levied on all non-Muslims.

During the siege of Babylon, the Muslims had camped to the north of the fortress and it was here that 'Amr founded Fustat, a garrison city, for the control of the Nile Valley.

> *Arabic began to replace Greek as the language of government, culture and commerce in the city and in time filtered down to the rural population, causing the Coptic language to be forgotten.*

The Abbasid caliphs

The rapid growth of the new Islamic Empire brought in its wake a host of problems. Tribal differences among the Arabs began to reassert themselves as various factions fought over the spoils of conquest and the leadership of the Ummah. These conflicts, usually expressed in religious terms, deeply divided the Arabs and resulted in more than 100 years of rebellions and civil wars.

A semblance of Muslim unity was eventually re-established in 750 when the Abbasid family seized control of the empire. Brought to power by a coalition of Arab and Iranian forces, the Abbasids established a more international state, which was centred on Baghdad and which drew upon the services of all Muslims.

In Egypt a new administrative capital was built to the north of the former capital Fustat. Known as Al-Askar or "the Cantonments", this military suburb became the official residence of the provincial governor, his attendant army and the large bureaucracy.

During the first 200 years of Muslim rule, Egypt was a pawn rather than a true participant in the wider political issues that dominated the affairs of the Islamic Empire. Controlled by a series of military governors appointed by the caliphs in the east, most of the country's great agricultural wealth was channelled into the coffers of the central treasury. The power of these governors was severely curtailed by short terms of office and by restrictions placed upon their internal authority to prevent the establishment of an independent state in Egypt.

The result was oppressive taxation and widespread official corruption, which brought Egypt to the verge of economic collapse in the early 9th century. This state of affairs also reflected the progressive decline of Abbasid authority throughout the empire, which was simply too large to be effectively ruled by one man.

In order to hold their state together the caliphs in Baghdad began to employ Turkish slave armies to act as a counterbalance to their turbulent Arab and Iranian subjects. Far from being slaves in the Western sense of the word, these Turks were groomed as a ruling caste, loyal only to the Abbasids. The power of the Turkish generals became so great and the upkeep of their armies so expensive that the caliphs were compelled to distribute whole provinces to them in lieu of pay. In this manner Egypt became a private fief of the new Muslim military elite in 832. Unwilling to leave the political nerve centre of Iraq, which might result in a loss of influence, the generals appointed their own governors for Egypt, who acted independently rather than as agents of the caliphs.

Independence under Ibn Tulun

The most famous Turkish governor was Ahmad Ibn Tulun. The son of a Turkish slave, he had been raised and educated in the Abbasid court and was posted to Egypt in 868 at the age of 33. Taking advantage of rivalry among the Abbasid family and its Turkish armies, Ibn Tulun was able to gain total control of the provincial government, establishing the first autonomous Muslim state in Egypt. By drastically reducing the imperial tribute to Iraq and by reinvesting the country's wealth in his new domain, Ibn Tulun brought about a period of prosperity. One of his first actions as independent sovereign was the creation of a strong army made up of Turkish, Greek and Sudanese slaves, with which he conquered all of Syria in 878.

In order to celebrate his independence Ibn Tulun built a new royal city to the north of Al-Askar called Al-Qatai or "the Wards" after its division into separate districts, each housing a different contingent of his multiracial army.

Ibu Tulun died in 884 and was succeeded by his 20-year-old son Khumarawayh. With his father's army he extended the borders of the Tulunid state to the Euphrates, forcing the Abbasids

Tunisia, however, demanded a more effective form of government in the Nile Valley. The Abbasids were therefore compelled to allow the establishment in 935 of a new semi-autonomous state in Egypt, founded by Muhammad Ibn Tuglij, known as "the Ikhshid". His main task was the creation of a strong Egyptian buffer state to prevent further Fatimid eastern expansion.

On his death in 946, he was nominally succeeded by his young sons, but the real power was held by their regent, the Nubian eunuch Kafur. Kafur's strong rule held the Ikhshid state together, but on his death it fell when faced by the Fatimid invasion of 969.

to recognise his sovereignty. In 896 Khumarawayh was murdered by slaves from his harem and was succeeded by his two sons and a brother, notable for the extravagance of their lifestyle and incompetence of their rule. After exhausting the state treasury and alienating the army, they were deposed and murdered, leaving Egypt too weak to resist the reestablishment of direct Abbasid rule in 905.

For the next 30 years Egypt was again ruled by a series of oppressive and ineffectual provincial governors, appointed from Iraq. The growing threat of the Shi'a Fatimid dynasty, centred in

LEFT: engraving in the mosque of Ibn Tulun.
ABOVE: the Fatimid period gave rise to many splendid buildings in Cairo.

The origins of the Fatimids

The Fatimids were a radical Shi'a sect that believed their imams (leaders) were the only rightful rulers of the Muslim world. Basing their claim on their direct descent from the Prophet Muhammad through his daughter Fatima, they viewed the Abbasids as usurpers, and dreamed of uniting all of Islam under the banner of Shi'a Islam.

The conversion of the Kutama Berbers of Algeria by an Isma'ili agent in the early 10th century supplied the Fatimids with an army and a North African kingdom, but their dreams were set on Egypt. The death of Kafur and the consequent downfall of the Ikhshid state supplied the Fatimid caliph Al Mu'izz with the chance he had been waiting for.

The founding of Al-Qahirah

In 969 Egypt fell to General Jawhar, a military slave of European origin, whose first action was the construction of a new royal enclosure to house the victorious Al-Mu'izz and his Shi'a government. The new Fatimid capital was named Al-Qahirah, "The Subduer", later corrupted by Italian merchants into Cairo.

The Fatimid imams controlled a vast secret organisation, the Da'wa, which sent highly trained agents throughout the Muslim world, winning converts and preparing the way for the eventual takeover of the Isma'ili caliphs. But the initial military success of the Fatimids was short-lived. After

The followers of Al-Hakim were eventually driven out of Egypt and forced to flee to Lebanon, where they founded the Druze religion, a sect that still believes Al-Hakim to have been the incarnation of God.

gaining control of Palestine and the holy cities of Mecca and Medina, they encountered stiff Byzantine resistance in northern Syria. To offset their military failure the Fatimids turned to the realm of trade. Fustat became a major trade emporium, and Fatimid Egypt became fabulously wealthy.

Plans for the conquest of the Abbasid Empire were postponed indefinitely and little effort was made to convert the Christian and Sunni Muslim native population to Shi'a Islam. As a minority sect in Egypt, unconcerned with proselytising, the Fatimids were extremely tolerant, employing Sunnis, Christians and Jews equally.

The mad caliph

The shift to a conservative and materialistic state deeply concerned the third Fatimid caliph, Al-Hakim (996–1021). Described as insane by medieval Arab historians, he was preoccupied with revitalising the spiritual mission of the Isma'ili movement and with the maintenance of his personal power in the face of governmental opposition. His fervour resulted in measures that were both extreme and brutal, but rarely without a purpose.

Decrees aimed against women, forbidding them from leaving their houses or possessing independent wealth, besides being a concession to public morality, were probably directed against his sister, Sitt al-Mulk, who was an influential opponent of his policies. When he allowed a group of extremist Iranian Isma'ilis to proclaim his divinity in 1017, he was only carrying the spiritual pretensions of his family to their ultimate limits..

The Fatimid hierarchy eventually decided the imam had to go. While he was riding his donkey alone in the Muqattam Hills at night, Al-Hakim mysteriously disappeared, almost certainly murdered on the orders of his sister and the Fatimid elite, who now took over the reins of government.

Famine and threats

During the reign of Al-Mustansir (1036–94), Fustat reached the peak of its prosperity. With a population of almost half a million people living in five-storey buildings, with running water and so-

ABBASIDS VERSUS FATIMIDS

The origins of the rivalry between the Abbasids and the Fatimids date back to the first years of the Islamic era, when the early Muslims were divided over who was to succeed Muhammad on his death in 632. The majority of his followers, who were to become the Sunnis, favoured the election of one of them as caliph, while a minority, who became known as the Shi'a, supported a hereditary principle, which would preserve the caliphate within the Prophet's family. Among the most extreme of the various Shi'a sects that grew out of this conflict were the Isma'ilis, of whom the Fatimids were the most successful members, and who believed their imams were the only men capable of leading the Ummah to perfection.

phisticated sewer systems, it was one of the great cities of its age.

Despite its wealth the Fatimid state rapidly began to decline. The Turkish troops, who had largely replaced their Berber rivals, were unruly and a constant threat to internal security. A series of seven low Niles between 1066 and 1072 plunged the country into further chaos. Famine and plague spread throughout the Nile Valley, reducing the people of Fustat to cannibalism. The Turkish soldiers looted the Fatimid palaces on the pretext of arrears of pay, and Al-Mustansir secretly called in Badr al-Jamali, the Fatimid's Armenian governor at Acre in Palestine, to restore order.

few years earlier. The crusaders were themselves divided into four, often hostile, principalities, more concerned with their individual short-term needs than with the establishment of a single, strong Christian kingdom.

The rise of the Zangids of Mosul, who began absorbing their Muslim neighbours and preaching jihad in the first half of the 12th century, meant it was just a matter of time before the Christians were encircled and picked off one by one.

Saladin

The Fatimids tried to play one side against the other, but in 1169 were compelled to submit to

A surprise attack on Al-Qahirah in 1072 crushed all opposition and won Badr al-Jamali full dictatorial powers. He now had to face an impending invasion by the Seljuk Turks and the enclosing walls of Al-Qahirah were rebuilt, incorporating massive new gates, to withstand the expected siege. The sudden break-up of the Seljuk Empire after 1092 saved the Fatimids from certain defeat, but left the Middle East crowded with petty Muslim states. Their lack of unity facilitated the victories of the first Crusade of 1099, launched in response to the Seljuk conquest of Jerusalem a

LEFT: 12th-century depiction of the Fatimid cavalry attacking a Crusader fortress. **ABOVE:** the Mosque of Al Hakim today.

INSIDE THE ROYAL ENCLOSURE

Separated from the predominantly Sunni population of Fustat by a mile of wasteland, Al-Qahirah's high walls could be penetrated only by the Isma'ili elite. Within were two great palaces, the home of the imam and his court bureaucracy. Its religious and intellectual centre was the mosque of Al-Azhar, the headquarters of the Da'wa and the main congregational mosque of the city. The rest of Al-Qahirah's 120 hectares (300 acres) were filled with gardens.

Secluded in the luxury of their fortress city, the Fatimid imams underwent a dramatic change and the more radical aspects of their esoteric teachings were toned down.

the Zangid general Salah-ad-Din (Saladin), who abolished the Fatimid caliphate in 1171, re-establishing Sunni Islam in Egypt. The Fatimids were the last Arab dynasty to rule Egypt. From this point on the country would be under the control of Turks and related peoples from the eastern Islamic

> *Though weakened by dynastic and military rivalries, Egypt was incredibly wealthy.*
> *The key to victory in the various power struggles was that who ever controlled its vast resources could dominate the whole region.*

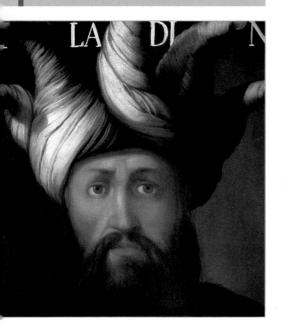

world, a situation that would continue until the 1952 revolution.

In theory Egypt was now a part of the Zangid Empire, ruled by Nur ad-Din, a man dedicated to jihad against the crusaders; in reality it was firmly in the hands of his Kurdish general, Saladin. Refusing to leave Egypt until it was secure from crusader attack and Fatimid resurgence, Saladin fell out with his master, who wanted Egypt's resources for his own war effort.

Sending only apologies and excuses, Saladin set about building a power base. His enlarged army was stationed in the newly constructed Citadel, situated about halfway between Al-Qahirah and Fustat. The two urban centres were linked to the new fortress by a series of walls, to facilitate the defence

of the Egyptian capital, setting the stage for the future development of one unified city.

Resisting the Crusades

The death of Nur ad-Din in 1174 and the subsequent break-up of this empire left Saladin undisputed master of Egypt. He spent the next 13 years conquering the divided Zangid principalities of Syria and placing them under the control of his family, the Ayyubids. With Egypt and Syria once again united, Saladin turned his attention to the crusaders, who were decisively defeated in 1187.

The capture of Jerusalem and Palestine established Saladin as a champion of Islam, but also triggered the Third Crusade. Led by Richard the Lionheart of England and Philippe II of France, the Christians retook Acre, but were unable to advance further. The peace settlement of 1192 recognised Saladin's gains, leaving the crusaders in possession of a small coastal strip of Palestine. Saladin died the following year a satisfied man.

The Ayyubid Empire created by Saladin was a federation of sovereign city-states, loosely held together by family solidarity. The rulers of Egypt, the wealthiest and most centralised of the provinces, exercised a vague suzerainty over their kinsmen, which they used to try to limit the endless intrigues and power struggles that dominated Ayyubid politics. As the head of the family, the sultans of Egypt had the right to demand military aid from their brothers and cousins in Syria, but this was often reluctantly given, the minor princes being more afraid of their Ayyubid neighbours than of an external enemy. The sultans, as a result, were hesitant about engaging in serious warfare, preferring to use diplomacy to achieve their aims.

The Sultan Al-Kamil (1218–38) was able to defeat a Christian invasion of the Nile Delta in 1221, but to avoid a repetition of the experience came to a peaceful agreement with the Holy Roman Emperor Frederick II in 1229, whereby Jerusalem was declared an open city, accessible to Muslims and Christians alike. This solution to the crusading problem proved unpopular with religious fanatics on both sides and hostilities were soon resumed.

The last major Ayyubid sultan, As-Salih (1240–49), whose ruthless rise to power had alienated most of his relatives, could no longer rely on the support of his Syrian kinsmen. Faced with the threat of a Mongol invasion from the east, As-Salih began building a Turkish slave army, loyal only to him, to defend the Ayyubid state.

The fighting abilities of As-Salih's new military slaves or Mamluks were put to the test in 1249, when the Sixth Crusade of St Louis IX of France invaded Egypt. During the course of hostilities As-Salih died, but news of his death was concealed by his wife and the Mamluk emirs, to allow his son, Turan Shah, to reach Egypt and claim the sultanate. Turan Shah arrived in time to witness the defeat of the French king by the Mamluks in 1250. Alarmed by the growing power of the Bahris, the new sultan began to replace them with his own men. But the Mamluks were not to be ousted so easily. Instead, they murdered Turan Shah and seized control of Egypt.

negotiating a second marriage with a princess of Mosul. Unwilling to share her power with another woman, Shagar Ad-Durr had her husband murdered. Aybek's Mamluks, enraged by the death of their master, seized his queen and handed her over to the former wife of Aybek, whom he had been compelled to divorce by Shagar Ad-Durr upon becoming sultan. Egypt's only woman sultan was then beaten to death in front of her rival.

The Mamluks had proved their military prowess against the crusaders and the Ayyubids, but were now called upon to face a far greater threat; the heathen Mongols, who in 1257 swept through Iraq into Syria, crushing all Muslim resistance. Unde-

The Bahri Mamluks

To legitimise their coup, the Mamluks proclaimed Shagar Ad-Durr (As-Salih's widow) as sultan. The Ayyubid princes of Syria, refusing to accept the loss of the richest province of their empire to a woman, prepared for war. Needing a man to lead her army, Shagar ad-Durr married the Mamluk commander, Aybek, who ruled with her as sultan. The Ayyubids were defeated in 1250 and Aybek, encouraged by his victory, conquered Palestine.

To strengthen his position, in 1257 Aybek began

The Mamluks' Maristan hospital was ahead of its time. There were wards for all known diseases, baths, kitchens, laboratories and a lecture hall for interns.

feated in battle, the Central Asian hordes seemed on the verge of extinguishing Muslim civilisation in the Middle East. Only the Mamluks remained to stop them and at the battle of Ayn Jalut in 1260 they did, becoming the saviours of Islam.

Under the sway of their first great sultans, Baybars al-Bunduqdari (1260–79) and then Qalawun (1279–90), the Mamluks emerged as the foremost military power of their age. Kept in top fighting

LEFT: Saladin (1138–93) depicted by the Renaissance painter Cristoforo dell'Altissimo. **ABOVE:** the Battle of Hattin, 1187, in which Muslim forces under the command of Saladin vanquish the crusaders.

shape by the constant threat of the Mongols, now centred in Iran, the Mamluks recaptured Syria and expelled the last of the crusaders from the Palestinian coast.

The Mamluk system

The political system created by Baybars was based on a military slave oligarchy. Young Qipchaq Turks would be brought to Egypt as slaves, converted to Islam and given a military training. On completion of their education they would be freed and enrolled in the private army of one of the great Mamluk emirs, who collectively controlled all of Egypt's resources and governmental positions. The most

Position within the Mamluk hierarchy depended on slave origins. The sons of Mamluks were not allowed to follow their fathers' military careers so a steady flow of new slaves was required to replenish army ranks.

ruler without power, allowing the emirs time to determine who was the strongest without resorting to civil war. In this manner Qalawun's son An-Nasir Muhammad was made nominal sultan in 1293, at the age of nine. After ruling for a year he was deposed, but then reinstated in 1299,

powerful amir would be chosen as the sultan.

The foundation of the system was the intense loyalty the individual Mamluk felt for his military house (*bayt*). His political fortunes were linked to those of his emir. If his *bayt* was successful, the common Mamluk could expect to be promoted to the rank of emir and even to the sultanate. The political environment was therefore dominated by intrigue and constant striving for power among the *bayts*. The sultan tried to manipulate these conflicts to maintain his position but if he was unsuccessful he would be destroyed by his emirs' ambitions.

The reign of An-Nasir Muhammad

The one exception to this rule was that the son of a sultan often succeeded his father as a stopgap

when the emirs fell out amongst themselves.

Having been raised in an atmosphere of intrigue and double-dealing, An-Nasir emerged at the age of 25 as a ruthless, suspicious and absolutely despotic sultan. Resolving to rule alone after enduring the miseries of his youth, he murdered the emirs of his father one by one, replacing them with his own men. Unwilling to trust even the emirs of his own *bayt*, An-Nasir inaugurated an era of peace to prevent arming a potential rival with the command of an army. A period of trade and great prosperity ensued, the apex of Muslim civilisation in Egypt.

An-Nasir's success in mastering the Mamluk system brought about the beginning of its decline. So firmly did he grip the reins of power that, on his death in 1340, none of the emirs was strong enough to replace him. Instead he was succeeded by a series of ineffective sons and grandsons.

An-Nasir's policy of peace filled the state's treasury but caused the Mamluks to neglect their military training. A whole generation grew up without having fought a major war, a serious deficiency for a state founded on martial superiority.

The Circassian Mamluks

For 41 years after the death of An-Nasir, 12 of his direct descendants ruled Egypt as nominal sultans. But in 1382 the emir Barquq (1382–99) seized control and distributed all positions of power to his fellow Circassians. This second Mam-

new central Asian conqueror devastated their Syrian province. Repeated outbreaks of plague during the 15th century reduced the ranks of the Mamluks, whose replacement was both costly and difficult. The threat of strong neighbours and the chronic outbreak of factional fighting at home further drained the treasury, forcing the sultans to adopt the short-sighted economic policies of excessive taxation, debasement of the currency and the introduction of state-owned monopolies.

The chief failing of the Circassians, however, was their refusal to adopt modern military methods. Bred to be a cavalry elite, they despised gunpowder as unmanly. Their major rivals in the early

luk dynasty maintained the same political system as the Qipchaq predecessors. An important difference, however, was that the Circassians were brought to Egypt not as boys, but as young men. Instead of being moulded by the rigours of a Mamluk education, they arrived in Cairo with clear ideas of how to manipulate the system to their own benefit. Ambitious, unruly and deficient in their military training, they were a terror to the inhabitants of Egypt, but poor soldiers.

Unable to defeat the invading Tamerlane in 1400, the Circassians watched helplessly as the

LEFT: Mamluk soldiers and a Mamluk official.
ABOVE *The Turkish Patrol*, by Alexandre Gabriel Decamps, painted in 1831.

THE BLACK DEATH

The reign of the Mamluk sultan Hasan (1347–61) saw the outbreak of the Black Death, which rocked the economic foundations of Egypt by drastically reducing its population. Whole districts of Cairo were completely wiped out, indirectly benefiting the sultan, who inherited the property and valuables of the plague's numerous victims. With this unexpected windfall Hasan financed his great mosque, which was completed in 1362 and considered the grandest of all Cairo's Mamluk buildings. This was no small distinction: the Mamluk sultans' lust for political power was matched only by their love of luxury and the number and splendour of their grand buildings.

16th century, the Ottoman Turks, had no such snobbish qualms. When the two forces finally clashed at the battle of Marj Dabiq in 1517, the Mamluks were blown off the field by superior cannon fire. Following this victory, the Ottoman Sultan Selim the Grim conquered the Mamluk sultanate and Cairo became the provincial capital of a new Muslim empire centred in Istanbul.

Egypt as an Ottoman province

The Ottomans, engaged in continual warfare with Iran and the Christian West, could not afford to spare the necessary men to uproot the Mamluks from Egypt completely. Instead the Mamluks were incorporated into the Ottoman ruling elite and held in check by a provincial governor and a garrison of crack Ottoman troops, the Janissaries.

In the 17th century, military defeats brought steady decline to the Ottoman Empire. Rampant inflation, caused by the flood of Spanish silver from the New World, upset the balance of power in Egypt. The office of governor was sold to the highest bidder, then resold at the first opportunity, to supply the central treasury with a steady flow of cash. The governors, rarely ruling for more than three years, could never establish effective control over Egypt. The Janissaries, forced into local trade by the steady devaluation of their salaries, became little more than armed shopkeepers and artisans.

The rise of Ali Bey al Kabir (1760–72) saw the remergence of the Mamluks as an international power. By destroying the rival *bayts*, the governor and the Janissaries, Ali Bey became master of Egypt. He was on the verge of re-establishing the Mamluk Empire when he was betrayed by his lieutenant Abu'l-Dhahab. Deprived of its

strong leadership, the Mamluk *bayt* of Ali Bey fragmented and Egypt was plunged into a devastating civil war which lasted until 1791. Although order was restored by the victory of Murad Bey and Ibrahim Bey, the economy of the country was in ruins. In this unsettled state, Egypt was invaded in 1798 by the French under Napoleon Bonaparte.

The French expedition

On the morning of 21 July, 1798, the combined musketry and artillery of 29,000 French troops smashed an onslaught of Mamluk cavalry. This, known as the Battle of the Pyramids, marked a turning of the tide against the East. It also roused

NAPOLEON'S SAVANTS

A scientific mission consisting of 60 savants accompanied the French expedition up the Nile in 1798. Their task was to compile a complete dossier on Egypt's antiquities, its people, topography, flora and fauna, producing a massive *Description de l'Egypte*, which became a runaway success when published between 1809 and 1813.

The task of the savants, who comprised intellectuals and scholars, was to learn and record as much about Egypt and its ancient monuments as they possibly could. Their number included specialists in every conceivable discipline from astronomy to zoology, and none of them was more colourful – or destined for

greater fame – than Dominique Vivant Denon, an impoverished minor aristocrat, failed lawyer, temporary diplomat, antiques dealer, archaeologist and interior decorator. Among his friends he included Voltaire and – more relevant to his inclusion in the party – Josephine, Napoleon's wife.

The military did their best to accommodate the group in their attempt to absorb and record the sights, and sometimes provided a squad of soldiers to protect Denon when he fell behind the French column to make sketches. On 1 February 1799 the French reached Aswan, from where Denon returned to Cairo loaded with drawings and notes.

Egypt from the slumber of 300 years as an Ottoman province.

Bonaparte's expedition was doomed right from the start. Within seven days of raising the *tricolore* over Saladin's citadel, the British had sunk the French fleet off Abu Qir and the Mamluks under

months, while Bonaparte's army was depleted by malaria and dysentery.

Despite the propaganda churned out in Arabic by his printing press – the first in modern Egypt – his attempt to portray the Palestine débâcle as a victory was not greeted with enthusiasm in Cairo. With communications to Paris cut by the marauding British and his own troops disillusioned, he concluded that his personal ambitions were unlikely to be served by lingering. Fourteen months after his arrival, Bonaparte slipped home in such haste that General Kléber, his second-in-command, received news of his appointment as the new General-in-Chief scrawled on a scrap of paper.

Murad Bey had fallen back to Upper Egypt, from where they continued to conduct a successful guerilla war.

Hoping to regain momentum and impress his constituency in France, Bonaparte embarked on a campaign in Palestine. Again, superior French artillery brought quick victories. These efforts to terrorise their opponents into submission failed, however, and at the fortress of Acre in northern Palestine the French were brought to an abrupt halt. Reinforced from the sea by a British fleet, the Turkish garrison maged to hold out for two

LEFT: Napoleon roused Egypt from its slumbers.
ABOVE: detail from the *Battle of the Pyramids*, painted by Louis-François Lejeune.

Although the French remained in Egypt two more years, defeating two Turkish attempts to dislodge them, the hopelessness of their mission finally forced them to succumb. Kléber was assassinated at Azbakiyyah in June 1800 and the task of negotiating with an Anglo-Ottoman force that landed in the Delta in the autumn of 1801 was left to his successor. The French, now numbering only 7,000, were allowed to return to France. In three years of occupation, they had failed to meet any of their strategic objectives. Britain still dominated the seas, the Ottomans had reinforced their hold on the Levant, and the Egyptians, though impressed by the power of European science, technology and military organisation, had rejected what little they saw of the infidel's civilisation. ❑

MUHAMMAD ALI AND MODERN EGYPT

Western intervention may have put the brakes on Egypt's expansionist projects but it indirectly led to the modernisation of the country's infrastructure

Muhammad Ali Pasha, who ruled for nearly half a century, is credited with having laid the foundations of modern Egypt. In addition to building an empire, he carried out reforms aimed at modernising Egypt and founded the dynasty that was to rule for a period of almost 150 years, until the revolution of 1952.

Muhammad Ali was born in 1769 in Kavalla, Macedonia, in what is now part of modern Greece but then belonged to the Ottoman Empire. He entered Egypt as second-in-command of an Ottoman army sent to join the British in expelling the French, who had occupied the country since 1798. After the French and British troops left Egypt, the Ottoman troops stayed on to reassert the sultan's authority.

During the four ensuing years, however, Egypt was reduced to a state of anarchy, with Mamluk beys fighting against one another and against the Ottomans, who were themselves divided along ethnic lines. In 1805, having had enough of chaos, the people of Cairo finally turned to Muhammad Ali to restore order, naming him the new viceroy. Such an appointment was the prerogative of the sultan

The Mamluk beys who managed to escape to Upper Egypt were hunted down and killed. Mamluk power came to a definitive end and Muhammad Ali's hold on power was secured.

in Constantinople, but the sultan, presented with the *fait accompli*, confirmed the Cairenes' choice.

Nevertheless, Muhammad Ali's position as viceroy was tenuous. Defeating a British force at

LEFT: engraving (1818) of the great Muhammad Ali (1769–1849). **RIGHT:** Muhammad Ali with his retinue.

Rosetta in 1807 consolidated his power, but bold steps were still required. Boldest and bloodiest was his extirpation of the rebellious Mamluk beys (officers). On March, 1811, he invited 470 Mamluks to a ceremony in the Citadel. Assembled to take their leave, the departing Mamluks had to pass through a narrow passageway to a locked gate, where the pasha had arranged for their massacre. For the next 37 years his authority was absolute in Egypt.

Among Muhammad Ali's best-known exploits are his military conquests. In 1811, at the request of the Turkish sultan Mahmud II, he sent troops into the Arabian province of the Hijaz to combat the Wahhabi movement, a fundamentalist sect of Islam that threatened the sultan's authority. In 1816 Egyptian troops entered the Nejd, the Wahhabi's homeland, and by 1818 all of western and central Arabia was under Egyptian control.

After the Arabian campaigns, Muhammad Ali sent an expedition under one of his sons up the Nile to gain control of the Sudan's mineral resources and its active slave trade, which he saw as a possible source of military manpower. Next came campaigns in Greece. At the request of the sultan, an army commanded by his son Ibrahim was sent to Crete in 1822 to quell an uprising against Ottoman control.

In 1824 a second expedition, again commanded by Ibrahim, sailed from Alexandria for the Morea, now known as the Peloponnese. This reassertion of Ottoman power provoked the major European

> By 1840 Muhammad Ali had planted more than 16 million trees and built roads and bridges where none had ever existed.

states, Britain, France and Russia. An allied fleet sent to mediate ended up sinking the entire Egyptian fleet at Navarino in 1827.

Syria gained

Muhammad Ali's last successful expansionist venture was his Syrian expedition of 1831. Using a quarrel with a governor as a pretext, he sent in Ibrahim with an army of peasant conscripts. At the end of 10 months all Syria had acknowledged him as overlord. In 1832 Ibrahim pushed on into Anatolia, defeating the Ottomans at Konya. Before he could occupy Constantinople, however, Russian intervention again brought European interests into play; and in 1833 an agreement was signed between the sultan and his unruly vassal, by which Egypt was formally accorded rule over Crete and Syria in return for an annual tribute.

With the Sudan, the Hijaz and these new acquisitions, the Egyptian Empire rivalled the Ottoman in size, although Egypt itself was still nominally a part of the Ottoman Empire and Muhammad Ali still only a pasha, the sultan's viceroy. In 1839 the sultan attempted to regain Syria by force.

Ibrahim's own crushing victory over an Ottoman army at Nezib was followed by the desertion of the Ottoman Navy to Alexandria and these two events led to a European crisis. Britain, Russia and Austria sided with the sultan, while France supported Muhammad Ali. A catastrophe was averted when Muhammad Ali signed an agreement by which his rule was to be made hereditary, but which also confirmed the sultan's suzerainty, the terms of which were agreed under European pressure in 1841.

Modernising on all fronts

Shorn of his acquisitions abroad, the pasha turned his remaining energies back to the task of modernising Egypt. The benefits to his country were enormous. They include the massive upgrading and extension of Egypt's irrigation system and the introduction of a multitude of exotic plants. Rice, indigo and sugar cane were massively encouraged, as well as the cultivation of long-time staple Egyptian cotton, which later became the country's principal export.

HEALTH OF THE NATION

The one subject on which Muhammad Ali was known to have been fanatical was public health. Swamps were drained, cemeteries were moved, hospitals, infirmaries and asylums were built, a school for midwives was established, and French-trained physicians were appointed as public-health officers in all provinces. In Cairo accumulated rubbish was cleared and seasonal ponds, like the one at Azbakiyyah, were filled, while a start was made on a street system that would allow the use of wheeled vehicles. This was extremely far-sighted at a time when the links between sanitation, dirt and disease were only just being recognised and addressed in Europe.

Land tenure and tax systems he reformed by nationalising all property, making himself titular owner of all land and eliminating the iniquitous tax-farming system that had prevailed earlier.

Muhammad Ali also created modern industries in Egypt. Beginning with an industrial complex at Bulaq, the Nile port of Cairo, where the famous Bulaq Press was set up, he built shipyards, foundries and armament factories. Textile mills, the basis of the European Industrial Revolution, soon followed. Since a primary aim was to avoid dependence upon Europe, the infant textile industry was protected by embargoes and subsidies, but this step toward economic independence was foiled,

experts recruited during his early years in power.

In Alexandria Muhammad Ali established a Quarantine Commission, thus identifying the city once again as the country's main port of entry. And it was here that the pasha died in 1848, 80 years old, but predeceased by his son, the gallant Ibrahim, to whom he had given the viceregal throne 11 months before.

Muhammad Ali's successors

Ibrahim had shown himself to be a good leader but his nephew, Abbas, the only son of Muhammad Ali's second son, Tussun, became viceroy and immediately rejected all his policies. While Muham-

like his foreign policy, by European interests: the provisions of 1841 made Egypt subject to the tariffs that prevailed through the Ottoman Empire, allowing cheaper imports, mainly from Britain, to flood into Egypt.

In other respects his efforts were more successful. The Bulaq Press was to become the most distinguished publisher in the Arab world. Its production of printed books was an essential element in the creation of a new intellectual élite, which would gradually replace the European

LEFT: equestrian statue of Ibrahim Pasha (1789–1848), Muhammad Ali's adopted son, Azbakiyyah Garden, Cairo. **ABOVE:** *Grand Cairo*, painted by the orientalist David Roberts.

mad Ali had been eager for Western agricultural and technical ideas, particularly those of the French, Abbas was xenophobic, disliking the French in particular and favouring the British, to whom he granted a railway concession. He summarily expelled all the French advisors upon whom his grandfather had depended, closed all secular or European schools, and turned for support to religious leaders. He was as autocratic as his grandfather, but earned the gratitude of the Egyptian peasants by his negligence, which left them in comparative peace. Apart from the British railway completed after his death, the sole positive relic of his six-year rule was that he left full coffers and no foreign debt.

When Abbas was murdered in 1854 by two of his personal bodyguards, his uncle Said succeeded him. Said again reversed the direction of the government, favouring a return to his father's programmes and to abandoned projects in irrigation, agriculture and education.

Open to European influences, Said is perhaps best known for his friendship with Ferdinand de Lesseps, to whom he granted a concession for the Suez Canal. As originally granted in 1854, this concession was one of the great swindles of all time, with terms extremely disadvantageous to Egypt. Recognising the enormity of his error later, Said managed to renegotiate and got somewhat more favourable terms, but only at the cost of an indemnity of more than 3 million Egyptian pounds.

To pay this sum he was forced to take Egypt's first foreign loan, thus not only setting a dangerous precedent, but planting a time bomb under Ismail, the third of Ibrahim's four sons, who became viceroy on Said's death in 1863.

Ismail the Magnificent (1863–79)

Under Ismail's rule the modernisation begun by Muhammad Ali moved forward with new dynamism. Reviving his grandfather's policy of independence from the sultan, Ismail sought to transform Egypt into a country Europe would respect. In 1866, through payments to the sultan - and an increase in tribute, he secured a change in the hereditary principle from seniority to primogeniture, thus guaranteeing the throne to his own line, and permission to maintain a standing army of 30,000. The same year he summoned the first Chamber of Deputies, a move that pleased the Europeans as representing a step towards constitutionality. The following year he obtained the Persian title of khedive (sovereign), borne by his heirs down to 1914, as well as the right to create institutions, issue regulations and conclude administrative agreements with foreign powers without consulting Constantinople. His new independence was signalised in June 1867 by Egypt's autonomous participation in the Exposition Universelle in Paris.

Foreign debts come home

The sultan's response to the festivities at the canal opening was to send Ismail a decree forbidding him to undertake foreign loans without approval. A massive bribe secured confirmation in 1873 of all rights obtained earlier, as well as permission to raise a large army.

TRANFORMING THE COUNTRY

Ismail had been sent as a student to Paris by Muhammad Ali in 1844. He was one of a delegation of 70 that also included a young man named Ali Mubarak, who would later serve Ismail as minister of education, director general of the state railways, minister of endowments and minister of public works. Ismail and Mubarak had thus known Paris as it was before the Second Empire: an essentially medieval city, largely consisting of slums and only partially touched by modernisation under Bonaparte.

When Ismail saw the transformation wrought by Haussmann – the new city, with its parks and broad tree-lined boulevards – he was dazzled; and on his

return to Egypt he sent Mubarak to Paris to see for himself, and appointed him minister of public works in the meantime. The result was the transformation of Cairo. The changes made in Cairo during the few months leading up to the opening of the Suez Canal, in 1869, were the culmination of five years of feverish modernisation not just in Cairo but throughout the country. Two other major canals had already been completed. Municipal water and gas companies had been set up in 1865, telegraph linked all parts of the country and Cairo's main railway station had been inaugurated in 1867, the same year that Ismail opened the Egyptian exhibition at the Exposition Universelle in Paris.

The American Civil War had brought wealth to Egypt by raising the price of cotton, enriching the new class of landowners that Said and Ismail had created. This was not enough, however, even coupled with Egypt's tax revenues, to keep pace with Ismael's ambitions. In the confusion of public and private exchequers, colossal debts had been run up, prompting alarm in Paris and London, where Ismail's independence was already regarded as a threat to the status quo.

Most of the debt was the result of swindles perpetrated by European adventurers. The largest of these, like the first of the debts, was an inheritance from Said: the Suez Canal, built using the

Foreign occupation

His son Tawfiq, whom Ismail himself described as having "neither head nor heart nor courage", was no match for the adversaries who had defeated his father. But the army made a stand. The chief spokesman, a senior officer named Ahmad 'Urabi, was appointed minister of war and thus found

> The khedive and his family owned around one-fifth of the cultivable land, and as the price of cotton rose on international markets much of the new wealth came his way.

corvée, at Egyptian expense. In 1875, Ismail was forced to sell his shares in the canal company to Britain. An Anglo-French dual control set up to oversee his finances began creaming off three-quarters of the annual revenues of Egypt to pay European creditors.

Ismail was forced to liquidate his personal estates and to accept British and French ministers in his cabinet. Playing the few cards left to him, he evaded a complete takeover of his government until finally the Europeans lost patience. Putting pressure on the sultan, they had Ismail deposed.

LEFT: Khedive Ismail, a visionary ruler.
ABOVE: *The Opening of the Suez Canal*, by William Pape (1859–1920).

himself at the forefront of resistance to further European intrusion.

Presented abroad first as a military dictatorship, then as a danger not only to European interests, but also to the sultan's, this situation provided the final excuse for intervention. Over the sultan's protests, British warships bombarded Alexandria on 11 July 1882. Hoping to regain status after repeated humiliations through the instrument of these invaders, Tawfiq abandoned his own government and put himself under their protection. Support for a provisional government also melted away. Near the end of August, 20,000 redcoats were landed on the supposedly sacrosanct banks of the new Suez Canal and two weeks later the Egyptian Army under 'Urabi was crushingly defeated at Tell al-Kabir.

> *Egypt's role within the British Empire was essentially to supply raw materials and a market for manufactured items, like any other colony or possession.*

Thus came to an end 19th-century Egypt's experiments with modernisation, twice halted by European displays of power. The many cultural, social and even physical marks left on the country by Muhammad Ali and Ismail have, however, so far proved indelible.

British rule

Evelyn Baring, who became Lord Cromer in 1891, first came to Egypt in 1879 as the British financial controller during the dual control of France and Britain but later returned in 1882 as the consul-general. In 1882, the British government promised an early evacuation of its troops, but they lingered on and, since the British refused to formalise their presence, the British consul-general became the de facto ruler of Egypt, with absolute authority in both its internal and foreign affairs.

Cromer discouraged both industrialisation and higher education, putting an end to the kind of autonomous development that before the occupation had made Egypt, with Japan, unique among countries of the non-Western world. It is therefore not surprising that the British occupation helped to solidify nationalist awareness in Egypt.

This awareness received added stimulus after 1892, when Abbas Hilmi Tawfiq's 18-year-old son succeeded as khedive. Educated at a Swiss school and at the celebrated Theresianum in Vienna, Abbas II was typical of the new Egyptian elite that had been created by Muhammad Ali's and Ismail's educational designs. In Egypt under Cromer, however, there was no real role for this elite or even for Abbas himself, as the consul-General made humiliatingly clear to the young khedive at the earliest opportunity. Abbas' response was to seek out the young nationalist leaders and provide them with financial support.

Secular nationalism drew growing strength between 1890 and 1906 from the country's enormous prosperity, derived almost exclusively from cotton. The landowning class created by Said and Ismail grew even richer, merging with the old and new elites. Greeks and Italians chiefly, but also Britons, Frenchmen, Swiss, Germans and Belgians, all received privileges under the Ottoman capitulations that granted them immunity from Egyptian laws and taxes.

The Dinshawai Incident

As Cromer approached retirement from Egyptian service in 1906, he contemplated changes to allow for more self-government, but his autocratic rule had left him few friends in the country. In that year the Dinshawai Incident occurred when a group of British officers were casually shooting domestic pigeons that belonged to peasants in the Delta village of Dinshawai. The villagers tried to stop them, and in the skirmish a woman and four men were wounded. Outraged villagers sur-

TRANSFORMING AGRICULTURE

The most important achievements during British rule were the completion of the Delta Barrage in 1890 and the building of the first Aswan Dam (still sometimes called the British Dam) in 1902. Begun under Muhammad Ali, the Delta Barrage made double and triple cropping possible in the Delta, while the Aswan Dam, coupled with barrages at Asyut (1903) and Esna (1906), extended the same system to Upper Egypt, reducing dependence on the annual flood. By the early 20th century, cotton had become the mainstay of the Egyptian economy. Other food crops continued to be grown and Egypt was still able to feed its growing population without depending on imports.

rounded the officers, beat them and held them until the police arrived. One officer escaped and ran through the noon-day heat to a British army camp, but died of sunstroke just outside the camp entrance. A peasant who had tried to help him was beaten to death by British soldiers. This murder was subsequently forgotten. To consider charges against the villagers of Dinshawai, however, a special tribunal was set up.

The tribunal met in Dinshawai for 30 minutes then sentenced eight villagers to lashes, 11 to periods of penal servitude ranging from one year to life, and four – including a 17-year-old boy and a 60-year-old man – to hanging. Though public exe-

dive, whom he permitted to wield increased power, and undertook several reforms. Egypt's first secular university was allowed to open in 1908 and the provincial councils were encouraged towards more autonomy. Unfortunately, Gorst's arrival coincided with a worldwide economic slump. Blamed for the ensuing crash, his policies were resented by British civil servants in Egypt and misinterpreted as weakness by the Egyptian population. In 1910, recognising their failure, he resigned and Lord Kitchener succeeded.

Kitchener had served as commander-in-chief of the Egyptian army and knew Egypt well. He introduced regulations for censorship, school

cutions had been outlawed in Egypt two years earlier, the villagers of Dinshawai were forced to witness these sentences being carried out.

Nobody connected with this incident – to which Egyptians could only respond with helpless grief – was ever forgiven.

Change at the top

Cromer's successor as consul-general, Sir Eldon Gorst, spoke Arabic, having lived many years in Egypt, and was ready to effect change in British policy. He cultivated a friendship with the khe-

LEFT: cartoon of Lord Kitchener of Egypt.
ABOVE: contemporary cartoon showing anti-British riots in Aswan in 1919.

discipline and the suppression of conspiracy. Once again the Khedive came under the consul-general's strict authority. In 1913, however, he introduced what seemed to be a liberal reform: a new constitution that provided for a Legislative Assembly. It had met on only one occasion before World War I broke out.

The Protectorate (1914–22)

The outbreak of the war was the catalyst for a series of important events. Severing the 400-year-old Ottoman connection, Britain declared Egypt a protectorate, thereby finally formalising the authority it had had for the past 32 years. Abbas Hilmi, who had been in Constantinople when the war started, was forbidden to return, then declared

> There was little enthusiasm in Egypt for either side in World War I, but much resentment of the arrogance of British power. During the war, opposition to British rule crystallised among Egypt's elite.

a traitor and deposed. His two young sons were excluded from succession, and his uncle, 60-year-old Husayn Kamel, was made ruler, with the title of sultan, by the British.

At the end of the war, the nationalist movement was stronger than ever and a dynamic leader had emerged to direct its efforts. Saad Zaghlul was an

only hardened nationalist sentiment, and by early 1919 the demands were for nothing less than complete independence, with representation at the Peace Conference in Paris. Following demonstrations in Cairo, Zaghlul and three other nationalists were exiled to Malta.

This provoked the successful uprising that Egyptians refer to as the Revolution of 1919 *(see box below)*. A field-marshal, Lord Allenby, was sent to replace Wingate, recalled because of his support for the Egyptians' demands. After appraising the situation, however, Allenby promptly brought Zaghlul home from exile, and gave him permission to go to Paris. With other members of the

Al Azhar-educated lawyer of Egyptian peasant ancestry. Imprisoned briefly for participation in the 1882 resistance, Zaghlul later practised law. During this period he married the daughter of a pro-British prime minister, and was shown favour by Cromer, who appointed him minister of education. It was not until the Protectorate was declared in 1914 that Zaghlul joined the nationalist ranks, angered by Kitchener's treachery to the constitution he had supported in 1913.

Emergence of the Wafd

As soon as the armistice was signed, Zaghlul asked the British Government to be allowed to go to London to present Egypt's case for independence, but London refused. This uncompromising position

THE REVOLUTION OF 1919

The uprising known in Egypt as the Revolution of 1919, provoked by the exile to Malta of Zaghlul and three of his colleagues, was a short-lived but bloody affair. Violence in Cairo, the Delta and the Nile Valley, especially around Asyut, was accompanied by a general strike. Many upper-class women also came out on to the streets to demonstrate, led by Safia Zaghlul, wife of Saad.

Several hundred Cairo citizens were killed in confrontations with British and Australian troops who had been unnerved, it is said, by delays in the demobilisation process. Forty British soldiers and civilians also died during the uprising, and railway and telegraph lines were destroyed.

Wafd, as his followers had come to be called (*wafd* means "delegation" in Arabic), Zaghlul attended the conference, but failed to secure his major objective. On the same day that the Treaty of Versailles was signed Allenby issued a proclamation reaffirming the Protectorate.

In November 1919, the British Government sent a mission to Egypt to study and make recommendations on the form of a constitution for the Protectorate. The mission's report recommended that, although Britain should maintain military forces in Egypt and control over foreign relations, the protection of foreign interests and the Sudan, Egypt should be declared an independent country. But the report was not published until the end of 1921, and meanwhile Zaghlul was arrested and exiled again.

For his part, Allenby had privately made conclusions similar to those of the mission. In February 1922, upon his return from a visit to England,

The Wafd spoke for the whole country during the interwar years. Its ranks consisted mostly of Egyptian professionals, businessmen and landowners, whose interests the Wafd represented until all the political parties were outlawed under Nasser.

he bore a proclamation that unilaterally ended the Protectorate, but reserved four areas of British control. Three weeks later, Egypt's independence was officially declared; and Sultan Fuad – who had been chosen by the British from among several candidates to succeed his brother, Husayn Kamel, upon the latter's death in 1917 – became King Fuad. A constitution based on that of Belgium was adopted in 1923.

Fuad as king (1922–36)

The Wafdists at first rejected this declaration of independence, with its four "reserved points". When Zaghlul was finally allowed to return, however, they sought to participate actively in the forthcoming elections, which they won by an overwhelming majority. And so Zaghlul became Egypt's prime minister in early 1924.

As prime minister, Zaghlul gave up none of his demands connected with completing independ-

LEFT: *The Egypt*, a paddle steamer operated by Thomas Cook for excursions on the Nile.
RIGHT: European dress was the norm for middle-class Egyptians in the 19th century.

dence, which included the evacuation of all British troops and Egyptian sovereignty over Sudan. His hopes for their fulfilment were raised when a Labour government came to power in Britain. Less than a year after the Wafd's landslide victory, however, the assassination of Sir Lee Stack, the British commander-in-chief *(sirdar)* of the Egyptian Army and governor-general of the Sudan, put an end to such optimism.

Allenby delivered an ultimatum to the Egyptian Government, though it had clearly not been responsible for the murder, making punitive demands. Badly shocked, Zaghlul accepted most of them, but refused withdrawal of Egyptian troops

from the Sudan, the right of Britain to protect foreign interests in Egypt, and the suppression of political demonstrations. Defiance seemed impossible, however, and he could only resign, leaving it to a successor to accept all the British conditions.

During this crisis, in December 1924, King Fuad took the opportunity to dissolve the Wafdist Parliament and rule by decree. Elections were held in March 1925 and the Wafd won by an overwhelming margin, so the king again dissolved parliament. A third set of elections in May 1926 also gave the Wafd a majority, but the British vetoed Zaghlul's reinstatement as prime minister. Already shattered by Stack's murder, Zaghlul's health deteriorated further. and he died a few months later.

Royal dictatorship

Mustafa An-Nahhas succeeded Zaghlul as the leader of the Wafd, and during the following four years the struggle between the Wafd and King Fuad took the same pattern, with the Wafd winning general elections and the king dissolving the Parliament to appoint his own ministers. In 1930, Fuad appointed Ismail Sidqi Pasha as prime minister and replaced the 1923 constitution with his own royally decreed one. Two successors managed to maintain Fuad's constitution until 1935, when combined nationalist, popular and British pressure finally forced him to restore the constitution of 1923.

In 1928, Hassan Al-Banna had founded the Muslim Brotherhood, the stated aim of which was to purify and revitalise Islam. But the brotherhood had political aspirations as well and began to take an active part in politics in the late 1930s. It has since been a force with which every Egyptian government has had to contend.

During the interwar period, agriculture remained the backbone of the economy, but the Egyptian middle class started to invest in factories. The process of industrialisation began again, in a modest way initially, but greatly stepped up after the end of World War II. Along with industrialisation inevitably came urbanisation.

Negotiations for an Anglo-Egyptian treaty concerning the status of Britain in Egypt and the Sudan had long been underway. It was finally signed in August 1936 and became the basis of the two countries' relations for the next 18 years.

King Faruq

After 1936, political leadership and the internal political situation deteriorated. Fuad died in April 1936 and his son, Faruq, still a minor, succeeded him. The Wafd split, and a new party, the Saad Wafd, was formed. Extremist organisations also emerged, such as Misr Al-Fatat, an ultra-nationalist pro-royalist group that combined elements of religious fanaticism, militarism and a deep admiration for Nazi Germany and Fascist Italy.

DECADENT RULER

Faruq epitomised the decadence of the final years of Egypt's monarchy. He was only 16 years old when he came to the throne, and had always been a spoiled child, indulged by his doting parents and several sisters. At the age of just 14 he was sent to the Royal Military Academy in London, as what was known as a "gentleman cadet", but this attempt to instil discipline in him failed.

Throughout his life Faruq was partial to practical jokes (including picking pockets), a childish trait he combined with playboy vices such as gluttony, womanising, gambling and a passion for cars, including, it is said, 10 Rolls Royces.

Population pressure in the rural areas encouraged large numbers of rural poor to migrate to the city. Beginning during the interwar period, this population shift has since made Cairo one of the most densely packed cities in the world.

World War II and its aftermath

When World War II broke out, in accordance with the terms of the Treaty of 1936, Britain took control of all Egyptian military facilities, although Egypt itself remained officially neutral for most of the war. The government necessarily supported the British, but many Egyptians did not, while clandestine army groups and Al-Banna's Muslim Brotherhood not only rejected the idea of co-operation but secretly plotted the government's overthrow. In February 1942, with tanks drawn up in front of Abdin Palace, the British installed – at gunpoint – their own candidate, the Wafdist An-Nahhas, as prime minister. This not only poisoned Anglo-Egyptian relations for more than a decade, but also discredited the Wafd itself.

At the end of the war, Egypt was in a precarious situation. Prime ministers and cabinets changed often; the Wafd, the Saadist party and the king were mutually hostile, and communist elements were gaining strength. In addition, a new political force had appeared, the Free Officer movement in the army, led by Gamal Abdel Nasser. Fiercely nationalistic, completely disillusioned with the government, it denounced what it saw as Britain's humiliating occupation of Egyptian soil. The leaders of the Free Officers were in contact with the Muslim Brotherhood and, although some of the two groups' aims coincided, the Free Officers refused Al-Banna's offer to join forces.

The disastrous defeat of the Arabs – the Egyptian Army at their forefront – in Palestine in 1948–9 fuelled the Muslim Brotherhood, whose volunteers had fought bravely, and its membership rapidly increased. The defeat also increased the disaffection of the army with both the palace and the government, which it accused of complicity in a scandal involving defective arms. Both the Muslim Brotherhood and the Free Officers plotted to take power; and to this end the

LEFT: King Faruq admiring a bust of his father King Fuad. RIGHT: King Faruq with his second wife and children in exile in Capri.

Brotherhood carried out a series of terrorist operations, including the assassination of the prime minister, Noqrashy Pasha, in December 1948. Aware of the danger that the Muslim Brotherhood represented, the government retaliated with massive arrests of its members and Al-Banna himself was assassinated in February 1949.

Black Saturday

In 1950, riddled with corruption and bad leadership, the Wafd was again elected to power. It instituted disastrous economic policies, but sought to hold onto popularity by releasing many members of the brotherhood, abrogating the 1936 Treaty and

calling for the evacuation of British troops from the Canal Zone. Resistance to the British troops in the canal area took the form of guerilla action with the tacit approval of the government. In January 1952, a second Dinshawai occurred when the British besieged and overran a post manned by Egyptian auxiliary police, who fought to the last man. Rioting broke out in Cairo, which the authorities either would not or could not control. On 26 January, the day known as Black Saturday, foreign shops, bars and nightclubs were burned and British landmarks such as Shepheard's Hotel and the Turf Club disappeared for ever.

The climax came in the night of 22 July, when the Free Officers took over key positions in a bloodless coup d'état engineered by Nasser and other members of his organisation. On the morning of 23 July, the people were informed that the army, commanded by General Neguib, had seized power. Disillusioned by their corrupt government and dissolute king, the Egyptians greeted the news with joy.

The Nasser Era (1952–70)

The young officers moved quickly to consolidate their power. On 26 July, King Faruq was forced to abdicate in favour of his son, who was only six months old. The constitution was repealed and all Egypt's political parties were suspended. In June 1953, the monarchy was formally ended and a republic was declared.

General Neguib, brought late into the Free Officers' plans to serve as a figurehead, was declared president and prime minister of the new republic. Other Free Officers were installed as his ministers, Nasser becoming deputy prime minister and minister of the interior. Neguib tried to assert the authority he nominally held, but by May 1954 Nasser was prime minister and virtual dictator.

Nasser's first important public act as prime minister was the amicable negotiation of a new Anglo-Egyptian treaty that provided for the gradual evacuation of British troops from the Canal Zone. The agreement was signed in October 1954 after six months of negotiations. Although his

THE SUEZ CRISIS

The turning point in political orientation away from the West came in June 1956, after the United States withdrew its financial backing for the High Dam at Aswan. Nasser nationalised the Suez canal and announced that he would use the revenues from it to build the dam. This provoked the fury of France and Britain, whose nationals owned the Canal, and together with Israel they launched a tripartite attack on Egypt. The invasion was ended by the intervention of the United States and the Soviet Union, which forced the three aggressors to withdraw. Nasser had won an important victory with very little effort and came to symbolise the defiance of imperialist domination.

opponents grumbled that it was not favourable enough to Egypt, since it provided that the British could use the canal base in times of war, Nasser was generally hailed as the leader who finally ended foreign occupation in Egypt.

In April 1955, Nasser attended the Bandung Conference of Afro-Asian states. Soon afterwards he announced Egypt's commitment to positive neutrality, or non-alignment, and its refusal to join the Baghdad Pact, a military alliance including Iraq and Turkey, which the United States and Britain hoped to establish in the Middle East as a way of maintaining Western influence. With Nehru, prime minister of India, and Yugoslavian leader Tito, Nasser became one of the founding leaders of the Non-Aligned Movement.

Arab socialism

It was not until July 1961, five years after the Suez War *(see box below left)*, that Nasser adopted a comprehensive programme of rapid industrialisation, to be financed in part by nationalisation of all manufacturing firms, financial institutions and public utilities. Created to further the new programme decreed that year, the Arab Socialist Union was to remain the only legal avenue for political activity open to the Egyptian people for more than a decade.

As Nasser built respect for Egypt abroad, he began to wave the banner of Arab unity. This led in 1958 to a union between Egypt and Syria, later joined by Yemen, called the United Arab Republic.

> *Syria, initially the most enthusiastic partner in the United Arab Republic, soon became disenchanted. A new military regime took Syria out of the union in 1961 but Egypt retained the name until Nasser's death.*

demanded that UN troops stationed in the Sinai be withdrawn and announced a blockade of the Straits of Tiran. Probably only bluff on Nasser's part, these moves were quickly taken advantage of by Israel. On 5 June, it launched a sneak attack on Jordan, Syria and Egypt, wiped out the entire Egyptian Air

Nasser's next unfortunate undertaking in the name of Arab unity was his five-year embroilment in Yemen. He sent troops to help out the republican forces there in 1962, while Saudi Arabia aided the royalists. But both countries remained put until 1967, when they were forced to come to an agreement in order to face a common enemy: Israel.

The Six-Day War

The Arab-Israeli war of June 1967 was a blow from which Nasser never really recovered. Following growing tension in the area, in May 1967 he

LEFT: images of President Nasser. **ABOVE:** Egyptian prisoners of war held in Gaza during the Six-Day War with Israel in 1967.

REDISTRIBUTION OF WEALTH

One of Nasser's first policies was the institution of radical land reform. At the time, Egypt's farmland was in the hands of a tiny land-owning elite. Under his new laws, ownership of land was limited to 80 hectares (200 acres), and holdings beyond this limit were subsequently reduced many times and redistributed among the dispossessed peasants *(fellaheen)*.

In addition, private property was confiscated from foreigners, members of the royal family and the rich in general. Bank accounts, land, houses and personal effects were all seized in an effort to deprive the upper classes of their capital assets, political influence and the culture that had set them apart.

Force on the ground, and in six days had occupied the Golan Heights, Gaza, Jerusalem, the West Bank and Sinai. Israeli troops crossed the Suez Canal and were ready to march to Cairo. Only a cease-fire quickly worked out by the United States and the USSR prevented further disaster. After the Six-Day War Nasser resigned, but resumed his post the next day following mass demonstrations for his return.

However popular he remained, the old charisma was gone and Nasser was a broken man. Efforts to salvage a wrecked economy, no longer even agriculturally self-sufficient, proved fruitless. His last important act was an attempt to reconcile King Hussein and the Palestinians after the bloody events of

than a decade. After a long period of close relations with the Eastern bloc, Egypt was turning toward the West.

Sadat's boldest initiative was his launching of the fourth Arab-Israeli war in October 1973. The outcome of this was by no means a total victory, but it did allow Egypt to regain its pride and gave Sadat enough prestige to ignore Arab unity and seek a separate peace with Israel *(see box below)*.

Sadat's economic policies, encouraging foreign investment and private enterprise, created high inflation and widened differences between the new rich and older salaried classes, as well as the poor. The drain of Egyptian brains and brawn to oil-

Black September 1970, when the king tried to crush the PLO in Jordan. Later that month he helped negotiate an accord by which Hussein, Arafat and other Arab leaders agreed to end the fighting. He died of a heart attack the day after the signing of the accord.

The Sadat era

On Nasser's death, Anwar Sadat, his vice president, succeeded to the presidency. No-one expected him to last long in this position, but he proved more skilful than his opponents. In May 1971, in what he called a "corrective movement", he consolidated his power by dismissing high-ranking government officials who opposed him. The following year he expelled Soviet teachers and advisors, who had been in Egypt for more

CAMP DAVID ACCORDS

The fourth Arab-Israeli war gave Sadat the prestige to seek a separate peace with Israel. The process began with his visit to Israel in 1977 and resulted in the Camp David accords, the result of 13 days of intense negotiations, signed under US patronage (President Carter) in March 1979.

Furthered by infusions of US aid, the accords were greeted in Egypt with euphoria, a mood that dissipated as differences between Egyptian and Israeli interpretations became clear. Fellow Arab countries meanwhile were appalled by this development; they denounced the accords and expelled Egypt from the Arab League.

rich countries meanwhile became a torrent. Remittances from abroad emerged as the most important factor in the economy. Property prices soared as returning Egyptians sought to invest in something safe. The impact of these revenues was ignored by government planners, whose economic models were geared solely to public-sector revenues.

The high-handed style of Sadat's government, in an atmosphere of corruption and crony capitalism, alienated many. Overt opposition gathered around the new political parties, including a revived Wafd, while less public hostility crystallised in Islamic revivalism. The Muslim Brotherhood had regained most of its freedom of action, but there were other more radical groupings, one of which was responsible for Sadat's assassination on 6 October 1981 during a ceremony commemorating the crossing of the Suez Canal.

The Mubarak years

Vice president Hosni Mubarak, a former air force commander, succeeded Sadat as president. He tried at first to promote more democratic government, and his greatest challenge came from the Islamic Group (Al-Gama'a al-Islamiya), who aimed to turn Egypt into a fundamentalist Islamic state. Their attacks on tourist sites in the 1990s caused tourism to plummet, further increasing unemployment and discontent. The government reacted with a harsh crackdown, and hangings of convicted terrorists – the first since the aftermath of Sadat's assassination – resumed in 1993.

Security was tightened even further a decade later, following the bomb attack on the Taba Hilton in 2004 which killed more than 30 Israelis on holiday in the Sinai resort. And in July 2005 bombs planted at the Red Sea resort of Sharm el-Sheikh killed 88 people and injured some 200 more – an attack for which two separate organisations claimed responsibility.

Although Mubarak first tried to curtail the corruption of the Sadat years, it became a feature of his own regime, causing discontent among the masses. At the same time, the freeing of exchange rates, easing of import controls, creation of an Egyptian stock exchange and the repatriation of large sums privately invested abroad have helped the middle class.

LEFT: Sadat with Israeli prime minister Menachem Begin in 1977 and with Margaret Thatcher in London.
ABOVE RIGHT: President Mubarak with French president Nicolas Sarkozy.

> *Mubarak remains a valued ally of the US, who are understandably keen that his successor will be somebody with whom they can have a similar working relationship.*

In 2005 amid growing discontent and huge pressure from the US, president Mubarak called for a constitutional amendment to introduce contested presidential elections. However, a few restrictions were retained to prevent serious opposition candidates from running, and in the summer election Mubarak won a landslide victory. But the political

ferment stirred by sometimes violent campaigning made the process towards democracy more likely. One of the strongest opposition voices belonged to a new party, Kifaya ("Enough" in Arabic), which staged hundreds of protests demanding change. The other strong force was the Muslim Brotherhood, which organised street protests across the country.

The current regime does not have an unblemished human-rights record: members of labour organisations and homosexuals have received a particularly raw deal in recent years. Mubarak is now an old man, and cannot be in power for much longer. Many assume that his younger son, Gamal, will succeed him, but the subject is so sensitive that a newspaper editor was threatened with arrest for suggesting that the president's health was failing. ❑

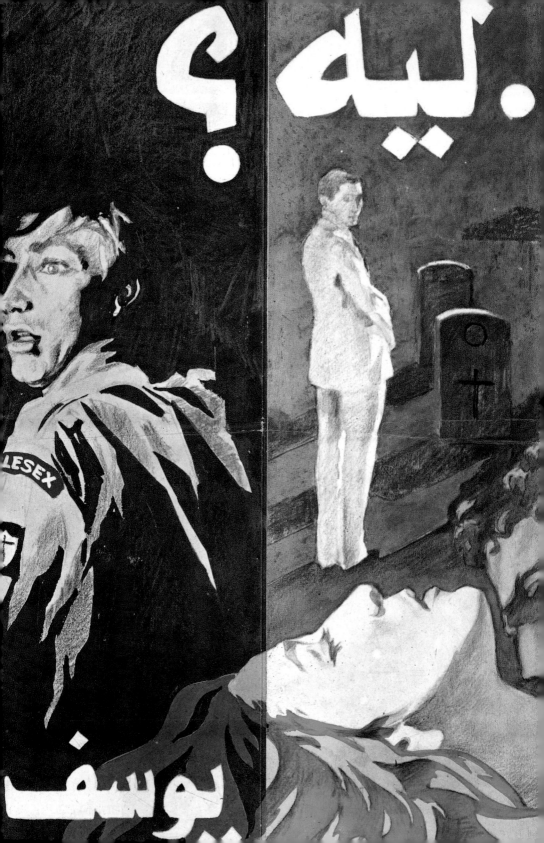

كندريه

أفلام مصر العالمية

POPULAR CULTURE

Egypt has long been regarded as the hub of popular culture in the Arab world. From films to fiction, and soaps to song it has led the way. Contemporary music has accommodated Western influences in recent years and a new visual-arts scene is flourishing

In *The One Thousand and One Nights*, Cairo is called "the mother of the world", a phrase that Egyptians nowadays tend to modify to "Mother of the Arab World". Although in politics that may no longer be true, Egypt can still claim to be in the forefront as far as popular culture is concerned: from Damascus to Casablanca, Egyptian films and television are screened, books by Egyptian writers are read, its singers are given radio airtime and, to a lesser extent, its theatre is respected.

The written word

The year 1988 was one of celebration for Egyptian writers, for that was when Naguib Mahfouz won the Nobel Prize for Literature. But even Mahfouz himself was astonished. Although a world-class writer, he was seen as a traditionalist – Dickens was a major influence – and the works cited by the Nobel committee were written more than a quarter of a century earlier.

Mahfouz (who died in 2006) and Taha Hussein (1889–1973) were the grand old men of Egyptian letters. Other central figures in the development of modern Egyptian literature are Tawfiq al Hakim

The traditional storyteller has now become a rarity. Occasionally you can still see these masters of memory performing to a public who now – too late – appreciate an art that has all but disappeared.

(The Prison of Life), who defined Egyptian autobiographical writing (died 1987), and the Alexandrian-Greek poet C.P. Cavafy (1863–1933)

(Collected Poems) whose explorations of sexuality, memory and history have a universal appeal. They and their younger contemporaries – like Abdel Rahman al Sharqawi *(Egyptian Earth)*, Sonallah Ibrahim *(Zaat)*, Ahdaf Soueif *(Aisha, In the Eye of the Sun)*, Gamal al Ghitani *(Zayni Barakat)*, Nawal al Saadawi *(Woman at Point Zero)*, Yusuf Idris (died 1991; *The Cheapest Nights)*, Ibrahim Abdel Meguid *(No One Sleeps in Alexandria)* and Bahaa Taher *(Love in Exile)* – created a tradition of modern storytelling, rich in folklore and heavy in allegory (a necessity given the censorship laws).

In 2008, Bahaa Taher won the Booker Prize for Arab Fiction with *Sunset Oasis*, published in Cairo in 2007, which explores the themes of

PRECEDING PAGES: cinema poster.
LEFT: Alaa al-Aswany, author of *The Yacoubian Building*. **RIGHT:** Adhaf Soueif, novelist and journalist.

occupation and subjugation. Taher, now in his 70s was an exile in Switzerland for 17 years before returning to Egypt in 1995.

Post-independence writers have taken different routes. The work of Edward al Kharrat *(Girls of Alexandria)* and Yahya Taher Abdullah (died 1981; *The Mountain of Green Tea)* move away from Western literary traditions, but Ahdaf Soueif and Waguih Ghali (died 1969; *Beer in the Snooker Club)* write in English and have not been translated into Arabic. The 1990s saw some important new women writers: Miral al-Tahawi *(The Tent)*, and Somayya Ramadan *(Leaves of Narcissus)*. One of the biggest international suc-

cesses in recent years is Alaa al-Aswany, who famously worked as a part-time dentist before turning to writing full-time. *The Yacoubian Building* (2002) follows the fictional relation-ships between the inhabitants of a downtown office-cum-apartment block (actually inspired by the real Yacoubian Building containing al-Aswany's dental surgery).

The novel, which is an engrossing metaphor for the ills of Egyptian society, touching several taboo subjects, was made into a star-studded film in 2006, directed by Marwan Hamid and with Adel Iman *(see page 97)* playing the lead role, and then a television series in 2007.

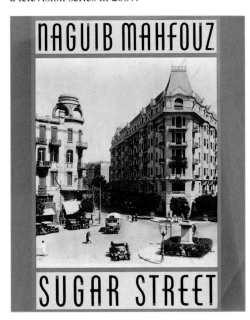

NAGUIB MAHFOUZ
SUGAR STREET

Cairo, cinema city

In 1927, Aziza Amir released the first Egyptian-made film, *Laila*. Much of Egypt's claim to cul-tural supremacy in the Arab world has been due to the phenomenal success of the film industry, which developed in the mid-20th century and peaked in the 1960s, when a new film was released almost every day. Subjects ranged from historical epics to back-alley melodramas, and one of the most popular film forms was the musical, whose plots were often copied from Hollywood.

Singer Umm Kalthoum *(see box, page 98)* dominated here as she dominated Cairo's concert halls. Her most successful partnership was with the actor Farid al Atrash, who, like her, combined a talent for acting with an exceptional voice.

So important was the musical in the development of Egyptian cinema that critic Samir Farid noted: "The Egyptian cinema only became talking in order to sing, without which it would be silent today."

Salah Abou Seif made some of Egypt's most important post-revolution films, and won the Critics' Prize at the 1956 Cannes Film Festival with *La Sangsue*. Abou Seif directed the leading stars of his day, including the legendary belly dancer Tahiya Karioka, Hind Rostom, Omar Sharif and his wife Faten Hamama. Abu Seif's films very

set in ancient Egypt. Part of Chahine's success was due to his ability to convince European film bodies to provide money or facilities, which also guaranteed him an international audience. His work was recognised by a Lifetime Achievement Award at the 1997 Cannes Film Festival.

Few other Egyptian directors have achieved anything like Chahine's stature, with the exception perhaps of Yousri Nassallah, and the bulk of Egypt's output is low-grade melodrama and weak romantic comedy. Directors tread the fine line between titillating the audience and not offending the government's censors, who mostly succeed in keeping nudity, overt political criticism

much reflected the mood of the time – political, questioning, fiercely pro-Arab and anti-royalist.

Youssef Chahine, who died in 2008, had been directing films since the 1940s and did more than anyone to bring credibility to Egyptian cinema. Chahine created a broad body of work, from the realism of the black-and-white *Cairo Station*, in which the director took a key role as a station porter, to the more recent *The Emigrant*, an allegory about corruption, ignorance and injustice,

LEFT: the late Naguib Mahfouz and the jacket of *Sugar Street*, part of the Cairo Trilogy. **ABOVE:** Youssef Chahine, a radical influence on Egyptian film .

ABOVE RIGHT: still from *The Yacoubian Building*, based on Alaa al-Aswany's novel and starring Adel Imam.

and religious slurs off their cinema screens.

Adel Imam is probably the most successful leading male actor currently at work in Egypt. Several of his films have tackled serious and topical subjects, most notable, perhaps, being *The Terrorist*, a comedy about an ordinary man getting himself into extraordinary difficulties in the bureaucratic nightmare of Cairo's Interior Ministry building and being mistaken for a terrorist.

Released in 1994, when the government was struggling to control the activities of the fundamentalist groups, *The Terrorist* succeeded in making the public question why such people were driven to violent measures.

Rising costs, a lack of good cinemas, failure to control video piracy and the spread of satellite television have seen film production dwindle over the past 15 years, though the opening of a "Hollywood-on-the-Nile" with up-to-date film and TV production facilities 15 km (9 miles) southwest of Cairo is a sign of renewed confidence in the industry.

Live on stage

Many stars of Egyptian cinema appear regularly on stage in Cairo. Most Egyptian theatre is comedy or melodrama – particularly popular during the long nights of Ramadan – and carried off by the status of stars like Adel Imam and belly dancer Fifi Abdou. An alternative is provided by playwrights such as Mohammad Salmawy,

although his work owes more to European than Egyptian tradition. Hassan el-Geretly's El Warsha is one of the most convincing of Egypt's experimental theatre groups: their performances often mix storytelling with music and traditional shadow plays.

Television's revolution

It would be hard to overestimate the impact television has had on the lives of rural Egyptians. The promise Nasser and Sadat made to link every village in the country to the national electricity grid had an unforeseen effect and changed rural life for ever. With electricity came television and with television came late-night viewing and that, in turn, put an end to farmers getting into their fields before dawn.

Now satellite TV is widespread, and this has had another effect. In the 1960s and 1970s, Egypt was the major producer of film and television programmes in the Arab world. But with the increased availability of a wide variety of foreign programming, Egypt's dominance has begun to wane. This was first noticed in 1997, when an Egyptian journalist working on the BBC's World Service reported that for the first time Egypt's famed Ramadan serial, the *Fawazeer* – a jamboree of song and dance and extravagant costumes that runs each night throughout the month of fasting – had lost ground to Syrian and Jordanian programmes broadcast by satellite. The implication, the journalist suggested, was that soon Egyptian Arabic would no longer be the lingua franca of the Arabic world.

The sound of music

Evidence of Egypt's domination of the Arab cultural scene in the 1960s is provided by the music of the Egyptian singer Umm Kalthoum *(see box)*. Her contemporaries, including Mohammad Abdel Wahab, Abdel Halim Hafez and Farid al-Atrash, still have a large audience among the older generation. But, with over half of the 82-million population aged under 25, the biggest slice of Egypt's music market is taken by modern musicians.

Among the latest sounds to be heard is *shaabi* (people) music, developed by singer Ahmed Adawiya in the 1970s, mixing protest lyrics with a strong back beat. After a decade and more of phenomenal sales, Adawiya began singing about God, relinquishing his place as king of *shaabi* to Hakim and to the hugely popular Shaaban Abdel-Rahim.

UMM KALTHOUM

In the 1960s, when nationalism ran high, Umm Kalthoum, the singer with the trademark dark glasses, enjoyed the sort of pulling power now reserved for American TV soaps. Each month she performed a new song in her inimitable, passionate warble and, they say, the entire nation came to a standstill as people listened to the "Star of the East" on the radio. When she died in 1975, many of the leaders of the Arab world attended her funeral.

Her songs and voice remain popular today, all over the Arab world. There is a museum in her honour, with photographs, personal possessions and other memorabilia on Rawdah island in Cairo *(see page 135)*.

In contrast, *al-jeel* (the generation) music is a fusion of disco and local rhythms, its lyrics generally confined to enduring themes of love and nostalgia. Mohammad Foad and Hisham Abbas are two names to listen out for, but Amr Diab is the most popular.

The sound of Egypt that has reached the West is an eclectic mix of Arab, Egyptian, Turkish and Indian sounds, produced by musicians such as George Kazazian, Natacha Atlas and the popular Les Musicians du Nil, a group of Upper Egyptian musicians led by the folk singer Metqal, himself a mix of Sudanese, Nubian and Egyptian influences.

> The Prophet Muhammad said, "Those who will be most tormented on Judgement Day will be image-makers." Consequently, Muslims have traditionally frowned on the representation of living creatures.

Egyptian artists started by confronting their ancient traditions. As sculptor Mahmoud Mukhtar (1883–1934) said, "When I was a child, there had been no sculpture in my country for more than 700 years." The Neo-Pharaonists, as they were called, believed that a new Egyptian identity would

The visual arts

Because the Prophet Muhammad denounced "image-makers", visual art in Egypt cannot claim an ancient tradition. However, contacts with Western culture in the 19th century stimulated a debate, with the pro-independence nationalists being keen to promote a recognisable Egyptian style. Little advance was made until the early 20th century, when the mufti of Egypt suggested the Prophet's comment should be seen in context, having been made in an age of idolatry, and Prince Yusuf Kamal founded the School of Fine Arts in Cairo.

emerge by examining the past. The work of Modernist artists like Mukhtar, Mahmoud Said and Mohammad Nagui reflected this.

The Atelier of Alexandria – founded by Mohamed Nagui, his sister Effat Nagui and her husband Saad al Khadem, one of Egypt's most important folklorists – did much to further a purely Egyptian style in a European context.

The contemporary art scene is now blossoming, with the opening of the Town House Gallery in Cairo and numerous others. Popular artists are Anna Boghiguian, Chant Avedissian, Hoda Lutfi, Abdel-Ghany, Amal Kenawy, Sabah Naim and Shady el-Noshokaty. Some young photographers like Randa Shaath, Lara Baladi and Yousef Nabil are also receiving international recognition. ❑

LEFT: the much-loved Umm Kalthoum.
ABOVE: Les Musicians du Nil whose music is appreciated on the World Music scene.

Song and Dance

Belly dancers stand alongside pashas and postcard sellers among Egyptian stereotypes. Yet their appeal is deep-rooted and very real

Belly-dancing – or *raks sharqi*, Oriental dance, as those in the business prefer to call it – opens a window on Egyptian culture and poses a question: how can a conservative, Islamic society tolerate, much less adulate, curvaceous women dressed in sequin-covered bikinis making provocative gestures in public? The answer is less and less. Although belly-dancing is traditional, native, and probably much older than Islam, the growing number of fundamentalists in Egypt consider it unrespectable, and even threaten dancers at weddings or at home. Some even say that the art is slowly dying out in Egypt, as foreign dancers take over.

The origins of *raks sharqi* are unknown. Tomb paintings suggest that ancient Egyptians liked to dance. The legend of Salome, who danced so beautifully that she was granted a wish by the king and asked for the head of John the Baptist, confirms that dance was a court entertainment and that dancers have long commanded high fees.

Nineteenth-century writers, from Edward Lane to Flaubert, refer to the bad reputation of public dancers, Lane with disapproval, Flaubert with pleasure, having slept with one. Flaubert's line won out as far as foreign expectations go: Orientalist painters and modern Hollywood film-makers alike made this sort of dancing universally recognised.

The cinema has helped promote the popularity of public performances in Egypt as well. For a dancer's reputation to survive, she had to mix regular club appearances with screen roles. The most famous belly dancers of all time – Tahiya Karioka, Samia Gamal and Naeema Akef – were all successful actresses as well as brilliant dancers.

Above: a dancer catches the lens of a camera. Men will often join a belly dancer on stage, dancing with her while stuffing money into her cleavage. Men also enjoy dancing among themselves.

Below: one of the most famous dancers of the late 20th-century was Fifi Abdou. These days she rarely dances and instead concentrates on her career as an actress.

Left: the trademark wiggle. These days, however extravagant a dancer's costume – and some cost a fortune – they tend to be far less revealing than in days gone by.

A FOREIGN AFFAIR

In the 1940s and 1950s, during the heyday of belly-dancing when the great composers were still at work and cinema had a touch of glamour, it was unthinkable that foreigners would star in Cairo's clubs. The biggest names of Cairo's dance scene are still Egyptians, but an increasing number of foreign women are providing competition.

Some commentators have suggested that foreign women can never attain the heights scaled by Egyptian dancers because, however technically advanced they might be, they will never be able to respond to Egyptian melodies and movements in the same way as the daughters of the Nile. Since the wars in the Gulf and the rise of the Islamic movement, Egypt's nightclub scene has slumped, with dancers facing law suits on indecency charges and threatened by fanatics. With fewer dance jobs available, the competition has become fierce and many Egyptian dancers have retired or taken up the *hijab*, leaving the stage free for foreigners.

ABOVE: Nagwa Fouad photographed with Bolshoi ballerina Maya Plisetskaya in 1961. Nagwa Fouad, one of the great belly dancers of all time, reached her peak as a dancer in the 1970s. She was known for taking belly-dancing to a new level, with dramatic choreography that placed it at the centre of a spectacular show. In 1971 the famous Egyptian singer, Mohamed Abdel-Wahab composed a special piece for her, *Qamar Arb'tasher* (Full Moon).

TOP: the Brazilian belly dancer Soraya, performing at Mena House Oberoi Hotel.
LEFT: dancer in one of several nightclubs on the Pyramids Road, Giza.

A LOVE OF FOOD

Though not a bastion of haute cuisine, Egypt offers many tasty experiences, such as memorable mezes, great street food, succculent fruit and oriental pastries

In the Middle Ages, Egyptian cuisine enjoyed a high reputation all over the Islamic empire, but not many now travel to Egypt in search of a culinary experience. Those looking for the best of Middle Eastern cuisine will undoubtedly choose countries like Lebanon or Turkey. Nevertheless Egyptians love to eat – and to share a meal – and will endlessly discuss the delight of the dishes served, simple as they may be. As in most Arab countries the best food is found at home. Restaurants usually serve only the more common Egyptian dishes such as kebabs, meze and perhaps stuffed pigeon or *meloukhia* (a thick soup made of a deep-green leaf, similar to spinach). Over the past few years trendy restaurants in Cairo have rediscovered typical Egyptian dishes, including *fatta* (a mix of rice, bread and garlic), often accompanied by water pipes.

Food for the pharaohs

The Egyptians' sense of hospitality and their love of food goes back a long way, according to the evidence of many well-preserved wall paintings and carvings in tombs and temples around the

Egyptian cuisine shows signs of a long history of occupation: the Persians, Greeks, Romans, Arabs and Ottomans have all left their mark. More recently, European influences have also been added.

country, which depict large banquets and a wide variety of foods. Such images also provide proof that many of the dishes enjoyed in Egyptian households today were also on the menu in antiq-

uity. *Meloukhia* soup, roast goose and salted dried fish *(fasieekh)* are examples.

A poor man's table

However elaborate the cuisine enjoyed by Egypt's former kings and sultans, the majority of today's *fellaheen* (peasants) are far too poor to make the most of gastronomic opportunities. As in other Arab countries their diet consists mainly of locally grown vegetables, lentils and beans, with meat at weekends or on special occasions. With the huge influx of people from the countryside to towns and cities, this vegetable-based peasant cuisine has become common and most middle-class families will now elaborate on these basic recipes, adding more expensive ingredients when they can

LEFT: a feast of flavours. **RIGHT:** street food is often freshly prepared and delicious.

afford them. Even in Cairo's most upmarket quarters, colourful carts can be found on street corners early in the morning, where they serve steaming *fuul* (fava beans) for breakfast.

A warm welcome

"If people are standing at the door of your house, don't shut it before them" and "Give the guest food to eat even though you are starving yourself" are two of the many proverbs that insist that hospitality is a duty and that all guests should be offered food and drink. Whatever their social standing, an Egyptian family will always serve guests several salads and a few vegetable and

particularly appetising, but with familiarity the earthy dish can become quite addictive.

Fava beans are also used in another of Egypt's favourite dishes, *taameya* (deep-fried fava-bean balls, rather like falafels, which use chickpeas instead), which are often served with *fuul*. Another staple dish, usually sold as street food (which makes a delicious, inexpensive lunch), is *kushari*, a mixture of macaroni, lentils, rice and chickpeas, served with fried onions and topped with a generous dollop of hot tomato sauce. A familiar-sounding dish is *makarona* – pasta accompanied by a variety of sauces – which is also usually sold from a cart as lunch time street food.

meat dishes. Guests will always be handed the best morsels of fish or the finest cut of meat from the central serving dish or platter. Guests also have a well-prescribed role to play: at first they must refuse the offer, but must then relent after some pressure. They are expected to praise every aspect of the food, without inspecting it too closely.

Fuul above all

Fuul (fava or broad beans), stewed and eaten with bread, form Egypt's staple diet. Usually eaten for breakfast or as a sandwich between meals, *fuul* can just as well be served as lunch or dinner in some households. Some people who can't afford any other food will eat it several times a day. At first the brown muddy stew may not look or smell

BEAN FEAST

In her *Book of Middle Eastern Food*, Egyptian-born writer Claudia Roden reminisces about *fuul medames* (stewed fava or broad beans mashed with onions, tomatoes and spices): "Ceremoniously, we sprinkled the beans with olive oil, squeezed a little lemon over them, seasoned them with salt and pepper, and placed a hot hard-boiled egg in their midst... Silently, we ate the beans, whole and firm at first; then we squashed them with our forks and combined their floury texture and earthy taste with the acid tang of lemon, mellowed by the olive oil."

Beans are a staple food for Egyptians, especially in rural areas, where meat is eaten only rarely, and they make their way into many different street foods.

The evening air is often scented by the warm smell of roasting maize (corn on the cob), libb (melon seeds) and tirmis (lupin seeds), sold from street carts, in little paper cones.

Make a meal of meze

Of all the dishes on offer in Egypt it is a table full of meze, dips and salads that best reflects the Egyptian and Middle Eastern character. Meze are served with drinks as a light snack or as an appetiser before a meal. Egyptians love to sit and relax at home, on a terrace or in a café, chatting and

one day in the year when they are sure to get a taste of meat: Id al-Kebir, the 10th day of the last month of the Muslim calendar. In commemoration of Abraham's sacrifice of his son Ismail, rural families who can afford it will sacrifice a sheep or a lamb. The animal, which should be fat and young, is ritually slaughtered and roasted whole on a spit and usually some of its meat is distributed to the poor, according to the tenets of Islam. Sheep are also slaughtered to mark other important occasions such as death, birth or marriage.

Ramadan, the month of fasting from sunset to sunrise, is another occasion when more meat is consumed than usual. Families visit each other in

laughing with friends and savouring a few salads and small dishes. These can be anything from a plate of hummus (chick pea purée), pickled vegetables or elaborate *mahshi* (stuffed vegetables), to little meat pies. With such a variety of dishes, meze can easily turn out to be a pleasurable and leisurely meal on their own.

Celebrations

Meat has always been considered a food for the rich and aristocratic. Poorer Egyptians rely on a diet of wheat, beans and lentils and there is only

the evenings and celebrate the end of another day of fasting with a rich display of foods and sweets.

Many Egyptian recipes won't stipulate what sort of meat is to be used, as traditionally there was only sheep or lamb, and occasionally camel, goat or gazelle. Islam prohibits pork, but beef and veal are now widely available in Egypt. Meat is usually grilled as kebab or kofta (minced lamb) or used in a stew. Offal – particularly liver, kidneys and testicles – is considered a delicacy.

Sweet as honey

The traditional end to a meal at home is a bowl of seasonal fruit, but Western-style ice cream and crème caramel will also be offered as a dessert in most restaurants. Even though they are not usually

FAR LEFT: for lots of different dishes try mezze.
LEFT: delivering freshly baked flat bread.
ABOVE: sharing a meal with friends.

eaten as a dessert, there are some delicious Egyptian puddings, including *muhallabia*, a milk cream thickened by cornflour and ground rice, and *roz bi-laban*, a creamy rice pudding, both topped with chopped almonds and pistachio nuts. More elaborate is *umm ali*, a warm, comforting bread pud-

ding with coconut, raisins, nuts and cream. According to some sources, *umm ali* was introduced into Egypt by Miss O'Malley, the Irish mistress of the khedive Ismail.

Pastries are more likely to be served at parties and special, happy occasions such as weddings and births, than as a dessert. Baklava is the most famous oriental pastry, a filo wrapping stuffed with a mixture of nuts or almonds and covered with an orange-blossom syrup. More common are *basbousa*, a semolina cake of syrup and nuts, and the drier *kunafa*, angel hair filled with thick cream, ricotta cheese or chopped nuts and syrup. A woman who prides herself on making the best baklava or *kunafa* will often keep her recipe secret and only pass it on to her daughters.

Juicy drinks

Egyptians will tell you that "Once you drink water from the Nile, you will always come back to Egypt". A nice sentiment, but Nile water is more likely to curse than bless; stick to mineral water or fresh juices. Brightly coloured juice bars with their picturesque pyramids of strawberries and oranges and baskets of mangoes attract thirsty customers. Freshly squeezed *asir* (juice) is excellent and very cheap. The most widely available juice is *asir laymun* (fresh lemon or lime), usually served sweetened unless you say otherwise.

Usually there will also be a choice of *asir burtuqan* (freshly squeezed winter or summer oranges), *mōz* (banana), *gazar* (carrot) and *gawafa* (sweet guava). Depending on the season there could also be deep-red *asir ruman* (pomegranate juice), *farawla* (strawberry) and thick *manga* (mango). Some stalls also offer *asab* or *gasab*, the sweet juice pressed out of sugar-cane sticks.

Alcoholic pleasures

According to the Qur'an Muslims should not drink alcohol and, with religious tensions rising, much of Egypt is becoming dry. But you can usually get alcohol in hotels and Western-style bars and restaurants, except during Ramadan, when no alcohol is served to Egyptians even if they are Copts. Many bars close for the month; others may ask to see a passport before they serve alcohol to foreigners.

Locally brewed Stella beer is quite enjoyable, while the more expensive Stella Export and Stella Premium are stronger, as is the better Sakkara.

The quality of the local wine used to range from drinkable to downright dangerous, but quality has much improved since the Gianaclis Winery was privatised. Cru des Ptolémées is a white wine made from pinot blanc. Rubis d'Egypte is a rosé, while Omar Khayyam is a deep red from cabernet sauvignon grapes. Obélisque makes red and white wines from imported grapes. The more expensive Grand Marquis, red and white, is very palatable, and Egypt now has its own "champagne", Aida. In 2005, Egypt launched its first vintage wine, Château des Rêves. Imported wine is considerably more expensive than the local varieties.

Zibeeb, or arak, the Egyptian version of ouzo, is reliable, but local spirits with inspiring names such as Dry Din, Marcel Horse, Ricardo and Johnny Talker are best avoided. ❏

LEFT: Alexandrian cafés are famous for their sweet pastries. **RIGHT:** a street vendor selling butter beans.

EGYPTIAN COFFEE HOUSES

The coffee house is an essential part of urban Egyptian life, but coffee has had a chequered history in Egypt. Although now integral to the lives of thousands, it once invoked the wrath of the clergy who saw it as a dangerous drug

In crowded Egypt, Allah can be counted on for two great mercies: endless sunshine and abundant free time. Small wonder, then, that the street café, where much of these two great resources is spent, is so ubiquitous an institution. Few men let a day pass without spending time in their local, drinking coffee, exchanging jokes or discussing the events of the day.

Different atmospheres

The *qahwa* – Arabic for both "coffee" and "café" – is defined loosely. It can be anything from a bench, a patch of charcoal, a tin pot and three glasses to a cavernous saloon reverberating with the clack of dominoes, the slap of cards and the crackling of dice.

In Cairo, a café may serve as the headquarters of a street gang, the meeting place for homesick provincials, or the rendezvous of intellectuals. There are cafés for couples, musicians, black

In Edward Lane's Manners and Customs of the Modern Egyptians he judged the number of cafés in Cairo in the 1830s to be over 1,000. Given a similar ratio of one café per 400 people, Cairo today would contain more than 30,000 cafés.

marketeers, leftists, Muslim extremists, homosexuals, retired generals and pimps. There is even a café for the deaf and dumb, where absolute silence belies the animated conversation that is conducted by gesture alone.

The ideal café adjoins a small square in the backstreets of a popular quarter. The simple decor of its exterior will reveal the sense of style its patronage demands. The few outdoor tables will be shaded by a tree or vine, while the ground will have been sprinkled with water to keep down the dust. A pungent sweetness emanates from the interior, where sawdust covers the floor.

An elaborate brass *sarabantina*, which resembles a cross between a steam locomotive and a samovar, occupies pride of place on the counter at the back of the room, behind which striped glass jugs for smokers' water pipes line the walls. The patron will puff judiciously as he takes in the crime column of the morning paper, while the *qahwagi*, or waiter, keeps up a continuous banter with customers, between forceful shouts to the tea boy.

LEFT: veteran smoker of a *sheesha* or water pipe.
RIGHT: Café Riche, a famous Cairo coffee house.

Liquid incidentals

Atmosphere is only one of the pleasures the café offers. There is also the pleasure of indulging in a hot drink. Tea, introduced in the 19th century, has replaced coffee as the staple. The powerful Egyptian version of the brew takes some getting used to. Since cheap tea dust is the preferred variety, don't anticipate a delicate flavour. Tea is drunk as a fix, as strong and sweet as possible. It is best to make no compromises with local taste: sugarless Egyptian tea is unpalatable. Some connoisseurs say that the truly classic glass of tea should be only faintly translucent, with a mild aroma of kerosene from extended boiling on a Primus stove.

More traditional are the hot medicinal infusions still found in many cafés. The bases of these potations range from ginger, *ganzabeel*, which is recommended for coughs, *erfa* (cinnamon) and *yansun* (aniseed) for the throat, to *helba* (fenugreek) for stomach complaints. *Karkadé,* the scarlet tea of a hibiscus flower, is a speciality of Aswan. Packed with vitamin C, it is delicious hot or cold. *Sahlib,* a steaming cream, concocted from dried orchids and topped with chopped nuts, is a winter favourite. In summer, cafés serve cooler drinks, ranging from *laymun* (lemon), *tamar hindi* (tamarind), *ersoos* (liquorice) and *farawla* (strawberry), to the ever more pervasive Kukula, Bibsi

Arabic coffee is still prepared and served in centuries-old style, without the fancy gadgetry of European invention. Sugar, then powdered coffee are added to hot water and brought to the boil in a brass *kanaka*. The *qahwagi* brings the *kanaka* and cup on a tin tray and pours the liquid with solicitude, preserving the *wish* – the "face" or thick mud that sits on the surface before settling. In the better cafés, a dark blend spiced with cardamon is used. In all establishments, customers must specify how they want their coffee: *saada*, or sugarless, *'arriha*, with a dash of sugar, *mazbut,* medium, or *ziyada*, with extra sugar. In some "European cafés", *qahwa Faransawi* or French coffee is served, and newer, modern cafés have Italian espresso machines.

A HEADY BREW

The first recorded mention of the coffee plant was by an Arab physician in the ninth century. Embraced by the Bedu, to whom it is a vital part of welcoming friends and strangers, it gradually spread all over the Arab world, and was introduced to the inhabitants of Cairo by Sufi mystics in the 16th century. The dervishes' adoption of the stimulant to prolong their ecstatic trances angered the orthodox clergy, who saw it as inspiring deviant behaviour, and in 1532 the coffee bean was outlawed. As with tobacco, controversy raged for years before the weight of popular taste concluded the debate, and coffee became a respectable part of social intercourse.

and Shwibs, the commercially bottled soft drinks that have run old local brands off the market.

The formula of the traditional *qahwa* (coffee house) is increasingly popular with young, fashionable Cairenes. Several cafés, often open-air, have opened along the Nile or on ex-cruise boats, providing coffee, tea and *sheeshas*, as well as snacks and alcoholic drinks.

A smoker's paradise

The Egyptian café is a paradise for the serious smoker and has perfected the ultimate tobacco tool. The *sheesha*, or water pipe, cools, sweetens and lightens the taste of the burning leaves, makes

> *Until recently, hashish smoking in public places was not uncommon. The ghoraz (hash dens) of Cairo were famous. Official crackdowns, however, have relegated this activity to seedy back alleys and private homes.*

smoke, a cone of dry *tumbak* may take up to an hour to exhaust.

Live entertainment

Every café offers diversion in the form of cards *(kutshina)*, backgammon *(tawla)* and dominoes. But it

a soothing gurgle and provides a pleasant distraction for idle hands. It is an instrument of meditation to be savoured serenely.

The tobacco comes in various flavours. Most popular is *ma'assil*, a sticky blend of chopped leaf fermented with molasses. It is pressed in small clay bowls that are fitted into the *sheesha* and lit with charcoal. This tobacco is also sold with a smoother apple flavour *(tuffah)*, or sticky cherry, strawberry and even cappuccino flavours. *Tumbak*, another variety, is loose dry tobacco wrapped into a cone with a whole leaf. While *ma'assil* is easy to

LEFT: al Azhar Park has many new cafés with open-air terraces and far-reaching views. **ABOVE:** old-style café off the Qasabah beneath the Citadel.

is good conversation and companionship that draw regular crowds. Despite the mass media and the mobile phone, people still find that the best source of news – not to mention gossip, rumour, slander and fantasy – is found at the local café.

With the nation's characteristic penchant for nostalgia, aficionados will affirm that cafés are not what they used to be. Like the introduction of radio in the 1930s, which signalled the decline of storytellers, television has led to a decline in public entertainment. Luckily, most café owners leave their sets off except during major sports events.

The best time for dropping in on a café is the late afternoon, when the sun's dying rays turn duncoloured buildings to gold, and smoke drifts skyward from the *sheesha*. ❑

NINETEENTH-CENTURY TRAVELLERS ON THE NILE

Tourists had been visiting Egypt since the time of the Greeks, but there was a sense of rediscovery when 19th-century Westerners arrived in Egypt

It is hard for us to imagine the shock of arriving in Egypt in the 18th or 19th centuries. By the time we arrive, books, newspapers and television have shown us in minute detail what temples and tombs look like and the ways in which they functioned. Yet for all our information, early travellers were often better equipped to appreciate what they saw. After the French scholar Champollion deciphered hieroglyphics, many of them arrived having learned how to read ancient inscriptions. They would have read their Greek and Roman histories, and their early travellers, as well as the latest accounts.

Most Western visitors spoke no Arabic, though in Egypt few people spoke anything other than Arabic. Until the 1820s, foreigners travelled under constant threat in a country with no strong central authority, but there was romance as well as danger: new tombs and temples were being dug out of the sand, and until the mid-19th century they sailed on a river whose source remained a mystery.

ABOVE: When Napoleon invaded Egypt in 1798, he landed with an army of soldiers and 167 savants who spread across the country recording everything from antiquities to wildlife.

BELOW: After discovering the remains of ancient Troy German archaeologist Heinrich Schliemann went to look for the tomb of Alexander the Great. After visiting Alexandria, he concluded that popular tradition was right and that the tomb lay under the Mosque of Nebi Danial, but the Muslim authorities refused him.permission to excavate there.

RIGHT: Travelling incognito, the extraordinary Richard Burton perfected his disguise as Mirca Abdullah in Cairo before undertaking a pilgrimage to Mecca.

LADIES ON THE NILE

In 1849, Florence Nightingale (above) went to Egypt for the winter to recover her health and wrote, "One wonders that people come back from Egypt and live lives as they did before." She did not: by the time she got home she had written some of the finest letters from Egypt and also decided to devote her life to helping the sick.

By then people could sail on the Nile in comfort, but earlier travellers had not had it so easy. Elisa Fay, en route to India in 1779, was scared on the river up to Cairo, nearly suffocated under all the layers she was obliged to wear in public and was then robbed, along with the rest of her caravan, crossing the desert to Suez.

Sophia Poole, sister of Edward Lane, the Arabic scholar, lived in Egypt for seven years (1842–49) without having to compromise her Christian values, although she was a little shocked by the public baths. Miss Poole and her contemporary Harriet Martineau were among the first outsiders to write about women in Egypt, an insight furthered by the letters of Lucie Duff Gordon, who had been sent to the Nile for her health. In the year of her death, 1869, conditions were "soft" enough for Thomas Cook to launch the first package tour of the country.

BELOW: Between 1815–19 Giovanni Belzoni, circus strongman turned antiquity-hunter, opened the Second Pyramid at Giza and Abu Simbel's Great Temple, and discovered Seti I's tomb in Luxor.

ABOVE: Napoleon's savants were led by Baron Dominique Vivant. He published his own *Travels* in 1802, ahead of the *Description de l'Egypte* (1809).

BELOW: Egypt has long been a favourite place for adventurous writers. Among the crowd who visited in the 19th century, both Gustave Flaubert (right) and Mark Twain left classic accounts, though in Flaubert's case the wonders of ancient Egypt take second place after the marvels of its brothels and baths.

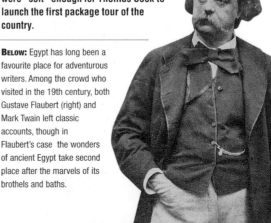

PLACES

A detailed guide to the country, with the principal sites
cross-referenced by number to the maps

Egypt occupies 1 million sq. km (385,000 sq. miles) of Africa's driest and most barren corner. It adjoins the Sinai peninsula, which is geologically African, but geographically belongs to Asia. South and west, beyond wide barriers of desert, stretches the great body of the rest of Africa, to which Egypt is umbilically connected, in addition, by the nourishing lifeline of the Nile. As it crosses the Sudanese border into Egypt, the Nile has already travelled 5,000 km (3,000 miles), carving a serpentine path through swamps, rock and sand and filling a massive artificial lake, with the Temple of Abu Simbel on one side. This lake, just south of Aswan, the world's largest, is Lake Nasser, a 20th-century achievement that changed the face of Egypt forever.

An ancient frontier town, where Africa and Arabia mingle, Aswan is the return point for most Nile cruises, although some companies are now operating in the waters of Lake Nasser. At Luxor the vessels pause in the centre of the largest agglomeration of ancient buildings in the world, anchoring between the east bank's great temple complexes of Karnak and Luxor and the west bank's vast funerary cities.

Further north, the river meanders on through fields dotted with water-buffalo. At length it swirls beneath the many bridges of Cairo. To the west are

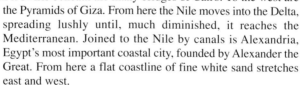

the Pyramids of Giza. From here the Nile moves into the Delta, spreading lushly until, much diminished, it reaches the Mediterranean. Joined to the Nile by canals is Alexandria, Egypt's most important coastal city, founded by Alexander the Great. From here a flat coastline of fine white sand stretches east and west.

The Places chapters in this guide begin in Cairo, then make their way steadily south to Upper Egypt with a detour to the oases en route. They then turn to the Delta and Alexandria and travel east to Suez, Sinai and the Red Sea. The main sites are numbered and can be cross-referenced to a map, which can be found on the page shown in the map logo at the top of each right-hand page. ❑

PRECEDING PAGES: views from Mount Sinai; inside the Temple of Abu Simbel; the landscape between Luxor and Esna. **LEFT:** a glimpse of the old city.
TOP: the Nile Valley. **LEFT:** wall hanging.

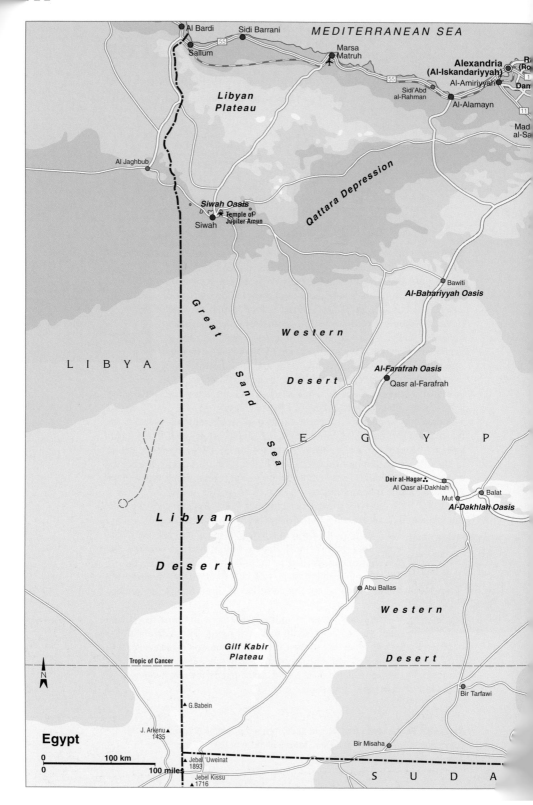

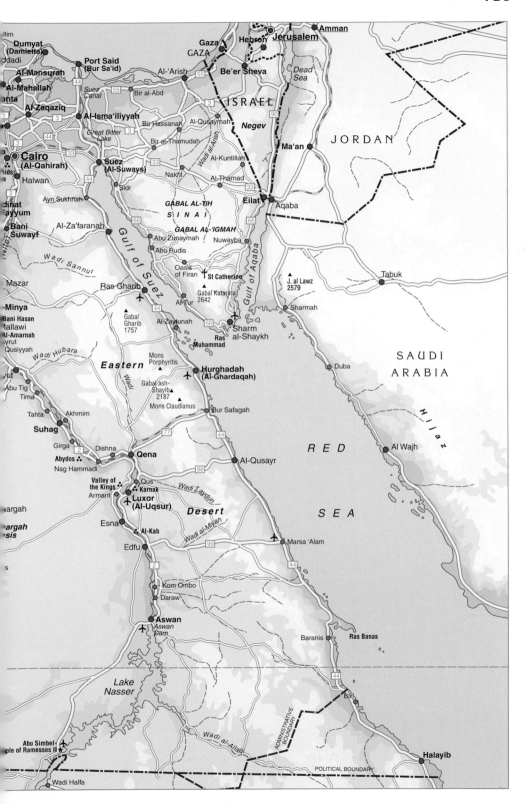

Recommended Restaurants on pages 156–7

CAIRO

A roaring metropolis of nearly 17 million people, Cairo is the cultural capital of the Arab world. Most visitors to Egypt spend at least a few days here, exploring its medieval mosques, sampling its fine museums and shopping in the labyrinthine Khan al-Khalili bazaar

When Ibn Khaldun, the great 14th-century Arab historian and social theorist, visited Cairo, he described it as "the metropolis of the universe, the garden of the world, the ant hill of the human species, the throne of royalty, a city embellished with castles and palaces, its horizon decorated with monasteries and with schools, and lighted by the moons and stars of erudition." What he was looking at was a city that had been devastated by the Black Death three decades earlier and had entered a long twilight of decline.

It remained nevertheless the greatest metropolis on earth, still larger in both population and extent than any city west of China. Enriched by the spice trade and the traffic in luxury goods, its sultans and amirs continued to adorn the city with extravagant architecture.

City of 1,001 Nights

It was during this period, sometime between 1382 and 1517, that *The Arabian Nights* were given their final form in the Cairo of the Circassian Mamluks. "He who hath not seen Cairo," says a character in one of these tales, "hath not seen the world. Her soil is gold; her Nile is a marvel; her women are like the black-eyed virgins of Paradise; her houses are palaces; and her air is soft, as sweet-smelling as aloe-wood, rejoicing the heart. And how can Cairo be otherwise, when she is Mother of the World?"

The Mother of the World is an old lady now, somewhat long in the tooth:

the gold in her soil has ceased to glitter, her Nile has been thoroughly tamed; and, though her women still have many admirers, her palatial houses are being rapidly demolished to make way for concrete high-rises, while her sweet-smelling air has achieved one of the highest pollution indexes in the world.

CENTRAL CAIRO

Modern Cairo spins on **Maydan at-Tahrir ❶**, a huge square from which all distances in Egypt are measured. The square was originally named Maydan

FAR LEFT: view over medieval Cairo from the Citadel.
LEFT: downtown Cairo.

Main attractions

THE EGYPTIAN MUSEUM, P.128
GAZIRAH ISLAND, P.132
  CAIRO TOWER, P.133
  MARRIOTT HOTEL, P.133
RAWDAH ISLAND, P.134
  MANYAL PALACE, P.134
  UMM KALTHOUM MUSEUM, P.135
  NILOMETER, P.135
OLD (COPTIC) CAIRO, P.135
MOSQUE OF IBN TULUN, P.140
GAYER ANDERSON MUSEUM, P.140
MEDIEVAL CAIRO
  MADRASAH OF SULTAN HASAN, P.142
  THE CITADEL, P.144
  AL-AZHAR PARK, P.146
  ISLAMIC ART MUSEUM, P.148
  MOSQUE-UNIVERSITY OF AL-AZHAR, P.149
  KHAN AL-KHALILI, P.150
THE CITY OF THE DEAD, P.151

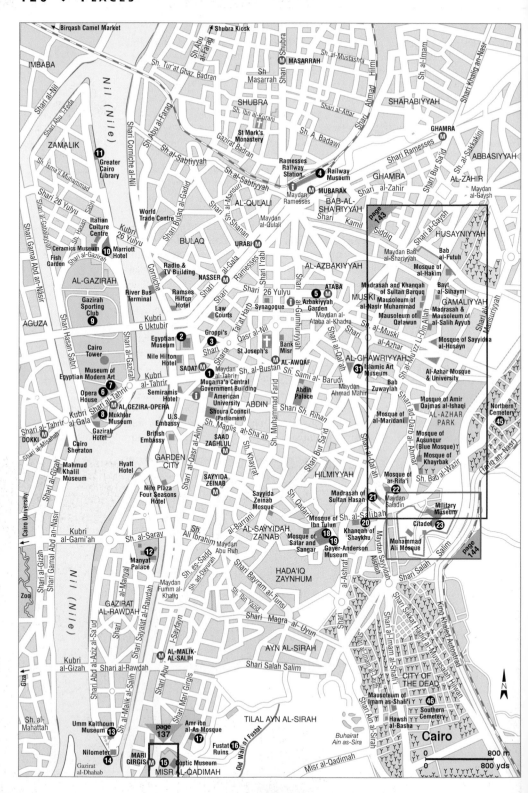

Cairo

Ismailiyyah, after Khedive Ismail. An open space, it demarcated one end of the new administrative, commercial and residential quarter of Maydan Ismailiyyah, which was laid out by Khedive Ismail in 1865.

Despite its strategic position near the Nile, Maydan Ismailiyyah did not achieve its present importance until after the July Revolution of 1952. Its name was changed and the mid-19th century barracks on its western (Nile) side, occupied throughout most of their history by British Guards regiments, were demolished and replaced by the **Corniche**, two new administrative buildings, and the **Nile Hilton**, the first major hotel built in Cairo since 1910.

On the south side of the Maydan the remains of a palace were knocked down and replaced by a concrete block known as the **Mugama'a**, accommodating various ministries issuing permits, licences, visas, expulsion orders and other bureaucratic forms. A Kafkaesque castle of red tape, it is notorious not merely for entrapment, frustration and delay, but also for the number of suicides that have occurred in its 14-storey-high stairwell.

Situated across the street from this monster, on the southeastern corner of the Maydan, is the only building left from Ismail's era, a small palace dating from 1878 which houses part of the American University, though the main campus has relocated to a new site on the eastern outskirts of the city.

Al-Qasr al-Ainy Street

One block south from here, on Shari' al-Qasr al-Ainy, is another set of government buildings including the **Shoura Council** (Parliament). Surprisingly, and to the dismay of the security guards, the **Ethnographic Museum** and the **Geographical Society of Egypt** are housed in the same complex and can be visited (Sat–Wed 10am–3pm; free; no camera; you must leave a passport or ID card at the guardhouse), though a fire in the Parliament in 2008 may have resulted in temporary closure. The ground floor holds a dusty collection of everyday items covering hundreds of years of life in Cairo, such as costumes, musical instruments, children's toys, jewellery, glassware, keys, locks and antique doors. Of special note are the

WHERE

To help you get to grips with street maps of Cairo, bear in mind the following:

bab = gate
bayt = house
kubri = bridge
madrasah = theological school/college
maydan = square
qasr = palace
shari' = street.

BELOW: Maydan Talaat Harb, downtown Cairo.

Model of Maket Ra in the Egyptian Museum.

bridal divan chair and a *mahmal*, an ornately decorated chest for carrying the new *kiswa*, the covering, renewed annually, for the *Kaaba* (the black box-like shrine in Mecca).

An African room full of spears and elephant tusks gives a flavour of the **Geographical Society,** centring on a beautiful wooden lecture theatre and reading rooms, on the first floor. The **Suez Canal Room** has a series of models of al-Isma'iliyyah, Suez and Port Said, showing the course of the canal through lakes and cuttings, as well as old photographs and prints.

The Egyptian Museum

On the north side of Maydan at-Tahrir stands the **Egyptian Museum ❷** (www. egyptianmuseum.gov.eg; daily 9am–6pm, admission charge, no photography allowed; a good guidebook to the museum is available from the museum shop and there is as a useful audio guide to the museum's masterpieces). Built in 1902 under Pasha Abbas Hilmi and dignified with Latin inscriptions, this museum holds the world's greatest collection of Egyptian artefacts. Unfortunately it is now far too small to house its massive collection and many of the exhibits are cramped and dusty, not to mention badly lit and labelled. Plans are on the way for a new and larger antiquities museum near the Pyramids of Giza, but that will not be finished until 2010 at the earliest.

On the ground floor large objects are arranged chronologically, running clockwise, so that a left turn from the foyer leads to the famous **Menkaure Triads** from Giza, showing King Menkaure (Fourth Dynasty) flanked by the goddess Hathor and another female figure representing Upper Egypt, while a right turn leads to Hellenistic painting and statuary.

No one should miss anything if time is not a consideration, but visitors in a hurry should turn left through the entrance to see the treasures of the **Old Kingdom**. Look out for the **Narmer Palette** in the first room *(see picture on page 35)*, recording the first unification of Upper and Lower Egypt by the legendary (and possibly mythical) King Narmer (also known as Menes), and generally considered to mark the beginning of Egyptian history and art

(*circa* 3,000 BC). Among other Old Kingdom highlights is a large black statue of Chephren, the builder of the second pyramid at Giza, seated on a lion throne. In Room 42, look out for the unusual wooden statue of Ka-Aper, known as **Shaykh al-Balad**, with rock crystal and alabaster eyes, as well as a painted limestone **seated scribe**, with vivid inlaid eyes. In the next room is the magnificent double sculpture of **Prince Rahotep and his wife Nofret**, a symbol of marital bliss, as well as the venerated dwarf **Seneb** with his family.

Reflecting a total revolution in Egyptian art under Akhenaten (*see pages 42 and 195*) is the **Amarnah art** in Room 3. More naturalistic than art previous to the Amarnah period, the pharaoh is depicted with lips, emaciated cheeks and a large belly. Akhenaten is usually seen with his family adoring the sun-god Aten.

Room 4 has a marvellous display of ancient **Egyptian jewellery**, while a few of the famous **Fayyum portraits**, faces painted on wooden panels placed over the mummy, are on display in Room 14.

From here, take the stairs up to the **treasures of Tutankhamun**. Discovered by Howard Carter in the Valley of the Kings in 1922 (*see page 159*), the items are displayed in two large galleries, and include 1,700 of the 2,500 objects found by Carter. As well as the famous gold death masks and lion throne there are cases of smaller items, such as the young king's boomerangs, bows and arrows and even wilting bouquets of flowers that were put inside his tomb. There is also some spectacular jewellery, and textiles, including the pharaoh's socks and shoes.

Rooms 53 and 54 on the upper floor contain a fascinating collection of **mummified animals and birds**, illustrating the animal cults of ancient Egypt, and in Room 43 there are objects from the tomb of **Yuya and Thuya**, including a magnificent gilded mask inlaid with gems.

The **Mummy Room** (separate admission charge) houses the mummies of

many notable pharaohs, found in a cache in Deir al-Bahri, Luxor, in 1875. Above all, they show the pharaohs' humanity, including their individual characteristics and defects.

Qasr an-Nil Street

Running northeast in front of the Museum is **Shari' Qasr an-Nil**, once the city's main shopping street and still displaying a few vestiges of the glamour that Ismail intended when he planned this part of the city. Up the street on the left is the **Automobile Club**, founded in 1924 and a haunt of King Faruq, who loved playing poker for outrageous stakes, and 100 metres/yds further on is **Groppi's Corner House** ❸ (1924), a once-luxurious catering establishment founded by an Alexandrian-Swiss family but now seriously dilapidated.

In the years before World War II, this branch of Groppi's sold Sèvres, Meissen, Lalique and silver as well as afternoon teas, aperitifs, confectionery, patisserie and delicatessen items. The handful of old Turkish ladies who remained faithful to the place long after its decline gradually found themselves elbowed out of the

Mummy of Tuthmosis II displayed in the Mummy Room at the Egyptian Museum.

Gold statuette from the treasures of Tutankhamun, on the first floor of the museum.

LEFT: one of several statues of Ramesses II in the museum,

TIP

Taxis are the best way of getting around Cairo. Though vehicles are often very battered and traffic jams can be horrendous, fares are extremely cheap. Although most taxi drivers speak only Arabic, you will usually manage to convey where you want to go successfully. Sharing a taxi is not unusual, particularly during rush hours.

BELOW AND BELOW RIGHT: Groppi's Corner House.

way by students, prostitutes and pimps, though the bar remained popular with local businessmen until the place was sold to a teetotaller in 1983.

The 1952 Revolution also changed the name and appearance of Talaat Harb Square in front of Groppi's. Until then it had carried the Arabic name, Sulayman Pasha, adopted by a Bonapartist officer, Colonel Anthelme Sève, who had entered Muhammad Ali's service after Waterloo, had converted to Islam and, as Sulayman Pasha al Faransawi ("The Frenchman"), carved a distinguished career. The north–south street running through the square likewise carried Sulayman Pasha's name, which is still used for both street and square by senior residents.

Across Talaat Harb Square, opposite Groppi's, stood the town house of one of Muhammad Ali's great-grandsons, which became the Savoy Hotel (no longer there), second only to Shepheard's during the Edwardian era.

The headquarters of the main banks and airline offices now line most of Shari' Qasr an-Nil. The north–south street that crosses Shari' Qasr an-Nil also has two names – Shari' Emad ad-Din or Shari'

Muhammad Farid – between which Cairenes choose according to age and politics. Down the next north–south street as you walk towards Azbakiyyah are **St Joseph's**, Cairo's biggest Catholic church, built in 1909, and, nearly opposite, its finest neo-Islamic building, the main branch of **Bank Misr**, built in 1922, with original woodwork and a splendid Mamluk-style marble floor still intact.

Azbakiyyah

Shari' Qasr an-Nil leads into **Shari' al-Gumhuriyyah**, formerly Shari' Abdin, which in turn leads to the **Abdin Palace**, Muhammad Ali's family's chief residence, part of which has been turned into a museum (Maydan Qasr Abdin; Sat–Thur 9am–3pm; admission charge) displaying a vast collection of weaponry and items relating to historic events.

At the other end of the street is the main station, where private royal trains are on display at the **Railway Museum ❹** (Maydan Ramesses; Tues–Sun 8.30am–1pm; admission charge).

An early 18th-century Ottoman mosque on the corner of Shari' al-Gumhuriyyah and Shari' Qasr an-Nil indicates the

Groppi's Corner House

Groppi is a name inseparable from downtown Cairo for anyone living in or visiting the city over the past 100 years. Established originally in Alexandria by a Swiss pastry cook and chocolatier by the name of Giacomo Groppi in 1890, it opened on Adly Street in Cairo in 1907. Throughout World War I and afterwards, the open gardens and tea-room became a favourite haunt of the British military stationed in the city. After World War II, if an event required refreshments there was only one thing to do– call Groppi.

Groppi's just about survived the nationalist bombings and attacks leading up to independence, but has gone downhill since then. There are now two locations: at Maydan Talaat Harb and Adly Street, the latter with a pleasant secluded garden. It is worth a visit to see the splendid period decor, especially the one at Talaat Harb, but the cakes and coffee are now second-rate, and likely to be a disappointment to anyone who remembers the great atmospheric Groppi institutions of the past.

overlapping of Ismail's new quarter with old Misr as it was before the French marched in; and a left turn into Shari' al-Gumhuriyyah leads to **Azbakiyyah**, which was founded as a pleasure zone in the 15th century but had evolved into an upper-class residential area by the time Napoleon established his headquarters here in 1798.

The focus of the area was a picturesque seasonal lake that filled during the Nile flood, and luxurious dwellings were built along its southern and eastern shores. Local resistance to the French reduced most of these to ruins, but under Muhammad Ali, Azbakiyyah was soon rebuilt and dotted with new administrative offices. After 1837, when the lake was drained and its site converted into a park, hotels began to move their premises into Azbakiyyah from the old European quarter along Shari' Muski to the east. One of them, the New British Hotel, was to become famous under the name of its first owner – Shepheard's.

In 1868 Ismail reduced the park to an octagonal garden and the remainder of the old lake site was opened for devel-

opment. New squares were created and public buildings were erected, the most striking of which was a theatre for opera. Built entirely of wood and completed within five months during 1869, the old Cairo Opera House saw the premier of *Aida* in 1871 and later became renowned for its collections of manuscripts, scores, costumes and sets, all of which were consumed by fire when the building burned down in 1971. The site is now occupied by a high-rise car-park. Behind this are remains of the department stores that were the great retail centres of their time. The Sednaoui Building is still in business, but the earlier Tiring Building is now almost derelict – its rooftop statues holding up a giant globe glimpsed whilst speeding away on the flyover towards al-Azhar.

Commissioned by Ismail and later erected in the square in front of the old Opera House is a heroic equestrian statue of Ibrahim Pasha. Two of Ismail's new streets, both still fashionable – Shari' Abdel Khaliq Tharwat and Shari' Adli, where the largest of Cairo's synagogues stands, as well as another branch of Groppi's – lead westward from Ibrahim's

The Tiring Building, an old Cairo landmark which once contained one of the city's top department stores.

BELOW: Azbakiyyah Garden.

BELOW: Cairo Opera House.

statue, while Shari' al-Gumhuriyyah continues north along the western edge of the **Azbakiyyah Garden** ➎. This well-kept octagonal garden, now closed to the public, was much larger in 1872 when it was elegantly designed by Ismail's French city planner in the style of the Parc Monceau in Paris.

Grand hotels

The now-closed **Continental Hotel** still overlooks the garden from the west, though it has been cut in half and concealed by a row of shop fronts. It was owned at an earlier stage (as the New Hotel) by Ismail himself and came to rank third among Cairo's hotels after the Savoy and Shepheard's.

Shepheard's itself, destroyed by fire in 1952 – the new Shepheard's Hotel on the Corniche has nothing in common with the old one but the name – originally tood on a site further north on Shari' al-Gumhuriyyah, now occupied by a high-rise building. In Ismail's time there were at least seven other hotels close by, plus half a dozen restaurants and a dozen or so foreign consulates.

The area had been known earlier for its

lively low-life, a reputation that did not diminish until long after World War II, during which the city was occupied by British and ANZAC troops eager for such diversions. **Shari' Clot Bey**, in particular, named, ironically, after Muhammad Ali's chief advisor on public health, was famous for its brothels until quite recently.

Further north and east of Azbakiyyah is an area where tourists never venture and few Cairenes visit, the old **Bab al-Bahr quarter**, identified with Christians and very traditional. Though it contains few historic monuments, its streets follow the 15th-century pattern surveyed in 1800 by Napoleon's savants, whose map remains the only accurate guide.

Gazirah and Zamalik

Newer districts, however, are not without appeal. On **al-Gazirah** (The Island), joined to the mainland by three bridges, two of them near Maydan at-Tahrir, are **Zamalik**, a suburb popular with wealthy Cairenes and European residents, as well several cultural attractions. The **Gazirah Exhibition Grounds** were replaced in 1982 as the site of the city's international expositions by the new Cairo International Fairgrounds at Madinat Nasr, but have since become the location of a Japanese-built cultural complex that Cairenes call the **Opera House** ➏.

The **Museum of Egyptian Modern Art** ➐ (Tues–Sun 10am–1pm, 5–9pm, Fri 10am–noon; admission charge) houses paintings and sculptures by 20th-century Egyptian artists. Two other permanent pavilions, including the **Hanager Art Centre**, have been set aside for temporary exhibitions by contemporary artists.

Across the road from the Gazirah Exhibition Grounds, in the park at the southern end of the island, is the **Mukhtar Museum** ➑ (Tues–Sun 10am–1pm, 3–5pm, Fri 10am–noon; admission charge; no photography), housing works by Mahmoud Mukhtar, Egypt's greatest modern sculptor and one of a handful of 20th-century Egyptian artists to achieve international recognition. Just up the road, the Saad

Recommended Restaurants, Cafés & Bars on pages 156–7

Zaghloul statue is one of his *(see picture on page 99)*, as is his giant sphinx and goddess entitled *Egypt's Awakening* on al-Gama'a Square at the entrance of the university and zoo *(see picture on page 153)*.

North of here is the 152-metre (500-ft) high **Cairo Tower** (daily 9am–midnight; admission charge), erected in 1957. When the lifts are working, the tower provides remarkable views of the city. A windy day, when some of the pollution is blown away, offers the best views, but queues can be long to access the tiny lift.

Further north are the grounds of two sporting clubs: the **National**, home of the national *(al-Ahly)* football team *(see page 28)*, with its own stadium, and the **Gazirah Sporting Club** ❾, which offers tennis, riding, golf, swimming and other sports. Arab horses from the best studs in Egypt race at the Gazirah track on alternate weeks in the season.

The name **Zamalik** covers all of Gazirah north of the Gazirah Sporting Club. Opposite the northern entrance to the club is a charming house built in the 1920s for *Nabil* (Lord) Amr Ibrahim, a great-great-grandson of Ibrahim Pasha, as a *salamlik* (reception suite) in the khedival style. It is now home to the **Gazirah Art Centre** (1 Shari' al-Marsafi; Sat–Thur 9am–1pm; admission charge; no photography;) with the **Ceramics Museum**, a unique collection of Islamic ceramics from the 9th century to the present day.

Immediately north, marked by a huge old banyan tree, one of Muhammad Ali's imported species, is the **Italian Culture Centre**. Behind is the **Marriott Hotel** ❿, standing just across Shari' Lutfallah immediately to the east. The central block of the hotel incorporates Khedive Ismail's palace itself. Legend says it was built for the Empress Eugenie to reside in during the Suez Canal inaugural celebrations of 1869, but it was actually begun in 1863 and opened in 1868.

The original vast grounds of the palace survive in two small portions: the enclosed garden attached to the Marriott Hotel, a popular meeting place in Zamalik, and the recently renovated **Fish Garden** (daily 9am–4pm; admission charge) 300 metres/yards to the west, between Shari' al-Gabalayyah and Shari'

Though not as exclusive as it used to be, the Gazirah Sporting Club offers all sorts of sports.

BELOW LEFT: the Museum of Egyptian Modern Art. **BELOW:** Art Deco Soliman House, Zamalik.

Zamalik Buildings

Gazirah Island, known as Zamalik, developed in isolation from the rest of Cairo. The sandy island continually altered its shape, size and position until the stabilisation of the Nile riverbank. It thus escaped development until the 19th century, when it became a retreat for Egyptian royalty who constructed expensive palaces and villas in a variety of styles, some of which can be visited today. The khedive's Gazirah Palace, built for the grand opening of the Suez Canal in 1869, is now part of the Marriott Hotel, while the Greater Cairo Library is located in the impressive former palace of a daughter of Sultan Hussein Kamel. The Gazirah Arts Centre (now Ceramics Museum), built in the 1920s, is another former palace with rooms dedicated to Fatimid, Turkish and Persian periods. Development along the eastern side in the 1930s saw the construction of mansions built in the popular Art Deco style of the period. Their names include Pyramid House, Nile View and Soliman House, and a few owners have completely refurbished in Art Deco style.

The Marriott Hotel incorporates the palace of Khedive Ismail and is set in extensive gardens. Its terrace is a lovely spot for afternoon tea or early-evening drinks.

BELOW: the palatial Greater Cairo Library.

Hassan Sabri. A public park since 1902, it still has the original estate's picturesque grotto-aquarium.

When the grounds were laid out in 1867, the Nile was diverted on the western side of the island and the resultant dry channel was turned into an irrigation canal for the gardens. Entire displays of masterworks were meanwhile bought at the Exposition Universelle in Paris to serve as the palace's furniture.

Foreign embassies

Along the eastern bank north of Shari' 26 of July Bridge are splendid mansions. These are mostly occupied by foreign embassies, but there is one that can be visited. The **Greater Cairo Library** ⓫ (Sun–Thur 9am–5pm; free; no photography) is housed in the impressive former palace of a daughter of Sultan Hussein Kamel (ruled Egypt 1914–17). Access for casual visitors is around the back of the building, and to the right, where a passport or ID must be left at the

gatehouse. It is very much a working environment, with rooms for study, but the refurbishment has been handled well and offers fine views across the river.

GARDEN CITY AND RAWDAH

Just south of Maydan at-Tahrir, the British and Americans have remained faithful to **Garden City**, laid out on the site of an old estate of Ibrahim Pasha's. The British consul general – now the **Residency** – was restored in the 1980s to its late-Victorian splendour. Full of banks and overcrowded with their customers during the day, Garden City recovers some of its charm at night.

Rawdah Island

The northern tip of Rawdah Island is dominated by the huge Hyatt Hotel, but there are some gems to be found on the island. Once belonging to the Muhammad Ali family is **Manyal Palace** ⓬ (daily 9am–5pm; admission charge) built between 1901 and 1929. It was left to the Egyptian nation in 1955 by Prince Muhammad Ali, the younger brother of Khedive Abbas Hilmi Pasha and a first cousin of King Faruq. It includes a

museum exhibiting Faruq's game-shooting trophies; the prince's own beautiful residence with its furnishings; and a 14-room museum housing family memorabilia. The gardens are being returned to their former splendour.

On the southern tip of Rawdah Island, but in fact much more easily accessed via the footbridge from the Corniche near Old Cairo *(see below)*, is the smaller Monastirli Palace. This contains the **Umm Kalthoum Museum ⓭** (daily 10am–5pm; admission charge), dedicated to the life and work of Egypt's best-loved singer *(see box on page 98)*. On show are her iconic sunglasses, good-luck handkerchiefs, photos and video clips of her performances.

In the same compound, at the southern tip of Rawdah Island, is the **Nilometer ⓮** (daily 10am–5pm; admission charge), clearly visible from across the river (it is distinguished by a conical cap). This is a reconstruction made in 1893 of a 17th-century Ottoman dome destroyed by the French in 1800; its interior is covered with fine Turkish tiles. The substructure, however, which is the Nilometer itself, dates from 861, which makes it the

oldest intact Islamic monument in Cairo and the only survivor from the Abbasid period. Comprising a calibrated stone column standing upright in a stone-lined pit with a staircase, it is particularly notable for the use of pointed arches at the highest intake level – 300 years before the appearance of such arches in Europe. Before the dams at Aswan were constructed, the Nile rose every summer and the strength of the inundation was shown by the level of water covering the niches cut into the central vertical column. The greater the depth of water, the more tax the farmers had to pay.

BABYLON – "OLD CAIRO"

The remains of Roman and Christian Babylon are found in the area known as **Misr al-Qadimah ⓯**, which confusingly translates into "Old Cairo" (though it should not be mistaken for representing more than a foretaste of Cairo's medieval glory). Here too are interesting remains from Egypt's Christian era, as well as one monument from the years immediately following the Arab conquest.

Cairo developed at a point halfway between Memphis and Heliopolis where

Umm Kalthoum, the Arab World's favourite diva. Her museum on Rawdah Island is well worth a visit.

BELOW:
the Nilometer, which measured the depth of the Nile, was built by the Abbasids in the 9th century.

The Coptic quarter of Misr al-Qadimah (Old Cairo) is easily reached on the metro. Get off at Mari Girgis (St George).

BELOW: film poster in Misr al-Qadimah.

that should not be confused with Mesopotamian Babylon, that probably derives from an Egyptian name such as *Pi-Hapi-n-On* or *Per-Hapi-n-On*, meaning "The Nile House of On". Under the emperor Trajan (AD 98–117), after more than a century of Roman occupation, during which Heliopolis had long been moribund, the old canal was reopened and a new fortress was built, one of three to control the whole of Egypt.

Egyptians themselves knew their country by many names, of which the most common during the Roman period was probably Kemet, "The Black Land". Throughout the rest of the Semitic-speaking Middle East, Egypt was called **Misr**, the name it still bears in Arabic today. When the Arabs conquered Misr in 641 AD and founded a new capital next to the walls of Babylon, this capital acquired the name of the country as a whole. This became more and more appropriate as new quarters with new names were added and it expanded to become the metropolis not only of Egypt, but of the Arab world, a huge city containing many distinct areas with their own names.

a road crossed the river, using the present island of Rawdah as a stepping stone. Since there were no other roads across the Delta, this one not only connected the Old Kingdom's administrative and religious capitals, but was the main passage into Egypt from the east, giving access to the rest of the country. During the Late Dynasty period a small fortress was built here and, after a canal linking the Nile with the Red Sea was completed by the Persian occupiers under Darius I (521–486 BC), the site became even more important. The Greeks called it **Babylon**, a name

Visiting Old Cairo

The remains of the Roman fortress of Babylon, which was largely intact until the British occupation, can be visited in conjunction with the churches and museum of the Coptic quarter. They can be easily reached by metro; the metro stop is **Mari Girgis** (St George) and stands opposite the modern Greek Orthodox church of the same name. A visit to the churches and the fortress is pleasant as the area is peaceful and picturesque, particularly following a thorough restoration of the quarter. The grounds of the **Coptic Museum Ⓐ** (daily 9am–4pm; admission charge) begin south of the tower and are entirely within the fortress walls. Founded by private benefactors on land belonging to the Coptic Church, the museum was taken over by the government in 1931. Though there are many ancient Christian sites in Egypt, there are none in which the churches themselves have not been abandoned, destroyed or rebuilt inside and out. It is therefore only the Coptic Museum that gives an idea of what the interior of a 5th-, 6th- or 7th-century church was like. Objects that were excavated in Upper Egypt and in the monastery of St Jeremiah at Saqqarah are of particular interest.

The museum's most prized relics are the Coptic textiles and the "Nag Hammadi Codices" *(see page 57)*, a collection of nearly 1,200 papyrus pages bound together as books – the earliest so far known with leather covers – sometime soon after the middle of the 4th century. Written in Coptic, the codices draw syncretically upon Jewish, Christian, Hermetic, Zoroastrian and Platonic sources and have thrown extraordinary light on the background of the New Testament, particularly the Epistles, by revealing that Gnosticism, hitherto supposed to be only a Christian heresy, was in fact a separate religion.

The churches

Babylon is mentioned in St Peter's first epistle, most scholars now concede, in connection with St Mark's Egyptian mission, and local legend claims it as one of the many places in Egypt where the Holy Family rested. The monks and martyrs who elsewhere created the heroic age of the Coptic Church seem to

The Western name "Cairo" derives from "Al-Qahirah", the name of a single quarter of Misr as understood by medieval Italian merchants, who mistook it for a complete city, like their walled towns.

BELOW: entrance to the Coptic Museum.

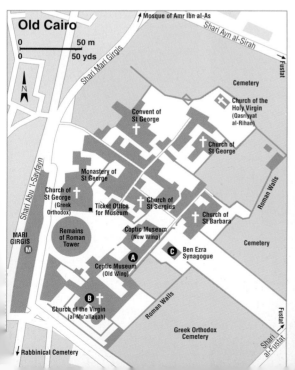

Old Cairo map:
- Mosque of Amr Ibn al-As
- Shari Ayn al-Sirah
- Shari Mari Girgis
- Fustat
- Cemetery
- Convent of St George
- Church of the Holy Virgin (Qasriyyat al-Rihan)
- Church of St George
- Monastery of St George
- Church of St George (Greek Orthodox)
- Ticket Office for Museum
- Church of St Sergius
- Shari Abu 'l-Sayfayn
- MARI GIRGIS Ⓜ
- Remains of Roman Tower
- Coptic Museum (New Wing)
- Church of St Barbara
- Roman Walls
- Cemetery
- Ⓐ Coptic Museum (Old Wing)
- Ⓒ Ben Ezra Synagogue
- Ⓑ Church of the Virgin (al-Mu'allaqah)
- Roman Walls
- Fustat
- Shari al-Fustat
- Greek Orthodox Cemetery
- Rabbinical Cemetery
- 0 50 m / 0 50 yds

THE COPTIC MUSEUM
القبطى

TIP

Coptic masses can be heard in the Church of the Virgin on Fridays 8–11am and on Sundays 7–10am. Churches are open 9am–4pm; donations welcome.

BELOW: interior and exterior detail of al-Mu'allaqah (The Suspended).

have passed it by, and there are no specific documentary references to any church structure earlier than the Arab conquest. Babylon could not have had much importance as a Christian centre until four centuries later, when it had long since been absorbed into Misr. The Patriarchate of St Mark, robbed of the saint's relics by Venetians in 828, was transferred there from a declining Alexandria sometime after 1048.

Churches and monastic settlements were scattered not only at Babylon but all over the future site of Misr. Many were later destroyed, but some were undoubtedly incorporated into later structures. Atop the two bastions of the southern gate of the Roman fortress, for example, is the **church of the Virgin** , referred to locally as **al-Mu'allaqah** ("The Suspended"), a seat of the patriarchate for centuries, one portion of which is claimed to date back to the 4th century; and within the walls are several others with an almost equal claim to antiquity – the **churches of St Sergius and St Bacchus**, **St Barbara**, **St Cyril and St John**; a second Church of the Virgin, known as **Qasriyyat al-Rihan**

("Pot of Basil"); and a **convent of St George**. Outside the fortress walls, but still within Old Cairo, are no fewer than a dozen more churches that were well documented in medieval times.

The oldest, finest and most portable objects have all been removed either to the Coptic Museum (see page 137) or to other collections around the world, but one of the sanctuaries of the Suspended Church has the remains of fine frescoes attributed to the 7th or 8th century, and the buildings of the convent of St George include an intact reception hall belonging to a Fatimid-period house, with magnificent wooden doors 7 metres (22 ft) high.

These churches are all Coptic Orthodox, but during Lent they become pilgrimage sites for Catholics as well. In the 17th and 18th centuries the Franciscan friars had the right to celebrate mass in the sanctuary of the Holy Family at the church of St Sergius and St Bacchus, which marks a traditional resting place of the Holy Family and is thus venerated by both Catholic and Orthodox believers.

Also within the walls of Old Cairo is the **Ben Ezra Synagogue**  (daily 9am–4pm; donations welcome), one of

Recommended Restaurants, Cafés & Bars on pages 156–7

Cairo's 29 synagogues, now under heavy security. It is a reminder of Egypt's role not only in fostering the Sephardic Rabbinical tradition but also in providing a home for Karaite Jews (before the 10th century) and Ashkenazi Jews (from the 16th century onward). Originally a church dedicated to St Michael the Archangel, the building was closed under the Fatimid caliph al-Hakim (996–1021), then sold to the Sephardic community. Among other functions it served as a genizah, a repository for documents made sacrosanct by being sworn under oath, which could not be casually discarded without sacrilege. It was discovered a few years ago during the restoration of the synagogue. Since these documents cover several centuries and include such mundane items as contracts, bills of sale and letters of credit, they constitute an extensive record of medieval Mediterranean trade.

The first Arab capital

Immediately to the east of Old Cairo, in an enormous area slowly being covered with new buildings, is the site of **Fustat** , the first Muslim capital at Misr, founded by Amr ibn al-As in the course of the Arab conquest. Excavations here have uncovered the remains of elaborate water storage and drainage systems, the foundations of private houses and apartment blocks, and thousands of objects made of wood, paper, ivory, glass, metal or ceramics, ranging in date from the 8th century to the 14th, and in provenance from Spain to China. The most significant of these objects may be seen in the Islamic Art Museum *(see page 148).*

There is little to see to suggest the importance Fustat still had as a residential, manufacturing and international trading centre even after the government had moved to new quarters further north. Coming from Old Cairo, you will notice, on the corner, the modern domed building of **Souq al-Fustat** containing shops and workshops of leading artisans.

Further along the street is the **mosque of Amr ibn al-As**  (daily 9am–4pm;

Fri closed during prayers noon–1pm). Erected in 641, it was rebuilt and enlarged several times and acquired its present size in 827, thus testifying to Fustat's rapid growth. After several centuries of neglect, it was rebuilt again near the end of the 18th century, just before the French invasion. After all this rebuilding, only an expert can now pinpoint the oldest areas of construction, but the site is important as it marks the first mosque in Africa.

EASTERN (ISLAMIC CAIRO)

In 872 the Abbasid caliph's name was removed from the Nilometer by order of the city's 38-year-old Turkish governor, Ahmad ibn Tulun, who would not only declare himself independent, but within 10 years make Misr the centre of an empire stretching from southern Turkey to Sudan. Cramped by the growth of Fustat, the Abbasid caliphs had already built themselves a new military quarter, **al-Askar**, to the north; but Ibn Tulun felt the need for something grander. The

Ben Ezra Synagogue (above) lies in the midst of the Coptic quarter. Beyond Old Cairo, 5 km (3 miles) to the southeast, is the considerably older Rabbinical Cemetery containing the tomb of Ya'kub ibn Killis, the Jewish vizier of the caliph Aziz (975–996).

BELOW: buying pottery, Fustat.

result was **al-Qatai'** ("The Wards"), a new town large enough to include a walled hippodrome, a hospital, a menagerie, mews, gardens, markets, baths, residential quarters (classified by nationality), reception and *harim* ("harem") palaces for Ibn Tulun himself, and a large governmental complex, which was attached to a great congregational mosque.

When the Abbasids repossessed Misr for the caliphate in 905, the **mosque of Ibn Tulun** (Shari' al-Salibah; daily 8am–5pm), rightly considered one of the architectural glories of the Muslim world, was the only building left standing in al-Qatai'. It is approached through the web of narrow streets that grew up around it, but most taxi drivers can find it. It has undergone several restorations, the first in 1297 and the latest very recently.

Built in the imperial style of the Abbasid court at Samarra in Iraq, where Ibn Tulun had lived as a young man, the mosque is built of red brick and stucco – original materials, rather than granite, limestone and marble borrowed from other sites, as is often the case in later

mosques. The mosque is impressive both for its simplicity and grand scale – its courtyard alone covers 2.5 hectares (6½ acres) and the sycamore-wood frieze of Qur'anic verses around the court is more than 2 km (1¼ miles) long.

The unusual spiral minaret was probably inspired by the minaret in Samarra, Iraq, although legend has it that a distracted Ibn Tulun rolled up a piece of paper and told the architect to use that as the design.

Gayer Anderson Museum

Adjoining the mosque's northeast corner is the **Gayer-Anderson Museum** (Bayt al-Kritliya, house of the Kretans, 4 Maydan Ahmad ibn Zulein; daily 9am–5pm, closed for Friday prayers; admission charge). Two recently restored houses, one from the 16th century, the other from the 17th, have been joined together to create a delightful larger dwelling with a *salaamlik* (reception suite) and *haramlik* (harem suite). Both are filled with *objets d'art* and antique furniture from all over the Middle East, the collection of Gayer-Anderson, a british major, who restored the houses

ABOVE AND BELOW: the 9th-century mosque of Ibn Tulun.

and lived here in the 1930s and '40s. The entrance to the museum leads from the mosque of Ibn Tulun.

About 500 metres/yds northwest is the **mosque of Sayyida Zeinab** (free), another revered site of pilgrimage, particularly for women. Amid a forest of columns the tomb of the granddaughter of the Prophet Muhammad is inside a shrine behind a solid-silver grille, dazzlingly illuminated.

Immediately across the road from the mosque is the free-standing **sabil kuttub of Sultan Mustafa**, which is still used as a Qu'ranic school.

Outside the Gayer Anderson Museum, Shari' Tulun leads eastward (left) after less than 100 metres/yards into **Shari' al-Salibah**, the start of the **Qasabah** *(see margin note)*, medieval Cairo's main street. The Qasabah linked all the city's parts on a north–south axis; at the height of Cairo's medieval prosperity this street was more than 13 km (8 miles) long.

Shari' al-Salibah

There is so much of the rest of medieval Cairo still to see that it is best to take the Qasabah piecemeal. The first major part

is rich in fine architecture. On the northeast side of Shari' al-Salibah is a delightful Ottoman-style *sabil-kuttub* (fountain school: *see box below*) built in 1867 by the mother of Abbas I, the successor of Muhammad Ali, and beautifully restored in 1984 by the Egyptian Antiquities Organisation.

Unmistakable just beyond the northeast and southeast corners of the intersection are the massive facades of two madrasahs (theological schools) built by the Amir Shaykhu, commander of the Mamluk armies under Sultan Hasan ibn an-Nasir Muhammad ibn Qalawun (1334–61), who ordered his murder in 1357.

Shaykhu's **madrasah** (built in 1349, on the left) and his **khanqah ❷⓪** (built in 1355, on the right) represent two classic Cairene architectural types, both introduced two centuries earlier by Saladin. Persian in inspiration, the madrasah provided a courtyard mosque made cruciform by four vaulted halls *(iwans)*, where instruction could take place in the four systems of legal thought regarded as orthodox by Sunni Muslims (Hanafi, Malaki, Shafi'i and Hanbali).

A *khanqah* is a Muslim "monastery",

WHERE

The great north–south thoroughfare called the Qasabah, medieval Cairo's main street, can still be followed on foot from Ibn Tulun northward for more than 5 km (3 miles), cutting through Islamic Cairo to Bab al-Futuh.

BELOW LEFT:
the *sabil-kuttub* (fountain school) of Sultan Mustafa.

Sabil-Kuttubs – Fountain Schools

To the early Arabs who brought Islam to Cairo from the harsh deserts of Arabia, water was one of the most precious commodities, to be harnessed and dispensed to all. The Prophet Muhammad is quoted as saying that the two greatest mercies were "water for the thirsty and knowledge for the ignorant", so that a continuous water supply and flow of knowledge were seen as essential for the wellbeing of these expanding Islamic communities. Within the crowded alleyways of Ottoman Cairo, small decorated buildings called sabil-kuttubs (literally meaning fountains of books) were provided by wealthy benefactors (often the Mamluk sultan himself) to quench the public's thirst for water and knowledge.

The *sabil* on the ground floor supplied free water to anybody who required it, whilst upstairs in the *kuttub* was a Koranic school and library for the education of children. Built from stone or marble and decorated with elaborately carved wood or finely wrought metal, each example of these delightful buildings is different from the next.

With the provision of a modern water supply system throughout the old city, most of these buildings have fallen into disrepair, but a number have been lovingly restored and there are now many fine examples scattered around the city.

a mosque with dwelling areas that serve as a hostel for Sufis (Muslim mystics). Shaykhu's recently restored *khanqah* accommodated some 700 Sufis in 150 cells of varying comfort, surrounding a mosque with a courtyard. These two buildings frame Shari' al-Salibah as one looks in the direction of the Citadel, creating a gorgeous Oriental-style vista.

Further up Shari' as-Salibah, towards the Citadel, is the first free-standing *sabil-kuttub* in Cairo (built by Qaytbay in 1479), beyond which the street emerges into the **Qaramaydan** (Maydan Salah ad-Din). This enormous square was the site of first Ibn Tulun's hippodrome and then the Mamluks' polo-ground, where their pageants, races, matches, musters and military displays took place under the gaze – and the guns – of the Citadel.

Madrasah of Sultan Hasan and the Rifa'i Mosque

At the northwestern corner of this square loom two colossal religious buildings, one on either side of the entrance to Shari' al-Qal'ah (generally better known under its former name as Shari'

Muhammad Ali): the **madrasah of Sultan Hasan** ㉑ (Maydan Saladin; daily 9am–5pm, till 6pm in summer; admission charge), built between 1356 and 1363; and the **Rifa'i Mosque** ㉒ (same hours and ticket as the Sultan Hasan Madrasah), which was built to complement it architecturally between 1869 and 1912. Visitors sometimes fail to understand that these two buildings were constructed more than five centuries apart, since the modern mosque shows perfect respect for its older neighbour across the street in fabric, scale and style.

Inside the Rifa'i Mosque Mamluk motifs have been reproduced with luxurious fidelity, demonstrating recognition of the Mamluk style as Cairo's trademark, an almost "official" style and thus particularly suitable in a mosque identified with the ruling dynasty. Originally endowed by the mother of Khedive Ismail, it houses her tomb as well as those of the khedive himself and four of his sons, including Husayn Kamil (1853–1917) and King Fuad (1868–1936). The former royal family is buried here, including King Faruq.

A great parade of Sufi orders, with chanting, banners and drums, takes place annually in Cairo on the eve of the Prophet's birthday. It traditionally begins here at the Rifa'i Mosque, marches down Shari' Muhammad Ali, up Shari' Bur Sa'id, then down Shari' al-Azhar – wide new European-style streets constructed by the dynasty between 1873 and 1930 – to end at the popular mosque of Sayyidna al-Husayn which was built by Khedive Ismail.

Sultan Hasan Madrasah, situated just across the street from the Rifa'i Mosque, provided a daunting model, since it is probably the greatest of the Bahri architectural monuments, and second only to Ibn Tulun's Mosque in grandeur of conception among all the historic buildings in Cairo. The walls are 117 ft (36 metres) high and so solidly built that the mosque was twice used as a fortress – first in 1381 during a Mamluk revolt and then again in 1517 during the Ottoman invasion.

Originally four minarets were planned, including two over the entrance portal, but in February 1360, while the building was still under construction, one of these

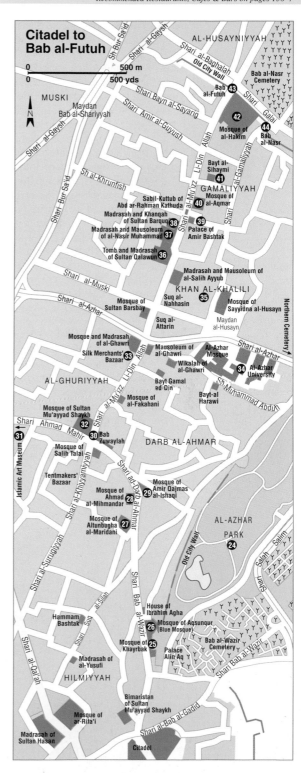

Twenty-seven varieties of marble were used for the floors of the madrasah of Sultan Hasan.

two fell, killing 300 people, and the second was never built. One of the two remaining minarets collapsed in 1659 and was replaced by the present smaller version, an Ottoman construction in the Mamluk style, in 1672, when the dome was also replaced. The architectural daring that caused the difficulties is made clear by the original minaret at the western corner; it is over 265 ft (80 metres), taller and larger than any other in Cairo.

The complex originally included a market, apartments and a well at its northern end. The original wooden doors at the entrance, covered with bronze and filigree silver in geometric patterns, were removed by Sultan Mu'ayyad Sheikh in 1416 to be used in his mosque near Bab Zuwaylah, where they are still visible, and most of the original marble floor was stripped by Selim the Grim for shipment to Istanbul after the Ottoman conquest. What is left, however, is stunning.

The Citadel

The **Citadel** ㉓ (daily 8am–5pm in winter, 8am–6pm in summer; admission charge), entered from **Bab al-Gabal** Ⓐ (also known as Bab al-Muqattam) reached from the Salah Salim highway, was begun by Saladin in 1176 as part of a grand scheme to enclose all of Misr within walls. In 1182, by which time he had gone north to fight his last campaigns against the crusaders, it was complete, and though it was later modified it was never without a military garrison.

In 1218 Sultan al-Kamil, Saladin's nephew, took up residence in the Citadel, and from that time until the construction of Abdin Palace in the mid-19th century it was also the home and seat of government of all but one of Egypt's rulers, including Ottoman viceroys. The Lower Enclosure contains the famous gate-passage where Muhammad Ali conducted a massacre of Mamluks in 1811 *(see page 77)*. It can be approached by an 18th-century gateway, restored in 1988, but it is best seen from the terrace of the Police Museum on the upper level, which contains the Southern and

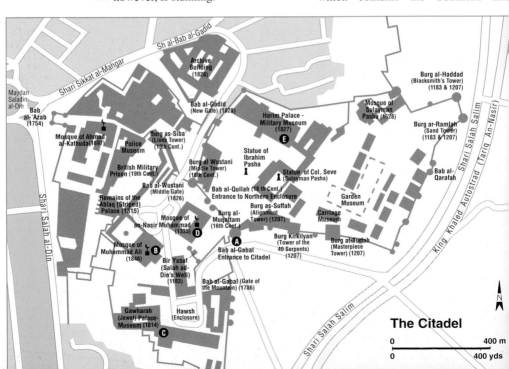

The Citadel

| 0 | 400 m |
| 0 | 400 yds |

Northern enclosures, nearly two-thirds of the Citadel's entire area.

Visible from nearly anywhere in the city below, on the pinnacle of the Southern Enclosure, is the **Muhammad Ali Mosque ⓑ**. Built between 1830 and 1848, it was not completed until 1857. Designed by a Greek architect in accord with Ottoman models, it owes nothing to Egypt but the materials from which it is made and a few intermingled Pharaonic and Mamluk decorative motifs, but it adds a wonderful picture-postcard element to the city's skyline. The clock in the courtyard was a gift made by Louis-Philippe of France in 1846, a belated exchange for the obelisk of Ramesses II from Luxor Temple, now standing in the Place de la Concorde in Paris, which Muhammad Ali had given the French in 1831. The pasha himself is buried here under a marble cenotaph.

The view from the belvedere near the mosque is remarkable on a clear day, when it is possible to see the Giza Pyramids. Across a little court is the **Gawharah Palace ⓒ**, built by Muhammad Ali in 1814, gutted by fire during a theft in 1972. The ruins have been in-telligently refurbished and converted into a museum of the mid-19th century, when it served as a vice-regal *salamlik* (reception) palace.

Below the Muhammad Ali Mosque, to the northwest, between the mosque and the gateway to the Northern Enclosure, is the great 14th-century **mosque of an-Nasir Muhammad ⓓ**, the father of Sultan Hasan. Built in 1318, enlarged in 1335, but stripped of its gorgeous marble by the Ottomans after 1517, it shows Persian-Mongol influence in its unique minarets, and an incredible variety of Egyptian sources in its columns: levied from Pharaonic, Greek, Roman and Coptic sites, they constitute a survey of Egyptian architectural styles.

North of the mosque of an-Nasir Muhammad are two gates: one downhill to the left leads into the Lower Enclosure; the other, around a corner to the right, leads into the Northern Enclosure. Within the Northern Enclosure is the **Military Museum ⓔ**, which is housed in Muhammad Ali's Harim Palace, built in 1827. The inside is packed with military memorabilia and historical weapons covering Egyptian Army

The distinctive silver-coloured domes of the Muhammad Ali Mosque are visible all over the city.

BELOW: the splendid interior of the Muhammad Ali Mosque.

history from Pharaonic times to the present, including one of Tutankhamun's war chariots.

In the far corner of the Northern Enclosure is the Suleiman Pasha Mosque, the first Ottoman mosque to be built in Cairo (1528). Nestled next to an old Fatimid tomb, it is set in a small garden, which must have afforded a cool and leafy touch of the Bosphorus to the homesick Janissaries who lived here after 1517.

Al-Azhar Park

The Aga Khan Trust for Culture undertook a formidable project in a city with one of the lowest ratios of green space in the world: they created the 30-hectare (74-acre) **al-Azhar Park** (daily 8am–10pm in winter, 8am–midnight in summer; small admission charge) near the Citadel. The project included the excavation and restoration of the 12th-century Ayyubid wall (which had been entirely covered in the accumulated rubbish of several centuries), the installation of three large freshwater tanks which provide for fountains and a lake with fantastic views over the medieval

city, and a formal garden. There are several good cafés and restaurants open until late in the evening.

A walk through medieval Cairo

Medieval Cairo can be known only on foot, and one of its greatest walks begins at **Bab al-Jadid**, the northern gate of the Citadel, and runs to Bab Zuwaylah. The street has other names – at-Tabbana, Bab al-Wazir – but is best known as **Darb al-Ahmar**. From outside the Citadel, Bab al-Jadid can be reached by walking up toward the Citadel from Maydan Saladin, then turning left to climb a road running parallel to its walls, bearing on to a shady street running downhill at the first intersection.

From here, the route to Bab Zuwaylah first runs through an area that was cleared for pleasure gardens by Saladin, then became fashionable during the reign of an-Nasir Muhammad, when many of his sons-in-law began building there.

First, on the left down a very short side street, for example, are the ruins of a medieval hospital (1420), the *bimaristan* **of Mu'ayyad Shaykh**; while on the

CAFES

Al-Azhar Park is a great place to escape from the bustle, heat and dust, buy an ice cream or a cold drink and gaze out over the seething mass of the city. Its cafés stay open long into the evening.

BELOW:
Tutankhamun's chariot in the Citadel's Military Museum.

Recommended Restaurants, Cafés & Bars on pages 156–7

right appear the **madrasah and tomb of Amir Aytmish al-Bagasi** (1348), the remains of the **tomb and *sabil-kuttub* of Amir Tarabay as-Sharifi** (1503), and the **tomb of Azdumur** (early 16th century). A hundred metres/yards further down the street on the right (east) is the **palace of Alin Aq** (1293), now under restoration, occupied and remodelled by the treacherous Amir Khayrbak, who built his tomb (1502), mosque and *sabil-kuttub* (1502) next to it, creating a northward view that is one of the most frequently photographed in Cairo.

This area is undergoing restoration by the Aga Khan Trust. Among the buildings being restored are the 14th-century Umm Sultan Shaban Mosque, the Khayrbek complex (encompassing a 13th-century palace, a mosque and an Ottoman house) and the Darb Shoughlan School. New jobs have been created and local housing has been renovated.

On the left (west) across the street from **Khayrbak's Mosque** ㉕ is the start of a 14-unit apartment house dating from 1522. Just beyond Khayrbak's mosque on the right (east), meanwhile, is a 17th-century house, with the 1347

mosque of Amir Aqsunqur ㉖ (9am– 5pm), one of an-Nasir Muhammad's sons-in-law, next to it. Adorned with Damascene tiles installed in 1652 by Ibrahim Agha, the first owner of the house, the mosque is also known as the "Blue Mosque".

Across the street from the mosque, next to the 16th-century apartment house, is a 17th-century *sabil* (fountain) and tomb, and on the east side another of Ibrahim Agha's houses (1652) with his adjoining *sabil* (1639). Beyond the *sabil* is a small Ottoman religious structure, with an Ayyubid minaret (1260). A little further down the street, another 17th-century *sabil-kuttub* appears on the left, and a 14th-century tomb on the right.

Jutting into the street from the left is the **mosque of Altunbugha al-Maridani** ㉗ (1340), notable for its woodwork and marble, which gives an idea of what an-Nasir Muhammad's mosque at the Citadel must have been like before the Ottoman conquest. Further along on the same side of the street is the **mosque of Ahmad al-Mihmandar** ㉘ (1325), which has a

TIP

Anyone – Muslim or non-Muslim – may wander into Cairo's mosques and madrasahs. The more important ones have opening times and an admission charge (otherwise tip the guardian). Visitors need to be respectfully dressed – no shorts, miniskirts or bare shoulders – and shoes should be removed. Women must cover their heads: at the more important mosques coveralls are provided (tip expected).

BELOW: fighter planes at the Military Museum.

The al-Ghuri Mosque was just one of many popular Cairo locations that Edinburgh-born artist David Roberts painted during his Oriental travels. He produced six folio volumes of 247 lithographs of Egypt, Nubia and the Holy Land, in the middle of the 19th century. Copies of his distinctive and atmospheric prints are to be found everywhere in Cairo.

17th-century *sabil-kuttub* next to it. Finally, on the right as the street turns a corner and Bab Zuwaylah comes into view, stands the exquisite funerary **mosque of Amir Qajmas al-Ishaqi** ㉙ (1481); it is connected with his *sabil-kuttub* by a bridge over a side street.

Darb al-Ahmar has undergone serious restoration in recent years. It runs east and west and leads – after a change of name – past **Bab Zuwaylah** ㉚ *(see below)* and the Tentmakers' Bazaar to the **Islamic Art Museum** ㉛ (Maydan Ahmed Maher, on the corner of Shari' Port Said and Shari' al-Qala'a; closed for restoration at the time of writing), containing one of the world's finest collections of Islamic applied arts, such as ceramics, woodwork, carpets and textiles, manuscripts, metalwork, stonework and arms.

North of Bab Zuwaylah

Built in 1092 as the southern gateway of al-Qahirah, the beautifully restored Bab Zuwaylah is the most distinguished of the old quarters. Originally a palace enclosure, it was opened to commercial development by Saladin. Through its

heart runs the Qasabah, at once the main artery of the medieval city and a single enormous bazaar, straddled at either end of al-Qahirah by splendid Fatimid gates.

High up on the wall next to the gate at Bab Zuwaylah hangs a mysterious collection of metal objects – weapons, tools, or Sufi instruments – which no-one has ever convincingly identified. Directly on top of the gate (daily 9am–5pm; admission charge) are two minarets. Belonging to the **mosque of Sultan Mu'ayyad Shaykh** ㉜ (1420), which stands just inside the gate to the left, they also demonstrate that by the end of the 14th century Bab Zuwaylah had ceased to be regarded as primarily military. There are far-reaching views over the city from the top of the minarets.

In this mosque the splendid doors of Sultan Hasan Madrasah *(see page 142)* were hung and can still be seen. Across the street, with an attached *sabil-kuttub*, is the facade of a caravanserai-emporium called **as-Sukkariyyah** (from the Arabic *sukkar*, the source of the word for "sugar" in several European languages)

BELOW: Bab Zuwaylah.

which has given this district just within the southern Fatimid walls its name.

Cruising up the Qasabah

From here northward the Qasabah has been devoted to buying and selling for eight centuries; 450 metres/yards up the street is another famous commercial district, the **al-Ghuriyyah**, named after Qansuh al-Ghuri, one of the last Mamluk sultans. His beautifully restored **madrasah** and **mausoleum** (1505; 9am–5pm, 6pm in summer) stand on the site of the **Silk Merchants' Bazaar** ㉝, a street market that was once the most famous in Cairo. At one time covered but now open-air, it is still bursting with textile trade.

At this point the Qasabah's north–south axis is dissected by the modern east–west traffic of **Shari' al-Azhar**, which was cut through old Misr in 1930 to provide a tram service for the greatest and most long-lived of the Fatimids' foundations, the **mosque-university of al-Azhar** ㉞ (9am–5pm, closed for Friday prayers; admission charge), lying a short distance down Shari' al-Azhar to the east. Built in AD 971, al-Azhar was the first mosque of Fatimid Cairo. It was also one of the first universities in the world, and it is still Egypt's supreme religious authority, attracting Islamic scholars from around the world. The entrance to the mosque is the splendid 15th-century **Barber's Gate**.

Several houses behind al-Azhar have been carefully restored and are now open to visitors. Coming out of the mosque, walk left and then turn left again; at the end of the street is **Bayt al-Harawi** (9am–4pm; admission charge), which is used as a cultural centre, and **Bayt Zeinab Khatun** (same opening hours), a smaller version of the Gayer-Anderson Museum.

Between the palaces

On the other side of Shari' al-Azhar, the Qasabah, here called Sharia al-Muizz li-Din Allah, continues north, until just beyond a 15th-century madrasah it is interrupted by another modern street, **Shari' al-Muski**. Traditionally associated with old Christian and European quarters, by the end of the 19th century it was lined with European-owned shops. Al-

> **TIP**
>
> The whirling dervishes of the At-Tannoura Egyptian Heritage Dance Troupe give performances at the Wikalat al-Ghuri on al-Azhar Road *(see page 321 in Travel Tips)*.

BELOW:
the prayer hall and courtyard of the mosque-university of al-Azhar.

Muski is now a chaotic and busy pedestrian street, where wholesale traders offer their wares to small merchants from all over Egypt.

The Qasabah itself still maintains its traditional character. Here, spices and scents are sold; beyond are goldsmiths; and the first major street to the right (east) leads to the **Khan al-Khalili ㉟**, famous formerly for Turkish goods and now the tourists' bazaar, where locals also buy jewellery and antiques.

Further north, to the right, is the magnificent complex built by three of the most important Mamluk sultans (daily 9am–5pm; admission charge). First to the left is the great *maristan* (hospital) tomb-madrasah built in 1285 by **Sultan Qalawun ㊱**, and next door are the madrasah and mausoleum built 40 years later by his son **al-Nasir Muhammad ㊲**. The next entrance through bronze-plated doors leads to the madrasah and *khanqah* of **Sultan Barquq ㊳**. The minaret of the **madrasah-mausoleum of Sultan as-Salih Nagm ad-Din Ayyub**, built by his widow, commands great views over the complex. This section of the Qasabah

was known even then as **Bayn al-Qasrayn**, "Between the Two Palaces", in recognition of the two huge Fatimid palaces that had stood facing each other on this site over a century earlier.

Appropriately, Cairo's principal slave market was also held here in the Bayn al-Qasrayn, where Mamluks and girls, mainly Circassian and Greek, continued to be bought and sold until the time of Muhammad Ali. Facing the huge complex are the remains of the 14th-century **palace of Amir Bashtak ㊴** (daily 9am–5pm; admission charge), with beautiful *mashrabiyyah* windows in a high plain facade.

On the crossroads is the elegant Ottoman *sabil-kuttub* **of Abd ar-Rahman Kathuda**, showing a mixture of Mamluk and Ottoman influences.

To the northern gates

Further north, in a stretch of the Qasabah where items such as copper bean-pots and finials for mosques are made, stands the 12th-century **Aqmar Mosque ㊵**, one of the few remaining Fatimid monuments and one of Cairo's oldest mosques. Around the corner at the

BELOW:
a *mashrabiyyah* window on an old Cairene property. Traditionally these enclosed windows provided privacy for the women of the house when they looked out upon the world.
BELOW RIGHT:
Khan al-Khalili.

Preserving Historic Cairo

So much of medieval Cairo is in a serious state of dilapidation that it is easy to think that nothing is being done to preserve the historic district. A serious eathquake in the 1990s, a rising water table, and the fact that many historic buildings have long served as homes, often to several families, all make conservation problematic.

However the government's Historic Cairo Restoration Project is at work on around 150 monuments, ranging from mosques and madrasahs to houses and caravanserais, and a further 500 monuments have been identified as historic buildings requiring restoration.

There has been criticism, especially from international quarters, concerning insensitive restoration by large companies inexperienced in conservation, the use of inappropriate materials, and failure to heed the needs of the local community. More successful in this last regard has been the Aga Khan Trust for Culture, whose holistic approach employs and engages with local people. The Al-Azhar Park is upheld as a shining example of this kind of work.

second turning afterwards, on a renovated and restored side street called the Darb al-Asfar, stands one of the best examples of an 18th-century Cairene town house, the **Bayt al-Sihaymi** ㊶ (daily 9am–5pm; admission charge). More typical but less furnished than the Gayer-Anderson house *(see page 140)*, it illustrates not only the standard division of rooms into a *salaamlik* (reception room) and a *haramlik* (family room), but also the ingenuity with which architects used courtyards, fountains set in sunken floors, high ceilings and north-facing wind-catchers on the roof to counter the stifling heat of a long Cairene summer.

Just before the Qasabah exits through Bab al-Futuh, one of the two northern gates of al-Qahirah, a space opens out to form another market, where once fine agricultural produce from the royal family's experimental farms was sold. Now mainly an onion and garlic market, it is bordered on its eastern side by the congregational **mosque of al-Hakim** ㊷ (9am–5pm), the Fatimid caliph. Finished in 1013, it was restored in 1980 by the Bohora, an Isma'ili Shi'ite sect who are based in Bombay but trace their ancestry back directly to the Fatimids, who have imported features that give the building a touch of India.

Bab al-Futuh ㊸, the great "Gate of Conquest" (daily 9am–5pm; admission charge; caretaker sits in the teahouse opposite the gate); **Bab al-Nasr** ㊹, the "Gate of Victory", the other northern gate of al-Qahirah; and the 330-metre (1,080-ft) stretch of wall between them – all built by the Fatimids' Armenian general Badr al Gamali in 1087 – have been restored and are worth touring if open. Badr's Armenian architects were skilled military specialists and their work originally made use of blocks quarried and carved under the pharaohs, some of which were scratched with Napoleonic graffiti more than seven centuries later.

Outside the northern gates is an open area, beyond which the Qasabah moves off north from Bab al-Futuh through the **Husayniyyah district**, known both as a butchers' quarter and a hotbed of

nationalism; its meat-cutters gave the French much trouble and were bombarded by them from the Fatimid walls. Adjoining the Husayniyyah on the east opposite Bab al-Nasr is a famous cemetery. Ibn Khaldun, a 14th-century historian from Tunis dazzled by the city, is among those buried here, and many people have made their homes among the graves.

The Northern and Southern Cemeteries

This fact makes it a good introduction to Cairo's **Northern** ㊺ and **Southern cemeteries** ㊻ (the larger tombs have their own guardians and fees; visitors should be respectfully dressed). Westerners delight in calling them collectively "The City of the Dead", though the cemeteries grew up at different times and are separated by the limestone spur on which the Citadel was built. That people live in these cemeteries is not solely to do with the city's housing shortage. As far as anyone knows, these cemeteries have always had inhabitants.

Gateway to the 12th-century Aqmar Mosque. Like al-Hakim Mosque, it was restored by the Bohora, an Islmaili sect which claims descent from the Fatimid dynasty.

BELOW:
pottery seller on the way to market.

SHOP

For a feel of how alive the cemeteries are, head for the Suq al-Gum'a, a Friday-morning market that starts under the Shari' Imam as-Shafi'i. Every kind of junk is sold here, including old cinema posters and kitsch souvenirs.

BELOW LEFT AND RIGHT: the mausoleum of Hawsh al-Basha.

Permanent structures demand caretakers and soon have communities around them. The tombs of popular Cairene saints are always thronged, but on Thursday evenings, Fridays and on major feast days the living Cairenes frequently visit their family tombs – just as ancient Greeks and Romans did or as modern Europeans used to do on All Saints' Day – and have family picnics among the graves.

This custom was elaborated by the Mamluk sultans and amirs. Every guest wore his most extravagant clothes: silks from China (like the cups, bowls and serving dishes) embroidered by the ladies of local harems, brocades manufactured in the Mamluks' own workshops. Flowers, incense and music accompanied the feasting but, if the tomb site was suitable there might also be horse racing, archery and hunting expeditions. The Northern Cemetery began life in the 13th century as a hippodrome and didn't evolve into a royal necropolis until later.

The **Southern Cemetery** is larger – it begins as far north as the mosque of Ibn Tulun – and much older. Several of the tombs have been pilgrimage sites for

centuries, particularly the 13th-century **mausoleum of Imam as-Shafi'i**, a descendant of the Prophet's uncle and founder of the most influential of the four orthodox schools of Sunni jurisprudence, who died in Egypt in 820.

Nearby is the **mausoleum of Hawsh al-Basha**, built by Muhammad Ali in 1816 for his favourite wife, where her three sons and other family members are also interred, alongside many of their retainers.

All around in every direction, interspersed with apartment blocks, are a multitude of other tombs. The most notable are those of Burgi Mamluk amirs, set within the remains of complexes that frequently included *khanqahs* and other large residential structures.

Impressive as it is, the complex can hardly compare with what the Mamluk sultans built in the **Northern Cemetery**. The Burgi period marks the high point in the development of both the carved stone dome and the three-stage minaret – with a square base, an octagonal second storey and a cylindrical upper storey, elaborately carved and topped by a bulb

set on colonettes – features that used to dominate Cairo's skyline.

Unhampered in this freshly opened necropolis by considerations of space, the Circassian rulers were free to indulge their tastes for piety and pleasure to the full. The results still visible are the remains of five huge monuments that may represent an epitome in Mamluk architecture. The most important are the **mausoleums of Farrag**, the son of Barquq, and **Qaytbay**, the most famous of the Circassians. Built between 1472 and 1474, they are the jewels of the period.

WEST OF THE NILE

Nearly a quarter of the 140-odd foreign embassies in Cairo are in Zamalik *(see page 134)*. Most of the rest are scattered along the Nile's western bank, in Giza, Doqqi, Aguza or Muhandesseen, which were still rural hinterland as recently as 1970. Though less green, less exclusively residential and far more crowded than it once was, Zamalik has many of Cairo's trendiest bars and restaurants. In recent years young, fashionable Cairenes have injected new life into the river bank, and many an old cruise boat has been turned into a sumptuous restaurant, bar, coffee house or nightclub. As Zamalik gets more crowded, many foreigners are opting to live in modern apartment blocks in **Muhandesseen**. The area has less character but has good shops, bars and restaurants.

In the nearby residential area of **Doqqi** is one of Cairo's quirkiest museums, the **Agricultural Museum** (Ministry of Agriculture, next to the 6th of October Bridge; daily 9am–2pm; admission charge). The oldest agricultural museum in the world, founded in 1938, it covers 11 hectares (27 acres) of gardens and several pavilions, including the Museum of Ancient Egyptian Agriculture, the Cotton Museum and a Museum of the Social Life of the Arab Nations.

Giza, in ancient times merely a stopover between Memphis and Heliopolis, is now a rapidly expanding

governorate in its own right. In 1908 the Cairo University was founded as a counterpart to the Islamic University of Al-Azhar, but it is now just as much a hotbed of fundamentalism as the latter.

Just opposite the University are the **Cairo Zoo** (Maydan al-Gama'a; 9am–4pm; small admission charge) and the **al-Urman Gardens** (Shari' Nahdat Masr; same opening times as the zoo; admission charge), designed by the Frenchman Barillet-Deschamps. Established in 1890, the zoo is one of the oldest in the world, with a comprehensive collection of animals, unfortunately now in a rather poor state.

Close to the river, next door to the Cairo Sheraton, a grand villa contains the rarely visited but fascinating **Mr and Mrs Mahmud Khalil Museum** (1 Shari' Kafour, daily 9am–6pm; admission charge). It houses a fine private collection of furniture and 19th- and 20th-century European art, including paintings by Delacroix, Gauguin, Pisarro, Renoir, Lautrec, Monet, Picasso

Egypt's Awakening *by Mahmoud Mukhtar (see page 99), situated at the entrance to the zoo on Maydan al-Gama'a.*

BELOW: houseboat beside the Corniche in Zamalik.

and Sisley, as well as work by Rubens and several Rodin sculptures.

Further south, on Jacob's Island on the Nile, is the kitsch but fun **Dr Ragab's Pharaonic Village** (Sakiet Miky, www.touregypt.net/village; daily 9am–5pm winter, till 9pm in summer; admission charge), offering a guided tour by floating amphitheatre past scenes re-enacted from Ancient Egypt.

This is also the new location for **Dr Ragab's Papyrus Institute**. Dr Ragab, an engineer by training, reintroduced the ancient art of papyrus rolling to Egypt in the 1960s and set up this museum. As well as displays explaining the process of making papyrus sheets, and occasional demonstrations, there is an extensive gallery and shop where better quality papyrus souvenirs are on sale.

NORTHERN CAIRO

To the north of the city towards the modern airport was ancient Heliopolis. It was the centre of the royal cult of Ra, the universal sun-god. Originally called On, the city the Greeks later called **Heliopolis** (City of the Sun) stood 25 km (15 miles) northeast of Giza and thus 32 km (20 miles) from Memphis, but on the opposite side of the Nile, in the modern district of al-Matariyyah. The primary theological centre of Old Kingdom Egypt, it was finally displaced in importance by Thebes, but not before its priests had developed elaborate rituals, liturgies and mythologies that revolved around the sun-god Ra and a host of lesser deities known as the Great Company.

It is recorded that Ramesses III (1182–1151 BC) endowed Heliopolis with some 12,000 serfs and over 100 towns, not to mention statues, gold, silver, linens, precious stones, birds, incense, cattle and fruit.

Even in ancient times, Heliopolis had begun to suffer a decline that led to systematic pillaging. Strabo, visiting in 24 BC, recorded its desolation and 14 years later a pair of obelisks erected by Tuthmosis III (1504–1450 BC) were removed by the Romans to adorn their new Caesarium, the Temple of Julius Caesar in Alexandria. Some 19 centuries later, during the reign of Khedive Ismail, these two monuments found their way out of Egypt and became the "Cleopatra's Needles" of London and New York (though they have nothing to do with any of the real Cleopatras). Only one obelisk, from a pair erected in the reign of Senusert I (1971–1928 BC) survives in situ (see below).

The Holy Family are said to have come here to escape King Herod and rested under what is known as the **Virgin's Tree** (daily 10am–4pm, admission charge). The original sycamore tree is long dead, but a third-generation tree is surviving quite well on the site. Paintings and biblical references of this journey are also to be seen inside the nearby **church of the Holy Family**. Both sites are about 800 metres/yds northwest of el-Matariyyah metro station on the way to El-Marg.

From the church of the Holy Family, continue up the busy road away from the Virgin's Tree for about 1 km/½ mile, to the only remains of ancient Heliopolis, the 1940 BC obelisk of Senusert I (daily 10am–4pm, admission charge) in a small

park but, as so often is the case in the suburbs, surrounded by rubbish.

Outlying attractions

The regeneration of the northern area for the influx of Europeans got underway at the beginning of the 20th century, when Baron Empain, a Belgian industrialist, developed modern "Heliopolis"(nothing to do with the ancient city of the same name). Some of the grand buildings of this time survive. The main road from the airport, for example, offers a brief glimpse of the **Baron's Palace**, not unlike an Asian temple, set back on the left-hand side. Built in 1906 to be the baron's own palatial residence, it is now a crumbling ruin.

On the same side of the road, closer into the city, is the October War Panorama (Wed–Mon; admission charge), in a circular building surrounded by fighter jets, missiles and tanks. Inside are sculptures showing famous battles throughout Egyptian history, ending with a 20-minute narration in Arabic (English on headphones) of the 1973 October War against Israel. Actual film footage is shown downstairs. The tomb

of the man behind that surprise attack on Israel is located about 2 km (1¼ miles) east of here along the busy al-Nasr highway, the main road to Suez. The **tomb of President Anwar Sadat** is below an open pyramid-style memorial, across the road from the scene of his assassination.

A recent addition for tourists is the newly restored **Muhammad Ali Pasha Palace** (daily 9am–5pm; admission charge) in northern Shubra (also known as the Shubra Kiosk), once connected to the Abdin Palace by a grand boulevard. Built as a pleasure palace for the Muhammad Ali family in 1821 by French and Italian architects, it features a large central pool where the pasha would entertain his wife and 125 concubines. Water from four lion fountains pours over carvings of fish, creating an illusion of them swimming. Surrounded by open colonnades, the rooms are built in various opulent Arab and Turkish styles, including the beautiful Diamond Room. The palace is just to the west of Koleyet el-Zeraah station, the penultimate stop on the metro line to Shubra el-Kheima. ❑

The ruins of the Baron's Palace, built in 1906 for Baron Empain, who developed the modern quarter of Heliopolis. Look out for the structure on your ride into town from the airport.

BELOW:
the tomb of Anwar Sadat on the main road towards Suez.

RESTAURANTS, CAFÉS & BARS

Restaurants

Prices for a three-course dinner per person with a half-bottle of house wine:
$ = under $20
$$ = $20–45
$$$ = $45–60
$$$$ = over $60

Egyptian/Levantine

Abou Shakra
69 Shari' Qasr al-Aini, Garden City
Tel: 02-2531 6111. **$$**
One of the best places in Cairo to eat kebabs, succulent leg of lamb and other meat dishes, preceded by *meze*. Good prices and good food.

Abu el-Sid
157 Shari' 26th of July, Zamalik.
Tel: 02-2735 9640.
$$$–$$$$

Atmospheric restaurant, that successfully recreates a colonial club feel with antique furniture and decor. Serves traditional dishes with style, to a funky Egyptian beat, and water pipes are available. Very busy at the weekends, so book ahead.

Akher Saa'a
8 Shari' al-Alfi, Downtown
Tel: 02-2575 1668. **$**
The "king of the *fuul*", open 24 hours, is renowned for its *fuul bisuyuk* (fava-bean stew with spicy sausages).

Alfi Bey
3 Shari' al-Alfi, Downtown
Tel: 02-2577 4999. **$$**
Old-style restaurant that opened in 1938. The Egyptian/Levantine dishes are hardly *haute cuisine*, but if you like

nostalgia. You'll be in seventh heaven. No alcohol.

Arabesque
6 Shari' Qasr an-Nil, Downtown
Tel: 02-2574 7898. **$$$**
Traditional Levantine restaurant, with faded Moorish interior, serving French and Egyptian dishes. Try the *meloukhia* with chicken or rabbit, or the grilled pigeon with Oriental rice, but definitely leave a space for the best *umm ali* (bread and butter pudding) in town.

Citadel View Restaurant
At the al-Azhar Park, Shari' Salah Salem
Tel: 02-2510 9151/50.
$$–$$$$
In an impressive Fatimid-style building, overlooking the formal gardens, with a magnificent view over historic Cairo and the Citadel, this is a perfect choice for lunch or a sunset tea or dinner.

Egyptian Pancake House
Between Shari' al-Azhar and Maydan al-Husayn. **$**
Delicious and cheap *fateers*, a pizza-cum-pancake. No alcohol.

Felfella
15 Shari' Hoda Shaarawi, Downtown
Tel: 02-2392 2751. **$$**
The original Felfella restaurant, which now has several branches in Cairo and other Egyptian cities. It started as a vegetarian restaurant and

still serves plenty of vegetable dishes and meze besides fare such as kofta, kebab and stuffed pigeon. The Cafeteria just around the corner serves good *fuul* and *taameya* sandwiches.

Morocco
Blue Nile, Corniche an-Ni, Zamalik
Tel: 02-2735 3314.
$$$–$$$$
Sumptuous Moroccan boat restaurant for well-heeled Cairenes, which turns into a trendy disco later in the evening.

Naguib Mahfouz Café, Khan al-Khalili Restaurant
Main street in the Khan al-Khalili
Tel: 02-2590 3788. **$$–$$$**
Excellent Egyptian-Turkish dishes, drinks and desserts in the heart of the bazaar.

Sabaya
Semiramis Inter Continental, Corniche al-Nil Garden City
Tel: 02-2795 7171.
$$$–$$$$
Excellent Lebanese restaurant serving traditional *meze*, the best *kibbeh nayyeh* (raw pounded lamb) in town and Lebanese specialities. Excellent wine list and an elegant contemporary Middle Eastern decor.

Seafood

Fish Market
Americana Boat, 26 Shari' an-Nil, Giza
Tel: 02-2570 9693. **$$–$$$**
Serves the best fish in

LEFT: Felfella has several branches in Cairo.

town, on the upper deck of a moored boat. Choose from the catch of the day and decide how you want it cooked. It will be done to perfection and served with Middle Eastern salads. Great views too.

Samakmak
92 Shari' Ahmed Orabi, Muhandesseen
Tel: 02-2347-8232. **$$$**
The decor may be uninspiring but Samakmak serves some of the best seafood and fish inland from Alexandria, and it's open 24 hours a day.

International
Aubergine
5 Shari' al-Sayed al-Bakri, Zamalik
Tel: 02-2735 6550. **$$$**
Popular meeting spot for vegetarian expats and young Egyptians before they move on to noisier places. Café Curnonsky on the first floor is a favourite haunt of foreign correspondents.

La Bodega
157 Shari' Yulyu, Zamalik
Tel: 02-735 6761. **$$$$**
Elegant bar-restaurant with several rooms, lounges and bars. The decor is inspired by Japan and the cuisine is fusion. There is also a cheaper but good brasserie.

Revolving Restaurant
Grand Hyatt Hotel, on the Corniche, Garden City
Tel: 02-2365 1234 . **$$$$**
Not only is this the restaurant with the best view in Cairo, as it is on the 41st floor, but it is the food is superb too. The tables are set around an open-plan kitchen where the chefs whip up French dishes with a modern twist. The dress code is formal. Book ahead.

Rotisserie Belvedère
Nile Hilton, Maydan Tahrir, Downtown
Tel: 02-2578 0444.
$$$–$$$$
Excellent, inventive French menu served in sumptuous surroundings with very formal service and great views over the Nile and Cairo.

Sangria
Casino al Shagara, opposite the World Trade Center, Corniche an-Nil, Bulaq
Tel: 02-2579 6511. **$$$**
Meze and à la carte menus featuring everything from pizza to sashimi. Offers a trendy indoor area and a terrace with great Nile views.

Le Tabasco
8 Amman Square, Muhandesseen
Tel: 02-2336 5583. **$$$**
One of the trendiest bar-restaurants in town. After 10pm the music and air con are turned on full and in come the young, rich and beautiful.

Villa d'Este
Conrad Hotel, Corniche an-Nil, Bulaq.
Tel: 02-2580 8000. **$$$$**
Villa d'Este is the best and most elegant Italian restaurant in Cairo, with northern Italian cuisine served in a romantic interior. A good choice for a special night out.

Asian
L'Asiatique
Le Pacha 1901 Boat, Shari Saray el-Gezira, Zamalik
Tel: 02-2735 6730. **$$$$**
This is an award-winning eatery offering Far Eastern, Italian, French and Egyptian restaurants onboard a pacha's private luxury boat. Also has bars and a café for lighter fare.

The Bird Cage
Semiramis Inter Continental, Corniche al-Nil Garden City
Tel: 02-2795 7171. **$$$**
Delightful Thai restaurant, serving well-prepared and beautifully presented Thai dishes. The decor is simple but elegant.

Buo Khao
9 Road 151, Maadi
Tel: 02-2350 0126. **$$$**
Genuine, well-prepared Thai food served in attractive dining room.

Peking
14 Shari' Saraya al-Azbakiyyah, Downtown
Tel: 02-591 2381. **$$**
Well-prepared Chinese food served in pleasant surroundings.

Cafés and Bars
After Eight
6 Shari' Qasr an-Nil (in a small alley), Downtown
Tel: 02-2574 0855. **$$**
Hard to find, down a small alley off Shari' Qasr an-Nil, but worth looking for. Cosy restaurant that turns into a jazz club at night. Very busy on Thursday and weekends.

Bam-Bu Lounge Club
Casino al Shagara, Corniche an-Nil, Bulaq
Tel: 02-2579 6511. **$$**
Overlooking the Nile. Very lively on Thursday and Saturday nights.

Beano's
8 Maydan Sheikh al-Marsafy, Zamalik. **$**
Popular with Zamalik residents, serving good coffee and pastries.

Blues
60 Shari' an-Nil, Giza
Tel: 02-2335 5552. **$$$$**
Trendy bar with live lounge music, good food and beautiful people.

La Bodega
157 Shari' 26th of July, Zamalik
Tel: 02-2735 6761.
$$$–$$$$
Cool bistro with Mediterranean dishes, from North African *tagines* and couscous to home-made Italian pastas and tapas.

Café Riche
17 Shari' Tala'at Harb, Downtown
Tel: 02-2392 9793. **$**
Riche is drenched in history. This is where Umm Kalthoum started her career, and where Gamal Abd an-Nasser planned his revolution. Nowadays there are fewer leftist intellectuals, but it is still a good place to meet for a drink or a light lunch.

Cilantro
157 Shari' 26 Yulyu, Zamalik
Tel: 02-736 1115
Also at: 31 Shari' Muhammad Mahmoud, Downtown. **$**
Trendy coffee shop selling excellent salads and sandwiches as well as juices, coffees and American-style pastries.

Jazz Up
Nile Hilton, Maydan al-Tahrir
Tel: 02-2578 0444. **$$**
Lively and smoky club, with jazz, reggae, rock and sometimes classical music.

Simmonds Coffee Shop
112 Shari' 26 Yulyu, Zamalik.
$
Good spot for cappuccinos and juices.

White
25 Shari' Hassan Asem, Zamalik
Tel: 02-230 4404. **$$$**
One of Cairo's most fashionable venues, with the latest music and expensive drinks.

EGYPTIAN MUSEUM

The museum, one of Cairo's greatest attractions, contains a breathtaking display of objects, from statues to mummies, jewellery and mosaics

The Egyptian Museum was first established in 1857 by a Frenchman, Auguste Mariette, founder of the Egyptian Antiquities Service. Mariette's tomb and a memorial to him can be seen outside this grand neoclassical building. It was Mariette who, in 1860, excavated the incredible black diorite statue of Pharaoh Khafre (Chephren), which is still one of the highlights of the collection. Originally located in the suburb of Bulaq, the museum relocated to Giza in 1891 and the present building was opened in 1902 to house the ever-expanding collection. There are so many objects within the storerooms that most have little opportunity of being seen by the public and even the experts are left to rediscover important pieces that have been "lost" in the museum for years. But the very best examples of statues, carvings, paintings, funerary objects, mummies, jewellery and mosaics are on display here. A new museum is under construction at Giza, and the artefacts will be distributed between the two sites.

The most popular attractions are the amazing objects from the tomb of King Tutankhamun, but the small dark room containing his death mask often becomes uncomfortably crowded. If this is the case, take the opportunity to see the wonderful objects from the lesser known Royal Tombs nearby, discovered unplundered at Tanis in the northern Delta in 1939. The golden objects are simply stunning, dating to the 21st and 22nd dynasties (around 1000 BC) when Tanis was the capital of kings who originated in Libya to the west. Coinciding with the outbreak of World War II, this discovery went almost unnoticed, and even today few people know about these gorgeous objects. Had they been discovered at any other time these finds would have been as famous as Tutankhamun's relics. Tanis has since gained notoriety as the fictional setting of the original *Indiana Jones* film, where the Ark of the Covenant was "rediscovered".

ABOVE: dwarfed by colossal limestone statues of Amenophis and his wife, Ti, visitors to the museum stand in awe at the remarkable collection of antiquities within the Egyptian Museum. But it is rare to see the rooms so empty – usually they are thronged with visitors, many of whom, overwhelmed by the sheer size of the collection, concentrate on the Tutankhamun exhibits and the ever-popular Mummy Room.

RIGHT: original pieces of papyrus give Egyptologists additional information about inscriptions and tomb paintings. On the staircases of the museum are some wonderful examples, with colours that are still remarkably fresh. Upstairs in Room 29 are ornamental texts from the *Book of the Dead* and samples of the writing equipment used.

LEFT: the funerary death mask of King Tutankhamun was probably very lifelike and indicates that he was a young man. Above his face on the gold and blue striped wig, is the vulture and *uraeus* (a cobra signifying royalty), while a false beard has been attached to his chin.

THE TOMB OF KING TUT

One of the great events of 20th-century archaeology was the discovery of the intact tomb of King Tutankhamun in 1922. Howard Carter was on the brink of giving up his long search in the Valley of the Kings, when a single step leading to the tomb's doorway was uncovered below the debris of another tomb. Over the following years, thousands of delicate objects were removed to the safety of the Egyptian Museum. Since the discovery there have been rumours of a "curse" upon those individuals who dared to enter the tomb, which perhaps began when the man who financed Carter's excavations, Lord Carnarvon, died soon afterwards at his Cairo hotel.

King Tut's worldwide appeal is so great that his Egyptian motifs and designs are inspirations for fashion, jewellery, decoration and architecture, beginning with the 1930s Art Deco period. Highlights of the collection regularly tour the world and are exhibited in some of the greatest museums.

ABOVE: it was not only human bodies that were mummified, so too were animals that were considered sacred because of their association with important gods, such as the falcon-headed Horus or the cat goddess Bastet. Room 53, on the upper floor, has a fascinating collection of mummified animals including cats, snakes, baboons and even a 6-metre (18-ft) long crocodile. Animal mummies are usually popular with children, and the museum has initiated an adopt-an-animal-mummy project.

RIGHT: the wooden statue of dignitary Ka-Aper dates from 4,500 years ago, and is now known as Shaykh al-Balad or the "village mayor". When the statue was excavated, the workmen thought it looked remarkably like the headman of the village of Saqqarah.

ISLAMIC CAIRO

**Centuries of Muslim rule have left
Cairo with an astonishing legacy of
Islamic architecture in its madrasahs
and mosques and given it the title of
the city of 1,000 minarets**

The army of Muslim general 'Amr ibn al-As crossed
into Egypt from Palestine in 639, and after the success
of his siege of Babylon two years later the rest of the
country surrendered to Muslim rule. 'Amr founded the
garrison city of Fustat, but when the Abbasids seized
control of the empire in 750 they built a military suburb,
al-Askar, near the city, establishing the trend of
developing a new suburb whenever the regime changed.
This protected older buildings rather than demolishing
them, and left us a great legacy of Islamic architecture.

In the late 9th century, Ahmad Ibn Tulun established a
new city, al-Qatai, to the north of Fustat, but all that
remains of this centre is his mosque, considered to be
one of the greatest Islamic monuments in Egypt.

During the 10th century, under the Fatimids, a new
walled city, known as al-Qahirah (Cairo), was built, but
this time purely for Shi'a officials, soldiers, servants and
slaves. Some of the important landmarks of this new
city are still to be seen today – al-Azhar, Bab Zuwaylah,
the main gateway in the south and Bab al-Futuh in the
northern wall. It was under the young Ayyubid leader
Salah ad-Din (better known as Saladin) who came to
power in 1171, that Sunni control was re-established as
he began a system of madrasahs or religious schools, in
order to prevent the return of Shi'a influence. Ayyubid
control ended in 1250 when the Mamluks rose up under
a series of strong rulers like Sultan Qalawun. Cairo
became a modern capital with hospitals, monumental
mosques and mausoleums that stand today as the peak
of Mamluk architecture. Their greatest leader,
Muhammad al-Nasir, urbanised the area between the
walled city at Bab Zuwaylah and the isolated Citadel,
where Sultan Hasan later built his madrasah.

The greatest building from the later Mamluk period is
the mosque of Sultan Mu'ayyid, built on the site of a
prison where he himself was once held prisoner, just
inside the Bab Zuwaylah.

ABOVE: mosques built around tombs of important religious figures
have become sites of local pilgrimage. The tomb of Sayyida Zeinab,
granddaughter of the Prophet Muhammad, and the patron of Cairo,
is inside a large mosque in one of the busiest parts of the city and is
always crowded with women. The mosque is one of the most popular
pilgrimage sites and up to a million people gather here in the first two
weeks of October, when Sayyida is especially venerated.

RIGHT: this beautifully decorated niche, known as a mihrab, indicates
the direction for prayer. Inside his madrasah, Sultan Hasan wanted
worshippers to pray not only towards Mecca, but also towards him.
His tomb lies just behind the mihrab, but sadly his body is not inside,
as it disappeared immediately after his assassination in 1361.

THE AL-AZHAR MOSQUE

The al-Azhar was the first mosque to be built by the Fatimids in AD 972. The Fatimids were a Shi'a sect that originally came from Tunisia, claiming descent from Fatima, daughter of the prophet Muhammad, from whom they took their name. The bright courtyard of the mosque is surrounded by ziggurat-topped arches, supported by single, double and triple columns and dominated by three minarets and a dome. A forest of columns inside the prayer hall leads to the delicate geometrical designs inside the mihrab.

The main gateway is known as the Barber's Gate, because it is where students had their heads shaved before entering the attached al-Azhar University. This is acknowledged as the world's oldest university, dating from AD 988, and most of the infrastructure came from an earlier centre of learning at Zebid in Yemen, at a time when the Fatimids controlled the entire Red Sea region. Interestingly, the al-Azhar is now considered to be the highest seat of learning of Sunni religious thinking.

ABOVE: for over a thousand years the muezzin has climbed this spiral staircase five times a day between dawn and nightfall to announce the call to prayer for the inhabitants of the old al-Qatai' suburb of Cairo. In the majority of mosques today the calls are recorded and played over loudspeakers, but the sound is as evocative and haunting as ever.

RIGHT: the continuity of Islamic architecture in Cairo is shown by the Rifa'i Mosque, built just a century ago. Across the road is the Sultan Hasan madrasah, the grandest of Cairo's Mamluk buildings, dating from the 14th century, which it complements perfectly.

Recommended Restaurants & Cafés on page 175

GIZA, MEMPHIS AND SAQQARAH

The Pyramids of Giza are the most famous symbol of Egypt. And among the country's other highlights are the Step Pyramid and the decorated tombs of Saqqarah, all accessible on an easy day trip from Cairo

The modern city of Cairo occupies a position at the head of the Nile Delta that has been of strategic importance for some 5,000 years and that has consequently seen many urban foundations, of which Cairo itself is merely the largest and the latest.

Many visitors are told by guides to consider the west bank of the Nile as the land of the dead and Giza as the necropolis of Cairo, in the way the Valley of the Kings was to Karnak and Luxor. But it is important to remember that the first capital of Egypt, Memphis, was itself on the west bank. Sadly, there is precious little to see of Memphis but its necropolis at Saqqarah and a string of later pyramids and burial constructions offer plenty to interest visitors. With Cairo so crowded and polluted, it is a joy to drive through the stretches of verdant countryside and open desert that run south and west of the capital. And horse riding, readily available at the Pyramids, can be a pleasant distraction to walking around the ancient sites, if only for an hour or two,

A day's tour

If you are travelling independently, it is worth hiring a taxi for a day to take you on a tour of Giza, Memphis and Saqqarah. This can be arranged at the reception of your hotel. It is also worth spending some time trying to understand importance of the locations on the t bank before seeing the sites selves, even if you are on an organised tour, for the speed of such tours can make it hard to grasp the history and chronology of the sites.

It is also important to plan your visit. If you want to enter the Great Pyramid of Khufu, for example, you need to get there early, as numbers are restricted (tickets are sold from 8am each day).

GIZA

The only survivors among the Seven Wonders of the World, the Pyramids of Giza (called *al-Ahram* in Arabic) are not hard to find. Standing at the end of a

Main attractions

THE PYRAMIDS OF GIZA, P.164
MEMPHIS, P.168
SAQQARAH, P.169
DAHSHUR, P.173
MAYDUM, P.174

LEFT: quintessential Egypt. **BELOW:** close-up of the Great Pyramid of Khufu.

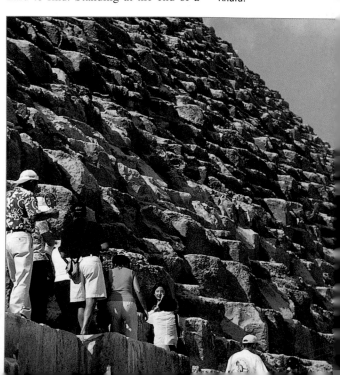

The Mena House Oberoi at the foot of the Pyramids is a great place for a leisurely lunch before or after a visit to the Pyramids.

boulevard (Shari' al-Ahram) on the desert plateau above the western edge of Giza, across the river from Cairo, can frequently be glimpsed from the city centre, shimmering in the distance through the haze of heat and durst.

At the foot of the Pyramids, on the road leading up to them from Shari' al-Ahram, is the **Mena House Oberoi Hotel**, once one of the most celebrated hotels in the world. Connected by a tramline to Cairo in 1900 shortly after its opening, it soon rivalled the famous Shepheard's Hotel, entertaining statesmen at three historic international conferences. The hotel's old wing is the only place in the world where you can wake up with a full view of the Pyramids.

The Pyramids

The most striking aspect of the **Pyramids of Giza ❶** (daily 7am–7pm

for the plateau, 8.30am–4pm to enter the Pyramids; admission charge) is their size. But even with all the facts and figures, it is still hard to believe that these ancient structures remain in such a good state of preservation. The vision and workmanship of people 4,500 years ago in creating structures that would be the world's tallest until the 14th century is staggering.

The **Great Pyramid of Khufu ❹** (Cheops in Greek, ruling approximately 2589–2576 BC) was originally 150 metres (480 ft) high and incorporates some 2.3 million stone blocks averaging more than 2½ tonnes in weight. The second ruler of the Fourth Dynasty, Khufu took pyramid building to a completely new level. Building on the experience of his father King Snefru, who constructed the first "true" pyramid at Dahshur (*see page 173*), Khufu envisaged a tomb on such a gigantic scale that it would preserve him for eternity.

Contrary to popular belief, however, the Great Pyramid is neither the biggest pyramid in the world – that distinction belongs to the Quetzalcoatl pyramid at Cholula, south of Mexico City, which

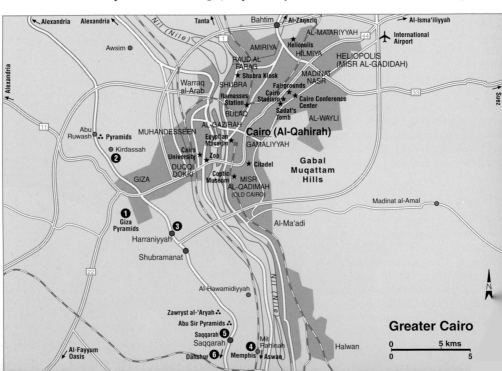

Greater Cairo

Recommended Restaurants on page 175

covers an area more than three times as extensive – nor was it built by slaves. Teams of skilled labourers on three-month hire were supplemented by a permanent workforce of local quarrymen. Other crews cut limestone and granite construction blocks at Tura, (near modern-day Cairo) and Aswan and transported them across or down the Nile to the building site.

Other stones – as recent excavations at the so-called "Lost City of the Pyramids" show – were quarried from just below the Pyramids, about 400 metres/yds south of the Sphinx. This quarry was then filled with the debris from the demolished mud construction ramps. Excavations of the workman's camp have revealed the houses, bakeries and tombs of the Pyramid builders, with inscriptions. Analysis indicates that the workforce comprised around 20,000 skilled builders over a 20-year period, contradicting Herodotus's 5th-century BC account of an estimated 100,000 slaves labouring for over 30 years.

Stripped of their smooth white Tura limestone upper casing and extensively quarried lower down for granite from the 11th century onwards, the sides of the Great Pyramid slope at an angle of 52 degrees, the approximate gradient for all the pyramids built after Snefru's Bent and Red pyramids at Dahshur. The four sides of the pyramid are only slightly off the cardinal points, at a time when the magnetic compass was unknown.

Except for their size, the isolated silhouettes of all the later large pyramids in Egypt would have looked exactly like the Great Pyramid. Each would have also stood within an enclosed complex, like Zoser's at Saqqarah *(see page 170)*, and would have been particularised by inscriptions, and by a painted or gilded cap.

Emerging from the Great Pyramid. The internal passageways are tight and the descents are steep. Claustrophics or anyone suffering from breathing problems should give the experience a miss.

Entering the Great Pyramid

The interior of the Great Pyramid can be visited and includes a grand gallery with a corbelled roof that is itself regarded as one of the most remarkable architectural works of the Old Kingdom. Entry is restricted to a few hundred people each

BELOW: aerial view of the Pyramids.

TIP

Each evening the Pyramids host three performances of a sound and light show in which an actorly voice relates their history in one of seven languages. An English-language performance is held every evening except Sunday. For a timetable, ask at your hotel or tel: 02-2386 3469;www.soundandlight.com.eg You can easily arrange for a taxi to take you there, wait and return.

BELOW: the reconstructed Solar Boat.

day. Tickets can only be bought on the day, from 8am from the ticket office.

The tunnel which was forcibly hacked out by treasure seekers leads initially to the "Ascending Corridor" and then the remarkable "Grand Gallery". The main burial chamber is a small room built of red Aswan granite, as is the large open sarcophagus that still remains in the centre. Shafts leading upwards from here point towards heavenly bodies.

East of the Great Pyramid is the site of Khufu's mortuary temple, identified by the remains of a basalt pavement, north and south of which are two boat pits *(see box below)*. Near its base are two more pits, one of which was excavated in 1954, when a complete dismantled river barge was found, probably secreted there in connection with the sun cult.

Beautifully reassembled, the cedarwood vessel can be admired in the **Solar Boat Museum** ❸ (daily 9am–4pm; admission charge). Photographs and explanations documenting the 13 years of excavation and reconstruction can be examined on the ground floor, together with original grass ropes and reed matting

from the double-roofed cabin of the boat.

The causeway leading from the Great Pyramid's mortuary temple to its valley temple is largely ruinous and cannot be excavated at its lower end, thanks to the encroachment of modern buildings. But just south of it, close to three subsidiary pyramids, the only undisturbed tomb thus far found of the Old Kingdom was uncovered in 1925. The sarcophagus was empty, but it was identified as the **tomb of Queen Hetepheres**, wife of Snefru and mother of Khufu, and yielded extraordinary objects, including a carrying chair and a portable boudoir, with linen curtains as well as a gilt bed and chair.

Pyramid of Khefre

The next pyramid belongs to Khufu's son, **Khefre** ❸ (Chefren, *circa* 2576–2551 BC), which looks taller than his father's but is actually smaller (it lies at a higher elevation, on a platform cut out of the sloping hill side, and is built at a steeper angle than the Great Pyramid). Look towards the top, where a lot of the outer limestone casing is still to be seen. The internal structure of passages is much simpler than that of the Great

Solar Boats

Between the two largest Giza pyramids is a glass building containing one of the solar boats that was buried alongside Khufu's pyramid. It was discovered in 1954, in a dismantled state comprising 1,224 pieces of polished cedar, buried in a narrow pit. The rebuilt solar boat is suspended above, with several walkways and platforms allowing views of the remarkable workmanship. A slightly smaller boat, also dismantled in antiquity, was discovered in another nearby pit, but this has been kept in-situ and resealed for preservation.

The real use of these boats is unknown, but they might have been used on the Nile to transport the king's body (there is a faint watermark), or fo symbolic use in the afterlife.

Recommended Restaurants on page 175

Pyramid, leading to a single chamber.

The Pyramid of Khefre is the most complete in relation to its surrounding complex, which includes the **Sphinx** . Intended originally to represent a guardian deity in the shape of a lion, the Sphinx had Khefre's face (it is said to be disfigured and beardless thanks to Mamluk artillery practice). Later associated with the sun-god and with Horus of the Horizon, as a Greek drinking song scratched on one of its toes during the Ptolemaic period attests, the Sphinx was the object of pilgrimages, especially during the 18th Dynasty.

In front of the Sphinx stands a granite stele set up by order of Tuthmosis IV (1423–1417 BC), who records a dream he had when still a prince: while he was resting under its shade during a hunting expedition, the Sphinx spoke, promising Tuthmosis the kingdom if he would clear away accumulated sand from around its feet. For many centuries the story has circulated as a folk tale or joke involving later rulers: in one 20th-century version the hero was Gamal Abdel Nasser and the Sphinx asked for an exit visa.

Pyramid of Menkaure

The third of the royal pyramids at Giza was begun by **Menkaure** (Mycerinus, *circa* 2532–2504 BC), the successor of Khafre. By far the smallest, it was apparently left unfinished at Menkaure's death and hurriedly completed by his son, Shepseskaf, whose own tomb is at Saqqara. There are signs of haste throughout the complex, even in the pyramid itself. Brick was used to finish off the mortuary temple, causeway and valley temple, though they were begun in limestone and some of the blocks

The mysterious Sphinx, guardian of the Pyramid of Khefre, has entranced visitors for centuries.

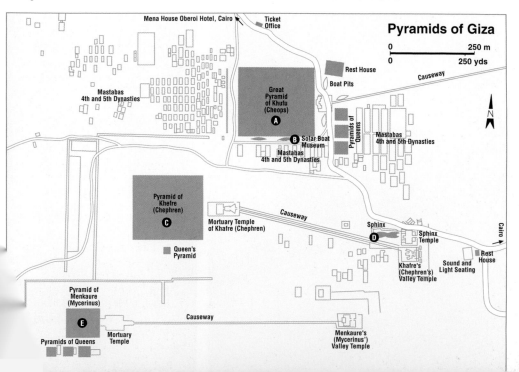

If you are an experienced rider, consider hiring a horse for a canter around the Pyramids (there are plenty of opportunities). Even novice riders can enjoy a gentle trek.

BELOW AND BELOW RIGHT: fertile fields and fruitful date palm near Memphis.

weigh 200 tonnes, showing that the failure to complete it in limestone was by no means due to a decline in technical mastery.

The great period of pyramid building, with its huge use of man-power and commitment, blossomed during this early period of Egyptian history and was never achieved again. There are smaller pyramids from later periods, but these are poor imitations.

About 1 km/½ mile beyond the Men-kaure pyramid is a **viewpoint** on the edge of the desert. Organised groups are driven there to take photographs, and to get hassled by souvenir sellers and camel-ride touts. Take a look around this viewpoint as there are some fossils in the sandy depressions, showing that this area was once under water.

Security for visitors is tight at the Pyramids, and it is impossible to wander too far off the beaten track, making it difficult to fully appreciate the scale of the Giza Pyramids area. Tourist police

with machine guns perched on camels, provide a photo that many tourists take back with them.

Local weaving

Kirdassah ❷, situated at the end of an old caravan route to Libya, 5 km (3 miles) north of Shari' al-Ahram, formerly supplied goods for desert traders and has become a centre for weaving, textiles and ready-made clothing, including the typical flowing *gallabiyas*.

Harraniyyah ❸, 5 km (3 miles) south of Shari' al-Ahram on the road to Memphis and Saqqarah, is the esteemed **Wissa Wassef tapestry workshops** (tel: 02-2381 5746; www.wissa-wassef-arts.com; daily 9.30am–5pm, weavers work Sat–Thur 9.30am–noon and 2–5pm) in a group of buildings that have won international acclaim for their architecture. The workshops export wool and cotton tapestries worldwide

MEMPHIS AND SAQQARAH

The most important of Cairo's predecessors was the city of **Memphis ❹** (daily 8am–5pm; admission charge), founded by Narmer (also known as

Recommended Restaurants on page 175

Menes), traditionally regarded as the first king of the First Dynasty, and said to have been the first to unite both Upper and Lower Egypt. The city was built on land reclaimed from the Nile in about 3100 BC and lies 24 km (15 miles) by road south of Cairo on the western side of the Nile.

Memphis can be reached by driving down the eastern side of the Nile and crossing the river south of Halwan. Another way is to cross the river directly into Giza and then drive south, either along the main highway to Upper Egypt, or along the attractive agricultural road that runs south from the Giza Pyramids.

The ruins of Memphis surround the village of **Mit Rahinah**, which derives its name from a temple of Mithras built here under the Romans, long after the days of the city's greatest glory when the cult of Ptah was worshipped here at a temple adorned by huge statues. But even when power transferred to Thebes, Memphis remained an important city.

There is little to see at Memphis except the **Alabaster Sphinx** and one of Ramesses' two colossi. The legs of this statue have been eroded, but the upper body, head and arms are beautifully carved and adorned with the king's cartouche; the workmanship can be appreciated at close quarters.

Most of the constructions at Memphis were of mud brick, which after centuries of neglect have simply dissolved back into the earth. Any heavy stone buildings either sunk slowly into the soft Nile silt or their blocks were re-used elsewhere.

More finds have been brought to light in recent excavations, and are scattered around, but visitors will probably want to enjoy the serenity of the surrounding groves of date palms, meditate briefly on the perishability of power, then push on up the road to Saqqarah, the great necropolis of the ancient capital of Memphis. The famous Step Pyramid of Zoser can be seen appearing over the tops of the many palm-tree groves as you approach from the Nile Valley.

Saqqarah

The site of **Saqqarah** ❺ (daily 8am–4pm, admission charge) lies on the

The finely carved head of the colossus of Ramesses II (see below).

BELOW:
the colossus of Ramesses II at Memphis.

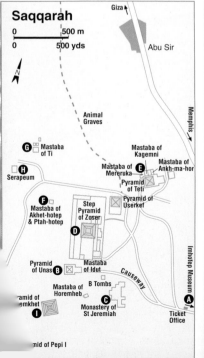

Saqqarah

0 ____ 500 m
0 ____ 500 yds

Giza ▲

Abu Sir

N

Animal Graves

Memphis

G ▢ Mastaba of Ti

Mastaba of Kagemni

Mastaba of Ankh-ma-hor

H
Serapeum

Mastaba of **E** Mereruka

Pyramid of Teti

F ▢
Mastaba of Akhet-hotep & Ptah-hotep

Step Pyramid of Zoser

Pyramid of Userkef

D

Pyramid of Unas **B** ▢

Mastaba of Idut

Causeway

B Tombs

Mastaba of Horemheb

C

Monastery of St Jeremiah

Ticket Office

A

Imhotep Museum

ramid of emkhet

I

nid of Pepi I

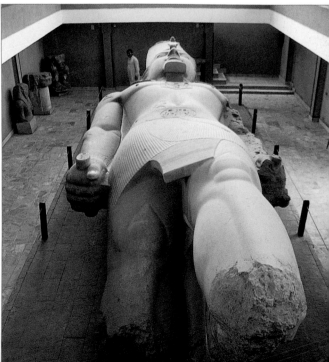

Statue of Ptah Hotep, a vizier of the Fifth Dynasty, in Saqqarah's excellent Imhotep Museum.

BELOW: limestone relief of the Starving Men of Unas, in Saqqarah's Imhotep Museum.

desert plateau about 3 km (2 miles) west of Memphis. This vast cemetery, which spans a period from the 27th century BC to the 10th century AD, is possibly named after Sokar, god of the burial sites.

A welcome new addition to the site is the modern **Imhotep Museum** Ⓐ (admission is included in that of the Saqqarah site; no flash photography), opened in 2006 in an attempt to redistribute many of the treasures in the Egyptian Museum to more relevant locations. Of the many highlights are objects found inside Saqqarah's pyramids and tombs, including a delightful wooden model of a rowing boat with human figures from the tomb of Khennu, a royal scribe of the Middle Kingdom. The mummy of King Merenre I, who ruled for five years from 2297 BC, is the oldest complete mummy yet found. Don't miss the haunting limestone bas-relief of the "Starving Men of Unas" from the causeway ramp of Fifth-Dynasty King Unas; it shows the ribcages of the starving Bedouin before they are given food by the king.

Allow plenty of time to visit the museum, as it really helps to explain the importance of the Saqqarah site.

The ticket office at the entrance to the necropolis stands above the valley temple attached to the **Pyramid of Unas** Ⓑ. Built by the last king of the Fifth Dynasty (*circa* 2375–2345 BC), this houses the earliest pyramid text. The ceremonial causeway linking the two has been excavated and the pyramid at the end is one of the least difficult for visitors to enter. Quite close to the parking space below the enclosure on the opposite side of the causeway to the Pyramid of Unas are the ruins of the **monastery of St Jeremiah** Ⓒ, founded in the 6th century and destroyed in the 10th. The monastery was the source of most of the objects in rooms 6 and 7 of the Coptic Museum in Cairo.

Dominating the whole area, however, is the **Step Pyramid of Zoser** Ⓓ (Third Dynasty, 2668–2649 BC), the earliest of all the pyramids and the first great monument in the world to be built of hewn stone. The entire complex within the enclosure, including shrines, court-yards and the Step Pyramid itself, was the conception of a single man, Imhotep,

Zoser's chief of works, who some consider to be the first recorded genius in history. An inscription left behind by a New Kingdom tourist venerates him as "he who opened the stone". He was later identified with magic, astronomy and medicine, finally becoming deified in the 6th century BC. Translating motifs from more perishable materials, such as wood or papyrus reeds, into stone, the Zoser complex displays many features that became a permanent part of the Egyptian architectural vocabulary and a few that have apparently remained unique.

The Step Pyramid can be entered only with special permission (a tour takes several hours), but a cross-section would reveal its complexity, arising from the fact that it began as a mastaba (from an Arabic word, meaning "bench" that refers to the usual oblong shape), a one-storey tomb of common type. Even here Imhotep showed his originality, for his mastaba was square rather than oblong and built of stone rather than the usual mud brick.

Looking at the pyramid, you can clearly see the separate interior structures where the outer casing has collapsed. It is possible that the surrounding life-after-death structures are copies of real buildings used by the king in Memphis. One curious small stone annexe at the rear of the Step Pyramid, known as the *serdab*, contains a statue of the king (not original) able to look out at the world through two eyeholes cut in the wall. The strange slope of this front wall is at the same angle as the pyramid, which serves as the *serdab's* back wall.

Viziers' tombs

Not to be missed, no matter how short your visit, are two Sixth-Dynasty *mastabas*, the **tombs of Mereruka and Kagemni** Ⓔ, who were both viziers of King Teti (*circa* 2345– 2333 BC). Nestled next to the Pyramid of Teti, northeast of the Zoser complex, these two structures promise nothing on the outside, but contain the most outstanding tomb reliefs of the Old Kingdom. Carved with lively scenes of domestic life, they show the interests and pursuits of the Old Kingdom nobility: hunting, horticulture, husbandry, music and dancing, preparations to ensure that the next world would be as bountiful as this one. The artist's

TIP

If you have plenty of time to spare, it is worth spending a whole day in Memphis and Saqqarah. You could follow local tradition and take a picnic to enjoy in the ruins of the monastery of St Jeremiah.

BELOW: Imhotep's Step Pyramid, built for King Zoser at Saqqarah.

Imhotep

The exact role of Imhotep is unknown but he is seen as the first engineer, architect and physician in history as well as being a high priest and official of King Zoser. For the tomb of his king, Imhotep initially built a mastaba in stone blocks, which needed precise cutting and handling. Having completed it, there was enough strength to build another on top, and so on. His achievements were recognised by later dynasties, and he was elevated to a god; later on, Greeks identified him with Asklepios, their god of medicine. Imhotep's undiscovered tomb is probably somewhere near Saqqarah and may contain many of his secrets. To cinema fans, Imhotep is better known as the inspiration for the series of films entitled *The Mummy*, showing him coming back to life and wreaking havoc.

When the cult of Serapis, combining the characteristics of Osiris and Apis (identified with the Greeks' Zeus), was invented under the Ptolemies, the Funerary Temple of Apis became a centre of pilgrimage for Greeks and Romans.

carved workmen exchange hieroglyphic one-liners; and such is the acuteness of his observations that over 50 different species of fish have been identified by modern experts.

Almost as satisfying are the scenes in the mastaba of **Ankh-ma-hor** (known as the "Doctor's Tomb"), a few steps away, which show similar pursuits but are best known for their depictions of craftsmen (jewellers, metalworkers, sculptors) and also physicians conducting surgical operations.

Directly west of the Pyramid of Teti, a kilometre away and connected with it by a dirt road parallel to what was once an avenue of sphinxes, is a rest house serving cold beer and soft drinks. Close to here, to the left of the dirt road, is the Fifth-Dynasty double **mastaba of Akhet-hotep and Ptah-hotep** (his son) **F**, high officials under the kings preceding Unas.

On the right-hand side of the road is the **mastaba of Ti G**, their slightly older contemporary. Here, too, more remarkable scenes from daily life are depicted, including children's games (Ptah-hotep) and boat building (Ti).

The Serapeum

Below the rest house is the **Serapeum H** (closed indefinitely), the catacomb of the sacred Apis bull, whose rites were witnessed by Herodotus during his 5th-century BC sojourn in Egypt. Inside the labyrinthine tunnels, the mummified bulls were buried in huge stone sarcophagi set in subterranean galleries.

Situated immediately to the north are graveyards containing the mummies of other animals: baboons, now extinct in Egypt, though they can still be found in the Sudan; and ibis (three species were known to the ancients, identified by modern experts as sacred, bald and glossy: *see pages 236–7*), now very rare, though the name is frequently given locally to the cattle egret, which are seen everywhere in rural Egypt, often perched on the backs of water buffalo and cattle.

Further tombs

Just south of the Zoser complex, across the causeway of Unas, are the recently opened **B Tombs** (separate admission charge). Not as impressive as the tombs north of the Step Pyramid, but much quieter and still beautiful, are the joint **tomb of Niankhkhnum and Khnumhotep**, overseers of the royal manicurists to Pharaoh Niuserre (Fifth Dynasty); the **Tomb of Neferherenptah**, the overseer of the royal hairdressers, with a fine bird-hunting scene; and **tomb of Irukaptah**, overseer of the royal butchers.

Further along are the **Persian Tombs** (525–404 BC), some of the deepest tombs in Egypt.

Beyond here is the unfinished **Step Pyramid of Sekhemkhet O**, Zoser's successor (2649–2643 BC), overlooking an area where there has been a great deal of archaeological activity. Here in 1975, while looking for the tomb of Maya, an official of Tutankhamun, the Egypt Exploration Society discovered a tomb prepared for Horemheb, Tutankhamun's general, who would become a pharaoh himself (1343–131 BC). Eleven years later, Maya's tom was finally found, but not before

BELOW: entrance to the funerary complex at Zoser, Saqqarah.

Recommended Restaurants on page 175

enormous amount from other burials had been revealed.

Further south, accessible on foot, by donkey, horse or camel (which can be rented at the resthouse) or by a vehicle with four-wheel drive, are the **pyramid complex of Pepi I** I (2332–2283 BC); the **pyramid complex of Djedkare Isesi** (2414–2375 BC) with the pyramid of a queen nearby; the **tomb of Shepseskaf** (2504–2500 BC); the **pyramid complex of Pepi II** (2278–2184 BC); and three other pyramids, one belonging to Userkare Khendjer (*circa* 1747 BC).

In the Saqqarah area alone, in fact, no fewer than 15 royal pyramids have been excavated, creating a zone more than 5 km (3 miles) long. And what has been discovered thus far is only a tiny fraction of what lies still buried under the sands, including – somewhere – the tomb of Imhotep, the great architect.

The relationship of all these monuments to Memphis is made clear by the fact that "Memphis" is derived from one of them: the pyramid of Pepi I, which was called Men-Nefer, "Established and Beautiful". But the Saqqarah monuments are only part of the Memphite

necropolis, which actually extends north along the desert plateau beyond Giza to Abu Ruwash and southward to Dahshur and Mazghunah, a total distance of about 33 km (20 miles). The two pyramids to be seen from Saqqarah south across the desert in the distance are the Bent and Red pyramids at Dahshur.

DAHSHUR

The peace and quiet beauty of the palm groves around **Dahshur**  ❻ have attracted many of Cairo's professional class, who have built rural retreats here. The most pleasant time of year to visit the site (open daily 8am–4pm winter, till 5pm summer; admission charge), is midwinter, when a lake forms within an artificial embankment below the Black Pyramid.

The **Black Pyramid** was built of brick but unused by Amenemhet III (1842–1797 BC), one of Egypt's most colourful kings. The dark colour that gives it its name arises from the fact that it has been systematically stripped of its original white limestone covering. The view of the pyramid across the lake is one of the most charming in Egypt,

BELOW:
the Bent Pyramid
at Dahshur.

Within the pyramid enclosure at Dahshur were the tombs of two Middle Kingdom princesses, containing gold and turquoise jewellery, now in the Egyptian Museum in Cairo.

BELOW: the Collapsed Pyramid, of King Snefru at Maydum.
RIGHT: the Mena House Oberoi.

worth the 5-km (3-mile) drive from Saqqarah. Its inscribed capstone is in the Egyptian Museum in Cairo.

There are two other 12th-Dynasty pyramids here, another from the 13th Dynasty, and a third not yet identified. Most striking, however, are two 4th-Dynasty pyramids, built by Snefru (2613–2589 BC). The southernmost of the two is the third-largest pyramid in Egypt and is easily distinguished, standing about 300 metres/yds further into the desert, beyond the Pyramid of Amenemhet III, not only by its bulk, but by its shape, which has led to it being called the **Bent Pyramid**: the 54-degree slope of its sides changes halfway up to an angle of 43 degrees, for reasons that may be rooted in religious symbolism, or may simply be because it had to be finished in a hurry.

The Bent Pyramid made internal use of cedar trunks imported from Lebanon, still intact, as beams, and is externally the best-preserved of all the pyramids, thanks to an ingenious construction method that made stripping its surface particularly difficult.

About 600 metres/yds northwest of the Bent Pyramid, between it and the Red Pyramid, are the remains of Snefru's mortuary temple, rededicated to Snefru during the Middle Kingdom and under the Ptolemies. Snefru was the father of Khufu, better known as Cheops, the Greek form of his name, builder of the Great Pyramid at Giza.

Visible about 2 km (1½ miles) away almost directly north is the pyramid's companion, sometimes called the **Red Pyramid**, which uses a 43-degree angle throughout its height. This is the earliest known pyramid to have been completed as a "true" pyramid, built less than 60 years after Imhotep's great discovery.

Khufu's own immediate successor, Djedefre, constructed a pyramid at **Abu Ruwash**, 10 km (6 miles) northwest of Giza, which marks the northernmost limit of the Memphite necropolis; and 5 km (3 miles) south of Dahshur, at **Mazghunah**, are two ruined pyramids possibly marking the southernmost limit of the necropolis.

MAYDUM

Out on a limb, 55 km (34 miles) south of Saqqarah is the **Pyramid of Maydum** (daily 8am–5pm; admission charge), which probably dates from the end of the Third Dynasty or early Fourth Dynasty and represents the transition from the Saqqarah-type step pyramid to the "true" pyramidal forms found at Giza. This structure, with its burial chamber above ground, could have been built by an earlier king and finished by King Snefru. Also referred to as the **Collapsed Pyramid** due to the removed outer casing, it looks like a ruined tower surrounded by rubble.

The Egyptian security forces are nervous in this former military area with its easy access to trouble spots further south, and a police escort is provided for the 2-km (1¼-mile) drive off the Nile Valley road. The site ticket includes entry inside the pyramid, as well as the nearby mud-brick mastaba No. 1 containing a red granite sarcopha-with some mummy remains, but inscriptions.

RESTAURANTS

Restaurants

Prices for a three-course dinner per person with a half-bottle of house wine:
$ = under $20
$$ = $20–45
$$$ = $45–60
$$$$ = over $60

Giza

Andrea's Restaurant
On the left bank of the Maryutiya Canal, towards Kirdassah, Giza
Tel: 02-3383 1133. **$$**
Good range of meze and succulent chicken served with rice. Mainly outdoors under the trellises, with simple furniture.

Barry's
2, Shari' Abu Aziza, next to the AA stables, in the village Nezlat es-Semaan.

Tel: 02-3388 9540. **$$–$$$**
Wonderful Egyptian restaurant, run by an American woman and her Egyptian husband. The food is mainly traditional Egyptian with good meze and grills plus tagines (Moroccan stews), but the best thing is the cold beer and superb views over the Pyramids of Giza, especially at sunset.

Christo
10 Pyramids Road, Giza. Tel: 02-3382 4333. **$$$**
Extensive range of seafood with fabulous views of the Pyramids from the terrace. Near the Mena House Oberoi.

Moghul Room
Mena House Oberoi (near the Giza Pyramids) Tel: 02-383 3222. **$$$**

The Mena House Oberoi (see picture below) is an obvious place to go for lunch or afternoon tea before or after a visit to the Pyramids. But a good option for dinner is its Moghul Room, where you can sample freshly prepared Indian food in plush surroundings, with live music.

Panorama Restaurant
Gawharet Alahram Hotel 103 Pyramids Road, Giza. Tel: 02-3771 7111. **$$**
Great views of the Pyramids from the top floor.

Pyramids Tivoli
Off Al Remaya Square, Haram, Cairo–Alexandria road.
Tel: 02-3382 6555. **$$–$$$**
Café-lounge bar, restaurant and nightclub with belly dancing. One of several similar establishments in the vicinity.

Seasons
Four Seasons Hotel, 35 Shari' Giza, Giza
Tel: 02-573 1212. **$$$$**
Elegant restaurant serving Egyptian specialities with a twist as well as superb international and fusion-style cuisine.

Saqqarah

Cataract Pyramids Resort
Al Haraneya, Saqqarah Road, Giza. Tel: 02-3771 8060 www.cataracthotels.com **$$$**
Situated between the Pyramids and Saqqarah, this hotel is set in lush grounds. La Pergola, its outdoor terrace restaurant, makes a pleasant stop on a hot day.

THE PYRAMIDS

The magnificent Pyramids of Giza, tombs of the ancient pharaohs, are the only survivors of the Seven Wonders of the World

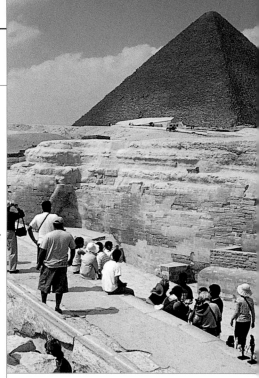

The builders of the Pyramids were kings of the 3rd–6th dynasties of the Old Kingdom (2686–2181 BC). About 80 structures have been identified, but most are in a poor state of preservation. Their use is still debated, but most experts agree that they were the tombs of pharaohs. The evolution of burial sites from early mastaba ("bench" in Arabic) to step pyramid, on to the "true" pyramids, is a fascinating journey of spiritual ideals and "hit and miss" engineering. One theory for the pyramid shape is that it represents the benben, a triangular-shaped stone found in early temples, associated with the sun-god Ra and the creation of life. In hieroglyphics, the benben is represented as a pyramid shape.

Throughout this pyramid-building period, there were five major developments. The first was Zoser's step pyramid at Saqqarah, which had six steps and a burial chamber below ground. Half a century later this was copied by King Snofru, first king of the 4th dynasty, who planned an eight-stepped pyramid covered in limestone blocks, known as the Maidum or "Collapsed" Pyramid. He also built the "Bent" Pyramid at Dahshur further north, then embarked on a third and final one, known as the Red Pyramid – the first "true" pyramid. Built with much shallower angles, this is a graceful construction, containing a single burial chamber above ground. Snofru's son Khufu learned from his father's experiments and embarked on the fifth version, which became the Great Pyramid at Giza.

In his marvellous 1947 book *The Pyramids of Egypt* I.E.S. Edwards says that "the temptation to regard the true pyramid as a material representation of the sun's rays and consequently as a means whereby the dead king could ascend to heaven seems irresistible".

LEFT:the tiny entrance into the Red Pyramid leads to steep internal passageways with almost no air circulation inside.

ABOVE: the sphinx, with a lion's body and a man's head, was carved out of a harder block of stone, exposed when the causeway to Khafre's pyramid was being built.

ABOVE LEFT: the Step Pyramid of King Zoser was the vital link between a mastaba tomb and the first "true" pyramid. The idea of this massive tomb being a "stairway to heaven" for the king's *ka* or spirit, can be clearly understood.

LEFT: this temple tomb standing at the foot of the Great Pyramid of Khufu is typical of the smaller constructions built around the tomb of the pharaoh. These are the burial chambers of nportant ministers and viziers or other mbers of the royal family.

BUILDING MATERIALS

The pyramids that we see today would have looked very different when they were built. All the major pyramids had coverings of highly polished stone at one time, but over the millennia these have been stripped away, leaving the rough surfaces of the limestone construction blocks, which each weigh around 2 tonnes. The best remaining examples of this covering are the "Bent" Pyramid at Dahshur and towards the top of the Khafre Pyramid at Giza. The most popular covering material was polished white limestone from the Tura quarry in the Muqattam Hills, on the opposite side of the Nile overlooking Cairo.

Occasionally darker granite from Aswan was used, but because it was very hard and difficult to smooth – and because of the additional costs of transporting it along the Nile – the granite was laid in smaller bands. The best example of this is along the lower level of the Menkaure Pyramid at Giza. There is evidence that some pyramids also had small granite caps (pyramidia), often covered in electrum (gold, silver and copper mixture) to reflect the rays of the sun.

ABOVE RIGHT: a fanciful image of a young Khufu, who grew up to build the Great Pyramid.

LEFT: this unfinished mastaba No. 17 at Maydum, south of Saqqarah, is an early type of tomb that eventually developed into the pyramid shape. Several burial chambers are hidden within this mastaba, from which some fine statues and friezes were recovered; they are now in the Egyptian Museum.

BELOW: the Pyramids of Giza comprise one of the most famous silhouettes in the world. Contrary to popular opinion they were built not by slaves but by teams of skilled labourers and local quarrymen.

THE OASES AND THE FAYYUM

Since at least 5000 BC man has been exploiting nature's gifts in this curve of oases in Egypt's Western Desert, the most remote of which retains its distinct culture and language

he very word "oasis" conjures a string of romantic images – swirling sands, covered-up Bedu, mirages, the thirsty caravan stumbling into a pool of sweet water set amid swaying palms. Little of this vision has any foundation in modern reality: the caravans have all but vanished, banditry has (mostly) been suppressed, and the Bedu have traded in their camels for Toyotas. Not even the vestiges of modern man, however, in the form of asphalt, high-tension wires and water pumps, are capable of concealing the truths of a harsh climate, where shifting sands can block roads for days and where the foolhardy can still meet death by thirst, exposure or the sting of a scorpion. Nor have 21st-century wonders obscured the essential miracle of water, gushing hot or cold from barren rock to irrigate acres of garden in the midst of a wasteland.

The Sahara

From the Nile, the Sahara stretches 5,000 km (3,000 miles) westward to the Atlantic. The world's greatest expanse of desert is broken only by dots of green, where human habitation has survived the spread of sands. Contrary to popular imagination, oases generally lie in rocky lands where wind and time have scratched out vast depressions whose depths allow natural underground aquifers to reach the surface.

In Egypt's Western Desert a single aquifer flows north from Sudan, running an arc of five oases roughly parallel to the Nile. Prehistoric remains show that man has been exploiting nature's gift since at least 5000 BC. Under the pharaohs the four Nileward oases – al-Khargah, al-Dakhlah, al-Farafrah and al-Bahariyyah – formed a useful line of defence against Libyan tribes.

These days the desert and the oases are popular with wealthy Cairenes and ex-pats who happily exchange the city's noise and pollution for a weekend of peace and quiet in the desert. The government is slowly becoming aware of the area's potential for adventure

Main attractions
AL-FAYYUM, P.181
SIWAH, P.184
AL-BAHARIYYAH, P.185
AL-FARAFRAH, P.186
AL-DAKHLAH, P.186
AL-KHARGAH, P.188

LEFT: looking out over the desert.
BELOW: utilising the natural springs.

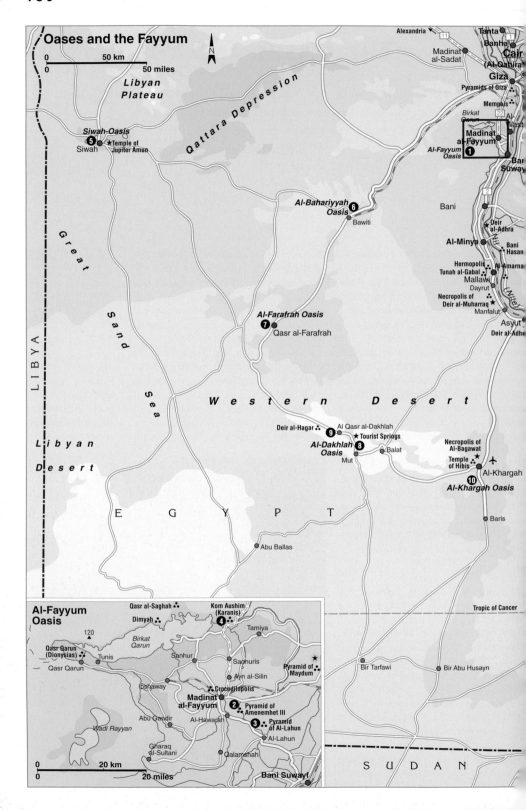

Oases and the Fayyum

0   50 km
0   50 miles

N

Libyan
Plateau

Qattara Depression

Siwah-Oasis
5 ★Temple of
Siwah   Jupiter Amun

Al-Bahariyyah
Oasis **6**
Bawiti

Great

Sand

Sea

Al-Farafrah Oasis
7
Qasr al-Farafrah

L I B Y A

Libyan

Desert

Western   Desert

Deir al-Hagar ❖ Al Qasr al-Dakhlah
9 ★Tourist Springs
Al-Dakhlah **8**   Balat
Oasis
Mut

Necropolis of
Al-Bagawat
★
Temple ✈
of Hibis
Al-Khargah
10
Al-Khargah Oasis

E   G   Y   P   T

Baris

❖ Abu Ballas

Alexandria

11

Tanta
Banha
Cai[r]
(Al-Qahira)
Madinat
al-Sadat
Giza
Pyramids of Giza
Memphis
22
Birkat
Qarun
Al-
Was[t]
Madinat
al-Fayyum **1**
Al-Fayyum
Oasis
Ba[n]
Suway[f]

2

Bani

Deir
al-Adhra
Al-Minya
Bani
Hasan
Hermopolis
Tunah al-Gabal   Al-Amarna
Mallawi
Dayrut
Necropolis of
Deir al-Muharraq ★
Manfalut
Asyut
Deir al-Adh[ra]

Tropic of Cancer

Bir Tarfawi   Bir Abu Husayn

S   U   D   A   N

**Al-Fayyum
Oasis**

Qasr al-Saghah ❖   Kom Aushim
(Karanis)
Dimyah ❖   **4**
120 ▲   Tamiya
Birkat
Qarun   Sanhur
Qasr Qarun
(Dionysias) ❖   Tunis
Qasr Qarun
Saqhuris
Ibshaway   Ayn al-Silin
Pyramid of ★
Maydum ❖
Crocodilopolis
Madinat
al-Fayyum **2**
Abu Gandir   Pyramid of
Al-Hawarah   Amenemhet III
3 ❖ Pyramid
Wadi Rayyan   of Al-Lahun
Gharaq   Al-Lahun
al-Sultani
Qalamshah
Bani Suwayf

0   20 km
0   20 miles

tourism. In coming years the oases are likely to feel a lot less remote.

History of the region

The camel, the only beast capable of five days march without water, was introduced by invading Persians in the 6th century BC and provided the oases with their first great leap forward, matched in importance only in the 20th century with the introduction of electricity and the car. The camel helped to revive the desert economy. The new beast was no help to the Persian emperor Cambyses, however, when he dispatched his army from al-Khargah across the desert to Siwah in 525 BC. According to Herodotus, all 50,000 men were buried in a sandstorm.

The Ptolemies, who administered Egypt like a vast agricultural estate, set about improving the productivity of the region. Archaeological remains show that cultivation grew to its furthest extent under their rule; new wells were dug with Alexandrian technology and the complex systems of water distribution that still persist were brought into use. The Roman conquest led to a reversal of fortunes. The internal unrest of the late Roman period saw banditry increase at the expense of sedentary agriculture, while persecutions forced Christians to take refuge in the desert. Wells that had been regularly repaired and cleaned were allowed to dry up, as a general decline in population, lasting up to the 20th century, set in.

Al-Fayyum

Sprouting from the west bank of the Nile like a tender leaf, **al-Fayyum ❶**, some 100 km (62 miles) southwest of Cairo, is referred to by some as Egypt's largest oasis. Others deny that it is an oasis at all, as it is fed not by springs but by the Bahr Yusef, an ancient Nile canal. An excellent road across the desert connects al-Fayyum to Cairo, two hours away (leaving Cairo from behind the Giza Pyramids). Alternatively, it can be reached from the more scenic Nile road to Upper Egypt. Some 48 km (30 miles) south of Cairo's edge the road draws parallel to the Pyramid of Maydum *(see page 174)*.

Ancient history

In prehistoric times al-Fayyum was a marshy depression that collected the

TIP

The security forces are concerned about the safety of tourists in Nile towns to the south of Cairo. As access to the oases is close to these areas, there can be delays at checkpoints whilst the police work out the level of protection required. This might amount to a police car accompanying you on your journey or an armed policeman or soldier joining you in your vehicle.

BELOW LEFT AND RIGHT: enduring features of al-Fayyum, a water wheel and a pigeon house.

SHOP

Two Swiss potters,
Evelyne Porret and
Michel Pastore, have a
pottery school in the
Fayyum, where you can
buy the school's
striking ceramics.
Alternatively you can
buy them from Nagada,
a textile and interior-
design shop in Cairo (13
Shari'Refa'a in Dokki;
tel: 02-3748 6663;
www.nagada.net).

BELOW: herding in
the Oases.

Nile's overflow during the flood season. Its wetlands were a favourite hunting ground of the Old and Middle Kingdom pharaohs until the 12th Dynasty's Amenemhet I (1991–1962 BC) drained the swamps, building a regulator at al-Lahun, the point where the river periodically breached its banks, and allowing the formation of a permanent reservoir, Lake Moeris to the Greeks, now called Lake Qarun (Birkat Qarun).

With this lake at the depression's northern end stabilised, agriculture could be introduced, and al-Fayyum began to flourish. It received a further boost under the Ptolemies, who reclaimed more than 1,200 sq. km (450 sq. miles) of fertile land, reducing the lake to about twice its present size. Improved agricultural methods were introduced, and new-fangled Greek hydraulics – water wheels of a unique type still seen today (see picture on page 181) – permitted extensive terracing.

The Fayyum experienced an influx of Greek settlers during the Ptolemaic period. The so-called Fayyum Portraits – portraits painted on wood and attached to the faces of mummies – in the Egyptian Museum in Cairo and frequently seen in other museums around the world, show typical Graeco-Roman influences.

Al-Fayyum was an early and highly successful effort at land reclamation. Further improvements in the 19th century turned it into the "Garden of Egypt", but the 20th century unfortunately brought with it overpopulation and salinisation. Lake Qarun now measures only 40 x 9 km (24 x 5 miles) and is as salty as the Mediterranean, while Madinat al-Fayyum, the capital city (see below), is badly overpopulated.

Continuing southwest for 16 km (10 miles) across the desert, the road leads over train tracks and along the edge of an army camp. It then forks: the road to the right enters cultivation and ultimately goes to Madinat al-Fayyum, the main town of al-Fayyum; the road to the left goes on towards the **pyramid complex of Amenemhet III ②** (1842–1797 BC) at al-Hawarah (daily 7am–5pm; admission charge). This was the site of what Herodotus in the 5th century BC called the Great Labyrinth. Amenemhet III is unusual in that he built two

Recommended Restaurants on page 189

pyramids, the other being at Dahshur.

Southwest of al-Hawarah the road crosses a canal to reach the main al-Fayyum to Bani Suwayf road. Eight kilometres (5 miles) to the left, on a peninsula of desert, stands the 12th-Dynasty **Pyramid of al-Lahun ❸** (daily 7am–4pm; admission charge), the tomb of Senusert II (1897–1878 BC).

Turning right instead we reach **Madinat al-Fayyum** after 10 km (6 miles), occupying the site of ancient **Crocodilopolis**, where the reptiles were revered (see box). Strung out along the Bahr Yusef, it has lost much of its former charm, but in the central square an example of the al-Fayyum water wheel groans away. The main suq, its lanes cluttered with wares, has a rustic simplicity, but there is little to offer visitors other than the heavily eroded 12th-Dynasty obelisk of Senusert I (1971–1928 BC), on a roundabout. The railway also runs here, but the service is very slow and erratic.

Around Lake Qarun

Lake Qarun is the Fayyum's greatest attraction. The western end, approached through the villages of **Sanhur** and **Ibshaway**, is the more peaceful stretch. The village of **Tunis**, where artists from Cairo have built some beautiful houses, has a potters' school and workshop started by the Swiss potter Evelyne Porret (see margin, page 182). Further on are the Ptolemaic **temple at Qasr Qarun** (daily 8am–4pm; admission charge), the site of ancient Dionysias. South of here is a series of further lakes, with swimming at **Wadi Rayan**. Beaches at the lake's eastern end, where most of the hotels and fish restaurant are, fill up with Cairenes on holidays and weekends.

Past the eastern tip of the lake is **Kom Aushim**, ancient **Karanis ❹**. Dating from the Ptolemaic period are extensive ruins of a temple dedicated to the crocodile-headed god Sobek, a Serapis temple and a later Roman temple to Zeus Amun. Inside the ruined mud houses are old millstones and olive presses, and you can also visit a small museum (daily 8am–4pm; admission charge). Karanis was located on a desert caravan route running from Memphis to al-Fayyum. Again security is tight, with Western visitors having armed-guard escorts.

The remains of ancient Karanis. Its raised position gives good views of the surrounding oasis.

BELOW:
still waters, Lake Qarun.

Crocodile Worship

The great Nile crocodiles (crocodylus niloticus) were worshipped and sanctified in ancient times. The crocodile god Sobek, one of the most important of gods, is seen as a human figure with crocodile head on countless temple carvings, though the main centre of worship was at Crocodilopolis, which the Greeks renamed Arsinoe and is now Madinat al-Fayyum. Upon their deaths, both young and adult crocodiles were mummified.

In her 1877 book *A Thousand Miles up the Nile* Amelia Edwards indicates that crocodiles were only found south of the city of Asyut. Since the building of the Aswan High Dam they have survived only in Lake Nasser. Today their numbers are increasing and adults can grow up to 7 metres (22 ft) in length.

Siwah Oasis

The most mysterious of Egypt's oases, **Siwah ❺** was long off-limits to tourists thanks to troubles along the Libyan border, to which it is adjacent. At present, not even a visitor's permit is needed and foreigners can venture freely to the oasis. Daily buses now ply the asphalted 300 km (190 miles) between Siwah and Marsa Matruh on the Mediterranean coast (*see page 267*).

The most remote of the oases, Siwah is unusual in Egypt in that it has a distinct culture and its own language, related to the Berber languages of North Africa. It evolved as a well-watered stopping point in the desert, on the Haj pilgrimage route from the coast of northeastern Libya through to the Red Sea, and thus developed many Berber connections.

Unorthodox customs used to be tolerated, including homosexual marriages (they were banned in the 1920s but continued illegally up until the mid-20th century), but all this changed fast as a result of contact with the world beyond the desert. The biggest threat to Siwah's character today is a government plan for an airport.

The oasis' main population centre is in **Siwah** town, dominated by the remains of the ancient hill-top settlement known as Shali Fort, a tight collection of ruined mud-brick houses, to which the Siwis moved from the **fortress of Aghurmi** in the early 20th century. On the rock of Aghurmi, 4 km (2 miles) from the centre, sit the remains of the **temple of Jupiter-Amun**, home of the famous oracle that confirmed Alexander the Great in his status as a god. Bicycles, for rent in Siwah town, are the best way of getting to the main sites in the oasis.

Another major historical site is **Gabal al-Mawta** (Mon–Thur 8am–2pm, Fri 7am–noon; no official admission charge but baksheesh is expected), less than 1 km (half a mile) north of Siwah town, where tombs have been cut out of the rock of a conical ridge. Paintings cover some of the walls, especially in the tomb of Si-Amun, but much was destroyed when the tombs were used as shelters during the Italian air raids of World War II. The oasis was a strategic location for the Allied Long Range Desert Group as they penetrated deep behind German/Italian lines.

BELOW: view of al-Bahariyyah.

Siwah is famous for its lush gardens, and fruit orchards. It is the major producer of dates in Egypt – over 1 million palms fill the cultivated area – and it is also an important producer of olive oil

Among the orchards, palm and olive groves lie numerous springs, such as the **Ain al-Gubah**, the ancient **Well of the Sun**, whose waters were said to have purifying properties. Indeed, the water is so plentiful that large salty lakes have formed and drainage is a major problem.

Over the past decade Siwah has been at the forefront of environmentally friendly tourism, turning this once remote region into an area of up-market eco retreats. One of the best examples of these (across the lake from Siwah town) is the stunning eco lodge of Adrere Ammelal, built in the traditional Siwah materials of mud brick and salt crystals *(see Travel Tips for details on accommodation)*. One of Egypt's most respected writers, Bahaa Taher, won the 2008 Booker Prize for Arabic Fiction for his book *Sunset Oasis (see page 95)* which is set in Siwah.

Nearby is the **Great Sand Sea** with its spectacular dunes and hot- and cold-water pools and lakes. To the northeast is the Qattara Depression, one of the lowest points below sea level in the world.

Al-Bahariyyah

Al-Bahariyyah ❻ is reached from Cairo by an excellent road that leads westward off the al-Fayyum desert road behind the Giza Pyramids. About 330 rather dull kilometres (205 miles) later is a new settlement around Egypt's only iron mines. Not far beyond the mines the road descends into the **al-Bahariyyah Depression**. Here, near the town of **Bawiti**, archaeologists have revealed an ancient Egyptian cemetery, thought to be the largest ever uncovered. Excavation is in its early stages, but it is thought that there are as many as 10,000 mummies dating from the Greco-Roman period. The tomb complex, dubbed the Valley of the Golden Mummies *(see box)*, is not open to the public, but there is a small museum.

Bawiti sits atop a rock outcrop. To the

Though you will see many Toyota trucks and 4x4s most locals still get around by donkey and cart like this one in Siwah.

BELOW LEFT: pausing near Dakhla.

Valley of the Golden Mummies

Like many good discoveries, this one happened by accident in 1996 when the hoof of a donkey being ridden by the guardian of the Temple of Alexander at al-Bahariyyah disappeared into a hole. The result was the uncovering of four tombs containing over 100 mummies, many with beautifully gilded faces, dating from the Roman period of the 26th Dynasty, some 2,000 years ago. These important tombs were located close to the temple and several rooms, containing both male and female mummies, have now been excavated.

During the Roman period this region became wealthy from the production of wine, and this affluence is reflected in the high quality of workmanship and the gilding and painting on the sarcophagi. Some of the best examples of the mummies, including that of a woman with gold-plated breasts, are now on view at the small al-Bahariyyah Museum. The lighting is subdued to protect the delicate materials and no photography is allowed.

Excavations of this exciting site are continuing under the direction of Dr Zahi Hawass, secretary general of the Supreme Council of Antiquities. So far some 200 mummies have been uncovered, but it is anticipated that as many as 10,000 may lie in a cemetery comprising around 6 sq.km (2⅓ sq. miles).

Donkey riding through the quiet lanes of the oases.

BELOW:
the White Desert.

north, cliffs drop abruptly into a sea of palms. Bawiti's gardens spread for several kilometres along the base of this cliff. The view from the cliffs at the spring called **Ain Bishmu** is stunning. Here the water emerges from a gorge to flow into the surrounding orchards. Within the gardens, land is so precious that there are few walkways and it is often necessary to paddle through the irrigation channels. Dates, olives, oranges, apricots, lemons, pomegranates and tiny apples grow in jungle-like proliferation.

Around Bawiti and its sister village of **al-Qasr** are numerous ancient sites, not all accessible and not all interesting. More to the taste of tourists are the hot springs, some of which reach a scalding 47°C (115°F). Few things are as memorable as a moonlit bath under palm trees in the crisp air of the desert.

Al-Farafrah

From al-Baharriyah, a well-travelled road goes southeast, through 185 km (115 miles) of some of Egypt's most spectacular scenery, including the **White Desert** *(see box)* to the **al-Farafrah ➐**

oasis. Compared with the other oases, Al-Farafrah has a fairly small area of land under cultivation, but it has the greatest potential for land reclamation with more than 100 natural springs.

In spite of good road connections, **Qasr al-Farafrah**, the main settlement, feels a long way from anywhere (it is 200 km/120 miles from al-Dakhlah, the next town on the desert loop), and though no longer a hamlet is still very traditional. A village of some 3,000 inhabitants built up against the side of a hill, it has fine old mud-brick houses with wooden doors and elaborate locks. The private museum run by Badr, a local artist who has exhibited in Europe, is interesting, but the main attraction is the village itself. Wander around, visit the springs – Bir Sitta (No. 6) and Ain Bishoi are the most popular – and stroll through the gardens of olives and fruit trees.

Al-Dakhlah Oasis

Al-Dakhlah ➑ (The Inner) has a population of 80,000 and produces wheat, mangoes, oranges, olives and dates. The New Valley Project, an ambitious scheme to bring water from

The White Desert

West of the string of oases that make up the al-Bahariyyah settlements is a large expanse of exposed limestone known as the White Desert. Erosion by wind and rain over many thousands of years has sculpted these massive blocks into strange shapes that loom out of the desert landscape like monstrous white ghosts.

For visitors with 4x4 vehicles the area makes a popular weekend excursion from Cairo, spending a couple of nights camping in the desert. If you don't have your own vehicle, the best way to see this remarkable area is to join an organised tour from Cairo. It is also sometimes included in intineraries travelling overland from Siwah to Cairo via al-Bahariyyah, again spending the night camping under the stars.

Recommended Restaurants on page 189

Lake Nasser to irrigate the Western Desert, has more than doubled its size in recent years, but al-Dakhlah retains more of its original laid-back charm than al-Khargah, to which it is connected by a 190-km (120-mile) road and daily buses.

The first important village in the depression is **Balat**. In the 13th-century it was the terminus of a direct caravan route from Asyut in the Nile Valley, and a hive of mud-brick dwellings testifies to medieval prosperity. Using only mud and straw, builders attained a sophistication in architecture that combines utility, beauty and harmony with natural surroundings. Balat was also the seat of the oases' pharaonic governors; a French expedition is excavating extensive remains northwest of the village.

Al-Dakhlah's current capital is at **Mut**, some 35 km (22 miles) further west. The town contains most of al-Dakhlah's hotels. Provisions may be bought here and there are a number of decent restaurants, but there is little to see – the old town's mud-brick citadel has been allowed to fall into ruins. The town also has a small ethnographic museum

presenting oasis life. However, a new museum is planned which will focus on the desert sciences and the prehistoric monuments from the entire Western Desert region.

Just outside Mut, to the northwest, are the so-called **Tourist Springs**, with pool (charge) and rest house. In fact, many of the other warm sulphurous springs of the oases – most are around al-Dakhlah – are equally pleasant.

No trip to al-Dakhlah would be complete without a walk through its fields and gardens. Wheat is the main field crop while in the gardens grapevines vie for space with date palms, mulberry trees, figs and citrus.

Thirty kilometres (18 miles) beyond the Tourist Springs, the town of **Qasr al-Dakhlah ⑨** perches on a mound between the desert and the fields. Like Balat, it is a honeycomb of little lanes running between mud-brick houses. Although cement is gaining ground, mud bricks are often preferred since

Characteristic clay-brick mosque in Qasr al-Dakhlah.

BELOW: potters in al-Dakhlah.

TIP

Al-Dakhlah is the only place in Egypt where visitors can still see the construction of *saqiyas* (huge buffalo-driven water wheels constructed from palm timber and clay jars).

BELOW: buying and selling in al-Khargah.

they retain heat at night and coolness during the day. Qasr al-Dakhlah has wonderful gardens, a fortress and a mosque dating from the Ayyabid era and a restored madrasah (Qur' anic school).

In the desert 4 km (2 ½ miles) west of al-Qasr are some well-preserved Hellenistic tombs, one with a brightly painted zodiac on the ceiling. Further along the main road, at **Deir al-Hagar**, lie the ruins of a recently restored 1st-century AD sandstone temple.

Al-Khargah Oasis

Al-Khargah (The Outer) ❿ is the largest and most developed of Egypt's oases, by virtue of its proximity to the Nile and because it is the seat of the New Valley Governorate. Five kilometres (3 miles) north of Asyut, a paved road leads past industrial complexes up into the desert. Two hundred kilometres (120 miles) of barren gravel later, the road suddenly descends a magnificent cliff into the **al-Khargah Depression**, which extends southwards, narrowing at its extremity, for 100 km (60 miles). Descending from the plateau on the left-hand side are the

remains of the old railway track that once linked the area to the Nile valley.

As one crosses the flat bottom of the depression, a few straggly trees appear on the road side, inauspiciously announcing the beginning of cultivation. Then modern concrete and glass buildings and Nasserite housing blocks begin to sprout, marking the entrance to al-Khargah town. Visitors to the oases should realise it is merely an administrative centre and a showpiece of the New Valley Project, initiated by Abdel Nasser in the later 1950s, and has little of the appeal normally associated with oases such as Siwah or al-Baharriyah. The project, the aim of which was to use the vast potential of the oases' waters for land reclamation and new settlement, has met with only limited success. Much of al-Khargah's population consists of resettled Upper Egyptians; and the new hotels, duck farms and packaging industries point to some degree of prosperity.

The town's **museum** (daily 8am–4pm; admission charge) houses archaeological finds from al-Khargah and al-Dakhlah. Of most interest is a display, labelled in English, following the early

Recommended Restaurants below

history of the region. The desert town used to be an important stop on the famous Forty Days Road, a trade route connecting Sudan and the south with the oases and the north. Used to transport ivory, gold and slaves, as well as camels, it was a lucrative route, as the number of protective forts along its lenth testify. Camel traders still used the route until relatively recently, but these days most of the journey is completed by truck.

About 2 km (1¼ miles) northeast of the town, not far from the main road, lies a cluster of monuments. Chief amongst them is the **Temple of Hibis** (daily 8am–4pm; admission charge), important as one of the few remnants of Persian rule. Built of local sandstone, it was mainly built under Darius I, but the colonnade was not completed until the reign of Nectanebo II in the 4th century BC and other additions date from the Ptolemaic period. It is well preserved, having been buried in sand until its discovery in the early 20th century, and lies in a palm grove beyond the remains of a ceremonial pool and an avenue of sphinxes. The carving style within shows local influence, while the content of the reliefs – deities, the burial of Osiris and a winged Seth struggling with a serpent – follows a standard pattern.

At the edge of cultivation to the north of the temple lies the Christian **necropolis of al-Bagawat** (open daily 8am–4pm; admission charge), a huge area of mud-brick domes and vaults, some of which date back to the 3rd–7th centuries and therefore representing one of the earliest Christian cemeteries in the world. Some of the tombs have very vivid illustrations from the Old Testament, depicting the the stories of Adam and Eve, Noah's Ark, the Exodus and even Jonah being ejected out of the whale's stomach. It is worth engaging the services of one of the guardians (tip expected) to show you the highlights of the site. A kilometre's hike across the sands north of the cemetery leads to the ruins of **Deir al-Kashef**, a fortified monastery also dating from the early Christian period.

South of al-Khargah town a paved road extends through a string of smaller oases, past some minor antiquities, to **Baris**, site of a village designed by the renowned Egyptian architect Hassan Fathy which was never completed. ❑

BELOW:
waterside table,
Lake Qarun.

RESTAURANTS

Siwah

Abduh's
Main square
Tel: 046-460 1243.
$–$$
This is the oldest restaurant in town, always popular and with consistenly good, simple food. There's a large breakfast menu, tra-ditional dishes, pasta, vegetable stews, couscous and roast chicken.

Alexander Restaurant
Near Abduh's, off central market square. **$**
Similar to Abduh's, and also good value.

Serves a budget menu, including curries.

Kenooz
Shari' Seboukha, Siwah Town. Tel: 046-460 2399. **$–$$**
Egyptian and Siwan food served on a pleasant terrace under the stars and the palm trees.

Prices for a three-course dinner per person with one beer or glass of house wine:
$ = under $20
$$ = $20–45
$$$ = $45–60
$$$$ = over $60

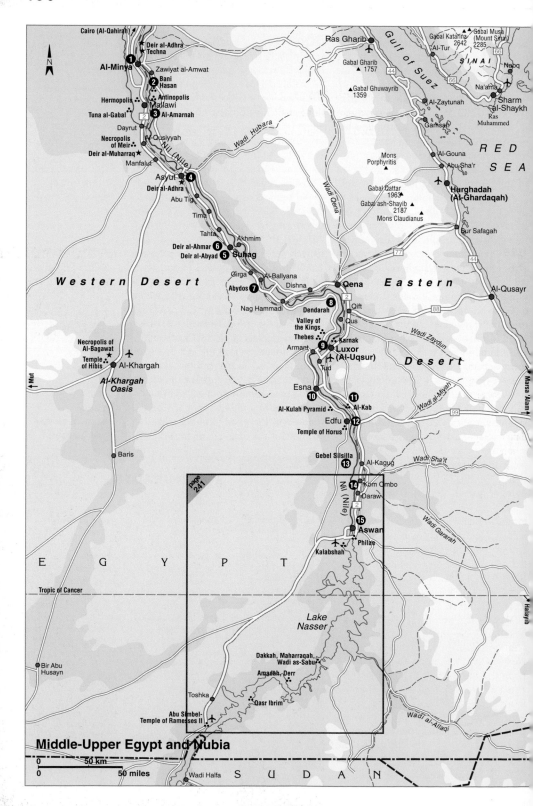

Middle-Upper Egypt and Nubia

Recommended Restaurants on page 201

MIDDLE EGYPT

A visit to Middle Egypt, a region little changed for
thousands of years until the building of the Aswan Dam,
helps to explain the Middle Kingdom shift of power from
Memphis to Thebes

Far or 19th-century visitors sailing along in their *dahabeyyahs* (sailing boats), their only means of reaching Upper Egypt, the lush countryside south of Cairo offered a first taste of adventure on their great journey up the Nile.

Even today Middle Egypt offers a rich and varied experience, and those with time to spare and patience will discover a place in Egypt far removed from the mass tourism evident in parts of Upper Egypt. Many spectacular ancient tombs and temples lie in a rural landscape that has barely changed in centuries, and where the majority of farmers still work the land by hand.

In addition, Middle Egypt provides many clues to understanding Egypt's ancient history. The Middle Kingdom tombs at Bani Hasan help to explain the shift of power from Memphis to Thebes, and the change in burial patterns from the Old Kingdom pyramids at Giza and Saqqarah to the tucked-away royal tombs in the Valley of the Kings at Thebes in Luxor.

Middle Egypt was also the chosen base for the most radical of all pharaohs, Akhenaten, who during the New Kingdom period moved his capital Akhetaten from Luxor to al-Amarnah, roughly halfway between the modern towns of al-Minya and Asyut. And just 50 years later Seti I built his magnificent temple complex at Abydos to confirm the restoration of the old regime that Akhenaten had tried to overthrow.

Security issues

However, at present, security issues prevent any cruise ships from making the two-week journey from Cairo to Aswan, and travel in the region is unpredictable. Outbreaks of violence in the region's sprawling towns in the 1990s, including a series of attacks on tourists and government officials by militant Islamic fundamentalists, have made much of the region a virtual no-go area for tourists. Security remains very tight and foreigners are only allowed to travel by rail or road in military convoy, making it diffi-

Main attractions
DEIR AL-ADHRA, P.194
TOMBS AT BANI HASAN, P.194
AL-AMARNAH, P.195
TOMB OF SETI I, ABYDOS, P.198
TEMPLE OF HATHOR, DENDARAH, P.201

BELOW: landscape near al-Minya.

TIP

The lack of foreign tourists in the area means that accommodation between Cairo and Luxor is basic. Al-Minya offers a few more up-market hotels.

BELOW LEFT: the Coptic cross is similar to the ancient Egyptian ankh, the hieroglyphic symbol for life. **BELOW RIGHT:** cotton traders

cult to visit the sights independently or spontaneously.

Although no foreigners have been attacked since the 1990s and the Interior Ministry has recently eased restrictions (and regularly promises to reinstate the cruises), local officials are still extremely cautious. Even rail travel is unpredictable: you may find that ticket clerks will not sell you a ticket to destinations between Cairo and Luxor, or that when you alight from the train you are unable to exit the station. If you do manage to leave the station you may or may not be given an armed escort (either of which could make you feel uneasy): the situation changes from place to place and from day to day. Certainly foreigners will be turned away at road blocks at the slightest sign of trouble.

Islamic extremism

The university of Asyut has long been associated with Islamic fundamentalism. President Sadat's attempt to suppress religious extremism in the 1970s led to a battle between security forces and Islamic groups which escalated to such a point that the president himself was assassinated in

1981. Little has changed since then. Over a million Egyptians returned home after losing their jobs in Iraq, on account of Egypt's involvement on the Allied side in the first Gulf War (1990–91), a situation that created a lot of anger and despair and an easy breeding ground for fundamentalist propaganda. In 1992 several groups, especially the Al-Gama'a al-Islamiya, embarked upon a programme of violence to achieve their goals – mainly to make Egypt an Islamic republic, and to deport all foreigners.

In a country much dependent on income from tourism, attacks on tourist sites proved an easy and effective way to destabilise the government. Militants attacked night trains, buses and cruise boats, with some injuries and deaths to foreigners. Most attacks occurred in the area around Asyut and Dayrut.

Changing lifestyles

Until the building of the Aswan Dam, which regulates the flow of the Nile and produces hydroelectricity, the lives of the *fellaheen* (peasants) had barely changed in thousands of years. Their routines were regulated by the annual

The Copts

Copts account for about one-fifth of the population in Middle Egypt, and the region is a stronghold for Coptic traditions. They believe that Deir al-Muharraq *(see page 197)* was one of the earliest churches in the world, and it is certain that the monastery had monks from the 4th century onwards. Until recently their cohabitation with the Muslim majority was held up as a model of Egyptian tolerance, but pressure on precious agricultural land due to population growth and the subsequent unemployment, has created tensions. These were made worse by the return of Egyptians who had fought with the Mujahedeen in Afghanistan during the 1980s and of Egyptian migrant workers from the Gulf States and Iraq, leading to violent clashes through the 1990s.

The tension shows itself in the heavy security outside Coptic churches, and also in the region's architecture, as Copts and Muslims build new churches and mosques, each time trying to outdo the other, with spires and minarets towering ever higher and brighter above the landscape.

rise and fall of the river and the sowing and harvesting of crops, occasionally interrupted by a *mouled* (local saint's festival). Over the past few decades many things have changed. The towns and cities have massively expanded, often over precious agricultural land; educational opportunties have improved, offering children life chances other than farming; and almost every household now has electricity and satellite TV. Whereas it used to be the sun that dictated the pattern of the day, it is now more often than not foreign or Egyptian soaps on TV that draw the *fellaheen* home in the evening.

Al-Minya

The first place of much significance on the journey south of Cairo is **Bani Suwayf**, but this is an administrative hub and of little interest to visitors. More worthy of attention is the provincial capital of **al-Minya ❶**, on the west bank of the Nile, 245 km (153 miles) south of Cairo. Known as "the Bride of Upper Egypt", on account of it lying on the cusp of Lower and Upper Egypt, it has an important university and some fine

colonial architecture from a time when Greek and Egyptian cotton barons did business in the area. With a good choice of hotels and a more relaxed atmosphere than the other cities in Middle Egypt, it makes a good base for exploring the surrounding sights of Deir al-Adhra (just north of the town: *see below*), Tuna al-Gabal, Bani Hasan and Hermopolis Magna. The town itself offers pleasant walks along the Nile, but has no sights at present; a new **Minya Museum** is due to open in 2010, displaying treasures from nearby Amarnah.

Across the Nile on the east bank is al-Minya's vast and impressive cemetery, **Zawiyat al-Mayitin** (Corner of the Dead), with several hundred mud-brick domes in the Muslim cemetery and just as many crosses in its Coptic counterpart. It is said to be one of the largest cemeteries in the world. Until recently, when a long-awaited bridge was built across the river, the dead were transported to their final resting place by felucca.

Deir al-Adhra

Twenty-one km (12 miles) north of al-Minya on the east bank of the Nile (ferry

> The mayor of Al Minya was a fresh-faced, alert, twinkling Muslim in a dazzling loose snowy gown...He dined with us in the garden of the hospitable Coptic house.
>
> Freya Stark
> *East is West*, 1945

BELOW:
growing rice near Bani Suwayf.

The Middle Kingdom tombs at Bani Hasan are cut into the desert cliff well back from the river. The best way to get to the tombs is to take a taxi from al-Minya.

available) brings the curious traveller to an extraordinary monastery, the **Deir al-Adhra** (monastery of the Virgin), perched on top of a cliff, 130 metres (426 ft) above the river, and approached by 66 steps hewn into the rock. It is said to have been founded in AD 328 by St Helena, a dubious attribution, but one that corresponds in date at least to the archaeological evidence and the plan of the church. Coptic tradition says that the Holy Family rested here on their flight from the Holy Land, and many miracles are ascribed to its picture of the Virgin, said to weep holy oil. Hundreds of Coptic pilgrims flock here on the week-long feast of the Assumption in August and make the precipitous ascent.

The tombs of Bani Hasan

On the east bank of the Nile 18 km (11 miles) south of Al-Minya, and approached by a battered old ferry, is the village of **Bani Hasan** ❷, above which 39 Middle Kingdom tombs have been cut into the cliffs (open daily 8am–5pm; admission charge and tip for the guard who unlocks the tombs).

The powerful feudal lords who are buried here ruled almost independently of the Middle Empire during the 11th and 12th dynasties (2125–1795 BC). Twelve of the tombs are decorated with scenes similar to those at Saqqarah, but painted in fresco rather than carved in relief. Biographical accounts describing the military and administrative pursuits of the aristocratic owners are depicted, as well as pastimes, occupations and trades such as hunting, fishing and dyeing cloth.

The best tombs are open to the public, including the tomb of **Baqet**, an 11th-Dynasty monarch, which in addition to scenes of hunting and harvesting depicts a catalogue of 200 wrestling positions; the tomb of Baquet's son, the governor **Kheti I**, presenting interesting depictions of daily life in the Middle Kingdom; the particularly grand tomb of **Amenemhat**, which has a portico and a courtyard as well as fine paintings; and the beautiful

Recommended Restaurants on page 201

tomb of **Khnumhotep**, which includes vividly coloured scenes of his family life, trading and hunting.

Mallawi and Hermopolis

Sixteen kilometres (10 miles) south of Bani Hasan, and back on the west bank, are the scant remains of the ancient town of **Antinopolis**, founded by Hadrian in memory of his friend and favourite, the beautiful boy Antinous, who was drowned here, perhaps willingly, as a human sacrifice.

At **Mallawi**, a few kilometres further on, a road leads to the right, bending northwards through fields of sugar cane, where a little railway runs in and out to transport the crop to a nearby molasses factory. The road passes through the village of Al-Ashmunayn, which partially covers the ruins of ancient **Hermopolis**, city of Thoth, the god of wisdom and writing and the reckoner of time, and therefore equated by the Greeks with Hermes. Ancient Egyptians believed that this site was the primeval hill from where the sun-god Ra emerged to create the world out of chaos.

It is worth taking the time to wander around the rather confusing overgrown hummocks, which are all that remain of this once-flourishing provincial capital. The ruins of a huge **Temple of Thoth**, two giant quartzite baboons and a church of the Virgin are about all that can be identified.

Across the fields on the edge of the desert, 7 km (4½ miles) west of Hermopolis, is the necropolis called **Tuna al-Gabal** (daily 8am–5pm; admission charge) containing several interesting graves, in particular that of Petosiris, which illustrates the link between Egyptian and Greek art. Petosiris belonged to a family of high priests of Thoth during the time that Alexander liberated the Egyptians from the hated Persians at the end of the 4th century BC. In the decoration of his fine tomb he chose to have the conventional offering scenes depicted in the fashionable new Greek style. Here the stiff virgins characteristic of the New Kingdom are

replaced by a parade of buxom young women in fluttering see-through draperies, and the men are wearing hitched-up *gallibiyas* and straw hats, not unlike the people visible on the roads of Middle and Upper Egypt today.

Al-Amarnah

Returning to the main road and heading south, another 10 km (6 miles) will bring motorists to the turn-off for **Al-Amarnah ❸** (daily 8am–4pm Oct–May, to 5pm in summer; admission charge), the open plain on the east bank of the Nile where the rebel pharaoh Akhenaten and his wife Nefertiti made their brief bid to escape from the stuffy and over-bearing establishment of Thebes in the 14th century BC. Their new capital Akhetaten, the Horizon of Aten, was the capital of Egypt for only 30 years, until Akhenaten's death in 1336 BC. His successor moved back to Thebes, and this city was abandoned forever.

Though the story is appealing and romantic, the site of Akhetaten in the hot dusty bowl of the Amarnah plain can be disappointing, as the ruins are hard to understand, even though the orig-

One of two giant quartzite baboons at Hermopolis. Baboons were sacred to the ibis-headed Thoth, god of scribes, learning and intellect and the reckoner of time.

BELOW:
carving at Hermopolis.

Head of the beautiful Nefertiti. Many such portrait heads were found in the work-shop of an al-Amarnah sculptor called Tuthmosis.

BELOW: limestone carving from the tomb of Ay, al-Armanah, depicting Akhenaten and his wife presenting Ay with a golden collar

inal outlines of the buildings are still discernible. Archaeologically, however, it has yielded a vast amount of information and some beautiful objects, including the famous head of Nefertiti (now in Berlin: *see margin note*).

The site is extensive, as the city of Akhetaten spread out over 14 km (9 miles). At the time of writing the special bus for the site was not running, and the only way to visit the site was to hire a taxi from Mallawi and take the irregular car ferry. Make sure you tell the taxi exactly which tombs you want to see and how long you are staying. There are 25 tombs but not all are open to the public, and only five have light, so bring a torch.

From what remains of buildings and frescoes, Akhetaten seems to have been a bright and cheerful place reflecting the king's delight in his family and the everyday world. "Because Thou has risen," he says in his wonderful *Hymn to the Sun*, found in the tomb of Ay, "all the beasts and cattle repose in their pastures; and the trees and green herbs put forth their leaves and flowers. The birds fly out of their nests; and their wings praise

Thy Ka as they fly forth. The sheep and goats of every kind skip about on their legs; and feathered fowl and birds also live, because Thou hast risen for them."

From the landing stage at At-Till, a dirt track follows the original Royal Road which cuts straight to the centre of Akhetaten. Remains of the Great Temple of Aten (now covered in Muslim tombs), the Archives where the famous Amarnah letters were found, and the Royal Palace, are discernible just south of At-Till.

A pedestrian bridge, from where the royal couple waved at their subordinates, connected the Royal Palace with the State Palace across the Royal Road. The famous unfinished head of Nefertiti (now in Berlin) was found in a sculptor's workshop in the residential quarters, now mostly covered by sand.

Of the 19 southern tombs, located about 8 km (5 miles) from the landing, that of Ay (prepared during Ay's lifetime but never used, as he was actually buried in Thebes) is undoubtedly the finest, with wall paintings depicting street and palace scenes, and Akhenaten and his wife presenting Ay with a golden collar *(see picture, page 196)*. The tomb

of Mahu, Akhenaten's chief of police, is the best-preserved on the site.

To the north, outlines of Nefertiti's Northern Palace and courtiers' villas can be traced. Incorporating reception rooms, bedrooms, bathrooms with basins and toilets, kitchens, and storerooms, the houses were surrounded by gardens with trees and pools. Air conditioning was effected by wind catchers which faced the northerly breezes. These architectural details can be seen in paintings in the Egyptian Museum in Cairo. The seven northern tombs often show depictions of daily life in Akhetaten, as well as the royal couple and their family.

Asyut

A few miles further south, on the west bank, **Asyut ❹**, the most important town in the region, stands on a bend in the river, 378 km (236 miles) south of Cairo. In the 19th century it marked the end of the Forty Days Road from Darfur in Sudan, and in its important market slaves from Sudan and the Libyan desert were sold.

Thanks to the cotton boom during the late 19th and early 20th centuries, its wealthy merchants built palatial villas here and lived on a grand scale, with black-tie dinners and weekly races. Most of these families eventually moved north, however, and Asyut is now rather provincial, though it has a university, a huge cement plant and rug factories. A Presbyterian mission has been established here for over 100 years and there are many Coptic churches and communities.

The large Coptic community takes care of several early monasteries north and further south of the town. The **Deir al-Muharraq** (Burnt Monastery), 12 km (7½ miles) north of Asyut, is believed to be where the Holy Family stayed for six months, their longest stay in Egypt. Copts believe that the **church of al-Azraq**, consecrated in AD 60, is the oldest church in the world. There are still about 120 Coptic monks in residence.

Suhag

South of the town of **Suhag**, 115 km (71 miles) south of Asyut, are two of Egypt's most visited monasteries. The **Deir al-Abyad ❺** (White Monastery; daily 7am–dusk), founded in the 5th century by St Shenuda, one of the fathers of Coptic Christianity, has many striking similarities with pharaonic temple design. The monastery was once home to over 2,000 monks, but these days only four remain.

Nearby **Deir al-Ahmar ❻** (Red Monastery; daily 7am–midnight) was founded by Besa, one of Shenuda's disciples, and is dedicated to St Bishoi . Monasticism started in Egypt around AD 320, after Pachom from Esna founded the first community. He first served in the Roman Army, which convinced him that his monks should be strictly disciplined and of service to the community. Shenuda, at the end of the 4th century, went even further and introduced strict rules for every aspect of a monk's life.

Abydos

Abydos ❼ (daily 7am–6pm; admission charge; bring a torch), 165 km (103

After Akhenaten's death, his successor, Tutankhaten (later to change his name to Tutankhamun) abandoned Akhetaten for Memphis and Thebes and reinstated Amun-Ra as the chief god of Egypt. Akhetaten quickly went into decline.

BELOW:
Deir al-Abyad (the White Monastery) near Suhag.

miles) north of Luxor, near al-Balyana, is one of Egypt's most spellbinding spots. The area was used as a burial place from *circa* 4000 BC until well into Christian times, around AD 600. The site has been systematically excavated since 1977, and many important finds have come to light, including the tombs of kings from before the First Dynasty, causing Egyptian chronology to be extended by a zero dynasty. In 1991 two large ships carrying the dead were found, thought to be 5,000 years old. The earliest known tomb of a pharaoh, dating back to around 3150 BC, was discovered in 1993, containing some of the oldest known examples of hieroglyphic writing.

In the dawn of history, Wepwawet, the jackal deity and the original god of Abydos, roamed the desert's edge guarding the ancestral burial grounds below the dip in the western hills. At sunset the ancients imagined the golden glow to be the staircase to the afterworld and they wished to be buried at its foot.

Place of pilgrimage

But most of all, Abydos is associated with the legend of Osiris. From the Middle Kingdom onwards, every pharaoh as well as hundreds of thousands of pilgrims left some token of their presence or a false stele at Abydos, hoping to gain favour with Osiris in his capacity as Judge of the Court of the Hereafter. The area is thus a mass of funeral stele, burial grounds, former temples and memorials. But it was the New Kingdom pharaoh Seti I (1291–1278 BC) who was responsible for the most beautiful tribute to Osiris, his seven-sanctuaried temple, the Great Temple of Seti I.

Seti came to power around 1291 BC, some 40 years after the monotheistic regime of Akhenaten at al-Amarnah had collapsed. The nation was still recovering from the shock of this apostasy, and Seti wished to reaffirm his faith in the traditional gods and restore them to their former pre-eminence. To this end he rallied all the resources of the land to build and adorn a new temple at Abydos, in which he recorded his devotion to the six main gods: Osiris, his wife Isis, their son Horus, Amun-Ra, Ra-Hor-Akhty and Ptah. He also honoured his forebears by recording

BELOW: relief in the Great Temple of Seti I, Abydos, depicting Osiris with characteristic crook and flail, with Isis. **BELOW RIGHT:** the First Hypostyle Hall, the Great Temple of Seti I, Abydos.

The Osiris Legend

Legend relates how the just and much-loved ruler Osiris was killed by his evil and jealous brother Seth. Isis, Osiris' weeping sister/wife, faithfully searched the banks of the Nile for his dismembered body. The pieces of Osiris were buried at different places in both Upper and Lower Egypt, but importantly his head was believed to be buried at Abydos. She eventually found all the pieces, except for the penis which had been swallowed by a fish, and bound them carefully together with strips of cloth. Isis used her magical powers to revive her husband just long enough to conceive their son Horus. She fashioned a phallus from Nile mud, turned herself into a bird and, hovering over the body of her husband, became pregnant.

It was at Abydos that Osiris was resurrected and assumed his powers as the lord and judge of the afterlife. Their son Horus grew up and resumed the struggle with Seth.

their names in a list of kings. This assemblage of 76 cartouches has been of immense importance to researchers and historians.

Temple of Seti I

The temple is entered through a mostly ruined pylon leading into the **First Hypostyle Hall**, which was completed by Seti's son Ramesses II. Beyond this is the **Second Hypostyle Hall** with 24 papyrus columns, and decorated with some of the finest reliefs in the whole country. These exquisite reliefs on fine white limestone show Seti engaged in performing a multitude of rites in honour of Osiris and the company of gods. The reliefs on the walls on the right are particularly noteworthy.

Further on are the seven sanctuaries of the six mentioned gods and of Seti himself; these would have contained their barques behind closed wooden doors. Seti himself died before the temple was completed, leaving his son Ramesses II to finish the decoration of the courtyards and colonnades, in a clearly less sophisticated way.

In the south wing of the temple,

entered from the Second Hypostyle Hall is a long passage known as the **Gallery of the Kings**, where Seti I and his son Ramesses are shown honouring all the kings that came before them, from King Menes to Seti I. North of Seti's temple is the much less well preserved **Temple of Ramesses II**, his son, dedicated to the same gods.

The cult of Osiris and Isis later moved south to the Cataract Region, but the annual festival of Abydos lingered for

Horus depicted on the wall of the temple of Ramesses II at Abydos.

BELOW:
Hall of Osiris, the Temple of Sethos, Abydos.

almost 400 years. Every January the great drama was re-enacted, with a cast of thousands and crowds of pilgrims came from all over Egypt to participate. A gold-plated image represented Osiris; the pharaoh himself took the part of Horus; and the priests and priestesses masqueraded as Wepwawet, Seth, Isis, Nephthys and supporting cast.

The Christians finally sacked the temple in AD 395.

Vestiges of powerful magic still cling to the sacred precincts. It is not unusual to see local women circling the pool of the mysterious building, often said to be the burial place of Osiris but in fact a cenotaph of Seti I, called the **Osireion**. In more

recent times the temple attracted the Englishwoman Dorothy Eady, who believed she was the reincarnation of a temple priestess and Seti's lover. She spent the last 25 years of her life living at Abydos, where she provided archaeologists with details of how temples worked in ancient times. Known as Umm Seti, the Mother of Seti, she died in 1981.

Dendarah

Excursions from Luxor and the longer Nile cruises include the **Temple of Dendarah** ❽ (daily 7am–6pm; admission charge), near **Qena**, on a bend in the river about halfway between Abydos and Luxor. Like those of Esna, Edfu, Kom Ombo and Philae, and others lost under Lake Nasser, the temple dates from the Ptomelaic period, and is around 1,000 years more recent than the New Kingdom temples.

The temple is dedicated to Hathor, the cow goddess, known as "The Golden One", goddess of women, who was also a sky and tree goddess, sometimes equated with Aphrodite by the Greeks. As in Kom Ombo and Philae, the sick

RIGHT: carving of Hathor the cow goddess at the Temple of Dendarah (**BELOW**).

travelled here to be cured by Hathor's healing powers.

Despite being damaged by the Christians, who chipped out the faces and limbs of many figures, Dendarah is one of the best-preserved Egyptian temples and its adjunct structures can all be easily identified. It has retained its girdle wall, its Roman gate, two birth houses and a sacred lake, as well as its crypts, stairways, roof and chapels.

Its most distinctive feature is its great hypostyle hall, with its 24 Hathor-headed columns and a ceiling showing the outstretched Nut, the sky-goddess, swallowing the sun at evening and giving birth at morning. The zodiac on the ceiling is the best-preserved in the whole of Egypt. The hall was decorated during the reign of Tiberius and is dated AD 34.

The dark courts and crypts in the interior give evidence of various festivals in which Hathor was involved. The most important of these feasts was the annual New Year Festival, during which the goddess was carried up the western staircase to the roof for the ritual known as the "Union with the Disc", returning down

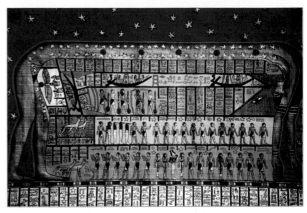

another staircase to the east. On the walls of the stairways the order of procession of the gods in full regalia is clearly shown. There are interesting graffiti on the roof, including names of Napoleon's soldiers. On the back wall of the temple is one of the very few contemporary representations of Cleopatra with Caesarion, her son by Julius Caesar.

Beside the birth house stand the ruins of one of the earliest structures of the Christian era, a basilica built in sandstone, the interior of which features a beautifully carved niche. ❑

Papyrus copy of the ceiling in Dendarah's New Year Chapel. It depicts the outstretched sky-goddess Nut swallowing the sun in the evening and giving birth to it in the morning.

RESTAURANTS

Al Minya

Banana Island Restaurant
Corniche an-Nil
Tel: 086-234 2993. **$$**
The main restaurant of Al Minya's Aton Hotel has an indoor section and a pleasant outdoor terrace. The food is simple but tasty Egyptian fare, including meze, kofta and kebab, lentil soup and traditional Egyptian desserts.

Dahabeyya House Boat
Corniche an-Nil
Tel: 086-236 3596. **$**
This recently refurbished old riverboat has been serving well-prepared Egyptian fare for many years, and it is still going

strong. The restaurant is now on the upper deck, and there are a few rooms underneath, though very few people stay here.

Kushari Nagwa $
This is the town's favourite *kushari*, specialising in a tasty mixture of pasta, rice and lentils topped with fried onions and spicy tomato sauce.

Savoy
Maydan al-Mahatta. **$**
A popular restaurant with locals and visitors alike, the Savoy, serves Egyptian fast food such as kebabs, sandwiches and rotisserie chicken with salads. Rapid turnover.

Asyut

Assiutel
146 Shari' an-Nil. Tel: 088-231 2121. **$$**
This hotel restaurant beside the Nile doesn't have a lot of atmosphere but it is one of the best places in Asyut to eat and one of the town's only bars (Asyut being a notoriously conservative city). The food is Egyptian, with roasted meats, meze, *etc*.

Casablanca Sweets
Shari' Muhammad. Tawfik Khashaba. Tel: 088-233 7762. **$**
This is a good place to order Egyptian *fteer*, a tasty cross between a pizza and a pancake which comes

with a range of sweet or savoury fillings. The menu also includes mediocre pizzas and quite good crepes as well as the sweets promised by its name.

Koshari Galal
Shari' Talaat Harb. **$**
This bustling kushari situated in the centre of town is packed with locals from midday through to the evening. Good for a cheap, tasty and filling meal.

Prices for a three-course dinner per person with a half-bottle of house wine:
$ = under $20
$$ = $20–45
$$$ = $45–60
$$$$ = over $60

UPPER EGYPT

The monuments of Upper Egypt are breathtaking.
The great temples of Luxor and Karnak and the funerary
complexes of the west bank form the largest
agglomeration of ancient buildings in the world

D uring the 19th century, as more and more archaeological discoveries were being made and the mystery of hieroglyphics unravelled, wintering in Egypt became fashionable for the well-to-do. They would hire a private houseboat, complete with crew and cook, at the port of Cairo, and sail upstream, stopping here and there to explore the ruins and visit local dignitaries. Their impressions were conscientiously set down day by day in letters home or in morocco-bound diaries, as they sat under the awning on deck, glancing up to watch the palm-fringed shore slipping peacefully by.

Luxor (ancient Thebes) was the high point on their journey, a concentration of magnificent temples and tombs, with comfortable hotels that offered the chance to get off the boat and relax in the superb winter climate.

It is still possible to spend a fulfilling week or two in Luxor, relaxing by the Nile, visiting the temples on the east bank and making forays over to the west bank to see the ancient necropolis of Thebes. But for a truly memorable visit, make time to travel south of Luxor to Aswan, along a 215-km (135-mile) stretch of river that is both picturesque and rich in ancient sites, Esna, Edfu and Kom Ombo all offer spectacular Ptolemaic temples, and Aswan, the regional [capital] and an important university town, [has] one of the most beautiful settings in [Egypt]. It is also the gateway to Africa. [With] fewer monuments it is the ideal

place to end your trip, shopping in the hassle-free suq or circling its many islands with a felucca.

The best time to make the journey is between October and April. Most of the luxury cruise boats run three-, five-, or eight-day trips starting from Luxor or Aswan *(see page 226)*.

LUXOR

Luxor ❾, 675 km (420 miles) south of Cairo, is the most important and the most spectacular site in all Egypt. Al-Uqsur (the Palaces) is the Arabic name for

PREVIOUS PAGES:
balloon rising over
Luxor, with the
Temple of Luxor in
the foreground.
LEFT: Luxor Temple,
with views over to
the West Bank.
LEFT: boat trips.

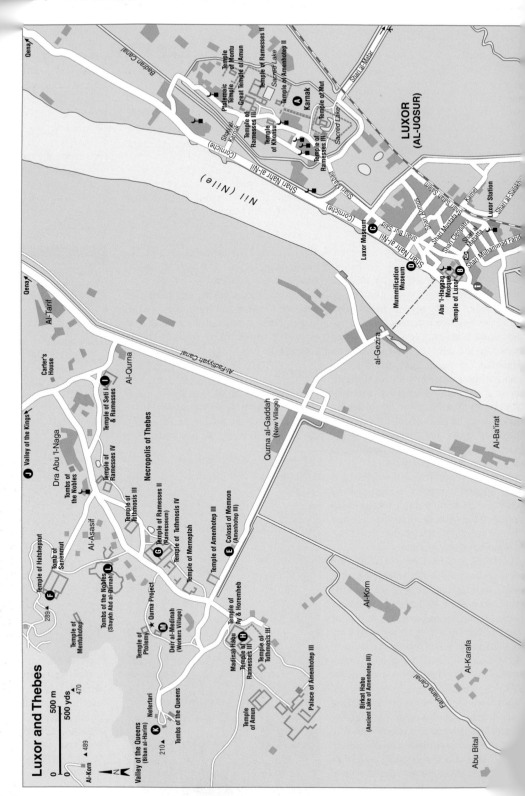

Luxor and Thebes

Qena

Qena

Qena

Badran Canal

Shari' al-Matar

LUXOR
(AL-UQSUR)

Sacred Lake

Temple of Montu

Temple of Ramesses II

Great Temple of Amun

Temple of Amenhotep II

Ptolemaic Temple

Temple of Ramesses III

Temple of Ramesses III

Shari' Karnak

Temple of Khonsu

Temple of Mut

A Karnak

Sacred Lake

Shari' al-Nil (Corniche)

Nil (Nile)

Shari' Karnak

Shari' Nahr al-Nil (Corniche)

Shari' al-Nil (Corniche)

Luxor Station

Shari' al-Salakhr

Shari' Maabad al-Karnak

Shari' al-Salah Salem

G Luxor Museum

Mummification Museum

Shari' Bur Sa'id

Shari' Yusuf

Shari' Mustafa Kamil

Shari' Cleopatra

Saad al-Maabata

D

B Shari' Muhammad Farid

Abu 'l-Haggag Mosque

i

Temple of Luxor

Al-Tarif

al-Gezira

N

Al-Fadliyyah Canal

Carter's House

Al-Qurna

Necropolis of Thebes

Qurna al-Gaddah
(New Village)

Al-Ba'irat

I Valley of the Kings

Dra Abu 'l-Naga

Tombs of the Nobles

Temple of Seti I & Ramesses

Temple of Ramesses IV

Temple of Tuthmosis III

Temple of Ramesses II
(Ramesseum)

J

G

Temple of Tuthmosis IV

Temple of Merneptah

Temple of Amenhotep III

E Colossi of Memnon
(Amenhotep III)

Al-Asasif

Tomb of Senenmut

Temple of Hatshepsut

F

289

Temple of Mentuhotep

Tombs of the Nobles
(Shaykh Abd al-Qurnah)

L

Qurna Project

Temple of Ptolemy

Deir al-Medinah
(Workers' Village)

M

Temple of Ay & Horemheb

Madinat Habu

Temple of Ramesses III

H Temple of Tuthmosis III

Palace of Amenhotep III

Al-Kom

Birkat Habu
(Ancient Lake of Amenhotep III)

Famina Canal

Al-Karafa

Abu Bital

Valley of the Queens
(Biban al-Harim)

K Nefertari

Tombs of the Queens

210

Temple of Amun

470

489

Al-Kom

500 m

500 yds

0

0

N

ancient Thebes, the splendid capital city of the New Kingdom (1570–1070 BC) rulers, whose glory still glowed in the memories of classical writers a thousand years after its decline. Here the booty of foreign wars, tribute and taxes poured into the coffers of the pharaohs of the 18th and 19th dynasties, each of whom surpassed his predecessor in the construction of gorgeous temples and tombs, creating a concentration of monuments that rivals that of any imperial city before or since.

Orientation

The east bank, where the sun rises, was the side of the living, and the location of the two great temple complexes of Luxor and Karnak, the first in today's city centre and the latter a 30-minute walk north. Today, most of the hotels and restaurants, are on the east bank, as well as the suqs, banks and offices. The west bank is the place of the dead, a vast necropolis containing the tombs and mortuary temples of the New Kingdom pharaohs. There are fewer hotels and restaurants on the west side, but it is favoured by independent travellers who want closer contact with the locals or peace and quiet away from the many tour groups.

A ferry (from the landing near Luxor Temple) runs between the east and west banks, and there is also a road bridge, 6 km (4 miles) south of town.

City changes

At the time of writing Luxor was undergoing a major facelift, under a new governor who was keen that the city's visitor facilities should match its monumental splendour. His plans for clearing the areas around the sites have been controversial, particularly the bulldozing of the old village of al-Gurna in the Valley of the Nobles *(see page 219)* and the demolition of 19th-century houses in the centre of Luxor to lay bare the Avenue of Sphinxes connecting Luxor Temple with Karnak.

Good management is certainly needed, as the number of visitors grows larger. Every day in winter the town

is brought to a standstill by more than 100 coach-loads of foreigners visiting the town from the Red Sea resorts, while hundreds of cruise boats, moored several vessels deep, block the view of the Nile. Plans are underway to move parking further away from the sites, and move the moorings for boats south of the town.

This tour of Luxor begins in Luxor itself, visiting Karnak, the Temple of Luxor and the museums, and then crosses the Nile to the west bank.

Luxor's Temples

Under the New Kingdom pharaohs, when Thebes became the seat of power, Amun, once just a local god, took on the qualities of Ra, the sun-god of Heliopolis, becoming Amun-Ra and rising to a position of ascendancy over all the multifarious gods of Egypt. With his consort Mut and his son Khonsu he formed the Theban Triad.

Two tremendous temple complexes were established in honour of these gods, the Temple of Karnak and the Temple of Luxor. Both were built over extensive periods of time and were constructed

TIP

The wealth of sites in and around Luxor make sightseeing both exhilarating and exhausting. To get the most out of your time wear light and loose cotton clothes, comfortable shoes, sunglasses, sunhat and sun lotion, take plenty of water with you, and try to read up on the sights beforehand. A torch for dark corners is also useful.

BELOW: three men wearing *gallabiyahs* in Luxor Temple.

TIP

The Karnak sound and light show, which is one of the best in Egypt, is held three or four times a night. As at the Pyramids, performances are held in different languages, with English performed every night of the week. To get to Karnak in the evening, hire a taxi or calèche. Your driver will wait while you watch. For more information, tel: 02-2386 3469; www. soundandlight.com.eg.

BELOW: Karnak Temple and lake.

from the inside outwards; the original founders built sanctuaries on spots that had probably been venerated for centuries, and successive pharaohs added progressively more grandiose courtyards, gateways and other elaborations.

The temple complex of Amun-Ra at **Karnak Ⓐ**, 3 km (1¾ miles) north of the centre of Luxor (daily 6.30am–5.30pm in winter, 6am–6pm in summer; admission charge; to get there, walk north along the Corniche or take a taxi or calèche) and its neighbouring buildings constitute the most awe-inspiring of all the Egyptian monuments. Apart from the immense conglomeration of elements that makes up the temple itself, it also has a particularly complicated plan. Unlike most other temples in Egypt, it was developed over many centuries on both an east-west axis, with six pylons, and on a north-south axis with four pylons. These 10 pylons, together with intervening courts, halls and enclosures, surround the nucleus of the sanctuary.

Karnak, known as Ipet-Sut, "The Most Esteemed of Places", was one of the most important religious and intellectual centres in antiquity, and for over 13 centuries successive pharaohs were proud to enhance its magnificence.

Put aside two half days to see the most important monuments, one starting early in the morning to be seduced by the temple's mystery, and one in the afternoon when the stones and carvings glow in the sun.

The local god Amun-Ra became more important during the early Middle Kingdom, and during the 12th Dynasty several temples were erected in his honour. Their foundations were found underneath the later temples. The origins of the Karnak Temple as we now see it are attributable to the royal family of the 18th Dynasty (1150–1290 BC), who made Amun-Ra the state god, and whose rise to power brought the city of Thebes to the heights of glory. Three Tuthmoses and Queen Hatshepsut, were responsible for most of the inner parts of the temple.

An avenue of ram-headed sphinxes leads to the unfinished **First Pylon**, built by Nectanebo I during the 30th Dynasty. The **First Court**, enclosed by colonnades on both sides, includes several shrines: the **Temple of Seti II**

Temple Structure

Temples in general all followed the same principles. For the ancient Egyptians the precinct represented a little replica of the cosmos at the time of the creation. It was set apart from the everyday world and demarcated by a mud-brick girdle wall. Usually, but not always, the temple had an east-west axis, so that the rising or setting sun could strike right into its innermost recesses. Giant wedge-shaped pylons or gateways flanked tall gold-plated doors and were decorated on the outside with enormous reliefs of the pharaoh symbolically subduing his enemies.

Within the gates were courtyards, with small kiosks or barque stations (storage places for the boats of Egyptian gods) for visiting gods. Other shrines appeared in later times, including the birth rooms in which the divine progeniture of the pharaoh was established. Before the entrance of the covered part of the temple stood enormous statues of the pharaoh in human or animal form and/or obelisks. Inside was a hypostyle hall with a forest of columns. All was lavishly decorated.

Proceeding through a vestibule into the offering court and then the inner parts of the temple, the ground rises by degrees, the roof gets lower until the sanctuary, which represents the mound of creation, is quite dark. Only the pharaoh and the priests were allowed into this holy of holies, where a gold-plated image of the presiding god was kept.

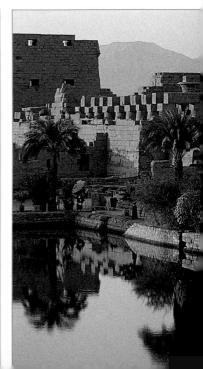

Recommended Restaurants & Bars on pages 234–5

the **Colonnade of Taharga** and the **Temple of Ramesses III**. The **Second Pylon**, built using blocks from earlier structures, leads into one of the architectural marvels of the world, the **Great Hypostyle Hall**. Seti I (1291–1278 BC) completed the mighty work started by Amenhotep III, and built the largest hall of any temple in the world, with 137 huge columns, covering an area of 6,000 sq. metres (19,685 sq. ft). It was completed under Seti's son, Ramesses II (1279–1212 BC), who placed the colossi of himself at the entrance. The northern walls are decorated with remarkable bas- reliefs of Seti I's battles in Syria and Lebanon, while the southern walls show similar themes, in a much cruder style, of Ramesses II's Battle of Kadesh.

Behind the Fourth Pylon lies the inner core and oldest part of the temple, starting with the Hypostyle Hall of Tuthmosis III. In this court stands one of the obelisks erected by his stepmother Hatshepsut (the second toppled over centuries ago and has been placed near the **Sacred Lake** *(see page 216)*. Hatshepsut dominated the family after

her husband and brother Tuthmosis II's death in 1518 BC. Tuthmosis III despised his co-regent/ stepmother, and as soon as she was out of the way proceeded to hack her name away from cartouches, substituting his own. He walled up most of the 320-tonne obelisks that she had erected, thus unwittingly preserving her work in pristine condition.

Tuthmosis III (1504–1450 BC) proceeded to reign long and brilliantly, waging 17 successful campaigns and extending the Egyptian Empire from Syria to the Sudan. He brought back thousands of prisoners and immense quantities of booty, as well as new varieties of trees and plants, new ideas and new fashions. The annals of his career are inscribed on the walls surrounding the **sanctuary** and extend to his great **Festival Hall** and to the southern courts.

Succeeding generations added new pylons, courts and subsidiary temples, all lavishly and colourfully illustrating their conquests, like a great stone history

A calèche heads past Luxor Temple. Caléches are a great way of travelling along Luxor's lengthy Corniche, especially if your cruise boat docks a long way from the centre.

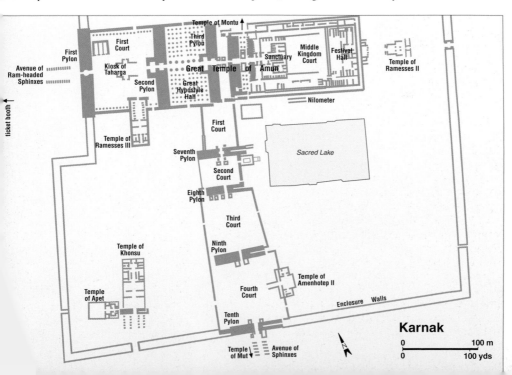

Karnak

0   100 m
0   100 yds

book. Amenhotep III contributed a pylon and the **Temple of Mut**.Though the capital moved away to the Delta and the importance of Thebes declined thereafter, Karnak continued to be expanded and embellished, such was the awe in which Amun-Ra was held. At the end of the Ramesside line the **Temple of Khonsu** was built, in which reliefs clearly show the rise to kingly status of the priests.

In the 6th century BC the Persians did a certain amount of damage when they sacked Thebes, but the incoming Greeks set things to rights. Alexander, his brother Philip Arrhidaeus (who replaced the original sanctuary with one of rose granite), and subsequently the Ptolemies restored and continued to make additions to the temple.

Luxor Temple

Luxor Temple ❸ (daily 6am–9pm, 10pm in summer; admission charge) is relatively long (230 metres/780 ft) and narrow, and lies in the centre of Luxor. Like Karnak Temple, to which it was connected by a 3-km (1¾ mile) long processional Avenue of the Sphinxes,

which is now being excavated, it was dedicated to the Theban Triad, but Amun of Luxor had a slightly different form and function, as a divinely fertile figure. Known as the "Harem of the South", Luxor Temple was the residence of Amun-Ra's consort Mut and her son Khonsu, while the statue of Amun was kept in Karnak. During the annual Opet Festival his statue was brought in a procession of holy barques to be reunited with his wife. Nowadays, during the annual *mouled* (festival) of Abu 'l-Haggag (Luxor's patron saint), feluccas are carried up to the mosque of Abu 'l-Haggag *(see below)* in a ceremony that is a survival of the ancient festival.

Nineteenth-century visitors to Luxor observed that the glorious city of Thebes had shrunk to a miserable village piled on top of metres of dirt and debris. Only the heads of the colossi of Ramesses, half the granite obelisk of Amenhotep and the capitals of the columns were still visible; and even these were battered and blackened with smoke. Excavations of the site started in 1885 when the houses were removed piece by piece, but the people of Luxor took a stand

when it came to removing the mosque of Abu 'l-Haggag, built in 1077, so it was left in situ, hanging above a corner of the courtyard built by Ramesses II. It has recently been restored.

The Temple of Luxor is easier to grasp than Karnak, as it is much smaller and the major part was built by one pharaoh, Amenhotep III (1386–1349 BC), with substantial later additions by his successors. The gigantic **First Pylon** on which were displayed his triumphs, was built by Ramesses II. It was fronted originally with six colossi of the pharaoh, but only one standing and two seated statues remain. One of the obelisks still stands in place, but its twin, presented to the French in 1829 , adorns the place de la Concorde in Paris. **The Great Peristyle Court**, which today incorporates the medieval mosque, was also added by Ramesses II, and in the southern half stand more of his colossal granite statues.

Amenhotep III, who built the **colonnade** with papyrus-bud columns, was succeeded by his son, Akhenaten 1350–1334 BC), the revolutionary pharaoh who moved the capital away from Thebes to Al-Amarnah *(see page 195)*. His reforms collapsed immediately after his death, however, and the capital returned to Thebes, the old hierarchy of priests was re-established, and his successors Tutankhamun and Horemheb dutifully took up the embellishment of the Luxor Temple again. On the walls of the processional colonnade, the skilful sculptors of Tutankhamun depicted the annual Opet Festival *(see pages 210 and the margin note, page 212)* showing the gods of Karnak, accompanied by a procession of priests, musicians, singers, dancers and sacred cows, parading down to Luxor on the west, and going back to their own temple on the east.

During the restoration of the **Second Court**, also built by Amenhotep, a large cache of statues was found, now in the Luxor Museum *(see below)*. Beyond this, the **Hypostyle Hall**, with 32 columns representing papyrus bundles, leads into a smaller hall. In Roman times this was converted into a church, and some of the Christian frescoes are still visible.

The **sanctuary** area dates from the reign of Amenhotep III. In the **Birth Room**, his mother Mutemwia is shown

Karnak's monumental statue of Ramesses II, with one of his daughters nestling at his feet.

BELOW:
the mosque of Abu 'l-Haggag, Luxor Temple.

Temple Columns

You will see two main types of column in Egypt's ancient temples. The first imitate natural vegetation, with bases and capitals shaped like bundles of papyrus or lotus flowers (depicted either closed or open) or palms (very common in the Ptolemaic temples). Sometimes, in hypostyle halls, they are clustered thickly together to represent the marsh of creation, a conception that was often completed by a ceiling adorned with pictures of heavenly bodies to recreate the sky. Some of the best examples of vegetal columns are found in the hypostyle halls in the Karnak and Luxor temples.

The second type of column is the more functional polygonal column, an early form of the Doric column, often with fluted sides.

Relief showing the Opet Festival on the colonnade in the Temple of Luxor. During the festival the sacred statue of the god Amun-Re was taken out of the sanctuary at Karnak and transported by sacred barge to the Temple of Luxor.

BELOW: *shabti* from the tomb of Tutankhamun in Luxor Museum.

being impregnated by Amun and giving birth to the infant pharaoh, whose body and spirit are formed on the potter's wheel by the ram-headed creator-god Khnum. The facts of life are indicated with delicate symbolism. A return to the floodlit temple at night allows one to take a better look at its magnificent reliefs.

Luxor Museum

Luxor Museum ⓒ (daily; 9am–1pm and 5–10pm in summer, 9am– 9pm in winter; admission charge), north along the Corniche, houses a small but impressive collection found in the Luxor area. The objects have been carefully placed and lit, and are well labelled, so that every single item looks like a masterpiece. Most of the museum's ground floor is dedicated to the period of the New Kingdom, and works include a beautiful bust of the young pharaoh Tuthmosis III and a fine wall painting of Amenophis III. A new wing is devoted to the glory of

Thebes during the New Kingdom and two royal mummies.

The upper floor of the museum has interesting reliefs from Akhenaten's temple in Karnak as well as spectacular heads of the same pharaoh in the typical Amarnah style *(see page 42)*, and a variety of smaller objects found in Tutankhamun's tomb, including *shabti (see picture below)*, models of servants that were intended to serve the pharaoh in the afterlife). In 1989 excavations in Luxor Temple, near the Birth Room of Amenophis III, revealed an important cache of statues, now displayed in the museum's **New Hall** (extra admission charge).

Mummification Museum

The **Mummification Museum** ⓓ (daily 9am–1pm and 4–9pm winter, 9am–1pm and 5–10pm summer; admission charge) houses a 21st-Dynasty mummy and a well-documented array of tools and materials used in the ancient art of mummification, including the tools to extract the vital organs and the Canopic jars in which the removed lungs, stomach, intestines and liver were placed. Only the heart – considered to be the essence of a

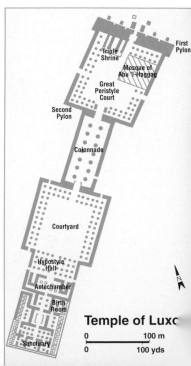

Triple Shrine

First Pylon

Mosque of Abu 'l-Haggag

Great Peristyle Court

Second Pylon

Colonnade

Courtyard

Hypostyle Hall

Antechamber

Birth Room

Temple of Luxor

Sanctuary

0   100 m
0   100 yds

human being – was left inside the body, ready to be weighed by Anubis against the feather of truth in the afterlife. There were four jars in all, each presided over by a son of Horus: Amset, human-headed; Hapi, baboon-headed; Duamutef, dog-headed, and Qebehnsenuf, hawk-headed.

Also on display are some of the more essential goods the deceased would want on the final journey to the other world; familiar from other museums in Egypt, their function is finally made clear.

The west bank

The Nile valley is wide at Luxor and the mysterious pink limestone mountains about 4 km (2½ miles) across the lush green plain west of the Nile are so honeycombed with treasures and secrets, that the average day or two spent among them is unlikely to be enough.

The west bank of the Nile was the necropolis of Thebes for more than 3,000 years. The New Kingdom pharaohs chose to be buried in the hidden Valley of the Kings, and they built their mortuary temples on the edge of the cultivation so that they would be remembered for eternity. The queens and royal children were buried in the nearby Valley of the Queens, the nobles and courtiers in the Tombs of the Nobles, and even the workers who laboured on the royal tombs had their own cemetery, the Workers' Village, known as Deir al-Medinah. Most of the tombs were cut deep in the rock, hidden in the valleys of the Western Desert hills.

Getting to the west bank

The west bank can be reached by local ferry (last ferry back 9.30pm in winter, 11pm in summer) from the landing opposite Luxor Temple, or by taking one of the launches for private hire moored along the bank. From the ferry landing you can either take a taxi for the day to transport you from site to site or rent a bicycle. (Note that it does get very hot in summer and cycling is only advisable between October and May).

Alternatively, a bridge, 6 km (3.5 miles) south of Luxor town, connects the east and west banks and makes it possible to visit the west bank by taxi from Luxor: the journey can take between half an hour and an hour.

An early start is recommended: the

Canopic jar in Luxor's Mummification Museum. The jars were used to store the body's organs, extracted from the body via a hole in the skull.

BELOW:
the Valley of the Nobles in the hills of the west bank.

Queen Hatshepsut, the only female pharaoh, was thought to have been the daughter, sister, wife and stepmother of the first three Tuthmosis. Hatshepsut reigned for 15 years.

BELOW: Temple of Hatshepsut.

monuments are better seen by oblique sunlight rather than direct vertical rays and the convoys of tour buses from the Red Sea won't have arrived (they get there around 10.30am).

Part of the governor's new plan is that each of the west bank's sites will have its own ticket office, but at the time of writing tickets for most of the site – except for the temple at Deir al-Bahari, the Valley of the Queens and the Valley of the Kings – were obtained from the ticket booth beside the Antiquities Inspectorate's office at the crossroads beyond the Colossi of Memnon; check if this is still the case when you get there. All sites are open daily 6am–4pm, until 5pm from June–Sept unless otherwise stated, and an admission charge is payable for each one.

Mortuary temples

The pharaohs of the 18th Dynasty broke with the pyramid tradition and began to hide their tombs deep in the mountainside, hoping to elude tomb robbers. On the edge of the valley, at some distance from their resting places, each pharaoh constructed his own mortuary temple.

The mortuary temples of Hatshepsut, Seti I, Ramesses II and Ramesses III still stand (those of other pharaohs have mostly collapsed). The two **Colossi of Memnon** , standing in the fields by the side of the road, are the most visible reminder of the Temple of Amenhotep III, the famous Memnon. After the one on the right was hit by an earthquake in 27 BC, it made a gentle singing noise at dawn which the Greeks believed to be Memnon singing for his mother Eos. The Roman emperor Septimus Severus had it restored in AD 199, after which the singing stopped.

Temple of Hatshepsut

The **Temple of Hatshepsut** (1498– 1483 BC) is somewhat different from the other temples, being set back in a spectacular natural amphitheatre. Three gracefully proportioned and colonnaded terraces are connected by sloping ramps. The sanctuary areas are backed up against the mountain and partially hollowed out of the rocks. On first approach the temple looks strangely modern, but it is easy to imagine how grand the complex must have been when

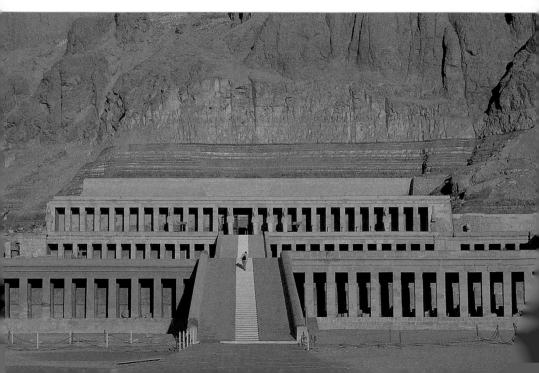

he courts were filled with perfumed plants, fountains and myrrh trees.

Hatshepsut's divine birth and exploits are recorded on the walls behind the colonnades of her temple. They include an expedition to Punt in Somalia, from where frankincense trees, giraffes and other exotica were brought back to Egypt. The cutting and transportation of the two great obelisks set up by Hatshepsut at Karnak are also recorded. The temple was designed by Senenmut, evidently a great favourite of the queen. His portrait is hidden behind a door; and his own tomb is nearby

The upper ramp has opened again after many years of restoration. The sanctuaries of Hatshepsut and of the sun how some fine reliefs, while the central sanctuary of Amun, dug into the rock, points towards her tomb in the Valley of the Kings. It was at this temple, in 1997, that 58 foreigners and four Egyptians were gunned down by Islamic terrorists.

The Ramesseum

Some of Ramesses II's (1279–1212 BC) mortuary temple, the **Ramesseum Ⓖ**, is in ruins, but like other monuments of this pharaoh (who reigned for over 60 years and had 80 children) what remains is majestic. In front of the Hypostyle Hall lie parts of the largest granite colossus on record, the statue of Ozymandias (Ramesses' coronation name) which inspired the poet Shelley in his poem *Ozymandias*:

I met a traveller from an antique land who said:
Two vast and trunkless legs of stone
Stand in the desert...
And on the pedestal these words appear:
'My name is Ozymandias, King of Kings:
Look on my work, ye mighty, and despair!"
Nothing beside remains. Round the decay
Of that colossal wreck, boundless and bare
The lone and level sands stretch far away.

One foot alone measures 3.3 metres (11 ft). The famous Battle of Kadesh (1274 BC) is depicted on the pylons. More

interestingly is a representation of Thoth, the ibis-headed secretary god *(see pages 46–7)* writing Ramesses' name on the leaves of the sacred tree. Vestiges of the adjoining palace where the king came to spend a few days supervising work on his "Mansion of Eternity" can be seen.

Madinat Habu

Ramesses III (1182–1151 BC), however, is not eclipsed by his famous forebear. Although he modelled his mortuary temple, **Madinat Habu Ⓗ** (daily; 8am–5pm in summer; admission charge), 1 km (⅔ mile) southwest of the Ramesseum, on that of his father's, the scale of it is even more extravagant. The surrounding mudbrick walls may have partly collapsed but the temple is one of the best-preserved in Egypt, and the easiest to understand as it reflects all the principles of the classical temple. In ancient times it was known as the "Mansion of Millions of Years".

The temple is not on the tour-group circuit, and in fact not much visited at all. In the late afternoon, in the last glow of the sun, one can still feel something of the awe and spirituality the place

Ceiling in the Ramesseum depicting Ramesses II with Amun.

BELOW: head of Ramesses II at the Ramesseum.

BELOW: the Ramesseum.

must have inspired in ancient times.

The enclosure is entered through the Syrian-style gatehouse from which stairs lead to the pharaoh's private apartments (closed at the time of writing). The grand **First Pylon** is decorated with reliefs glorifiying the king's military victories. Religious ceremonies took place in the First Court, flanked by colonnades on either side. On the south side the colonnade with papyrus columns formed the facade of the adjoining Royal Palace. Coptic Christians later used the Second Court as a church and carved their symbols on the pillars, but a few Osiris figures survived as well as coloured reliefs under the western colonnade. Only the lower part of later buildings remains; the upper part, including three small hypostyle halls and 52 side chambers, was used as a quarry by builders.

To the right of the entrance portal is a small **18th-Dynasty temple**, the oldest part of this complex, which is built over even earlier structures. The site of Madinat Habu enclosed the sacred site known as the Mound of Djeme, where it was believed the eight gods of creation were buried. Further east is a **Sacred Lake**.

Mortuary temple of Seti I

The well-restored small **Mortuary Temple of Seti I**  is where 19th-century visitors began their west-bank tour, and it was a favourite subject for painters, but these days it is well off the beaten track and rarely visited. The setting is wonderful, overlooking a palm grove, and the visitor finds a tranquillity that may have reigned in these sacred places in ancient times. Built by Seti I (1294–1279 BC), who also built the great Hypostyle Hall at Karnak and the superbly decorated temple at Abydos, it was dedicated to the worship of Amun and of Ramesses I. The first and second pylons and court are ruined, but the remaining walls have some exquisitely executed reliefs. Off the Hypostyle Hall are six shrines and a small chapel dedicated to Ramesses I, Seti's father, who died before having built his own mortuary temple. Archaeologists have recently found the earliest example of a palace within a memorial temple, as in the temple at Madinet Habu.

Valley of the Kings

After being embalmed and mummified the New Kingdom pharaohs were transported in solemn cortège to the **Valley of the Kings** , hidden in a secluded wadi in the Theban hills. They were buried in rock-cut tombs, bedecked with gold and jewels, and surrounded by treasures and replicas of all they would need in the afterlife.

As soon as a pharaoh ascended to the throne, he would begin to build his tomb which was intended to preserve the royal mummy for eternity. However, many died before the lavish decoration of their tomb was finished, which now gives an interesting insight into the different stages of the whole process. Although serious precautions were made to dissuade intruders, the treasures hidden inside were too much of an attraction to be left alone. As the power of the rulers of the 20th Dynasty decreased, breaking into tombs became commonplace, mainly by the craftsmen who had worked in them or by the supervisors themselves. B

the end of the New Kingdom the priests reburied the mummies in secret caches in the surrounding mountains, which were not discovered until the end of the 19th century.

The visitors centre

The entrance to the valley is now from the new **visitors centre** (6am–4pm in winter, until 5pm in summer; the standard ticket is valid for three tombs, and extra tickets are required for the tombs of Tutankhamun and Ay). In the air-conditioned hall, guides explain the history behind the Valley of the Kings, while visitors can see a model of the site, use the computers to find out more information or watch a short film about Howard Carter's discovery of Tutankhamun's tomb. A noddy train (another ticket) then takes visitors about 500 metres/yds to the entrance of the valley, but it is easy enough to walk.

There are 63 principal tombs, and undoubtedly more to be discovered. In most of the tombs, long, elaborately decorated corridors lead down through a series of chambers and false doors to the burial vault. The entrance passage is painted with texts and illustrations from mortuary literature and the *Book of the Dead*. In this, the pharaoh takes his last journey, passing through the 12 gates of the 12 hours of the night, beset by serpents, crocodiles and other malevolent beings. He arrives at the Court of Osiris where he is met by a delegation of gods; he makes his confession and his heart is weighed for its truthfulness and purity. A hideous monster waits to devour him should he fail the test but, evading the torments of hell, he is eventually received into the company of heaven.

Only a few of the tombs are open to the public at one time, as a rotation system has been introduced to protect the tomb walls from further deterioration caused by flashlights and respiration.

The Tomb of Seti I

The finest and largest tomb in the valley, now seemingly permanently closed to the public, is the **tomb of Seti I**. Like the carvings in his temple at Abydos *(see page 199)*, the tomb's walls are decorated with magnificent, subtly coloured reliefs, and the anteroom to the burial chamber has an important

Visiting the Valley of the Kings by donkey. The enclosed valley is extremely hot, so bring plenty of water, and a parasol or an umbrella for shade.

BELOW: the Theban necropolis is hot, stony and barren.

astronomical ceiling. The sarcophagus is now in the Sir John Soane Museum in London, and the mummy in the Egyptian Museum in Cairo.

The tomb of Tutankhamun

Only one of all these tombs miraculously escaped the attention of tomb robbers, who were already ransacking them within just a few years of their construction. The famous small **tomb of Tutankhamun** (1334–1325 BC), the boy-king, was not discovered until 1922, when Howard Carter, under the patronage of Lord Carnarvon, chanced upon it after a search of seven long years. The tomb (additional admission charge) contained over 5,000 precious objects buried with the young pharaoh, whose embalmed remains were still in situ in a complex system of gold and bejewelled mummy cases and coffins within coffins. A gilded chariot, beds, chairs, stools and headrests covered in gold leaf, alabaster lamps and vases, weapons, sandals, statues of servants *(see picture on page 212)*, amulets and all kinds of other objects in perfect condition were crammed into the small space of the tomb. The majority of the treasure is now in the Egyptian Museum in Cairo. This tomb, more than others because it is one of the smallest, has suffered from its popularity, and the colours have suffered from humidity caused by respiration.

The tombs of the Ramesses

Ramesses I ruled for only one year so his tomb is a simple affair, but the decoration in the burial chamber is superb with scenes of the pharaoh hanging out with the gods and extracts from the Book of Gates. The **tomb of Ramesses II** is the largest in the valley (his 67-year reign gave him plenty of time to work on it). Unfortunately he chose the wrong location as the tomb has been flash-flooded several times, and the decoration is in bad condition.

The longest tomb was built by **Ramesses III** and has beautiful painted sunken reliefs representing the various ritual texts. Closest to the entrance is the **tomb of Ramesses IV**, who died before finishing it. The tomb was robbed in antiquity and the paintings are not in good condition, but it has the valley's

> *A gasp of wonderment escaped our lips, so gorgeous was the sight that met our eyes: a golden effigy of the young boy-king, of most magnificent workmanship.*
>
> Howard Carter

BELOW RIGHT: the entrance to the tomb of Tutankhamun.

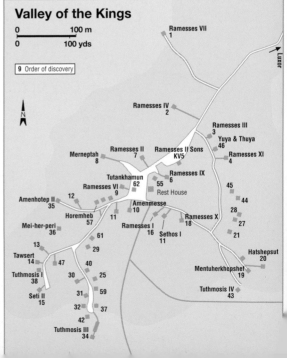

Valley of the Kings

0 — 100 m
0 — 100 yds

9 Order of discovery

Ramesses VII 1
Ramesses IV 2
Ramesses III 3
Yuya & Thuya 46
Ramesses XI 4
Merneptah 8
Ramesses II 7
Ramesses II Sons KV5
Ramesses IX 6
Tutankhamun 62
55
45
Ramesses VI 9
Rest House
44
Amenhotep II 35
12
Amenmesse 10
28
Horemheb 57
11
Ramesses X 18
27
Mei-her-peri 36
Ramesses I 16
21
61
Sethos I 11
13
29
Hatshepsut 20
Tawsert 14
47
40
Mentuherkhopshef 19
Tuthmosis I 38
30
25
Tuthmosis IV 43
Seti II 15
31
59
32
37
42
Tuthmosis III 34

Luxor

only image of the goddess Nut swallowing and spitting out the sun every day. The **tomb of Ramesses VI** has some fine astronomical scenes. The most visited tomb is that of **Ramesses IX**, which has colourful paintings from the Book of the Dead.

Other outstanding tombs

One of the earliest tombs open to the public belonged to **Thutmosis III**, but it takes quite a climb to reach it. It is unusual in that the decoration resembles the early papyri, and it looks almost like a cartoon. The **tomb of Tuthmosis IV** was also discovered by Howard Carter and it was the first tomb to use the technique of appying paint onto a yellow background.

The second-largest tomb in the valley, which belonged to Ramesses II's son **Merneptah**, has well-preserved reliefs in the upper part of the tomb.

The **tomb of Horemheb** was filled with furniture (now in the Egyptian Museum in Cairo). A steep flight of steps leads to a shaft decorated with images of Horemheb facing the gods.

The **tomb of Ay** (admission charge) lies 2 km (1¼ miles) up a dirt track, but it is worth seeing if it is open: the burial chamber has some spectacular scenes of hunting and fishing in the marshes.

Valley of the Queens

The royal wives were buried in the **Valley of the Queens Ⓚ** in the hills behind Madinat Habu. Very few are open to the public, but in 1995 the restored **tomb of Nefertari**, one of the most impressive monuments on the west bank, was opened for the first time since its discovery in 1904, albeit to a maximum of 150 people a day (it is again closed at the time of writing). Also buried in the valley are a number of princes thought to have been killed in a smallpox epidemic, including the nine-year-old son of Ramesses III. The young boy is shown being led by his father to meet the gods.

Tombs of the Nobles

Unlike royalty, who were buried with great solemnity, the priests, scribes and dignitaries of the court, whose tombs are scattered in the sandy foothills, departed this world surrounded with scenes of the joyous good living to which they had apparently been accustomed during their

TIP

The most recently discovered tomb in the Valley of the Kings, KV5 (the largest so far), a burial place for Ramesses II's many sons, with at least 110 chambers, was discovered in May 1995 (the excavation continues). To find out about the latest archaeological finds, log onto the website of the Theban Mapping Project: www.theba mappingproject.com.

BELOW: the tomb of the boy-king Tutankhamun.

TIP

The Tombs of the nobles are far less visited than those of the kings, but still well worth seeing. They are divided into five groups and each group requires a separate ticket (currently available from the Antiquities Inspectorate's Office *(see page 214)*.

BELOW: tomb painting of weeping women in the unfinished but finely decorated tomb of Ramose, Valley of the Nobles.

lifetime. Thousands of private **nobles' tombs** , from the 6th Dynasty to the Greco-Roman period, with the majority from the New Kingdom period, were found, but only about 19 are open to the public. Most consist of three rooms with a forecourt, a covered columned hall and a smaller room with niches in which were placed statues of the deceased. Many of the nobles's tombs are vividly painted with naturalistic scenes of agriculture, fishing, fowling, feasting and celebrating, thereby constituting a fascinating record of everyday life in ancient Egypt. Offerings were presented to the deceased in the court outside the tomb.

Tombs of Menna and Nakht

The **tomb of Menna** is tiny, but the decoration is extremely colourful and innovative, with the agricultural scenes particularly detailed and lively, as befits Menna's role as a scribe and overseer of the agricultural activities on the royal lands during the 18th Dynasty. The **tomb of Nakht** was possible decorated by the same artist. Though cramped, it is beautifully painted with scenes of a funerary banquet and agricultural tasks

such as ploughing and sowing. Nakht was a scribe and astronomer in the Temple of Amun in Karnak.

Tombs of Ramose, Userhet and Khaemwet

The decorations in the **tomb of Ramose**, although unfinished, reflect the fact that he was a governor of Thebes under both Amenhotep III and his son Akhenaten. While the walls show exquisite carvings in the style of the former, some low reliefs on the back wall reveal a clear influence from the Amarnah style.

Userhet was a scribe responsible for inventorying the wheat in the royal bakeries. The walls in this tomb are somewhat damaged but there are some unusual scenes of cattle branding and hunting. The decorations in **Khaemwet's tomb** are similar to those in the tomb of Ramose, but he added scenes particular to his function as overseer of granaries and the royal scribe.

Tombs of Sennufer and Rekhmire

Rekhmire was a vizier of Upper Egypt and mayor of Thebes during the reign of

Al-Qurna and the Tomb Robbers

The village of al-Qurna was built on top of the tombs of the Nobles, a situation that dated back to the early 19th century when locals providing services to European archaeologists excavating the Theban necropolis settled around the tombs. Inevitably, stories were rife about tomb robberies, and some villagers were rumoured even to have direct access to the tombs from their houses.

The Egyptian Government tried through the latter part of the 20th century to remove the villagers, and the world-famous Egyptian architect Hassan Fathy even designed a brand-new village for them at New Qurna, which still stands beside the road past the ferry landing, rather the worse for wear.

However, eventually, sewage from the village was deemed to be damaging the tombs, and in 2007 the governor of Luxor bulldozed al-Qurna's beautifully painted mud-brick houses, which had been part of the picturesque scenery of the west bank, almost overnight. The villagers were offered new houses several kilometres north of the Valley of the Kings. While some 3,500 families – eager to have their own homes rather than having to share with extended family as is the tradition in rural Egypt – accepted the offer, many members of the older generation still refused to go and were forced into much smaller concrete houses.

Tuthmosis III and Amenhotep II, a period of incredible prosperity for Egypt. He oversaw many great projects. Reflecting his status, his tomb is decorated with the finest paintings of arts and crafts, daily life and burial rituals. The **tomb of Sennufer**, mayor of Thebes and overseer of the Garden of Amon, has similar scenes and a ceiling painted with a vine laden with black grapes. It is an intimate tomb, giving a clear impression of the love between the deceased and his wife.

Tombs of Khonsu, Userhet and Benja

The decorations in these small tombs is fairly conventional with standard scenes of agriculture, hunting and offerings.

Tombs of Neferronpet and Nefersekheru

Also known as the **Khoka tombs**, these tombs, set apart from the others, belong to the New Kingdom scribes. They are brightly painted with strong yellow, blue and red tones. Their wives feature more prominently here than in other tombs. The adjacent tomb of Dhutmosi is closed to the public.

Deir al-Medinah, the Workers' Village

For some 500 years the village of Pa Demi (the Village) or Ta Set Ma'at (the Place of Truth) housed a community of architects, masons, painters and decorators who were kept segregated from the rest of the population for generations, in an effort to keep the whereabouts of the treasure-filled royal tombs a secret.

In Christian times, the small Ptolemaic **Temple of Hathor**, still there today, was occupied by early Christian monks, which is why the village became known as **Deir al-Medinah** Ⓜ, "Monastery of the City". There are very detailed records of the relatively humble lives of the 50 families of the workmen in the village, their salary and their work schedule.

Archaeologists have uncovered more than 70 houses here and many tombs, which the workmen decorated in their spare time. The most interesting is the **tomb of Sennedjem**, an artist who lived under the reign of Seti I; the paintings of everyday life in his tomb are exquisite. Other tombs worth visiting belong to **Peshedu and Ipy**.

BELOW:
tomb of Anerkhe, Deir al-Medinah.

The grape harvest, one of many agricultural details on the walls of the tomb of Paheri, al-Kab.

SOUTH OF LUXOR

The 215 km (135 miles) between Luxor and Aswan is one of the loveliest stretches of the Nile, and the best and most popular way of seeing it is from the deck of a cruise boat, with stops at the various sights along the way. The strip of fertile agricultural land on either side of the river becomes ever narrower, until it more or less gives way to the desert closer to Aswan.

The towns are still relatively small and picturesque: fishermen beating the water to scare the fish into a net, water buffalos wallowing in the mud, palm groves, farmers tilling the land with the same tools you see depicted in the tomb carvings. Most of the splendid monuments, temples and tombs date from the Greco-Roman period, but there are a few much older sites, including the remains of one of the oldest temples in Egypt, at al-Kab, and the quarry at Gebel Silsilla from which came the stone used in the temples in Luxor.

Esna

The small rural town of **Esna** ❿ lies 50 km (30 miles) south of Luxor and is built over the ruins of the **Temple of Khnum** (daily 6am–4pm Oct–May, until 5pm in summer; admission charge). A tourist suq leads from the Nile to the entrance of the temple. Only the Hypostyle Hall has been excavated and its foundation level is 8 metres (27 ft) below that of the street, an indication of the sand and debris that have piled up over the centuries since the temple was abandoned in the Roman period. Originally the temple would have been the same size as the temple in Edfu *(see page 223)* or Dendarah *(see page 200)*.

The temple is dedicated to the creator god Khnum, the main god of Esna, and it was built over an older structure by Ptolemy VI. The Romans added the **Hypostyle Hall**, which has 24 columns

with richly decorated floral capitals. It contains interesting reliefs and inscriptions, including the names and activities of Ptolemies and Roman emperors up until the time of Decius, murdered in AD 249. On the walls the emperors, dressed as pharaohs, are seen before the various gods of Esna, carrying out rituals related to the construction of the temple. French archaeologists have deciphered many details of the rituals of the worship of Khnum, as well as a calendar specifying when and how to celebrate. Just next to the temple is an old caravanserai, and south is a sesame oil press and the local suq.

Al-Kab

The site of **al-Kab** ⓫ (daily 8am–4pm Oct–May, until 5pm in summer; admission charge), ancient Nekheb, is 26 km (15.6 miles) south of Esna, and at the time of writing can only be visited by felucca or dahabeeyah, as the road convoy *(see box below)* is not allowed to stop here. In pre- and early dynastic times this was the capital of ancient Egypt, and the city's main goddess was the vulture goddess Nekhbet. The ruins of Nekheb are surrounded by an impressive mud-brick wall, and include several temples. Across the road, 500 metres/yds north of the ruins are several interesting rock tombs, mainly of local notables from the early 18th Dynasty. The **tomb of Paheri** has some colourful agricultural scenes. The **tomb of Setau** is similar even though it is 400 years younger than most of the other tombs here. In the desert east of Nekheb are several other temples and sanctuaries from the same period.

Edfu

A further 20 km (12 miles) south, on the west bank of the Nile, is the pleasant market town of **Edfu** ⓬. The Greeks called it Apollonopolis as the sun-god Horus-Apollo was worshipped here, for it was believed to be the spot where Horus won a major battle with the evil Seth to avenge his father Osiris *(see page 40)*. The Ptolemaic **Temple of Horus** (daily 7am–7pm in winter, until 8pm in summer; admission charge) is the most complete in Egypt and is in near-perfect condition, with its great pylon, exterior walls, courts, halls and sanctuary all in place. On the outer walls building is

Granite statue of Horus, the falcon god, one of two flanking the entrance through the pylon at the Temple of Horus in Edfu.

BELOW LEFT: visiting the Temple of Edfu. **BELOW:** docking beside Kom Ombo.

Travelling Between Luxor and Aswan

Most of the luxury cruise boats run three-, five-, or eight-day trips starting from Luxor or Aswan. Facilities and services vary from boat to boat, but most have well-trained guides speaking several languages. For the Egyptology buff, there are select tours led by university lecturers and archaeologists.

There are certain advantages to travelling between Luxor and Aswan by private taxi, but as long as it is necessary, under current regulations, to travel in military convoys, you should expect to see the sites in less than ideal conditions. It is only possible to have an hour-long stop at Edfu Temple, and this will be in the company of many other tourists, plus a short visit to Kom Ombo Temple.

Esna can be visited by convoy from Luxor, returning to Luxor by joining the afternoon convoy from Aswan, while sites such as Gebel Silsilla and al-Kab are only accessible by felucca or by dahabeeyah, as even the big cruise boats are not allowed to stop there.

Column from the Ptolemaic Temple of Kom Ombo. The temple's reliefs and decoration are among the most remarkable in Egypt, with traces of the original colour still evident.

BELOW: Gebel Silsilla.

recorded as having begun in 237 BC by Ptolemy III Euergetes (246–221 BC), and continued until decoration of the outer walls was finished in 57 BC. Built over a much older sanctuary, it was definitely one of the last attempts to build on a grand scale.

The massive First Pylon has carvings of King Neos Dionysos holding his enemies by the hair, in front of Horus and his wife Hathor. Regal carved-granite sparrowhawks, representing Horus, stand sentinel at the doors. The Court of Offerings has 32 columns with beautiful palm and flower capitals, and the walls are decorated with scenes of various festivals: the mock battle commemorating the victory of Horus over Seth; the joyful annual wedding visit of Hathor, who journeyed upriver from Dendarah to be reunited with her spouse, and the annual coronation of the reigning monarch who identified with Horus. A vestibule leads to a smaller and darker inner hypostyle hall, which has several antechambers with fine wall carvings, including one room, often thought to be a laboratory, with recipes for perfumes and ointments used in the

rituals carved into the walls. The sanctuary of Horus has the granite shrine that once contained the gold statue of Horus. In the eastern enclosure wall is a Nilometer which showed the level of the Nile flood, and thus helped predict the agricultural yield and taxes for the year ahead.

Gebel Silsilla

The Nile tapers to one of its narrowest points in Egypt at **Gebel Silsilla** ⓭, 42 km (25 miles) south of Edfu, known as Khenu, "Place of Rowing" in ancient times. It was an important centre for the cult of the Nile, as the current was very strong here during the inundation season. Stone from its sandstone quarries was used for the temples in Luxor.

The landscape is riddled with shrines, inscriptions and chapels left by pharaohs from different periods. The most impressive of these is the rock-cut chapel (furthest north) of **Speos of Horemheb** (1323–1295 BC). On the southern side of the site is a massive rock pillar, known as capstan, believed to have once had a chain around it that connected the east and west bank (hence the name *silsilla*, Arabic for chain). The only way to get to Gebel Silsilla at present is by felucca or dahabeeyah.

Kom Ombo

Kom Ombo ⓮ is situated 40 km (24 miles) north of Aswan, on a sandy bank where crocodiles used to sun themselves. The ancient city of Ombos owes its existence to its strategic position, on a promontory in a sweeping bend in the Nile, and to its role as an important stop on the caravan routes from Nubia to Egypt. Gold, copper, camels and African elephants were all traded here. It became more important during Ptolemaic times, when several temples were built in the city.

Most of the city is unexcavated, except for the **Temple of Haroeris and Sobek** (daily 7am–4pm in winter; until 5pm in summer admission charge), unusually dedicated to two gods: the falcon-headed god Haroeris, or Horus the Elder, and the crocodile god Sobek. Older structures

have been found on the site but the main temple was built by Ptolemy VI Philometer, while the decoration was finished by Ptolemy XII Neos Dionysos (80–58 BC and 55–51 BC).

The temple looks glorious seen from the river, despite the fact that part of the Roman forecourt has fallen into the river and parts of the rear of the temple are roofless. It is built on a double plan with symmetrical twin sanctuaries for Haroeris to the north and Sobek to the south of the central axis. South of the temple wall, near the entrance, is a small shrine to Hathor, in which are stored some mummified crocodiles found in a sacred animal necropolis nearby. Across the court is a birth house, with reliefs of Ptolemy VIII Euergetes's divine birth, and a small sacred lake where crocodiles were most probably raised.

There is a black diorite offering table for both gods in the middle of the forecourt. Two portals lead into the outer Hypostyle Hall, which has 10 columns with floral capitals and especially fine carvings. On the left-hand side is a very fine relief of Neos Dionysos being presented to Haroeris by the lion-headed goddess Raettawy and Isis under the guarding eye of Thoth.

From here, two doors lead into a shared inner hypostyle hall where the roof was supported by 10 papyrus columns. The walls here have reliefs showing Euergetes II and his sister Cleopatra VII in front of the gods. Three further vestibules are also decorated with beautiful reliefs, particularly on the rear wall of the third hall where there is a splendid carving of Philometer and Cleopatra standing in front of the moon god Khonsu, and Haroeris and Sobek. Only the foundations remain of the sanctuary of Sobek and Haroeris but behind them lies the inner temple gallery with seven chambers, closed to the public. On the walls of the outer temple gallery is a carving of medical instruments used in ancient times.

Daraw's Sunday-morning camel market is one of the biggest in north Africa.

Daraw, the camel market

The dusty town of **Daraw** on the road from Kom Ombo to Aswan (40 km/25 miles north of Aswan) distinguishes itself by hosting one of Egypt's largest camel markets (Souq el-Gimaal). Although this is a daily event, the best

BELOW: carving at Kom Ombo.

time to come is on Sunday morning (6.30am–2pm) when there are hundreds of camels and the market attracts huge numbers of traders. The camels are brought from the Sudan by the Sudanese and Rachidia herdsmen, through the Libyan Desert. This trail, known as the Darb al-Arba'in or the Forty Days Road, is one of the last surviving trading routes through the desert.

ASWAN

Ivory, ebony, rose and gold are the defining colours of **Aswan** ❶❺ (215 km/135 miles south of Luxor). Here, a wild jumble of glistening igneous rocks, strewn across the Nile, creates narrows between the highlands of the Eastern Desert and the sandy wastes of the Sahara. The barrier to navigation is known as the First Cataract; it was once where the civilised world stopped.

Aswan, for many at the end of a Nile trip, is a laid-back warm town where it is good to linger for a few days. The city has grown immensely in recent years, but the part to visit is still largely strewn along the Nile and on the islands. The suqs are more relaxed and less pushy

than in other Egyptian towns, and there is definitely a hint of Africa in the souvenirs for sale. Taking a felucca around the islands, sniffing the scents of the botanical garden and listening to the Nubian children sing is the perfect way to watch the sun go down behind the desert on the other side. Further south are some beaches where it is safe to swim on a hot day and you can roll down a sand dune.

Aswan is more than a tourist town it is the lively capital of the governorate and an important university town. To confirm its African identity the city now also has the Africa University for the study of African culture and science.

During the Old Kingdom a few travellers ventured further up the Nile in quest of gold, slaves and the occasional pygmy, leaving records of their missions inscribed on the rocks among the islands, but most expeditions were to Elephantine *(see page 229)*, the island in the middle of the river at the foot of the cataract. Yebu, the main town on the island, was the Old Kingdom border town, and as the Nile was believed to spring up from under the First Cataract,

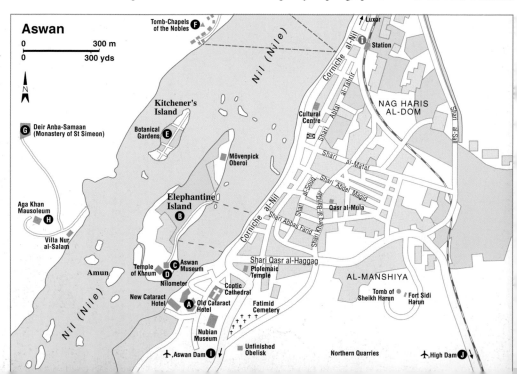

it was also an important religious centre.

The excellent winter climate and beautiful setting of Aswan were well-known in the classical world and were described by several writers. They mentioned the temples, the garden and the vineyards of Elephantine, which were supposed to produce grapes all the year round. Both the Ptolemies and the Romans maintained garrisons at this distant southern outpost.

The greatest geographer in antiquity, Eratosthenes (273–192 BC), who held a post as librarian in Alexandria under the Ptolemies, established the approximate circumference of the earth from astronomical observations made at Elephantine and Alexandria. He noted that at the summer solstice the sun's rays fell vertically to the bottom of a well at Elephantine, whereas on the same day in Alexandria an upright stake cast a shadow, indicating that the sun was seven degrees from its zenith. Since he knew the distance between the two cities, he could then proceed to work out the total circumference of the earth; and he came within a few miles of the truth.

Juvenal, the Roman satirist, died here in exile at the age of 80, towards the end of the 1st century AD. But it was the merchants, more than the scholars, scientists, poets and soldiers, who left the most abundant evidence, in the form of *ostraka*, or potsherds, inscribed with records of their transactions. Nineteenth-century travellers were able to pick up pocketsful.

In the second half of the 19th century tourists began to arrive by way of Thomas Cook steamers and *dahabeeyas*; and their many observations were noted in morocco-bound diaries.

Elegant hotels were built to accommodate the fashionable travellers who came to spend the winter at Aswan or to plan the future development of Egypt and the Sudan. The terraces of the **Old Cataract Hotel** Ⓐ must have been the scene of many a portentous discussion by these Victorian empire-builders.

The construction of the first **Aswan Dam** was successfully financed and the project completed in 1902. King Edward VII's younger brother came out from

Karkadeh, *a refreshing local drink, made with hisbiscus flowers.*

BELOW: Elephantine Island, Aswan.

A trader in Aswan's colourful and largely hassle-free suq.

BELOW: the Nubia Museum.

England for the opening with a host of onlookers, including the young Winston Churchill.

Aswan's Suq

Modern hotels have replaced the grand old ladies of the past, though the Old Cataract survives. A drink on the terrace at sunset is still a must, even though the hotel now imposes a minimum charge for non-residents, for the views over the islands on the Nile, the desert on the west bank and the picturesque ruins of Elephantine are unsurpassed.

On the shore below the hotel, as everywhere along the Corniche, feluccas dock, waiting for business. If you can't get on to the terrace of the Old Cataract, there are plenty of other café terraces on which to while away the hottest hours of the day in the shade.

Parallel to the Nile is the long stretch of Aswan's *suq,* which still retains a hint of Africa. The little shops sell cotton, *karkadeh* (hibiscus flowers for infusion,

the local drink here), Nubian baskets, dates, ebony cane and crocheted skull caps. The best time to visit is when the heat of the day has died down, late afternoon, or in the morning. Softly spoken Nubians while away their time in front of coffee shops, and women carry home the day's shopping on their heads, wearing their traditional thin black dresses with flounces trailing behind. Not so long ago, when they reached their villages by walking across the Nubian sand dunes, these flounces brushed away their footprints in the sand.

The Nubia Museum

Just south of the Old Cataract Hotel is the **Nubia Museum** (daily 9am–1pm and 5–10pm; admission charge), housed in a stunning modern building, built in Nubian style and surrounded by well-kept gardens. The importance of Nubian culture in Egypt has tended to be played down, even though the pharaohs of the 25th Dynasty came from south of Aswan. Since the flooding of Egyptian Nubia by the creation of Lake Nasser *(see page 233)*, and the Nubian diaspora that followed, there is a serious threat

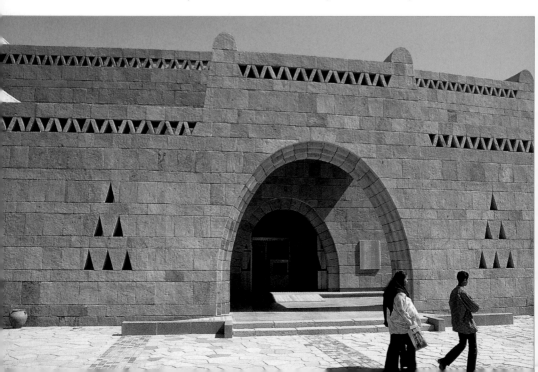

that Nubian culture could disappear altogether – hence the importance of this museum. Well designed and laid out, it throws light on Nubia's history and heritage, from 4500 BC to the present day. Highlights of the museum include the fine quartzite statue of a 25th-Dynasty Kushite priest, the splendid horse armour from the so-called Ballana Period (7th–5th century BC), centring on the region south of the First Cataract, and Nubian ceramics. A distinctive Nubian house and some prehistoric rock paintings can be found in the garden.

The Fatimid Cemetery

As in so many places in Egypt, Aswan has a multitude of burial grounds and memorials from different eras of Egyptian history. Near the Nubian Museum, for example, is a vast cemetery, known as the **Fatimid Cemetery**, with beautiful domed tombs from the Tulunid period. It is now fenced off but it is possible to enter from the main gate and walk across.

The Unfinished Obelisk

On the other side of the road, across from the cemetery, is one of Aswan's many quarries where the **Unfinished Obelisk** I (daily 8am–6pm in summer, 7am–4pm in winter; admission charge) can still be seen, attached to the bedrock. The 42-metre (137 ft) long obelisk would have been the single heaviest piece of stone in ancient Egypt had the workers not discovered a crack while hewing it out of the rock. Coloured granites, greywacke, syenite, alabaster and ochre were quarried and transported down the flooded Nile to the northern royal cities.

Elephantine Island

Opposite Aswan, in the middle of the Nile, is **Elephantine Island ❸**, much more built up than it used to be, but still pleasant with several Nubian villages and their gardens, and on the southern tip, the remains of ancient Yebu and a small **museum ❻** (daily 9am–6pm in summer, 8am–5pm in winter; admission charge). The museum, set in a lovely subtropical garden, is housed in the villa of Sir William Willcocks, who designed the first Aswan Dam. A gold-plated ram, ram mummies, precious stones, jewellery and amulets are on display.

The Unfinished Obelisk in Aswan. Obelisks, which later made their way to such places as Rome, Istanbul, Paris, London and New York, were ingeniously cut from Aswan marble.

BELOW: tomb in Aswan's Fatimid Cemetery.

Tomb Chapels of the Nobles · Luxor
Deir al-Saman (Monastery of St Simeon) · Kitchener's Island
Aga Khan Mausoleum · Elephantine Island · **Aswan**
Fort Harun ★
★ Unfinished Obelisk
Salugah
Northern Quarries
Scheyl
Unfinished Sarcophagus ★
First Cataract · Southern Quarries
★ Unfinished Colossus
Al-Shallal
Old Aswan Dam ❶
Awad
Agilqiyyah · Temple of Philae
Philae
Al-Hishah · Bigah

N

South Aswan

0 — 1 km
0 — 1 mile

Nil (Nile)

Soviet-Egyptian Memorial
Hydroelectric Station
Temple of Kalabshah, Bayt al-Wali · High Dam (Sadd al-Ali) · *Lake Nasser* · Terminus of Nile Valley Railway
❶

The Mausoleum of the Aga Khan III, which sits high above the west bank of the Nile.

The modern **annexe** next door has a wonderful collection of objects found on Elephantine, including weapons, pottery and household objects, with interesting labels in Arabic and English.

The entrance ticket to the museum includes the scant but rarely visited and therefore atmospheric remains of ancient Yebu, including the Temples of Khnum *(see below)*, on the tip of the island, and the **Nilometer ⓓ**. From the Old Kingdom onwards a strict watch was kept on the rise and fall of the Nile, and its measurement was one of the important functions of the resident governor of Elephantine and later

Aswan. Up until the 19th century, when western technology started to revolutionise the management of water, frequent and regular readings were taken from the Nilometer at the southern end of Elephantine Island, and the information was communicated to the surrounding region. Those responsible for the cultivation of crops and the maintenance of embankments and canals would thus know in advance what to expect, while other administrators could calculate tax assessments.

According to an interesting text at Edfu, if the Nile rose 24 cubits at Elephantine, it would provide sufficient water to irrigate the land satisfactorily. If it did not, disaster would surely ensue. Just such a failure, which lasted for seven years – though it is not the drought mentioned in the Bible – is recorded on a block of granite a short way upstream: "By a very great misfortune the Nile has not come forth for a period of seven years. Grain has been scarce and there have been no vegetables or anything else for the people to eat."

Archaeological remains of the **Temples of Khnum** on the southern end of

Recommended Restaurants & Bars on pages 234–5

Elephantine are sketchy, but there is evidence that Tuthmosis III, Amenhotep II, Ramesses III, Alexander IV (the son of Alexander the Great), Augustus Caesar and Trajan all had a hand either in their construction or maintenance. Parts of the temples were still standing when the French expedition arrived in 1798 *(see page 74)*, but were demolished about 20 years later by Muhammad Ali's son Ibrahim (at this time viceroy of Upper Egypt,) who subsequently used the temple's fine white stone to build himself a palace.

The nearby **Temple of Satet** was built by Queen Hatshepsut for the goddess of fertility and inundation. Beneath the ruins is a shaft leading to a natural whirl hole, the noise of which was revered as the "Voice of the Nile". Aramaic papyri found in the settlement record the presence of a large Jewish colony on the island.

Kitchener's Island and the west bank

The easiest way to see the sights on the west bank is to take a felucca. The feluccas also usually stop at the **Botanical Gardens E** (daily 8am–4pm in winter, 8am–5pm in summer; admission charge) on **Kitchener's Island**. In return for his military achievements in the Sudan, Consul-General Kitchener was presented with this island, for which he collected exotic plants and seeds from across the world.

In ancient times the hereditary governors of Elephantine and other high-ranking officials had their tombs cut out of the cliffs on the west bank of the Nile at a spot called Qubbat al-Hawa in Arabic, or Dome of the Winds. The **Tombs of the Nobles F** (daily 8am–5pm in summer, until 4pm in winter; admission charge) of the Old and Middle Kingdoms depict interesting scenes of daily life, and the views over Aswan and the Nile alone are worth the steep climb. It makes for a pleasant expedition combined with a visit to the **Deir Anba-Samaan G** (Monastery of St Simeon; daily 8am–5pm in summer, until 4pm in winter; admission charge).

The 6th-century monastery once provided for about 300 monks, but these days the ruins lie lost in the desert sands.

Aga Khan III, the grandfather of Kerim Aga Khan and distinguished leader of the Ismaili sect of Islam for many years, loved Aswan for its pleasant therapeutic, timeless tranquillity and had his domed mausoleum built high up on the bluffs overlooking the river. He was buried in the **Aga Khan Mausoleum H** in 1957. The building is a close relative of those of his ancestors, the Fatimids, whose followers' mausoleums are on the east bank. More recently, his wife the begum was also buried here. The tomb itself is closed to the public but the site commands wonderful views over Aswan. The couple's white villa can be seen just below the tomb.

Seheyl Island

Further south, just north of the Aswan Dam, is **Seheyl Island** (daily 7am–4pm in winter, to 5pm in summer; admission charge) with several Nubian villages. On the island's southern tip is a cliff with over 200 inscriptions from 18th and 19th Dynasty nobles who passed here on their

TIP

An afternoon walk through the sweet-scented lanes of the Botanical Gardens is the perfect antidote to a hot day. If you come by felucca, your captain will drop you off at one end of Kitchener's Island and then sail round to the other to pick you up.

BELOW: the Tombs of the Nobles on the west bank at Aswan.

The gardens and islands of Aswan are good places for spotting birds, among them the little green bee-eater, the pied kingfisher, the Nile Valley sunbird, black kites and the occasional Egyptian vulture (above). Binoculars are useful on a Nile Cruise.

BELOW: tree top on Kitchener's Island.

way to Nubia and wanted to make their mark. The **Kanzian House** (tel: 012-415 4902), a typical Nubian house, serves Nubian dishes and sells locally made crafts. The way to get there is by boat or felucca. On the way there is a great **beach** on the west bank opposite Salugah Island.

The Aswan Dam

The taming of the river's unpredictable moods and the year-round conservation of its waters have been at the core of Egypt's history and civilisation since its earliest beginnings. In primeval times, the unharnessed flood roared down annually from the Ethiopian highlands, swamping the valley for three months before it receded, leaving behind thousands of tonnes of fertile silt which, accumulating over millennia, created the 10-metre (33-ft) thick blanket of soil which constitutes the Valley and the Delta.

The flood, however, was unpredictable and occasionally failed to appear. The consequences were disastrous; and the co-ordinated planning required to deal with the recurring problem was an important factor in the development of ancient Egyptian civilisation. By systems of dykes and channels, water could be trapped in basins. These systems were improved by waves of conquerors who tried their hand at governing Egypt.

In the 19th century Muhammad Ali set about repairing and extending the canals and building barrages, which conserved enough water for a limited year-round supply. They made feasible the production of summer cash crops such as sugar, rice and cotton, which enormously increased the country's revenue.

Continuing this pattern of development, the British in their turn built the first **Aswan Dam ①** in 1902 at the head of the First Cataract, creating a reservoir 225 km (140 miles) long. At the time it was acclaimed as a great feat of engineering, and there was another marked increase in the prosperity of the country.

With the demise of the British occupation and the takeover of Egypt by Nasser's revolutionary government in 1952, the Nile Valley became a testing ground for international rivalries. The new regime focused its aspirations on the construction of a **High Dam ①** that would generate enough electricity for new industry and

Dahabeeyahs

Medieval historians described dahabeeyahs or "Golden Ones" as luxurious vessels that went up and down the Nile, sumptuously decorated with two masts, lots of staff and a few comfortable private cabins and bathrooms. The same wooden boats were favoured by 19th-century travellers too, who chose a boat and dragoman in Cairo, kitted it out and took about two months or more to sail up to Abu Simbel and back. The introduction of the Thomas Cook steamer and later the cruise boats put an end to dahabeeyahs until recently. A few years ago the dahabeeyah made a comeback, and it is undoubtedly once again the chicest and most pleasant way to travel up the Nile.

A few 19th-century vessels were restored, but others were newly built in the old style with between four and 10 cabins with en suite bathrooms. This is the slow way to travel: the cruise from Esna to Aswan takes six or seven days, a leisurely pace that includes the less visited sites of al-Kab and Gebel Silsilla, a swim in the Nile and a beach where the bigger ships can't stop. The boats can moor where they like, and the scenery is just as spectacular as it was a century ago. It is more expensive to travel on a dahabeeyah than on a regular cruise boat but in this age of mass tourism it is a privilege to see Egypt in all its tranquillity.

rural electrification, and provide enough water to bring millions of new acres under cultivation, but it needed financial and technical assistance to realise the project. The United States was ready to help, but withdrew its offer abruptly when Nasser refused to compromise his non-aligned status. The Soviet Union stepped in with loans and technology.

For 10 years 30,000 workers laboured on the dam. Hundreds of tonnes of rubble were shovelled into the Nile to make a barrier 4 km wide and 92 metres high (2½ miles x 300 ft). Four huge channels were cut through the granite on the west side to divert the water while 12 turbines were installed on the east. By 1972 the dam was finished. The High Dam straddles the Nile 13 km (8 miles) south of Aswan. Beyond it Lake Nasser stretches for 800 km (500 miles), deep into the Sudan, submerging many ancient temples and monuments *(see pages 228)* as well as Nubian culture.

The beneficial effects of the dam were immediately apparent, though it has fallen short of remedying all Egypt's ills. Had it not been for the water stored up behind it, however, Egypt would have suffered as disastrously as Ethiopia and the Sudan during the droughts of 1972 and 1984.

An additional 3 million *feddans* (1.2 million hectares/3 million acres) to Egypt's cultivable lands, irrigated by the new assured water supply, was planned, but the leaders were so closely identified with the project that they turned a deaf ear to seasoned advice. The new lands were on poor soil, which took years to attain marginal productivity at exorbitant cost. Eventually Sadat had to admit that grand schemes for land reclamation were unrealistic.

The containment of the flood has produced other results. Houses can now be built in places that were formerly under water for three months of the year; and in response to the huge explosion in Egypt's population the private sector has built on precious agricultural land. Moreover, other land is being lost through the use of excessive water, causing waterlogging and salinity. The drainage system that would remedy this defect is proving to be more costly than the dam itself. ❑

The Aswan Dam has brought many benefits but also some ills. There is a small visitors centre at the eastern end of the dam (take a taxi from Aswan).

BELOW:
waiting for the late afternoon rush.

RESTAURANTS & BARS

Restaurants

Prices for a three-course dinner per person with a half-bottle of house wine:
$ = under $20
$$ = $20–45
$$$ = $45–60
$$$$ = over $60

Aswan

1902 Restaurant
Old Cataract Hotel,
Shari' Abtal at-Tahrir
Tel: 097-231 6000.
$$$–$$$$
Aswan's finest restaurant serves a French-Levantine menu in a beautiful period dining room, with live Arabic music. The quality of the food can be a little erratic and the service is formal, but it still makes for a great evening out.

Aswan Moon
Corniche an-Nil
Tel: 097-231 6108. **$**
Floating restaurant on the Nile, which attracts many *fellucciyas*. Beer, fresh fruit juices and standard Egyptian fare in a relaxing atmosphere.

Biti Pizza
Midan al-Mahatta
No phone. **$**
This take away pizza place has a first-floor sit-down area, which is air-conditioned, calm and has views over the square. The pizzas are good and freshly made, perfect for lunch, and the *fteer*, an Egyptian version of pizza which comes sweet with nuts and raisins, or savoury with cheese or tuna, is excellent too.

Chef Khalil
Shari as-Souq, near the train station
Tel: 097-231 0142. **$$**
Simple but very popular fish restaurant that serves fresh fish, by the weight, from Lake Nasser and the Red Sea. The grilled or baked fish is served with salad and rice.

Makka
Shari Abtal at-Tahrir
Tel: 097-230 3232. **$$–$$$**
The best kebab and *kofta* in town, sold by weight, and served amid totally kitsch Islamic décor. No alcohol.

Nubian Beach
West Bank, past the Aga Khan Mausoleum.
Tel: 012-773 7885/012-169 9145. **$–$$**
Bordering the Nile at the foot of a huge sand dune, this Nubian café-restaurant is a delightful place for lunch, Lounging over a cool drink in the afternoon, or dinner. The food is simple but fresh and delicious, the service friendly. You have to get there by boat; call ahead for instructions.

Nubian House Restaurant
About 1km (½ mile) south of Nubian Museum, on the river bank
Tel: 097-232 6226. **$$$**
With beautiful views over the First Cataract and the Nile, this is a great place for afternoon tea, a *sheesha* or dinner with live Nubian music. Very relaxing atmosphere and friendly service.

Nubian Restaurant
Issa Island, south of Elephantine Island (free shuttle boat from opposite the Egypt Air office, from where you can also make your booking).
Tel: 097-230 2465. **$$**
Nubian restaurant located on its own island and providing local and Egyptian specialities accompanied by a good folkloric show.

Old Cataract Terrace
Old Cataract Hotel
Tel: 097-231 6000. **$$**
English afternoon tea is
served on the Nile-side
terrace from 4pm
onwards, following a
long-established tradition
of watching the sun set
on the West Bank.

Al Moudira
Daba'iyya, 15km (11 miles)
south of ticket office on the
West Bank
Tel: 012-325 1307/392
8332. **$$$–$$$$**
A great poolside restau-
rant with beautiful inside
rooms for colder days,
serving the best of West-
ern and Lebanese cui-
sine. Great for lunch or
for a romantic evening,
and definitely worth mak-
ing the effort to get
there. Book ahead.

The Bombay
Between the Isis and Shera-
ton hotels
Tel: 010-665 9505/010-294
8079. **$$$**
Great little Indian restau-
rant with all the classic
dishes for those who
want a change from
kebabs, *tagines* and Oriental salads. Simple but
pleasant décor and good
service.

Cafeteria Mohamed
Tel: 095-231 1014/012-385
0227. **$–$$**
Next to the Pharaoh's
Hotel, near the ticket
office on the West Bank.
Simple restaurant where,
with advance notice, the
proprietor will prepare
some real Egyptian food.
There is a small menu
but you can order
meloukhia, stuffed
pigeon or grilled kebabs,
all served with a cold
beer. Great place for
lunch.

Kebabgy
New lower Corniche oppo-
site the Old Winter Palace
Tel: 010-441 3834. **$$**
Good Egyptian fare
including *tagines*, grilled
meats and duck, all
served with salads and
rice. The stuffed pigeon
and duck with orange are
specialities. Slightly more
expensive than most, but
a great place to sit out
on the river.

Kushari Sayyida Nefisa
Shari' Mustapha Kamel
(near the suq). **$**
Serves the best *koshari*
(a mixture of rice, maca-
roni, fried onions, lentils,
and chickpeas) in town.

Lotus Restaurant
Shari' As-Suq
Tel: 095-238 0419. **$$**
A mixture of Egyptian and
international dishes. The
tagines are especially
good.

La Mamma
Sheraton Luxor Resort,
Shari' Khaled ibn al-Walid.
Tel: 095 237 4544. **$$–$$$**
In the courtyard of the
Sheraton Shopping
annexe, beside a pond
with pelicans and water
birds, is the pleasant terrace of La Mamma. Offer-
ing a welcome change,
this old-fashioned Italian
restaurant has home-
made pasta and excel-
lent pizzas, as well as
traditional main courses.
Save some space for the
dessert.

Memnon Restaurant
Opposite the Colossi of
Menon, West Bank. Tel: 012
327 8747. **$**
A small café-restaurant
opposite the Colossi of
Memnon which offers
good Egyptian dishes
and a few more adven-
turous but well-prepared

curries for a change. A
good place for a meal or
for a drink.

Metropolitan Café
Lower level Corniche an-Nil,
opposite the Winter Palace.
$$
Pleasant terrace with rat-
tan furniture, for a cold
beer or a cocktail at sun-
set or any time of the
day, looking over the Nile
and the Theban hills.
There is a large interna-
tional menu with *meze* to
go with the drinks, pas-
tas, salads and steaks.

Miyako
Sonesta St George Hotel,
Shari' ibn Khaled Walid
Tel: 095-238 2575.
$$$–$$$$
An excellent Japanese
restaurant with sushi and
sashimi prepared by a
Japanese chef. Dress
tends to be quite smart.

Mövenpick Restaurant
Crocodile Island
Tel: 095-237 4855. **$$$**
Pleasant terrace restau-
rant serving fresh pasta,
salads and grills as well
as excellent ice-cream.
Two indoor restaurants
offer a good buffet or
expensive French food *à
la carte*.

Nile Valley
Al-Gezirah at the ferry land-
ing. Tel: 095-231 1477. **$$**
Delightful rooftop terrace
overlooking the Nile and
the fields around al-Gezi-
rah. The menu includes
Egyptian meze, stews and
grilled kofta and kebab, as
well as international
dishes. The service is
swift and friendly.

Nur al Gurna
Opposite the ticket office,
Gurna
Tel: 095-231 1430. **$$**
Garden restaurant which
serves simple but well-
prepared Egyptian food

such as *meloukhia* (a
stew of spinach-like
greens and chicken or rab-
bit). Roast duck and
stuffed pigeon are often
on the menu, but it is best
to order before you go
sightseeing if you want
something special. No
alcohol.

Oasis
Shari' Labib Habashi
Tel: 012-336 7121. **$$$**
A relatively new restau-
rant, the Oasis is set in a
traditional building, with
cool tiled floors. There's
a good international
menu, but sandwiches,
coffee and pastries are
also served at all hours
of the day.

Oum Hashim
Shari' Yousef Hassan
Tel: 095-238 6521. **$–$$**
Down to earth place with
a good local feel. Stan-
dard Egyptian dishes
include good kebabs.

Sofra
90 Shari' Mohamed Farid, off
Shari' al-Manshiya.
Tel: 095 235 9752. **$$**
By far the best restau-
rant in Luxor, Sofra
serves excellent tradi-
tional Egyptian food at
reasonable prices. The
restaurant is set in an
old villa in a residential
area, with a lovely roof
terrace, and the furnish-
ings are local or col-
lected from junk shops.
There is no alcohol as it
is next to a mosque, but
it serves an array of
fresh juices. Very friendly
service.

Tutankhamun
Left of the ferry landing,
West Bank
Tel: 095-231 0118. **$**
Simple but very friendly.
The chef trained at one
of the five-star restau-
rants and his vegetable
stews are delicious.

LEFT: 1902 restaurant, Old Cataract Hotel.

STILL WILD AFTER ALL THESE YEARS

Despite the ravages made on Egypt's wildlife over the past hundred years, many of the creatures that the ancients revered are still found today

Before the building of the Aswan dams, the Nile flooded each year and its silt-rich water covered the valley. When the water subsided, the first creature that was seen to move was the scarabaeus, the dung beetle. This beetle also laid its eggs in dung or in the corpses of other beetles. Egyptians called it Kheper, and used it to represent the essence of existence, the god Kherpi. Scarab beetles can still be seen rolling their balls of dung, but many of the other animals that lived on land whose re-emergence the scarabaeus celebrated have long since disappeared.

Survivors

Egyptians used many living creatures to represent their gods, but where now are the Nile crocodile, the African elephant, the lions and ibises, green monkeys and baboons? Long since hunted out of existence or forced off the land as buildings gobbled it up.

Amongst the survivors that were common to the ancient Egyptians and are still found in Egypt today are the magnificent birds like the short-toed eagle, the long-legged buzzard, the hoopoe and the Egyptian vulture (all were used as hieroglyphics).

The Egyptians domesticated many animals including the cat, ox and cow, which feature on many tomb and temple decorations. In the river, grey mullet, catfish and Bulti fish would have been as familiar to the ancients as they are to Egyptians living by the Nile today.

Finally, while the scarab beetle reminds us of the eternal cycle that ancient Egyptians believed in, the pesky fly, also seen in hieroglyphics, reminds us that then, as now, there were trials and tribulations.

ABOVE AND RIGHT: the ibis was sacred to the highly regarded god Thoth, the scribe of the gods, who was believed to have introduced writing to Egypt. It was often mummified. Now extinct in Egypt, it is still found in parts of sub-Saharan Africa and in Iraq.

RIGHT: the Egyptian cobra was sacred to the goddess Wadjet. Egyptian cobras are still very common, and highly venomous. They often enter homes in search of food.

ABOVE: one of the great pleasures of wealthy Egyptians in antiquity was to go hunting in the papyrus marshes, particularly in the Delta. Egyptians hunted birds and other animals for sport, not to provide food, which was done using other techniques, such as ensnaring them in nets. Scenes of hunting and fowling are frequently depicted in tomb paintings. The Tombs of the Nobles in Thebes have some of the best examples.

PAPYRUS – THE FIRST PAPER

The papyrus plant *(Cyperus papyrus)*, a relative of sedge grasses, used to grow abundantly in Egypt, particularly in the marshy Delta. In antiquity Egyptians put papyrus to a number of uses. They wove it into mats, plaited it for ropes, bundled it together to form light rafts – perfect for fishing in the marshes – and pressed and wove it into a suitable medium on which to write. The creation of this technique was largely responsible for the explosion of literacy in ancient Egypt. Until then stone had been the main means of conveying the written word.

Making papyrus sheets was time-consuming and labour-intensive, so even in antiquity they were reserved for writing that was intended to last, for religious texts and important legal works. More ephemeral information was put down on slates or on pottery shards.

Because of its proliferation and importance, the papyrus was one of the symbols of Upper Egypt and its form was recreated in the shapes of pillars in several hypostyle halls.

Papyrus continued to be used for important texts into the 10th century, but the manufacturing technique was lost soon after paper was imported from the East and wasn't rediscovered until the 20th century, by which time papyrus had vanished from most of the country. Recently, there has been some replanting.

To see papyrus being made today, you can visit Dr Ragab's Papyrus Institute in Cairo *(see page 154)*, which also sells a wide range of high-quality copies of famous papyrus scenes.

LEFT: the jackal was sacred to the gods Wepwawet and Auamutef (one of the four sons of Horus), but it was its connection with Anubis, god and protector of the Dead and helper of Osiris, that earned the jackal such a prominent role in Tutankhamun's tomb. Anubis, with dog-like fidelity, was trusted with the protection of the mummy. Jackals are still found on the edge of the desert in Egypt, and as that is where Egyptians still bury their dead, the association between the jackal and Anubis continues. Egypt also has four species of fox, an animal closely related to the jackal.

ABU SIMBEL AND NUBIA

The temples and tombs of Nubia, lying south of the First
Cataract, were threatened with extinction by the Aswan
Dam, but thanks to worldwide cooperation many of
Nubia's treasures can once again be
viewed from the water

For thousands of years the First Cataract south of Aswan marked the border between Egypt and Nubia, the land south of Aswan up to Khartoum in Sudan. This arid sun-seared Nubian land, about 22,000 sq. km (8,500 sq. miles), is now dominated by Lake Nasser, the world's largest artificial lake.

After the building of the High Dam in 1971, Nubia disappeared under the lake's water, and its entire population of some 100,000 people were uprooted from their ancestral homes, with half relocated in Egypt (in Kom Ombo, about 14 km/9 miles north of Aswan, *see page 224*), and the rest in Kashem al-Girba in northeastern Sudan. Most of Nubia's major monuments were also transported to new locations, one as far afield as the Metropolitan Museum of Art in New York.

To the ancient Egyptians Nubia was known as Ta-Sety, the Land of Bowmen, as the Nubians were famous for their bows. The word Nubia is thought to have come from the ancient Egyptian word *nbw* (gold), for Nubia was an important source of ivory, copper and gold for the Egyptians. The area between the First and the Second Cataract is known as Lower Nubia (Wawat in ancient Egypt) and further south between the Second and Sixth cataracts is Upper Nubia (Kush).

Exploring Nubia

Many tourists include a day excursion to Abu Simbel in their programme, but increasingly, people are drawn to the lake itself for its beauty and tranquillity, far away from mass tourism. A few cruise boats tour the monuments around the lake, and in many cases this is the only way of accessing the temples that were salvaged from the water and located on higher grounds. Two companies organise fishing safaris *(see box, page 244)*, looking for the giant Nile perch and other fish, while a few companies offer a combination of visiting the sites, fishing, and trekking into the desert.

Abu Simbel can be visited by plane (Egypt Air operates several flights a day) and also by mini bus from Aswan.

Main attractions

PHILAE, P.241
TEMPLE OF KALABSHAH, P.243
AMADAH TEMPLE, P.245
QASR IBRIM, P.245
ABU SIMBEL, P.246

LEFT: inscriptions on a boulder on Sahil Island, near Aswan.
BELOW: the Temple of Kertassi, Kalabshah.

Historical Nubia

Mineral-rich but desolate, ancient Nubia traded iron ore, copper and gold for grain and other produce. As Egypt declined, so Nubia prospered

For many centuries Nubia was the link between Egypt and Africa, but it was not a regular trade corridor because of its inhospitable environment, and the natural barriers presented by the cataracts. But it was a largely barren land, while Egypt, on the other hand, had an abundant agricultural surplus, and so even in ancient times Nubians turned to their rich northern neighbour for vital food supplies, especially grain. And Egypt, though ever fearful of attack from the south, was ready to fulfil the Nubians' requirements in return for the right to exploit their rich mineral resources. During the New Kingdom when Egypt gained ascendancy over Nubia, much of the era's great wealth was derived from Nubian gold and copper.

Ancient Nubia

When the civilisation of ancient Egypt was in decline, the kingdom of Upper Nubia prospered, and around

600 BC the Nubians moved their capital from Napata southwards to Meroe (Shendi) in a fertile bend in the river, where, free from invasion, well-placed for trade, and rich in iron ore and in wood for iron smelting, they developed a culture that was at once a continuation of the Egyptian-influenced Napatan culture and a totally individual African entity.

The Meroitic kingdom spread northwards until, by the reign of Ptolemy IV (181 BC), the king of Meroe, Argamanic, controlled the Nile to within sight of Elephantine at Aswan. There the Nubians remained until the Roman conquest of Egypt in 30 BC, when the Romans signed a treaty with them, turning all northern Nubia into a buffer zone.

Nubia embraced Christianity between the 5th and 6th centuries, when numerous churches were built and some ancient temples were converted into churches.

From Christianity to Islam

When Egypt was conquered by the Arabs in the 7th century, they concluded a treaty with the Christian Nubian king and Nubia officially remained Christian until the 12th century, when many Nubians embraced the Muslim faith. Mass conversion to Islam was triggered when tribes from Arabia settled in Lower Nubia and began to impose their religion and political organisation on the people. They intermarried with Arabs and their children came to be called *Bani Kanz*, or the Kenuz tribe. Most of the resettled Nubian population in Kom Ombo belong to this tribe. By the end of the 15th century, Nubians, with the exception of only a few settlements, were Muslim.

Surviving documents in a host of languages, including "Old Nubian" (which has yet to be deciphered), Arabic, Coptic and Greek, provide a wealth of information about the Nubian people in the form of private and official letters, legal documents and petitions, which date from between the end of the 8th and the 15th century. Most of these documents come from Qasr Ibrim (*see page 245*). ❑

LEFT: the characteristic Nubian turban. **ABOVE:** Nubian homes are often exquisitely decorated.

The flooding of Nubia

When the creation of Lake Nasser threatened to swallow up many Nubian monuments, the governments of Egypt and Sudan launched an appeal to save and record as many of them as possible. The international response was impressive. Between 1960 and 1970, in the most concentrated archaeological operation ever undertaken, scholars, engineers, architects and photographers from more than 30 countries fought against time to preserve what they could, and 23 temples were saved. Many of these were left in Nubia but lifted out of harm's way: the Temple of Amadah, for example, was raised as a unit weighing 800 tonnes, put on rails and dragged up a hill to safety, while the Temple of Derr was rebuilt nearby, and another temple, built by Queen Hatshepsut, was dismantled, crated, loaded onto 28 lorries and taken to the Sudan, where it was reassembled in the National Museum at Khartoum.

Travel south of Aswan

From the High Dam south there is just the desert and **Lake Nasser**. The only places foreigners can get to by road beyond Philae and Kalabshah are Beit al-Wali and Kertassi. There are roads to the other temples further south (with the exception of Qasr Ibrim), but they are off limits for foreigners. Abu Simbel can be reached by road, but only by bus or minibus in a police convoy. Safety precautions are slowly easing up so it is worth checking current regulations with the tourist office in Aswan. It can be worth staying overnight, but book accommodation in advance (see page 315).

Philae

During the Ptolemaic period the cult of Isis moved 8 km (5 miles) south of Aswan to the island of **Philae ❶** (daily Oct–May 7am–4pm, June–Sept 7am–5pm; admission charge), near Bigah Island, identified with the burial place of Osiris (see page 47). On Philae, a particularly beautiful **temple** was dedicated to Isis and became the most important shrine in Egypt over the next 700 years. Pilgrims came from both north and south to invoke the healing powers of the goddess, and continued to do so long after Christianity had been adopted as the national and imperial religion. As

> I think riding up the Cataract was one of the most delightful moments of my life... the sense of power over the elements, of danger successfully overcome, is...one of the keenest delights and reliefs.
>
> Florence Nightingale
> Letters from Egypt,
> 1849–50

BELOW: one of several carvings of Isis on the Temple of Isis, Philae. Some of the depictions were deliberately damaged when the temple became a church in the 6th century.

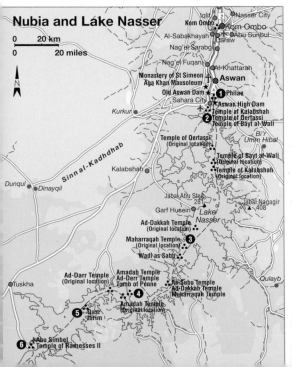

TIP

To Philae: Tickets for a return trip to Philae Temple are sold on the landing in Shellal (on the south side of the old Aswan Dam, reached by taxi). The trip by motorboat costs EGP10 per person; tip the boatman if you want to stay longer than the usual hour.

To Kalabshah: Boats to Kalabshah dock on the western side of the High Dam (reached by taxi). The return trip costs about EGP40.

BELOW:
Trajan's Kiosk, Philae

well as the Temple of Isis, many subsidiary temples, shrines and gateways were added to enhance the cult centre.

The construction of the first Aswan Dam in 1902 resulted in the partial submersion of Philae during eight months of the year. There were strong objections from conservationist quarters but, as Winston Churchill caustically observed, to abandon plans for the dam would have been "the most senseless sacrifice ever offered on the altar of a false religion". The dam was built, Philae was indeed inundated and, still more so in 1932 when the dam was heightened for the third time. But visitors were able to row and even swim about among the foliated capitals of the long colonnades and glimpse the ghostly reliefs on the walls in the water below.

When the High Dam was built between 1960 and 1971, Philae was threatened with total and permanent immersion. This time it was rescued by a huge international mission. A 1.6-km (1-mile) long coffer dam was constructed round the island, and all the water within was pumped out. Stone by stone the temples were dismantled, and transported to nearby Agilqiyyah Island, which had been levelled and remodelled to receive the masterpiece of reconstruction that visitors see today. The total cost was in the region of US$30 million, a fortune at the time.

Visiting Philae

Small boats take tourists from the boat landing at Shellal *(see margin note)*, in Aswan, to Agilqiyyah Island, where stairs lead from the landing to the oldest part of the Philae complex: the **Kiosk of Nectanebo I** (30th Dynasty) and the **Outer Temple Court**, flanked on both sides by colonnades. The entrance to the **Temple of Isis** is marked by the 18-metre (60-ft) high towers of the **First Pylon**, where reliefs show the Ptolemies in traditional pharaonic poses. To the left of the Central Court is the **Birth House of Ptolemy IV** (221–205 BC) with fine reliefs depicting the god Horus rising from the marshes. A stairway inside the **Inner Sanctuary of Isis** leads to the **Osiris Chambers**, decorated with exquisite reliefs illustrating the Osiris myth *(see page 40)*. Inside the sanctuary, reliefs show Isis suckling her son Horus as well as the young pharaoh.

To the right of the **Second Pylon** is the small **Temple of Hathor**, the patroness of music, with a good relief of musicians. On **Hadrian's Gate** an interesting relief depicts the source of the Nile as the Nile god Hapi, who pours water from two jars, a scene alluding to the ancient Egyptian belief that the source of the Nile was to be found at the First Cataract, from where it flowed both north towards the Mediterranean and south towards the Sudan).

The most photographed part of the temple is probably **Trajan's Kiosk**, (*circa* AD 100), displaying floral columns and reliefs of the Roman Emperor Trajan making offerings to Isis and Osiris.

The Temple of Kalabshah

For most of the year, the only way to get to the **Temple of Kalabshah ❷** (daily 8am–4pm; admission charge) is by boat (*see margin note, page 242*), but sometimes when the water is low, it can be reached via a 10-minute walk from Aswan's boatyard. However, seeing the temple in all its grandeur from the water is worth the extra expense and hassle.

The original site of Kalabshah, ancient Talmis, was 50 km (31 miles) further up the Nile, and today the temple lies somewhat forlorn in the shadow of the High Dam, where it was relocated in 1970. The temple, dedicated to the Nubian fertility god Marul (Mandulis to the Greeks), was built around 30 BC during the reign of Emperor Augustus, over an older Ptolemaic temple. During the Christian era it was used as a church. An impressive stoneway leads up to the First Pylon. The colonnaded court and hypostyle hall beyond the pylon have varied floral capitals, clearly suggesting a garden. Inside the sanctuary, the emperor is seen in the company of the entire Egyptian pantheon. A stairway leads to the roof, with magnificent views over Lake Nasser.

The smaller temple of **Bayt al-Wali** (House of the Governor), was also relocated here, having stood on a site near the original Kalabshah Temple. Carved into a sandstone hill, it was built by the viceroy of Kush to commemorate Ramesses II's successful military expeditions in Nubia. The well-preserved and brightly coloured reliefs show the victorious pharaoh receiving heaps of

TIP

A spectacular sound and light show, with three shows every evening (including an English-language show), relates the history of the Temple of Isis. For a schedule, ask at the tourist office in Aswan or consult www.sound andlight.com.eg

BELOW:
visiting the Temple of Isis, Philae.

The Cataracts

The First Cataract at Aswan is one of six original cataracts in the Nile, all found in the river's so-called "Great Bend" between Aswan and Khartoum, where due to tectonic shift the river veers away from its normal north–south course.

Although the word cataract derives from the Greek word *kataraktes* (meaning downfall of water), the cataracts are actually broad stretches of shallow water strewn with large boulders and islands rather than waterfalls, although they can incorporate rapids. They often create a very picturesque scene, as at Aswan, one of the loveliest stretches of the Nile. Presenting natural obstacles for boats, the cataracts hampered the Nile's navigability during antiquity except during times of flood. Today, the Second Cataract lies under Lake Nasser.

Not all of Nubia's temples found homes on the shores of Lake Nasser. Some were relocated abroad, including the Temple of Dabod, which is now in Madrid, the Temple of Dendur, now in the Sackler Wing of the Metropolitan Museum of Art, New York, and the two Roman temples of Tafa, which went to the Rijksmuseum in Leiden, the Netherlands.

BELOW: placid waters, near Qasr Ibrim. **RIGHT:** the 3rd-century temple at Dakkah.

exotic goods as tribute. Just north of the Kalabshah Temple are the picturesque remains of the **Temple of Kertassi**, with a few Hathor and papyrus columns.

Dakkah, Maharraqah and Wadi as-Sabu

The rest of the temples from here to Abu Simbel can only be visited by boat, as part of a cruise. Leaving from the Saad al Ali maritime station beside the Aswan High Dam, the cruise boats pass the temples of Kalabshah and Kertassi and the Bayt al-Wali, on the western shore, before heading into open water. The lake is broad here and the hills gently sloped, but further south the landscape closes in where the Nile used to run through a narrow passage between steep hills. It is a unique sight. Antiquities used to be spread along the Nile between the First and Second cataracts but, as with Kalabshah, many were grouped together during the salvage operation, which makes seeing them easier, even if it has taken some of the drama away.

The next group of **temples** ❸ – Dakkah, Maharraqah and Wadi as-Sabu – lies some 140 km (87 miles) south of

Aswan, also on the western shore.

Dakkah was begun, 40 km (25 miles) north of its present site by the 3rd-century local king Argamani, reusing stones from earlier buildings. Despite extensive additions under the Ptolemies and the Roman Emperor Augustus, the temple was never finished, as is apparent from the lack of decoration on parts of the pylon.

The nearby temple of **Maharraqah** originally stood 30 km (18 miles) north of its present site at the frontier market of Ptolemaic Egypt. It is a later building than Dakkah, constructed in the Roman period and dedicated to Isis and Serapis.

Wadi as-Sabu (the Valley of Lions) is the most complete of this group. The temple, originally located 2 km (1½ miles) further southwest, takes its name from an avenue of sphinxes that lead to a temple built by the viceroy of Kush for Ramesses II. Colossal figures of the pharaoh stand at the entrance and line pillars in the court. The outer areas of the temple were built of sandstone, but the vestibule, antechamber and sanctuary were carved out of the rock. The figures of Ramesses, Amun-Ra and Ra-Harakhte, which once occupied the

Fishing on Lake Nasser

As the sites along the Nile get more and more inundated by tourists, the attraction of a few days of peace and quiet on the very unspoilt and unvisited Lake Nasser has grown immensely. A few companies offer big-game freshwater fishing safaris on the lake, guaranteeing most people on the trip their biggest fresh water catch ever. The lake is home to the Nile perch, one of the largest freshwater fish in the world, as well as tiger fish and giant vundu catfish. The *Guinness Book Of World Records* lists a 232-kg (511-lb) Nile perch caught by local fishermen on Lake Victoria, while the largest recorded Nile perch caught on Lake Nasser weighed 176 kg (392 lb).

Companies offering fishing safaris include African Angler (25 Ahmed Maher Street, Aswan (near the suq); tel/fax: 20-97310907; www.african-angler.co.uk) and Lake Nasser Adventure (tel: 20-121040255; www.lakenasserad-venture.com), which also runs trekking trips in the Nubian desert between Aswan and Abu Simbel .

sanctuary, gave way to an image of St Peter when the temple was converted into a church.

Amadah trio

Forty kilometres (25 miles) south of Wadi as-Sabu, three monuments now stand near the original west-bank site of the Temple of Amadah. The small 18th-Dynasty **Amadah Temple** ❹ was built a couple of kilometres away from its present site by Tuthmosis III and Amenhotep II. The illustrations of planning and building the temple (in the innermost left-hand chapel) are worth finding. The nearby rock-cut **Temple of Derr** was moved 11 km (7 miles) north to its present site. Like the Wadi as-Sabu temple, it was dedicated to Amun-Ra and Ra-Harakhte; its figures were badly damaged by Christians using it as a church. Also here is the **tomb of Penne**, a local governor (1141–1133 BC), moved from Anibaah, 40 km (25 miles) south.

Qasr Ibrim

About 15 km (9 miles) north of Abu Simbel is **Qasr Ibrim** ❺. Now an island, before the flooding it was

situated on the eastern bank where three massive peaks of rock rose from the river. Crowning the middle peak were a ruined town, whose fortress commanded the valley for miles around in all directions.

This *qasr* (castle) is all that emerges above the level of the lake today but it must have been a striking landmark in pharaonic times when the first temple-fortress was built. Excavations have revealed inscriptions dating from the 16th century BC and there are remains of a significant Byzantine cathedral. It is known that the Romans, Saladin, the

As the number of cruise boats allowed to operate on Lake Nasser is limited, cruises on the lake have an air of exclusivity.

BELOW: fallen statue of Ramesses II at Wadi as-Sabu, built for Ramesses II by the viceroy of Kush.

TIP

It is well worth visiting Abu Simbel. The easiest and quickest way is to fly there direct from Cairo, Luxor or Aswan. There are up to three flights a day each way (only one on Sunday): www.egyptair.com. A cheaper way is to take a bus tour and go in police convoy through the desert. A multilingual sound and light show is staged daily at the temple at 7, 8 and 9pm in winter, and 8, 9 and 10pm in summer; www.soundandlight. com.eg

BELOW: the rock-hewn Temple of Ramessess II, Abu Simbel, with its four seated colossi.

Ottoman emperor Selim and Muhammad Ali all stationed garrisons here.

Abu Simbel

The mostly Nubian village of **Abu Simbel ❻**, 280 km (174 miles) south of Aswan, has some restaurants and cafés, as well as a few comfortable hotels. It is a relaxed kind of place, where people play backgammon in cafés or listen to Nubian music at night. The lake looks beautiful at different times of the day, but it's especially wonderful to visit the temple at the crack of dawn before the crowds arrive, or late afternoon.

The largest and most magnificent monument in Nubia, the famous **Temple of Ramesses II** (Oct–Apr 6am–5pm, May–Sept 6am–6pm, later if arriving planes are delayed; admission charge) was carved out of the mountain face between 1274–1244 BC, to confirm Ramesses II's might to all those who sailed down the Nile from the south, particularly the prosperous Nubians. The rock temple was dedicated to the main gods of Upper and Lower Egypt, Amun-Ra and Ra-Harakhte, but also to the deified pharaoh himself.

Over the centuries the desert sands covered up most of the temple's facade, and it was lost to the world until 1813, when the Swiss explorer Jean-Louis Burkhardt discovered it by chance as he travelled up the Nile. Only one head stuck out of the sand, and it took the Italian explorer Giovanni Belzoni several years to clear enough sand to enter the temple.

Salvaging the temple from Lake Nasser presented a formidable challenge to the rescuers. Unlike other temples, Abu Simbel was not freestanding; the facade was the cliff face itself hewn in imitation of a pylon and dominated by four colossi of a youthful Ramesses II. The salvage operation entailed sawing the temple into over 1,000 transportable pieces, some weighing as much as 15 tonnes, and reassembling them at a new site 60 metres (200 ft) higher than the original site. The ground was levelled and a great reinforced concrete dome was made to cover the temple.

The moving of the temple, which took over five years from 1966 to 1972, was regarded at the time as one of the wonders of modern engineering. The reconstruction is nearly perfect and every

year on 22 February and 22 October, only one day later than when the temple was in its original position, the dawn rays of the sun reach to the heart of the sanctuary to revive the cult statues.

The four seated 20 metre- (66ft-) high colossi of Ramesses II dominate the facade. The pharaoh considered himself a reincarnation of the sun-god Ra. At his feet are some of his children, and the supporting balustrade has kneeling and bound African captives on the south side and Asian captives on the north side. Look out for the graffiti left by earlier travellers, particularly on the two southern colossi; on the left leg of the second statue is a Greek inscription from mercenaries who passed by in the 6th century BC.

The **portal**, topped by a statue of the falcon-headed sun-god, leads into the **Great Hypostyle Hall**. This central hall is flanked by eight 10 metre- (33 ft-) high Osiride statues of the king in a double row facing each other, against a corresponding number of square pillars.

The **northern wall** of the Hypostyle Hall is decorated with the Battle of Kadesh in which the young Ramesses II confronted the Hittites in Syria. It is one of the most extraordinary and detailed reliefs to be found in the Nile Valley. There are over 1,100 figures and the entire wall, from ceiling to bedrock, is filled with activity: the march of the Egyptian Army with its infantry and charioteers, its engagement in hand-to-hand combat and the flight of the vanquished prisoners, leaving overturned chariots behind them. There are also scenes of camp life.

The reliefs on the **southern wall** are decorated with scenes of the king kneeling in front of several gods. The side chambers off the hall were used for storage and for keeping treasure. The much smaller **Second Hypostyle Hall** has just four large pillars and is decorated with scenes of offerings. Next is the **vestibule** which leads to the **sanctuary** carved out of the mountain to a depth of 55 metres (180 ft). Inside this is an altar and the seated statues of Ptah of Memphis, Amun-Ra of Thebes, the deified Ramesses II and

Ra-Harakhte, the sun god of Heliopolis; they are all the same size, indicating equality between the king and the gods.

Outside and south of the temple is a small **chapel** dedicated to Thoth, the god of learning, and five stele dedicated to high officials of Ramesses II. Unfortunately, at the time of writing it is no longer possible to enter the steel-enforced concrete dome that supports the temple (which gives a fascinating insight into the salvage process).

The small **Temple of Queen Nefertari**, which lay to the north of the great temple of her husband Ramesses II, was also saved. Nefertari was the most beloved of the wives of Ramesses II; and the pharaoh took the unprecedented step of having the facade of this temple decorated with statues of himself, his wife, and their children. The goddess Hathor, to whom the temple, is also dedicated, lovingly attends to the sun-god during his day's passage, so Nefertari is depicted watching admiringly as her husband kills his enemies.   ❏

Facade of the Temple of Nefetari, the beloved wife of Ramesses II.

BELOW:
detail from the Battle of Kadesh depicted on the northern wall of the hall of the Temple of Ramesses II, Abu Simbel.

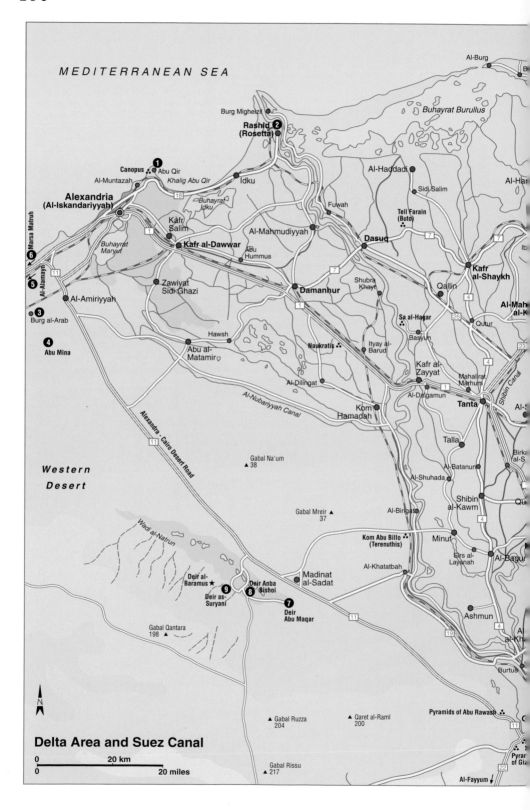

MEDITERRANEAN SEA

Al-Burg

B

ᵒ₀ᵒ *Buhayrat Burullus*

Burg Migheizil

Rashid
(Rosetta) ❷

Al-Haddadi

Al-Ha

Canopus ❶ Abu Qir

Sidi Salim

Al-Muntazah

Khalig Abu Qir

Idku

Alexandria
(Al-Iskandariyyah)

18

Buhayrat
Idku

Fuwah

Tell Farain
(Buto)

Marsa Matruh

Kafr
Salim

Al-Mahmudiyyah

Dasuq

7

Al-H

1

Kafr al-Dawwar

Abu
Hummus

Kafr
al-Shaykh

Buhayrat
Maryut

❻

Shubra
Khayt

Qallin

Al-Mah
al-K

Al-Alamayn

11

Zawiyat
Sidi Ghazi

Damanhur

7

Sa al-Hagar

26

Qutur

❺

Al-Amiriyyah

Basyun

Kafr al-
Zayyat

Al-Mah
al-K

❸

Hawsh

Naukratis

Ityay al-
Barud

4

Burg al-Arab

Abu al-
Matamir

Mahallat
Marhum

❹

Abu Mina

Al-Dilingat

Al-Dalgamun

1

Tanta

Al-S

Al-Nubariyyah Canal

Kom
Hamadah

Shibin Canal

Western
Desert

Alexandria - Cairo Desert Road

Talla

Birka
al-S

Gabal Na'um
▲ 38

Al-Batanun

Al-Shuhada

Shibin
al-Kawm

Qu

11

Gabal Mreir ▲
37

Al-Birigat

Kom Abu Billo
(Terenuthis)

Minuf

Wadi al-Natrun

Deir al-
Baramus ★

Deir Anba
Bishoi

Madinat
al-Sadat

Sirs al-
Layanah

Al-Bagur

❾

❽

Al-Khatatbah

Gabal Qantara
198 ▲

Deir as-
Suryani

❼

Deir
Abu Maqar

11

Ashmun

19

Al-Kh

Burtus

N

▲ *Gabal Ruzza*
204

▲ *Qaret al-Raml*
200

Pyramids of Abu Rawash

11

S

Delta Area and Suez Canal

Pyra
of Gi

0   20 km

Gabal Rissu
▲ 217

22

0   20 miles

Al-Fayyum

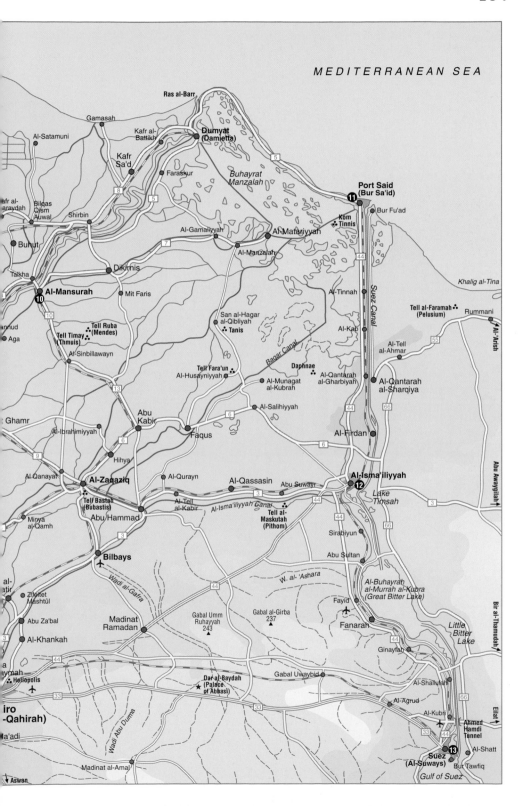

MEDITERRANEAN SEA

Ras al-Barr

Gamasah

Al-Satamuni

Kafr al-Battikh

Dumyat (Damietta)

Kafr Sa'd

Faraskur

Buhayrat Manzalah

Port Said (Bur Sa'id) ⑪

Bur Fu'ad

Kom Tinnis

8

afr al-araydah

Bilqas Qism Auwal

Shirbin

Al-Gamaliyyah

Al-Matariyyah

Buhut

7

Al-Manzalah

Khalig al-Tina

Dikirnis

44

Takha

Mit Faris

Al-Tinnah

Tell al-Faramah (Pelusium)

Rummani

Al-Mansurah ⑩

San al-Hagar al-Qibliyah

Tanis

Al-Kab

Al-Arish

10

annud

Tell Ruba (Mendes)

55

Aga

Tell Timay (Thmuis)

Al-Tell al-Ahmar

Al-Sinbillawayn

Bagar Canal

Tell Fara'un

Daphnae

Al-Qantarah al-Gharbiyah

Al-Qantarah al-Sharqiya

Ghamr

Al-Ibrahimiyyah

13

Al-Husayniyyah

Al-Munagat al-Kubrah

Abu Kabir

Faqus

Al-Salihiyyah

Al-Firdan

6

66

Al Qanayat

9

Hihya

Al-Zaqaziq

Al-Qurayn

Al-Qassasin

Abu Suwayr

Al-Isma'iliyyah ⑫

Lake Timsah

3

Minya al-Qamh

Tell Bastah (Bubastis)

Abu Hammad

Al-Tell al-Kabir

Al-Isma'iliyyah Canal

Tell al-Maskutah (Pithom)

44

Sirabiyun

66

Abu Sultan

3

Bilbays

Wadi al-Gafra

44

W. al-'Ashara

Al-Buhayrah al-Murrah al-Kubra (Great Bitter Lake)

atir

Zifeitet Mashtul

Madinat Ramadan

Gabal Umm Ruhayyah 243

Gabal al-Girba 237

Fayid

Fanarah

Little Bitter Lake

Abu Za'bal

Al-Khankah

aymah

Heliopolis

44

Ginayfah

Gabal Uwaybid

Al-Shalluah

Bir al-Thamudah

Eilat

33

Dar al-Baydah (Palace of Abbasi)

33

Al-Agrud

Al-Kubri

iro (-Qahirah)

Wadi Abu Dwma

66

a'adi

Ahmed Hamdi Tunnel

33

44

Aswan

Madinat al-Amal

Suez (Al-Suways) ⑬

Al-Shatt

Bur Tawfiq

Gulf of Suez

Recommended Restaurants, Bars & Cafés on page 269

ALEXANDRIA AND THE NORTHERN COAST

Modern Alexandria is the second-largest city in Egypt. Set on the shores of the Mediterranean, it has long been a popular holiday spot for Cairenes, a refuge from landlocked Cairo's searing summer heat

A visit to Alexandria, even if only for a day or two, is the perfect counterbalance to the intensity of Cairo. With its string of beaches and Mediterranean outlook, Alexandria is much more laid-back and a good place to relax. Here, the Nile is no longer the lifeblood of the community; instead the Mediterranean Sea and its maritime influences hold sway.

Modern attractions typical of the city's seaside location are what draw visitors to Alexandria, and the upgrading and expansion of these is regenerating the city and the surrounding area. Ambitious plans for tourist developments along the coastline to the west of Alexandria centre on the expansion of the Burg al-Arab international airport.

Alexander's legacy

When Emperor Alexander died in 325 BC, his remains were taken to Memphis for burial, but the priests sent the funeral cortège away. "Do not settle him here," they said, "but at the city he built at Rhakotis. For wherever his body must lie, that city will be uneasy, disturbed by wars and battles." So the conqueror of Asia was returned to the city he had established eight years earlier, where he was buried in a grave now lost somewhere below the foundations of modern Alexandria. And the priests were wrong: Memphis today is a sand heap littered with ancient fragments, while Alexandria, although buffeted by many wars and battles, has somehow stood the test of time.

Sadly there is very little left of the buildings and monuments that graced the city during the Hellenistic and post-Hellenistic period, making it the most renowned city of the ancient world after Athens and Rome. An odd column or two on the skyline, dank catacombs deep under modern pavements, a Roman pillar propping up the gateway to a pre-Revolutionary patrician villa and a growing inventory of masonry and columns and statues beneath the Mediterranean are all that is left of this glorious past. But over the past few years

Main attractions

ALEXANDRIA
  THE BIBLIOTHEKA
  ALEXANDRINA, P.257
  NATIONAL MUSEUM, P.258
  KOM AL-DIKKA, P.258
  FORT OF QAYTBAY, P.260
  TOMBS OF ANFUSHI,
  P.261
  POMPEY'S PILLAR, P.262
  CATACOMBS OF KOM AS-
  SHUQAFAH, P.262
  MUNTAZAH PALACE, P.264
  ROSETTA, P.264
  AL-ALAMAYN, P.266
  WADI AL-NATRUN, P. 267

PRECEDING PAGES: punts on Lake Idku, the Delta. **FAR LEFT:** Muntazah Palace and beach. **LEFT:** Alexandria is known for its cafés and patisseries.

TIP

Trains to Alexandria from
Cairo take about three
hours from Ramses
Station. Be sure to get
off at Masr, the central
station in Alexandria,
rather than suburban
Sidi Gaber Station.

the city, which has close to 4 million
inhabitants and is the Mediterranean's
largest urban centre, has recovered a
little of its former prestige. The new
Bibliotheka Alexandrina, inaugurated in
2003 *(see page 257)* is a symbol of the
city's renaissance.

A magnificent entry

When the 25-year-old Macedonian
conqueror Alexander the Great arrived
in Egypt in 332 BC, he realised that he
needed a capital for his newly conquered
Egyptian kingdom and that, to link it
with Macedonia, it would have to be
located on the coast. Early in 331 he
sailed northward from Memphis down
the Nile, then westward along the coast.
At a small fishing village called
Rhakotis, on a spit of land between the

sea and a freshwater lake, with limestone
quarries and easy access to the Nile, he
founded his city, gave orders to build it
and promptly departed. He never saw his
new metropolis completed, as he was
never to return, except in death.

After Alexander's death in 323 BC,
Egypt fell to a Macedonian general,
Ptolemy, who had been present at the
founding of Alexandria. He made it his
new capital and established a dynasty
that lasted until 30 BC.

The first Ptolemies busily set about
adorning their city. They also encouraged
scholarship, and under their rule
Alexandria became a haven and refuge
for intellectuals. The first two Ptolemies
meanwhile decided that they needed a
great monument in their new city, which
could be seen by ships at sea and provide

Recommended Restaurants, Bars & Cafés on page 269

a guide for sailors through the limestone reefs that line the shore. Thus the lighthouse on the island of Pharos, one of the Seven Great Wonders of the ancient world, came into being *(see box page 261)*. A fortress as well as a beacon, this huge lighthouse stood at the eastern end of Pharos, where it dominated both the Eastern Harbour, which sheltered the royal fleet, and the Western Harbour. Little remains of the lighthouse beyond a few Aswan granite blocks, although some if its statues and masonry have recently been found beneath the harbour *(see page 261)*.

The Mouseion

The Ptolemies' intellectual achievement was epitomised by the Great Library attached to the Mouseion in Alexandria. In many ways, the Mouseion, a shrine to the Muses, resembled a modern university, but the scholars, scientists and literary men it supported were under no obligation to teach. They could devote their entire time to their studies. The Great Library was, alas, burned down during Caesar's wars and the Mouseion's buildings have disappeared under subsequent rubble.

External threats, nationalist rebellion, intrigue at court and family strife made the Ptolemaic dynasty increasingly dependent on Rome. By 89 BC, thanks to the debts it owed to this new power, the Ptolemaic dynasty was under Roman control. In 51 BC, while rivals squabbled in the Roman Senate, a 17-year-old girl was crowned Queen Cleopatra VII in Alexandria. Three years later she was ready to play the temptress, first at Caesar's feet, then at Mark Antony's. And as long as she lived, Alexandria preserved its autonomy. At her death, it became a Roman city.

Centuries of decline

As Rome acquired increasing sway over its new colonies in the east, Christianity, a brand-new religious movement, drew disciples. More than any other city in the Roman Empire, Alexandria was the intellectual capital of the new religion.

The conflict between the Church and State came to its height in the first years of the 4th century under the emperor Diocletian, who demolished churches, demoted all Christian officials and enslaved or killed the rest,

Head in the Graeco-Roman Museum.

BELOW: late-Roman council chamber excavated in downtown Alexandria.

TIP

Central Alexandria is easily explored on foot, but for longer journeys, you might want to try the trams (they have one carriage reserved for women), which are good (albeit slow) for getting out to the east (blue trams Nos. 1 and 2 to Muntazah) and west to Ras al-Tin and Anfushi (yellow No. 15). Taxis are also plentiful and very cheap, and can be hired by the day.

BELOW: going for gold in the city's suqs.

as many as 60 a day for a period of five years, according to the traditions of the Coptic Church. This persecution prompted the Christian flight to the desert, which led to the founding of the first monasteries, and made such a strong impression on the Egyptian Church that the Coptic calendar (also sometimes called the Alexandrian calendar) begins at AD 284, marking the start of "the Era of Martyrs".

In 641, Alexandria fell to the Arab General Amr ibn al-As, who stormed into Egypt with an army of some 3,500 Bedu horsemen. They brought with them a new, rapidly growing religion, Islam.

This new religion would certainly have been hostile to a pagan Alexandria and was uneasy with a Christian one, but the Arab conquest was on the whole a humane affair and little damage was done to property. The city's two venerable libraries, which the Arabs are sometimes accused of destroying, had long been burned by pagans and Christians. But it was Cairo that would blossom under Egypt's Arab masters, while the once great, glittering city of Alexandria gradually dwindled, especially after a Frankish raid in 1365, when all the public buildings were destroyed and 5,000 citizens were carried off into slavery.

Renaissance and revolution

Modern Alexandria dates from the early 19th century and the reign of Muhammad Ali, who introduced its famous cotton industry and built the Mahmudiyyah Canal. This once more linked Alexandria to the hinterland, encouraging Egypt to look not only towards the Mediterranean again, but beyond it, to Europe. The cotton trade created great wealth, and a steady influx of Greeks, Italians, French and English turned Alexandria into a pseudo-European city, complete with wide, grid-planned streets, foreign schools, clubs, restaurants, casinos, businesses and banks.

The 1952 Revolution changed all that. The new government eventually expelled most foreigners and confiscated their lands or nationalised their businesses, while Egyptian capital and enterprise fled abroad.

Recommended Restaurants, Bars & Cafés on page 269

Using the mind's eye

A lot of the ancient city only came to light during a construction boom in the early 1990s. As old buildings were being demolished to make way for new ones, archaeological teams were allowed to excavate. One of the most important developments in understanding ancient Alexandria was the declassification of the harbour (ancient *portus magnus*) as a military zone in the 1990s. Underwater excavations have so far uncovered 2.2 hectares (5.5 acres) of buildings in the eastern section. Of special interest is the site of the Timonium, a small sanctuary used by Marc Antony in his retirement.

Bibliotheka Alexandrina

One of the most exciting developments in the city in recent years is the new **Bibliotheka Alexandrina** (www. bibalex.org; Sat–Thur 11am–7pm, Fri 3–7pm; separate admission charges for all the museums), a vast modern library inspired by the original Mouseion Library which was the pride of the ancient city and the world's first-ever centre for scientific research. The present library, located on the Corniche to the east of the Cecil Hotel, was inaugurated by President Hosni Mubarak in 2002, in the presence of a dozen other heads of state. Already there are almost 1 million visitors each year.

The impressive glass and steel building, an architectural evocation of the sun rising on the eastern Mediterranean, is intended to be an international centre of knowledge and culture, with the capacity to hold 8 million books in many languages, and 50,000 rare manuscripts.

There are actually six specialised libraries in total, including rare books and special collections; arts and multimedia; children's; microforms; and one for the visually impaired. The collection is far from complete, but the complex has given the city a renewed cultural focus. Many international stars perform in its concert hall (often in preference to venues in Cairo), and other facilities include a small antiquities section, a museum for local children and a planetarium. There is also an internet archive, nine permanent exhibitions on related subjects and space for four temporary exhibitions.

As soon as World War II was over the writing was on the wall for Alexandria's European community, and the far sighted were already getting out.

David Holdenk
Letter from Alexandria,
1963

BELOW:
Bibliotheka
Alexandrina.

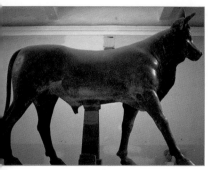

Apis bull in the National Museum of Alexandria.

BELOW: rehearsal at the Sayyid Darwish Theatre.

Museums

A good place to begin to unravel Alexandria's past is at the **National Museum of Alexandria** , in a modern villa at 110 Tariq al-Hurriyyah (daily 9am–5pm, public holidays 9am–3pm; admission charge). This new museum illustrates the city's history from antiquity to the modern day, with beautifully displayed and labelled artefacts that have been brought here from other museums in the city:, the Greco-Roman Museum, Qaytbay's fort and the Royal Jewellery Museum.

The layout is chronological, with the basement devoted to the pharaonic period, the ground floor to the Greco-Roman period, including a sphinx and other sculptures found in the Eastern Harbour, and the top floor is devoted to Coptic, Muslim and modern Alexandria. Interesting panels in every room explain various facets of religion and history.

Just around the corner, on Rue du Musée, is the entrance of the old **Greco-**

Roman Museum (closed at the time of writing for renovation). The museum fills the historical gap between the country's museums of pharaonic antiquities and Cairo's museum of Coptic and Islamic Art. Some of its Hellenistic sculpture and its wonderful Tanagra terracotta figurines collection have been moved to the National Museum of Alexandria *(see above).*

The Roman Odeon and Nabi Danyal

Return to Tariq al-Hurriyyah and find to the southwest of this street, near the Masr train station, the extensive excavations of **Kom al-Dikkah** (9am–5pm; admission charge). Here Polish archaeologists have been digging up Alexandria's past since 1959. Below Muslim tombs dating from the 9th to the 11th century, they have found baths, houses, assembly halls and the site where Christian mobs burnt objects from the Serapeum. The main attraction is the small 2nd-century theatre with well-preserved mosaic flooring. Some fine mosaic floors of a Roman villa, known as the Villa of the Birds, are

Recommended Restaurants, Bars & Cafés on page 269

also on show (extra admission charge).

Follow Shari' al-Nabi Danyal towards Tariq al-Hurriyyah. The point where the two streets meet has been the chief crossroads of the city for over 2,300 years. Here, from east and west, the Canopic Way (Shari' Tariq al-Hurriyyah) once ran from the Gate of the Sun to the Gate of the Moon. From north to south a street, now Shari' al-Nabi Danyal, once joined the harbour and its docks with Lake Mareotis.

A short walk up Shari' al-Nabi Danyal will bring you to the **Nabi Danyal Mosque ⑤**, on the left side of the street with an entrance set back. Mistakenly believed to lie over the tomb of the prophet Daniel, it is actually the burial place of Shaykh Danyal al-Maridi, who died in 1407. It is also falsely believed to be the site of the Soma, where Alexander is buried. Inside the mosque, an ancient caretaker will beckon you over to peer down a great square hole into the crypt where Danyal and one Lukeman the Wise lie, keeping company (it is alleged) with Alexander and some of his successors.

Almost straight opposite the Nabi Danyal Mosque some antique columns prop up the gatepost of what is now the French Cultural Centre.

The literary scene

Near the ancient crossroads, on Tariq al-Hurriyyah, is the **Sayyid Darwish Theatre**, a 19th-century opera house recently restored to its former splendour. During the early 20th century a literary revival took place in Alexandria, led by Constantine Cavafy (1863–1933), called "the poet of the city" by Lawrence Durrell. E.M. Forster, who lived in Alexandria and wrote its history, first met Cavafy in 1917 and was responsible for introducing him to the English-speaking world. The Greek poet's apartment at 4 Shari' Sharm al-Shaykh, off Shari' al-Nabi Danyal, is a **museum ⑥** (Tues–Sun 10am–4pm; admission charge). Lawrence Durrell's *Alexandria Quartet* was to a large extent inspired by Constantine Cavafy's poetry, and all the characters in the *Quartet* meet at least once at the Pastroudis café to drink *araq*.

Cavafy's flat may have been turned into a small museum, due to the efforts of the Greek Consulate, but **Lawrence Durrell's house** at 13 Shari' Maamoun

In ancient times the streets now called Shari' Tariq al-Hurriyah and Shari' al-Nabi Danyal were lined from end to end with colonnades.

BELOW: the 2nd-century theatre, Kom al-Dikkah.

Cleopatra's Needles

The Roman occupation of Egypt was closely followed by the looting of ancient artefacts to adorn the major piazzas and intersections of Rome. This led to there now being almost twice as many obelisks in Rome as there are in Egypt. However, not all of them made it to Rome. After defeating Cleopatra, Augustus Caesar ordered the removal of two granite obelisks outside the entrance of the Temple of the Sun at Heliopolis, but they only travelled as far as Alexandria. There they rested for almost 2,000 years until the late 19th century when Egypt presented one to London and another to New York. The ship carrying the obelisk to London almost sank and six men died. It was eventually raised beside the Thames in 1879. The other arrived a year later and now stands in New York's Central Park.

The Cecil Hotel is still going strong. The hotel was a setting for parts of Justine, *the first novel of Lawrence Durrell's* Alexandria Quartet.

BELOW: Fort Qaytbay.

in Moharrem Bey is under threat of being demolished. The city he describes, however, is still palpable. The **Cecil Hotel** Ⓖ is still there, and you can imagine Justine *(see margin note)* swinging in through the doors, however much the hotel has changed over the years.

At the heart of the former European zone, the Cecil Hotel overlooks the sea and Maydan Saad Zaghlul, a large square between **Ramleh tram station** *(al Raml)* and the **Corniche**. Here, in the lee of a few straggling palm trees, where the Romans built a temple to honour Julius Caesar, Alexandrians come to enjoy the cool of the evening.

The two obelisks that once stood here, the famous Cleopatra's needles, are now in London and New York *(see box, page 259)*. In the centre of the *maydan* is a statue of Saad Zaghlul, the nationalist hero who tried to negotiate Egypt's independence after World War I. The famous Pastroudis café closed down in 2004, but a few of the other patisseries where the writers and poets hung out are still there. The Trianon, Delices and Athineos are fine if somewhat forlorn examples of *fin-de-siècle* coffee houses.

The fortress and the Pharos

On the headland west of the Cecil Hotel is the **Fort of Qaytbay** Ⓗ. The best time to see the fort is just before dusk, when the warm reds and oranges of an Alexandrian sunset turn the sandstone building the colour of rich honey.

The trip out to Fort Qaytbay is of no particular interest except that it takes you along the sweeping bay to the site of the ancient Pharos lighthouse. On the Corniche side, you pass some dilapidated apartment buildings, gaily festooned with washing. Through the tightly packed buildings you might just catch a glimpse of the ornate mosque of Abu al-Abbas al-Mursi. On the sea side is the modern yacht club and a small fishing port, where nets are hung along the jetty to dry. The fort is at the end of a breakwater and has been restored since the British bombardment of Alexandria in 1882, the preliminary to the British invasion and occupation.

The lighthouse, constructed in 279 BC, was a marvel of its day. It rose to over 120 metres (400 ft) and hydraulic machinery may have been used for carrying fuel to the top. Within its square base were as

Map on page 254

Recommended Restaurants, Bars & Cafés on page 269

many as 300 rooms, to house mechanics and operators; above were an octagonal storey and a circular storey, topped by a lantern with a beacon.

The lantern collapsed as early as the 8th century, followed by the circular storey. In 881, Ibn Tulun made some restoration, but the 1100 earthquake toppled the octagonal storey and ruined his efforts. The Pharos still served as a lighthouse, however, until the square base was finally destroyed in another earthquake in the 14th century. In 1480, Sultan Qaytbay, built the fort that still stands on the site, incorporating some of the debris from the Pharos – you can make out granite and marble columns, for example, in the northwest section of the enclosure walls. The fort itself is an impressive piece of defensive architecture containing a not very interesting **naval museum**.

Ras al-Tin and Anfushi

Westward along the seafront 3 km (1½ miles) from the fort, is the 19th-century **palace of Ras al-Tin ❶** (Cape of Figs). Built by Muhammad Ali, but altered by later rulers of Egypt, this enormous pile is still used for official Egyptian government functions and cannot be visited.

East of the palace on Shari' Ras al-Tin, near the end of the tramline, and worth a look, are the Ptolemaic **tombs of Anfushi ❶** (daily 9am–4pm; admission charge). with decorations that marry Greek and Egyptian styles. Their stucco walls are painted to imitate marble blocks and tiles.

At this point, you can turn into the old Turkish quarter of **Anfushi** at the heart of what was once the island of Pharos.

Continuing southeast along Shari' Ras al-Tin you will reach **Shari' Faransa** (Rue de France). You are now in one of the most "native" parts of the city, where you may like to stop to look at the 17th-century **Tirbana Mosque**. It has a distinctive pale yellow exterior, with plaster over a red and black Delta-style facade of bricks and wooden beams. On its left side note the ancient columns at the entrance to the cellars. Two huge Corinthian columns mark the entrance to the mosque itself and support its minaret.

In ancient times Pharos was joined to the mainland by a causeway called the **Heptastadion**, which gradually became

> *...Few cities have made so magnificent an entry into history as Alexandria.*
>
> E.M. Forster

BELOW: tombs of Anfushi.

The Pharos

Besides the Pyramids, the other Ancient Wonder in Egypt was the lighthouse of Alexandria, the Pharos. Initially built by the Greeks to indicate the entrance of the harbour, it was turned into a lighthouse by the Romans. A floor mosaic of the Pharos found at a Byzantine church at Qasr Libya 900 km (560 miles) west shows that it was a hemispherical dome on top of a square building.

Contemporary descriptions talk of a mirror of polished steel, to reflect the sun by day and a fire by night, or describe a device made of glass, so fashioned as to enable a man sitting under it to see ships at sea that were invisible to the naked eye. If true, the latter suggests a kind of prism, the secret of which Alexandrian mathematicians may have discovered only for it to be lost when the Pharos fell.

Statue of Muhammad Ali overlooking Alexandria's Maydan al-Tahrir,

BELOW:
Pompey's Pillar.

a permanent broad neck of land. Along it to the south, Shari' Faransa runs into **Maydan at-Tahrir**, formerly Place Muhammad Ali. A statue of the pasha on horseback (by the 19th-century French sculptor Henri Alfred Jacquemart) still graces the *maydan*. The southern end of the square marks approximately the former mainland coastline and the sea-front of the village of Rhakotis.

The southern quarter

The hub of ancient Alexandria, **Rhakotis** is about 1.5 km (1 mile) southwest from the Corniche along Shari' Salah ad-Din and Shari' Amud al-Sawari. Simplest, perhaps, is to hail a taxi to **Pompey's Pillar ⓚ** – al-Amud as-Sawari, the Horse-man's Pillar (daily 9am–5pm; admission charge), at the bottom of a hill surrounded by a wall – this is now all that's left of the acropolis of the Ptolemies.

Long before Alexander arrived on the scene, this hill was the citadel of Rhakotis, dedicated to the worship of Osiris. The Ptolemies in their turn con-structed a temple of Serapis on its summit. Here, with a collection of around 700,000 manuscripts given to her by Mark Antony, Cleopatra endowed the second great Alexandrian library, which remained attached to the **Serapeum** until the temple itself was destroyed by a Christian mob. Not much remains: some tunnels in the rocks with crypts and niches and a few marble pillars.

The principal attraction is a solitary 30-metre (98-ft) high pillar of pink Aswan granite. When European travel-lers arrived in the 15th century it caught their attention and they named it after Pompey, saying that his head was enclosed in a ball at the top. It actually has nothing to do with Pompey: according to an inscription on its base, it was dedicated to the Emperor Diocletian in 291; it may once have had an equestrian statue on top, which would explain its Arabic name.

The catacombs

A short walk south of Pompey's Pillar are the **Catacombs of Kom as-Shuqafah ⓛ** (daily 9am–5pm; admission charge). Come out of the enclosure of Pompey's Pillar, turn right up a crowded street and at the top you will come to a small crossroads. Just beyond it is the entrance

to the catacombs. Immediately inside the entrance are four very fine sarcophagi of purplish granite. You are now on the Kom as-Shuqafah (Hill of Tiles) and the tombs here constitute the largest Roman-period funerary complex in Egypt. They date from about the 2nd century AD, a time when the old religions began to fade and merge with one another, as demonstrated in the curious blend of classical and Egyptian designs.

The catacombs are set out on three different levels, the lowest being flooded and inaccessible. The first level is reached by a wide circular staircase lit by a central well, down which the bodies were lowered by ropes. From the vestibule you enter the rotunda, with a well in its centre, upon which eight pillars support a domed roof. To the left is the banquet hall.

From the rotunda, a small staircase descends to the second level and the amazing central tomb is revealed. Here the decorations are fantastic and in a hotchpotch of styles. Bearded serpents on the vestibule wall at the entrance of the inner chamber hold the pine-cone of Dionysus and the serpent-wand of Hermes, but also wear the double crown of Upper and Lower Egypt, while above them are Medusas in round shields. Inside the tomb chamber are three large sarcophagi cut out from the rock. Roman in style, decorated with fruits, flowers, Medusas and filleted ox heads, none of them has ever been occupied and their lids are sealed. Over each of the sarcophagi is a niche decorated with Egyptian-style reliefs. Now turn and face the entrance. On your right stands the extraordinary figure of Anubis – with a dog's head, but dressed as a Roman soldier, with sword, lance and shield. On the left is the god Sobek, the crocodile god, with a cloak and spear.

Art and parks

Slightly out of the centre, on 27 Shari' Ahmed Yehya Pasha in Zizinia, is the palace of Princess Fatma al-Zahraa, now housing the **Royal Jewellery Museum** (closed at the time of writing). This superb collection of jewellery covers a period from Muhammad Ali to the abdication of King Faruq.

One stop further on tram No. 2 is **San Stefano**, which is home to Alexandria's

BELOW:
the catacombs of
Kom as-Shuqafah
combine Egyptian
and Roman
elements.

TIP

The Muntazah palace complex includes two palaces, the *harmalik*, the main palace, used for state purposes, and the *salaamlik*, a former royal guesthouse which is now the characterful El Salamlek Palace Hotel. It has luxurious rooms, suitably palatial suites, splendid public rooms and a small casino, as well as various restaurants. If nothing else, come for afternoon tea on the terrace and a walk through the grounds.

BELOW:
Alexandria's
Eastern Harbour.

latest museum. The **Modern Art Museum** (Shari' Mahmoud Said Pasha; daily 10am–6pm; admission charge) is housed in the villa of Mahmoud Said (1897–1964), one of Egypt's best-known modern artists. The museum contains his wonderful paintings and works by his contemporaries as well as paintings by today's artists, including Farouk Hosni, the current minister of culture.

At the end of the bay is Khedive Abbas II's **Muntazah Palace** **M**, now a presidential residence set in 140 hectares (350 acres) of pleasure gardens (admission charge), open to the public and a popular spot for a picnic.

Near the zoo and the Nuzha Gardens are the elegant **Antoniadis Gardens** **N** in Smouha (open daily 9am–sunset winter; 9am–9pm summer; admission charge). These peaceful formal gardens surround the 19th-century villa of the Greek philanthropist Sir John Antoniadis.

EAST TO ROSETTA

Alexandria's **Corniche** extends some 16 km (10 miles) eastwards. There are a number of public beaches between the Eastern Harbour and Muntazah, but they are crowded and polluted, and incessant building has turned most of the Corniche into an ugly string of high-rise buildings.

Eight kilometres (5 miles) east of Muntazah, with the gardens of the Muntazah Palace, is **Abu Qir** **1**, famous for battles fought here in 1798 and 1799. This seaside shanty town is home to some good seafood restaurants with open-air terraces right on the sea.

The next spot of interest is **Rosetta** **2** (Rashid), 65 km (40 miles) from Alexandria on the western branch of the Nile near the sea. It was here that the Rosetta stone, which enabled Champollion to decipher the hieroglyphics of the pharaohs, was discovered by Pierre Bouchard, a Frenchman working for Napoleon, in 1799. About the size of a gravestone, it was of very hard granite with three parallel bands of inscriptions. The defeat of the French by the British led to the stone passing into British hands and into London's British Museum. A replica of the original can be seen in the Egyptian Museum in Cairo.

The run-down town of Rosetta is famous for its 17th- and 18th-century houses, built in typical Delta style. Most of

Recommended Restaurants, Bars & Cafés on page 269

the houses have been renovated or are under renovation but a few are open to the public. The finest house is **Bayt Ramadan**, just west of the main square, which has a harem for the women in the household on the first floor, and a private hammam (bathhouse) on the top floor. Other traditional houses in the area include **Bayt al-Toqatli**, the impressive **Bayt Amasyali**, which has a splendid facade, and next door to it **Bayt Abu Shaheen**.

WEST TO BURG AL-ARAB

The coast road west of Alexandria is un-prepossessing for the first 30 km (18 miles) until you pass the **Agami**, which started out some decades ago as a few bathing huts and simple beach houses in a grove of trees, but has now mushroomed into an overgrown resort with swimming pools, discotheques and fast-food places.

Before the turn-off to the village of **Burg al-Arab** on the hill on your left, is the ancient **Temple of Taposiris Magna**, whose name is preserved in the modern Abu Sir. It is contemporary with the founding of Alexandria and was dedicated to the cult of Osiris. The ruined tower to the east is a Ptolemaic lighthouse, the first of a chain that stretched all the way along the North African coast. It looks, in miniature, very much as the Pharos, would have appeared.

To the south lies the lake bed of **Maryut** (ancient Mareotis), in spring vibrant with wildflowers. If you drive south across the lake bed, you can make out the remains of the ancient causeway, to your left, which connected ancient Taposiris with the desert.

Over the crest of the hill is the crumbling village of **Burg al-Arab ❸**, the brainchild of W.E. Jennings-Bramley, governor of the Western Desert under the British, who decided in the early 1920s to build a Bedu capital using stone from the ruins of Roman villas, which dotted the area. Modelling his village as a fortified medieval Italian hill town, he invited friends to build holiday homes within its turreted walls.

From here, you may want to continue inland and visit the ruins of the **monastery of Abu Mina ❹**. Drive south out of Burg al-Arab through an industrial development and turn left at the first crossroads you come to. This road will take you to the turn-off to the monastery.

The distinctive little water flasks that the monastery of Abu Mina produced (with their stamped depictions of St Mina standing between two kneeling camels) have been found as far afield as France and Spain.

BELOW:
Cleopatra' Baths,
Marsa Matruh.

The Cult of St Mina

Abu Mina was a young Egyptian officer, martyred in 296 during his service in Asia Minor because he would not renounce Christ. When his troops returned to Egypt, they buried him at the spot where the camel carrying his remains refused to go any further. Some time after this, a shepherd noticed that a sick lamb passing over the burial spot became well; so did another lamb, then a sick princess. The saint's powers were quickly recognised by Christians far and wide. A church was built over his grave in the 4th century, and this was then incorporated into a great basilica by Emperor Arcadius in the early 5th century.

For pilgrims, the site became the Lourdes of the Western Desert. The reason for this rapid popularity was probably the local water, which must have had potent curative powers, for in the shrine's heyday pilgrims flocked here by the thousands, filling little flasks, specially stamped with the saint's image, from the sacred source that flowed by his tomb. Over time houses sprang up, a baths complex was built, the land nearby was irrigated for agriculture, and a proper settlement evolved.

Conversions to Islam put an end to the cult, but as late as the year 1000 an Arab traveller saw the great double basilica still standing in the desert: lights still burned day and night at the shrine and there was a trickle of "the beautiful water of St Mina that drives away pain."

Before long you will spot the twin towers of a new monastery, founded in 1959, a popular pilgrimage spot for modern Copts. Drive on by and very shortly you will see a low line of hillocks to your right, the site of the ancient monastery of Abu Mina; the hillocks are the scrapheaps left behind by several generations of enthusiastic archaeologists. The foundations of the primitive church and the basilica of Arcadius can be discerned.

The crypt where St Mina was buried lies at the foot of a marble staircase, which was incorporated into the portico of the basilica, but his relics rest in the modern monastery. A baptistry with a font lies to the west. North of the basilica are the hospice and baths that were fed by healing springs, with cisterns for hot and cold water.

Al-Alamayn

Further along the coast road 105 km (65 miles) west of Alexandria, is **al-Alamayn ❺** (Alamein), the site of a series of battles that began in the summer of 1942 and turned the tide of war in favour of the Allies. Of the three main war cemeteries in al-Alamayn, the British is the first one you come to. It is on your left as you enter the town from the east. A walk around the simple tombstones, each of which carries an inscription, cannot fail to move. In the centre of town is a **War Museum** (daily 9am–4pm; admission charge) housing numerous artefacts of the battle. Beyond stands the stone monument to Germany's fallen soldiers, in a beautiful setting which overlooks the sea. Further down the coast is the Italian memorial, reminiscent of a railway station in a provincial Italian city.

Seaside resorts

From this point on, the coast varies between beautiful abandonment and heavy development of unfinished holiday resorts. On the left is the desert, enlivened by the occasional flash of colour from a gaily painted house or Bedu tent; to the right is the sea. If you long for a day on the beach, keep going to **Sidi Abd al-Rahman**, about 25 km (15 miles) past Al-Alamayn: some people claim it's the best beach on the coast. Out of season the hotel is rather

BELOW: the War Museum, al-Alamayn.

The Battle of al-Alamayn

For several months during early 1942, Allied troops had been forced back across North Africa under pressure from German and Italian troops intent on seizing the Suez Canal. In early July a defiant stand by the Allies under General Auchinleck halted this advance, but it was his replacement, Lieutenant-General Montgomery (Monty), who took the fight to the Axis powers. The 2nd Battle of al-Alamayn lasted almost two weeks and by November 4th 1942, Rommel, the German commander, ordered a retreat. The Allied Eighth Army pushed the Afrika Korps westwards, trapping the remaining German troops in northeastern Tunisia, leading to their surrender in May 1943. Some experts say that the Allied victory at al-Alamayn was the turning point of World War II.

Recommended Restaurants, Bars & Cafés on page 269

dismal, but there are also camping facilities. One of the main reasons that some tour groups travel along the coast to Sidi Abd al-Rahman is to then travel inland to visit the Siwah Oasis.

Alternatively, you can go to **Marsa Matruh ⑥**, 72 km (45 miles) further on, 280 km (175 miles) from Alexandria. Its seaside is lined with hotels, but the town has little character. You can visit **Rommel's Cave** (daily June–Sept 8am–5pm; admission charge), now a museum containing, among other items, the Desert Fox's armoury *(see box, page 266)*. The beach to the east, supposedly where Rommel went for his daily swim, is popular with families. There is an increasing stream of tourist traffic along the coast as the access to Libya continues to improve.

Wadi al-Natrun

To the west of the Delta, just off the Cairo-Alexandria desert road, the **Wadi al-Natrun**, or Valley of Natron, snuggles below sea level. It was once home to over 50 monasteries. **Deir Abu Maqar ⑦**, the largest, has in recent years been the seat of the Coptic Pope Shenouda III,

exiled here by the late President Sadat. It is closed to visitors unless they can show a letter of introduction from the Coptic patriarchate in Cairo (tel: 02-2282 5374). **Anba Bishoi ⑧** (tel: 02-2591 4448; daily, summer 7am–8pm, winter 7am–6pm; free), founder of another monastery, was a disciple of Abu Maqar (St Macarius). A third monastery, **Deir as-Suryani ⑨** (tel: 02-2592 9658; Mon–Fri and Sun 9am–6pm and Sat 9am–3pm winter, until 7pm plus Sat 9am–5pm summer; free), has 10th-century paintings and ivory panels in its church of Al Adhra. **Deir al-Baramus** (tel: 02-2592 2775; open daily, summer 9am–6pm, winter 9am–5pm; free) is the most remote.

Wadi al-Natrun's churches, like Pharaonic temples, have three distinct areas. The outer is reserved for laymen, the middle for initiates and the inner for clergymen. Visitors should on no account venture into the curtained inner sanctuaries. Monasteries are closed to

The mud domes of Anba Bishoi, Wadi Natrun.

BELOW: inside the monastery of St Bishoi.

the public during periods of fasting: Sexagesima Monday to Orthodox Easter (61 days), Advent (25 November–6 January), before the Feast of the Apostles (27 June–10 July) and before Assumption (7–21 August).

The Delta

The **Nile Delta** is lush with vegetation and veined with canals, From the Barrage at **Qanatir al-Khayriyyah** just north of Cairo, where parks surround locks and sluices built under the British occupation, to the marshy waters of lakes **Idku** *(see picture, pages 248–9)* **Burullus** and **Manzalah**, the Delta fans out like a palm tree reaching for the Mediterranean. To both the west and the east, deserts are receding in the face of extensive land-reclamation projects, while in the Delta *fellaheen* (farmers) pack their bags and leave to seek their fortune in Cairo or the oil-rich Gulf.

The prehistoric Delta was a swampy tidal estuary interspersed with islands. Centuries of effluvia built up a silty land mass that eventually split the river in two. During the annual flood, river water turned the Delta into a vast lake. The ancient Egyptians therefore built their towns on hills and hummocks which appeared like islands when the inundation was at its height.

Diligent canal building, after the union of Lower and Upper Egypt in the Old Kingdom, tamed the swamp. With the growth of trade and rivalry between Egypt, Phoenicia and the Greeks, the Delta grew in importance, encouraging later pharaohs to establish headquarters in the Delta near the sea.

Each area of the Delta has its particularity. **Al-Mansurah** ❿, the "victorious", was founded on the site of the Mamluks' triumph over crusaders under Louis IX. With its gracious Nile-side villas dating from the age when cotton was king in the Delta, the city is regarded as the queen of the Delta.

Dumyat (Damietta) rivalled Alexandria in the Middle Ages and is now the centre of Egypt's furniture industry; and **Disuq** is identified with a festival *(mouled)* in honour of its saint, Ibrahim ad-Disuqi. The Delta's largest town, **Tanta**, is known for its October *mouled*, drawing people from all over Egypt for the festival of Ahmad al-Badawi. ❑

BELOW: rural idyll in the Delta.

RESTAURANTS & BARS

Restaurants

Prices for a three-course dinner per person with a half-bottle of house wine:
$ = under $20
$$ = $20–45
$$$ = $45–60
$$$$ = over $60

Abu Ashraf
28 Shari' Safar Pasha, Bahari
Tel: 03-481 6597. $$–$$$
A 24-hour fish restaurant, very simple but with excellent fresh fish and seafood, straight from the market. Sea bass stuffed with garlic and herbs is a speciality, as is the creamy shrimp *kishk* (casserole).

Adoura
33 Shari' Bayram al-Tonsi, Anfushi
Tel: 03-480 0405. $$
Popular cheap outdoor restaurant in a quiet street. Excellent selection of fresh fish served with meze. No alcohol.

Bella Vista
Abu Qir beach. $$
Serves good seafood and fish by the beach.

Centro de Portugal
42 Shari' Abd al-Kader, off Shari' Kafr Abduh, Rushdy
Tel: 03-542 7599. $$$
Favoured by the local ex-pat community, the Portuguese Club is the place to go for good steak frites, veal esca-lope, a beer or a game of snooker. It can get rather loud, particularly at weekends, but the food is good, and there is a great garden in summer.

China House
Cecil Hotel, 16 Midan Saad Zaghloul
Tel: 03-487 7173. $$$
Alexandria's only Chinese restaurant. Chicken dumplings are excellent, as are the desserts and the views over the East-ern Harbour.

Cordon Rouge
Green Plaza Mall, 14th of May Bridge, Smouha
Tel: 03-420 8666. $$$
Very lively bar-restaurant in this busy shopping mall that serves good pastas, grills and salad.

Elite
43 Shari' Safia Zaghlul
Tel: 03-486 3592. $
Long menu of Greek and Egyptian dishes, and tables with a view on the world. Good value.

Fish Market
Al-Kashafa al-Baharia Club No. 26 on the Corniche
Tel: 03-480 5119. $$$
An upmarket fish restau-rant with a huge display of fresh fish, which is then cooked the way you want it. Good service, salad bar and a view of the harbour.

The Greek Club (Club Nautique Hellenique)
Shari' Qasr Qaytbay, Anfushi
Tel: 03-554 4512. $$
This old-fashioned Greek restaurant-bar is the best place to watch the sun set. In winter you can sit inside in the large, newly renovated rooms, but much recommended is the wide terrace with sweeping views over the bay. The beers are cold, and the atmosphere is truly Mediterranean.

Malek as-Samaan
Just south of the junction with Shari' Yousef, off Shari Attareen
Tel: 03-390 0698. $$
Only open from 8pm onwards, this is an open-air restaurant serving nothing but quail, sold by the pair with rice and salad. This experience is as Alexandrian as it gets.

Mamma Mia
Sheraton Hotel, Muntazah
Tel: 03-548 0550. $$
Good Italian with fresh pastas and pizzas. Kitsch Italian decor.

Mohamed Ahmed
17 Shari' Shakour Pasha off Shari' Saad Zaghloul
Tel: 03-487 3576. $
Serving the best *ful* and *tamia* in town and known as the Great Pyramid of Alexandria. No alcohol.

Samakmak
42 Qasr Ras at-Tin, al-Bahry
Tel: 03-481 1560. $$$
Excellent and unpreten-tious fish restaurant, opposite the boatyard and around the corner from the fish market. There is both indoor and outdoor seating, and diners choose from the fresh fish on display at the counter, specifying whether they want it grilled or fried.

Splash
Hilton Alexandria Green Plaza, Smouha
Tel: 03-420 9120. $$$
A relaxed Italian restau-rant in the heart of this shopping mall. Menu mixes classic and modern Italian cooking.

Tikka Grill
Al-Kashafa al-Baharia Club, No. 26 on the Corniche
Tel: 03-480 5119. $$$
Excellent fish kebabs and meat dishes and a salad bar. Good views.

Cafés and Bars

Athineios
21 Maydan Ramlak
Tel: 03-487 7173. $–$$$
Three-in-one establish-ment offers a patisserie, nightclub and a good restaurant with Levantine and Mediterranean fare.

Cap d'Or
4 Shari' Adib off Shari' Saad Zaghlul
Tel: 03-483 5177. $$
Art Nouveau bar serving a squid stew and fried fish. Attracts a loyal crowd of customers.

Coffee Roastery
48 Shari' Fuad
Tel: 03-483 4363/48. $$
Western-style restaurant-tearoom with great cof-fees, shakes, juices and a large snack and lunch menu. No alcohol.

Spitfire Bar
7 Shari' al-Bursa al-Qadima, off Shari' Saad Zaghloul
Tel: 03-480 6503. $
Smoky rock-and-roll bar with a mixed crowd of local die-hards and ex-pats.

Trianon
Maydan Saad Zaghlul
Tel: 03-482 0986. $–$$$
Elegant air-conditioned restaurant and bar, serv-ing Mediterranean-Levan-tine food. The patisserie next door has a good-value breakfast.

UNDERWATER ARCHAEOLOGY

Time and earthquakes brought down Alexandria's glorious waterfront, but over the past few years efforts have been made to raise it from the sea

Ancient Alexandria was one of the great cities of the world and befitting its role as a major Mediterranean seaport it had a grand waterfront, capped by the Pharos, wonder of the world. The Eastern Harbour, at whose entrance the Pharos stood, was fronted by the royal palace, which was constantly enlarged and embellished. Cleopatra built a new temple on the waterfront in honour of Mark Antony, which Augustus Caesar finished in honour of himself. In front of it stood two older obelisks brought from the south. This temple, the palace and all but a few stones of the Pharos disappeared in the aftermath of earthquakes.

Modern Alexandrians always knew they were sailing and swimming over the ruins of their city, but it wasn't until the 1960s that serious underwater exploration began. More recently, two separate teams have been at work beneath the Eastern Harbour. The site around the Pharos outside the harbour, from where blocks were recently lifted by a team led by the French archaeologist Professor Jean-Yves Empereur of the Centre d'Etudes Alexandrines (www.cea.com.eg), was first visited in the 1960s by Kamal Abu al Sadaat. He succeeded in bringing up a colossal female statue. The first underwater maps were made around that time by Honor Frost, a Briton working with unesco.

A second team under Frank Goddio worked inside the Eastern Harbour on what was dry land in antiquity, another site mapped by Abu al Sadat. The team working here claim to have discovered Cleopatra's Palace, but it might be hard to substantiate this.

In 2005 the open-air museum in the gardens of Kom ad-Dikka was reopened with some of the underwater finds from the Eastern Harbour.

ABOVE: of some 20 sphinxes discovered, only this one was intact, but even after desalination and restoration, its inscription is unreadable, its identity a riddle.

BELOW: among thousands of pieces of masonry found lying on the seabed, many had come from the palace and the Pharos which collapsed in the 14th century. This 40-tonne, grooved block has no inscriptions.

RIGHT: this uninscribed statue of a Ptolomy was found beside fragments from other statues which Professor Empereur believes were part of a group that stood on the Pharos and overlooked the port.

SAVING THE SALVAGE

The decision to raise blocks from the sea bed was a controversial one, with some archaeologists arguing that conservation would be impossible. So, having brought statues and masonry to the surface, the teams made conservation a priority. Blocks that had been soaking in saltwater for a couple of thousand years needed delicate handling to stop them crumbling when they dried out. The answer was to immerse them in desalination tanks installed in Alexandria several years ago, when a French team raised the remains of Napoleon's fleet in nearby Aboukir Bay. This time the desalination was done by an Egyptian team, with technical support from members of the French Institute of Oriental Archaeology (IFAO).

The first step was to immerse pieces in water that contained the same level of salt as seawater. The salt content of the water was then gradually reduced until the blocks were left standing in fresh water and the salts absorbed by the stone had been leeched away, a process that takes about five months. Here the colossal statue of a Ptolemy is shown soaking in one of the tanks at the start of its desalination treatment.

ABOVE: excavation work was often hampered by the sea. Archaeologists had to take into account underwater currents and surface conditions.

BELOW: a recovered sphinx make its way from a watery grave to a museum.

RIGHT: a diver from the Franco-Egyptian team exploring the open-sea site in front of Qaytbay's fort, which has yielded statues believed to have decorated the Pharos.

Recommended Restaurants on page 277

THE SUEZ CANAL

The Suez Canal is arguably the most vital traffic artery in the world. When it opened to shipping in 1869, it cut distances between Europe and India in half

Main attractions
PORT SAID, P.275
ISMAILIA, P.275
SUEZ, P.277

Picture a huge ocean-going ship drifting through a sea of sand. Seen across flat desert, the hallucinatory effect of the Suez Canal underlines the revolutionary impact the waterway has had not only on the nation of Egypt, but on the structure of international commerce. By the mid-19th century, with the expansion of both trade and empires, its economic potential was becoming increasingly obvious.

An old idea

The idea of building a canal that would link the Mediterranean with the Red Sea is ancient indeed. The first channel connecting the Nile and Red Sea might go as far back as the 12th Dynasty (*circa* 1800 BC). Certainly the 26th Dynasty pharaoh Necho II aired such a proposal at the end of the 7th century BC, with a project to join the Gulf of Suez to the Nile, down which ships could continue to the Mediterranean. According to Herodotus, an oracular pronouncement that he would merely be "labouring for the barbarians" dissuaded Necho from completing excavations. The job was therefore left to Egypt's Persian conquerors a century later, under Darius; their work was followed by Ptolemaic and Roman re-excavation.

During the centuries before the Arab conquest, however, this old canal silted up and the Muslims' brilliant general Amr ibn al-As, suggested that a new and better one should be cut across the narrow isthmus of Suez. Cautioned by

the caliph Omar that it would be hard to defend and that Greek pirates might use it as a route to attack the holy city of Mecca, he satisfied himself with renovating the existing canal. It flourished for another century before being blocked on orders of the Abbasid caliph al-Mansur.

It was not until the 19th century, with the growth of European power in the region and the energetic promotion of the French engineer Ferdinand de Lesseps, that Amr's idea could was brought to fruition. A Suez Canal

LEFT: canal traffic comes in all shapes and sizes. **BELOW:** fishing at Ismailia.

The Suez Canal

Engineered by the French, built by the Egyptians and coveted by the British, the Suez Canal has been a troubled but lucrative waterway.

Construction of the Suez Canal began in 1859. It took 10 years, with 25,000 labourers working three-month shifts, to cut the 160-km (100-mile) channel. The total cost, including the building of the Sweetwater Canal for drinking water from the Nile, reached £25 million, of which Egypt put up more than two-thirds. Amid extravagant fanfare, with assorted European royalty in attendance, the canal was opened to shipping in November of 1869, transforming trade and geopolitics as dramatically as the Portuguese and Spanish discoveries of the 15th century. At the same time Cairo acquired an extravagant new opera house and a new palace (now the Marriott Hotel) to entertain and accommodate the important guests who attended the opening.

However, Egypt's mounting debts forced the sale of its stake to the British Government for a paltry sum of £4 million sterling. As London's *Economist*

dryly commented in the year of its opening, the canal was "cut by French energy and Egyptian money for British advantage". The strategic importance of the canal to the British Empire was one of the excuses for occupying Egypt in 1882.

The fortunes of five wars

Britain imposed draconian measures on Egypt while defending the canal in both world wars. For Egyptians, foreign possession of the canal came to represent the major reason for the anti-imperialist struggle. Not until 1954 did Nasser acheive the withdrawal of British troops occupying the Canal Zone.

In 1956, hard up and seeking to finance the High Dam, Nasser turned as a last resort – having been refused financing by the United States – to nationalising the canal, from which Egypt received only a tiny portion of the revenue. Unreconciled to the rapid decline of its empire, Britain responded by invading, with the collusion of Israel and France, in what became known as the Suez Crisis. Only the intervention of the USA and the Soviet Union resolved the crisis, marking a turning point in international relations. Ten years later all that remained of Britain's empire were Gibraltar, Hong Kong and a few remote islands. Meanwhile Egypt had become dependent upon Russia.

In June 1967, the Israelis again attacked Egypt in the Six Day War, and held the Sinai Peninsula up to the edge of the canal. Heavy bombardment during the War of Attrition that followed the Israeli conquest shattered the canal cities and made refugees of their 500,000 inhabitants. For six years, until the successful Egyptian counterattack of the Yom Kippur War in October 1973, the waterway was closed to traffic.

The canal reopened in 1975, and has since been widened and deepened. However, despite these recent improvements, there are still limitations caused by the 70-metre (230-ft) clearance below the road bridge at al-Qantara and the 16 metre (52-ft) draft. ❏

ABOVE: the grand opening of the canal in 1869.
LEFT: visitors to the war museum in Port Said.

Recommended Restaurants on page 277

Company was formed by public subscription in Europe and an agreement was reached with the viceroy Said and his successor Khedive Ismail, whereby Egypt provided both capital and labour for the job itself.

The canal cities

Port Said ⓫ sits on an artificial landfill jutting into the Mediterranean and is named after the khedive of Egypt, Said Pasha. From here convoys of ships depart every morning at 1am and 7am, passing the green domes of the Suez Canal Authority building to begin the journey to the Red Sea.

Once the major point of entry for tourists stepping off the great Peninsular and Orient (P & O) passenger lines, Port Said is now the Hong Kong of Egypt, where Cairo consumers flock for duty-free goods. Despite the damage of three wars and the current emporium atmosphere, this resilient town retains a good deal of character, including some fine period buildings from the middle of the 18th century.

Fifty kilometres (30 miles) south of Port Said is **al-Qantara**, an important

battleground during World War I when British and Allied troops fought to stop the Ottoman Turks from taking the canal. Today it is the site of the **Mubarak Peace Bridge**, almost 10 km (6 miles) in length, which was built with Japanese assistance in the mid-1990s. Its construction was designed to improve communications with the Sinai and to repopulate the eastern bank of the canal, which had been abandoned during the wars with Israel.

Before reaching Ismailia, you will notice the first bridge across the canal carrying a rail line. It can swing out of the way to allow shipping to pass. It was built to replace the one destroyed in the 1967 war, again to try and redevelop the eastern bank of the canal.

Ismailia

Situated on **Lake Timsah** halfway between Port Said and Suez, **Ismailia (al-Isma'iliyyah)** ⓬ is the queen of the canal cities. With its tree-shaded avenues and colonial-style houses, it retains a

Memorial to Anwar Sadat, who was assassinated in 1981 while taking part in a military parade marking the Egyptian Army's retaking of the Sinai in 1973.

BELOW:
Mecca-bound pilgrims beside the canal at Suez.

Marble coffin from the Ptolemaic period in Ismailia's museum.

BELOW: the house of Ferdinand de Lesseps, the builder of the Suez Canal, Ismailia.

between the massive ships every 15 minutes transferring vehicles and people to the other side, where there is a war memorial and gardens.

There are few places in the world where you can watch giant tankers and container ships glide past at 15 km (9 miles) per hour so close and so quietly. The ships take between 11 and 16 hours to pass through, so you are almost certain to see a line of them at Ismailia around midday.

Ismailia has a few sights in addition to the canal. You can take a taxi to the small **regional museum** (daily 9am–4pm; admission charge), which has a good selection of mainly Greek and Roman finds, including a large 4th-century mosaic with mythological creatures. One of the most impressive items is a Hellenised face on a marble coffin from the Ptolemaic period.

certain gentility from the 1950s when British officers escaped the hardships of their desert postings to relax here at the French and Greek clubs. It is said to be the cleanest city in Egypt. There are a number of fairly good hotels and restaurants; and from uncrowded lakeside beaches ships transiting the canal can be watched.

To get a better view of the canal's activity, take a taxi to the dock for the local car ferry to Sinai. The ferry sneaks

Near the centre of Ismailia is the former **house of Ferdinand de Lesseps**, the builder of the Suez Canal, and close by a mosaic of the grand opening ceremony. In the central town square is the large new mosque of Abu Bakr Saddiq.

Recommended Restaurants below

South of Ismailia the canal enters the **Great Bitter Lake**, a small inland sea bordered by holiday villas and military installations. Halfway between the lake and Suez is the 5-km (3-mile) long **Ahmed Hamdi Tunnel** providing vehicle access to the Sinai. It was built by the British in 1983 but leakage problems necessitated serious repairs by the Japanese within the first decade. Such problems have halted plans for any further tunnels, hence the decision to build the massive Mubarak Peace Bridge at al-Qantara.

The port of Suez

Suez ⓭ (al-Suways), the canal's southern terminus, was Egypt's major Red Sea port for hundreds of years and it is thus an important transit point for millions of Muslims making the pilgrimage to Mecca *(hajj)* from North Africa and Turkey. The town has an important trading history as the main port at the northern end of the Red Sea. It was, for example, crucial in the coffee trade from the southern Red Sea port of Mocha in Yemen, for coffee accounted for over 60 percent of Egypt's imports

at the end of the 18th century. The wreck of a 17th-century cargo ship at Sadana Island at the entrance to the Gulf of Suez has been excavated to reveal a cargo of coffee, porcelain, pepper, spices and incense bound for Suez.

The port's harbour is now at **Bur Tawfiq**, an artificial peninsula where the canal meets the **Gulf of Suez**. Israeli bombardments flattened the town in the 1967 war, after which it was evacuated and hasty rebuilding has not enhanced its beauty.

Suez is best observed from the Sinai side of the canal, where scores of ships can be seen lining up in the Gulf ready to make the northward passage. It is an amazing sight. The modern canal is 192 km (119 miles) long and has a minimum width of 60 metres (197 ft), with no locks. Today about 10 percent of the world's shipping use it, earning Egypt over US$3 billion per year in revenue, making it Egypt's second biggest earner after tourism. ❏

Fishing in the Great Bitter Lake, south of Ismailia. The canal passes through two other lakes: Lake Timsah in the middle and Lake Manzala in the north.

BELOW LEFT: the mosque of Abu Bakr Saddiq, Ismailia.

RESTAURANTS

Port Said

Al Borg
Shari' Toreh al Bahr. **$$$**
On a street that is packed with restaurants, this one stands out. First-rate seafood, including great shrimp kofta, with huge salads.

Five Stars
Shar' al-Gumhurriyah. **$**
Inexpensive and excellent Egyptian fast-food.

Reana House
5 Shari' al-Gumhur-riyah. **$$**
Tasty Korean food served above the

atmospheric Cecil Hotel, which is well worth a night-cap afterwards.

Ismailia

Georges
11 Shari' Thawra.
Tel: 064 391 8327. **$$**
Reliable favourite serving a good range of shellfish and fish from Lake Timsah. Old-fashioned ambience; alcohol served.

King Edward
171 Shar' at-Tahir
Tel: 064 3369611.
$$
Good range of international fish and

meat dishes with some Egyptian specialities. Bustling ambience, and pizzas also available.

Nefertari
Shari' Sultan Hasan.
$$
Simple Egyptian fare such as grills, meze and salads, as well as some fish.

Prices for a three-course dinner per person with one beer or glass of house wine:
$ = under $20
$$ = $20–45
$$$ = $45–60
$$$$ = over $60

Recommended Restaurants, Bars & Cafés on page 289

SINAI

Whether treated as holy ground or as a
battleground fought over by classical empires
and modern nation states, the Sinai Peninsula
has always been special

olumes have been dedicated to this small desert poised delicately but obstinately between two continents. As a passage between Asia and Africa, it has weathered as many military crossings as it has peaceful occupations, thanks in part to a climate that precludes all but the sparsest settlement. Even its few prehistoric, ancient and medieval remains, however, have only been scratched at by archaeologists, while Biblical geographers' controversies over problematical routes and sites have created an academic kaleidoscope of fact and fantasy.

Sinai's transformation

It is only in the years since the latest of more than 50 recorded invasions of the Sinai that the region has ceased to be regarded by non-inhabitants as an empty buffer zone. Or as a dangerous crossroads where native Bedu and foreign powers controlled all access – effectively a barrier separating the two halves of the Arab world.

Sinai's 25,000 sq. km (10,000 sq. miles) of desert, ranging from the spiky granite mountains of the south to the central plateau of al-Tih, then to the rolling dunes of the northern coastal plain, are now fair game to back-packers, camel trekkers and busloads of tourists. The shock of the Israeli occupation and Israel's opportunistic development of the peninsula's tourist potential prodded Egypt towards a fierce determination to bind Sinai once again

to the Nile valley, this time inextricably.

Although the hotel infrastructure was originally geared to low-budget kibbutzniks, the Sinai now has some of Egypt's top hotels, best-maintained roads and certainly its most efficient bus services. Daily flights connect the capital to Al-'Arish, Taba and Sharm al-Shaykh, while a ferry and regular flights link Sharm al-Shaykh with Hurghadah and Luxor. Although public transport is reliable, there is no substitute for having one's own car – preferably with four-wheel drive.

PRECEDING PAGE:
beach idyll.
LEFT: Myos Harmes.
BELOW: family near
Hammam Fara'un.

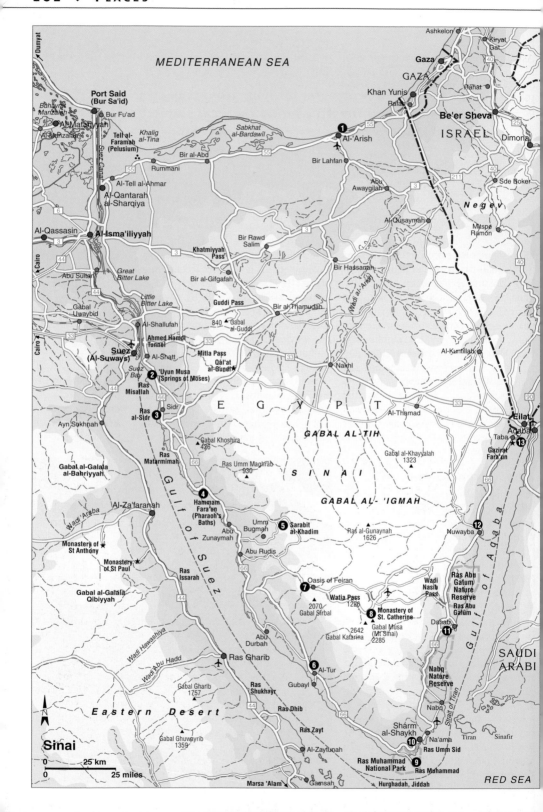

MEDITERRANEAN SEA

Dumyat

Bûhayrat Manzalah

Al-Matariyyah
Al-Menzalah

Port Said
(Bur Sa'id)

Bur Fu'ad

Tell al-Faramah
(Pelusium)

Khalig al-Tina

Sabkhat al-Bardawîl

Ashkelon

Kiryat Gat

Gaza

GAZA

Khan Yunis

Rafah

Rahat

Be'er Sheva

ISRAEL

Dimona

1 Al-'Arish

Bir al-Abd

Rummani

Bir Lahfan

Sde Boker

Al-Tell al-Ahmar

Al-Qantarah al-Sharqiya

Abu Awaygilah

Negev

Mitspe Ramon

Al-Qassasin

Al-Isma'iliyya

Bir Rawd Salim

Khatmiyyah Pass

Al-Qusaymah

Cairo

Abu Sultan

Great Bitter Lake

Bir al-Gifgafah

Bir Hassanah

Little Bitter Lake

Guddi Pass

Bir al-Thamudah

Gabal Uwaybid

Al-Shallufah

840 ▲ Gabal al-Guddi

Wadi al-'Arish

Al-Kuntillah

Cairo

Ahmed Hamdi Tunnel

Mitla Pass

Qal'at al-Gundi ★

Suez (Al-Suways)

Al-Shatt

Nakhl

2 'Uyun Musa (Springs of Moses)

Suez Bay

Ras Misallah

Al-Thamad

Ayn Sukhnah

Sidr

Ras al-Sidr **3**

E G Y P T

GABAL AL-TIH

Eilat

Aqaba

Taba **13**

Gazirat Fara'un ★

Gabal Khoshira 436

S I N A I

Gabal al-Khayyalah 1323

Gabal al-Galala al-Bahriyyah

Ras Matarmimah

Ras Umm Maghrab 930

GABAL AL- 'IGMAH

Al-Za'faranah

Wadi 'Araba

Hammam Fara'un (Pharaoh's Baths) **4**

Abu Zunaymah

Umm Bugmah

Sarabit al-Khadim **5**

Ras al-Gunaynah 1626

Nuwayba **12**

Monastery of St Anthony ★

Monastery of St Paul ★

Ras Issarah

Abu Rudis

Ras Abu Galum Nature Reserve

Ras Abu Galum

Gabal al-Galala Qibiyyah

Oasis of Feiran **7**

Watia Pass 1226

Wadi Nasib Pass

Dahab **11**

SAUDI ARABI

2070 Gabal Sirbal

Monastery of St. Catherine **8**

Ras Gharib

Abu Durbah

2642 Gabal Katarina

Gabal Musa (Mt Sinai) 2285

Nabq Nature Reserve

Wadi Abu Hadd

Wadi Hawashiya

Al-Tur **6**

Gubayl

Ras Shukhayr

Nabq

Strait of Tiran

Gabal Gharib 1757

Ras Dhib

Ras Zayt

N

Sinai

0   25 km

0   25 miles

E a s t e r n   D e s e r t

Gabal Ghuwayrib 1359

Al-Zaytunah

Ras Zayt

Sharm al-Shaykh **10**

Na'ama

Ras Umm Sid

Tiran

Sinafir

Marsa 'Alam

Gamsah

Ras Muhammad National Park **9** Ras Muhammad

Hurghadah, Jiddah

RED SEA

Recommended Restaurants, Bars & Cafés on page 289

North Sinai

Aside from seasonal Bedu encampments, North Sinai's population is concentrated on the provincial capital of **al-'Arish ❶**. From Cairo the main Ismailia highway leads to the Suez Canal. At Qantarah, north of Al-Isma'iliyyah, crossing to Sinai is made by a large bridge.

The road continues across the desert to the northeast, skirting the marshy lagoon of Lake Bardawil to reach Al-'Arish after 130 km (85 miles). This town of 40,000 is the biggest in the peninsula and much recent effort has been made to turn it into a palm-fringed resort with plenty of reasonably priced hotels and restaurants popular with Egyptian holiday-makers, though the once beautiful beaches are hemmed in with concrete. The local Friday suq has some good Bedu finds. Bedu crafts and jewellery are also on display at the local museum.

Just east of the town, the bare dunes begin. A few olive trees appear, marking the decline of the desert and the beginning of the fertile Palestine coastal plain. At 50 km (30 miles) the town of **Rafah** marks the current border. Beyond lies Gaza. Rafah's population is a mixture of local Bedu and Palestinian refugees. Their camp – built with Canadian government aid and consequently called Canada – was brutally bisected by the border fence erected after the area's return to Egypt in 1983. The border crossing at Rafah is now closed most of the time because of the situation in Gaza.

Between al-'Arish and Rafah a number of wadis, seasonal watercourses, lead back from the sea into the desert interior. The Bedu graze their goats and camels extensively in this region. Friendly and hospitable, they are wont to invite travellers into their ramshackle settlements – shacks slapped together with cans, boxes and the debris of four wars – for a glass of tea. The desert-dwelling women of north Sinai wear gorgeous embroidered dresses and heavy silver jewellery and are extremely friendly, so the opportunity to mingle should not be missed.

To the northeast of Suez and difficult to access, lie the ruins of a medieval fortress, **Qala'at al-Gundi**. Built by Saladin to protect trade and pilgrimage routes, these fortifications attest to the

Sinai is mostly inhabited by the Bedu, or Bedouin, who claim descent from tribes of the Hejaz (Saudi Arabia) on the Arabian peninsula, except the Jebeliya ("mountain people"), who are believed to be descendants of Caucasians.

BELOW LEFT: a heavy load in the Sinai desert.

Military Thoroughfare

The wilderness of Sinai is one of the most strategically important locations on earth. As the land bridge between Africa and Asia it has witnessed the marching feet of countless armies. It is where the ancient Egyptians under great military pharaohs such as Tutmosis III and Ramesses II attacked their eastern Mediterranean enemies, such as the hated Hyksos. In the other direction came the armies of Assyria, Persia, Greece and Rome, all intent on conquering the powerful Nile Valley civilisations.

With the building of the Suez Canal the region became even more important, with the Sinai essentially a "buffer zone" between east and west. During World War I there were several important battles fought by the Allies to stop Turkish forces seizing the canal as early as February 1915. From their base in Jerusalem, the Turks and Germans were attempting to stem the flow of men and supplies from the British Empire in the east.

After the establishment of the State of Israel in 1947, Egypt and its Arab neighbours fought the first Arab-Israeli war the following year. Other major conflicts followed, such as the Suez crisis of 1956 when British, French and Israeli forces attacked Egypt, the Arab-Israeli wars of 1967 (when Israel seized the Sinai from Egypt) and 1973, ending with the signing of the Camp David Peace Accord in 1978 which saw the eventual handing back of the Sinai to Egypt.

Colourful fish mosaic at Al Tur sums up one of the abiding attractions of south Sinai's coastal resorts.

BELOW:
'Uyun Musa (the Springs of Moses).

importance Muslim rulers attached to Egypt's Asian gateway.

SOUTH SINAI

With its two coasts, oases, mountains and historic sites, South Sinai is a much more popular destination. North of Suez, the Ahmed Hamdi tunnel carries traffic under the canal. Turning south, the main road follows the canal, veering eastwards opposite Suez. From here it descends 320 km (200 miles) along the breezy Gulf of Suez to Sharm al-Shaykh.

Along this route are **'Uyun Musa ❷**, the "Springs of Moses", a palm grove fed by two wells of brackish water where Moses is said to have rested with his flock, reached after 40 km (25 miles). Thirty-three kilometres (20 miles) further on, the road nears the coast at the wide sandy beach of **Ras al-Sidr ❸**, a favourite stopping place, and for some people worth the day trip from Cairo. Unlike the Gulf of Aqaba on Sinai's east coast, the Gulf of Suez is shallow and

sandy-bottomed. The marine life is abundant, and there are plenty of water sports on offer. Moon Beach in Ras al-Sidr is one of Egypt's top windsurfing destinations.

Beyond Ras al-Sidr the road bends away from the coast up into the mountains. A track to the right at this turn leads after a few hundred yards to **Hammam Fara'un ❹**, the hot springs known as Pharaoh's Baths. The seven springs produce boiling-hot mineral-rich waters that bubble from the base of the mountains right into the sea. It is a popular spot for Egyptian family bathing. The waters are said by local Bedu to cure rheumatism.

Ancient mining area

About 16 km (10 miles) into the mountains above Hammam Fara'un, a track leads left among palm trees. Negotiable only by four-wheel drive vehicles, it continues for 32 km (20 miles) to the site of **Sarabit al-Khadim ❺** (no facilities, ask for a Bedu guide at Abu Zunaymah), a 12th-Dynasty temple that was dedicated originally to the goddess Hathor. A second shrine, for the patron god of the

Recommended Restaurants, Bars & Cafés on page 289

Eastern Desert, Sopdu, was later added. The site, which covers approximately 0.4 hectares (1 acre), has yielded over 400 inscriptions, some of which praise Hathor, Hatshepsut or Tuthmosis III, and others give instructions regarding the mining of turquoise in the region (turquoise, malachite and copper were mined here).

Particularly interesting are the graffiti of the workers, some written in unknown scripts called protosinaitic. They form the link between hieroglyphics and the Phoenician alphabet from which Latin script developed. Also discovered here was the bust of Queen Tiy of the Old Kingdom, now displayed in the Egyptian Museum in Cairo.

Inscriptions at the mines of **Wadi Maraghah**, south of Sarabit al-Khadim, date back to the 4th Dynasty and the reigns of Snefru and Khufu (Cheops), builder of the Great Pyramid. The British caused much damage to the inscriptions here when they tried to reopen the mines in 1901.

From Wadi Maraghah a track running down the Wadi Sidri for 24 km (15 miles) rejoins the main road at **Abu Zunaymah**, where it descends again from the mountains to the coast. Beyond this ramshackle frontier settlement, where manganese from local mines of recent date is processed, the road continues to Abu Rudis. The Gulf of Suez is at this point dotted with beetle-like rigs shooting flames into the haze: this is the centre of Sinai's oil fields, most of them offshore. Pipes, fences, tanks and prefabricated housing clutter the shore town to Balayim 50 km (30 miles) further on.

The road again leaves the coast, heading towards the mountains of the Sinai range. A checkpoint marks the turn-off to St Catherine's Monastery (Santa Katarina), while the main road continues south to al-Tur and Sharm al-Shaykh. **Al-Tur** ❻, the capital and largest town in South Sinai, is reached after 75 km (45 miles) of hot driving through a wide valley. Settled in ancient times because of its good water supply and excellent

harbour, it was the chief quarantine station for pilgrims returning to Egypt from Mecca. Modern al-Tur, despite scattered palm groves and a beautiful beach, retains this way-station atmosphere. A peculiarity of the town is the racial mix of its inhabitants, many of them descended from Berber and African immigrants. From al-Tur it is 100 km (60 miles) to Sharm al-Shaykh (*see page 288*).

Going to St Catherine's

Turning instead up toward St Catherine's, you enter the **Wadi Feiran**. Narrowing as it mounts, after 33 km (20 miles) the dry ravine suddenly blossoms into a river of date palms. This is the oasis of **Feiran** ❼, the largest and most fertile patch of cultivation on the peninsula. Parched for most of the year, winter rains and melting snow send down short-lived torrents to water the valley. Scattered throughout the palm groves are clusters of Bedu huts. The wadi may have been the site of the biblical battle between the Amalakites and the Israelites. Within the mountain are the scattered

> Put off thy shoes from off they feet, for the place whereon thou standest is holy ground.
>
> Exodus, The Bible

BELOW:
visitors to
Hammam Fara'un.

The ossuary at St Catherine's houses the skulls of former monks.

remains of monasteries, chapels and hermit cells of early Christian monks who believed this to be the Elim of the Bible. Tranquil and serene, it is difficult to imagine that Feiran was a cathedral city in the Middle Ages. The ruins of the cathedral and ancient settlement are being excavated; you can often visit the small convent.

South of the oasis, approached most easily up the Wadi 'Aleayat, rises the peak of the **Gabal Sirbal**. At 2,070 metres (7,000 ft) it is not high for the Sinai range, but its isolation makes the view from its summit extensive. One school of Biblical speculators claims it as the true Mount Sinai.

From Feiran the road climbs into an open plain and after 32 km (20 miles) reaches the settlement of Santa Katarina, where there are hotels, a camp site and the bus stop. The **monastery** ❽ (open to visitors 9.30 am–noon, closed on Sun and all Greek Orthodox holidays; modest attire is required) is in a wadi between Gabal Musa – most popular candidate for

the site of the delivery of the Ten Commandments – and the Gabal al-Dayr just up the hill to the south.

The Roman emperor Justinian ordered the building of a fortress monastery on the site in AD 537 in order to protect the Sinai passes against invasion. Originally dedicated to the Transfiguration of Christ, the church built within the fortress was renamed after St Catherine (a 4th-century Alexandrian martyred for her derision of Roman idol-worship), after her body miraculously appeared atop Sinai's highest peak, apparently looking none the worse for wear. This miracle, coupled with the Crusaders' occupation of nearby Palestine, ensured the support of Christian rulers.

The monastery's fame spread, so that by the 14th century up to 400 monks lived there, as the grisly collection of skulls in the ossuary attests. In recent centuries Russia was the chief benefactor. The monastery now has around 20 resident monks, and remains the property of the Greek Orthodox Church.

The monastery

The path to St Catherine's leads past a

Recommended Restaurants, Bars & Cafés on page 289

walled orchard and an outer complex of buildings before reaching the monastery itself. An old basket-and-pulley system of entry has been abandoned and visitors now enter by simply walking through a portal. A small building on the left inside the wall is one of the original structures, diplomatically converted into a mosque in the 12th century. The Church of St Catherine is down the steps to the left just behind the mosque.

The church, built by order of Justinian in AD 527, is basilical in form, with great granite columns supporting the nave. The wooden bracing beams of the reconstructed ceiling are original and beautifully carved, one of them with a foundation inscription dating to Justinian. The doors leading to the sanctuary are flanked by two silver chests inlaid with precious stones. Both were donated by members of the Russian royal family, one in the 17th century, the other in the 19th. The sanctuary is adorned with 6th-century mosaics that are the monastery's greatest treasure. Within the arch and semi-dome of the apse is a portrayal of the Transfiguration of Christ: to his left stand Moses and St James, and on his right are Elijah and St John the Apostle.

Side aisles, lined with chapels dedicated to varied saints and decorated with ancient and modern icons, lead off from either side of the church. At the sanctuary end of the building a small alcove opens into the Chapel of the Burning Bush. Here, on a site marked by a small silver plate, God spoke to Moses whilst hidden in a flaming shrub. The monastery's other treasures, off-limits to visitors (unless they have a letter of introduction from the Greek patriarchate in Cairo), include a library of rare manuscripts and a museum (admission charge) containing a superb collection of icons.

Just behind the monastery a path leads ultimately to the summit of Gabal Musa. Steps mounting the cliff to the right should be avoided for the ascent. Instead, continue on the gently sloping main track, which curves behind the southern slope. The climb is fairly easy but coming down is trickier, and care should be taken. The view from the top is magnificent, particularly at dawn or sunset. Gabal Katarina, the highest point in Egypt at over 2,640 metres (8,500 ft), has an even better view. It is approached up the wadi on Gabal Musa's western side.

Sinai's mountains are very ancient, and their variety, in terms of texture, colour, shape and vegetation, is eternally fascinating – especially in the very early morning or early evening when their contours and colours are seen most clearly. The descent from St Catherine's to the east traverses enthralling landscapes all the way to the sea.

THE GULF OF AQABA

One of the earth's most dramatic interfaces, the Gulf of Aqaba is only 16 km (10 miles) wide, but in places as much as 1,800 metres (6,000 ft) deep. Indeed, it marks a long geological fault, running from the Dead Sea in the north to Africa's Great Rift Valley in the south. Coral reefs line the shores of the Gulf from Ras Muhammad at the peninsula's extremity

TIP

The mountain and wadi area around St Catherine's Monastery is a national park. The St Catherine Protectorate publishes brochures detailing walking trails, but all walks must be done with a Jebelliya guide, the only people authorised to work as guides in the area. Guides can be found at the Mountain Tours Office, run by Sheikh Mousa, www.sheikmousa.com, tel: 010-641 3575.

BELOW: a place of contemplation.

TIP

The resorts around
Dahab and Nuwayba
offer 4x4 and camel
trekking trips into the
hinterland. (You can
also negotiate directly
with the Bedu, a few
miles south of the hotel
strip.) Either way, the
trips are well worth-
while: many of the
Dahab's fertile wadis
(valleys) are extremely
beautiful.

BELOW: gateway
to the Ras
Muhammad
National Park.

to Taba on the Israeli border. Teeming with life and colour, they provide a striking contrast to the desolation of the land.

Ras Muhammad ❾ is a coral peninsula thrusting its head into the Red Sea. It is a nature reserve and one of the outstanding snorkelling and diving areas in the world. At the Shark's Observatory a coral ridge falls over 80 metres (262 ft) into the open sea and the wary diver or snorkeller can float along its edge (under 1 metre/3 ft deep at high tide) and look out into an underwater paradise.

North of Ras Muhammad, on a beautiful natural harbour much damaged by the ill-planned building of successive occupants, is the town of **Sharm al-Shaykh** ❿, international gateway to the region and the hub of a series of resorts that merge into one another – Ras Muhammad *(see above)*, Na'ama Bay, Coral Bay, Shark's Bay (a good family resort) and Ras Nasrani. **Peace Road** , running a little way inland, links all the bays together (taxis and minibuses ply the route).

Old Sharm lies a little way inland, as authentic a piece of Egypt as you will see

on this part of the Sinai coast, with small shops on backstreets and an unhurried atmosphere: it is well worth a visit.

Five miles farther on, **Na'ama Bay** is the centre of Sinai's tourist boom, with hotels, restaurants, camping grounds and diving shops. It is overdeveloped but it makes a good base for visiting local beaches. Some of the best for diving and snorkelling are The Tower, Ras Umm Sid, Ras Nasrani and Nabq. Equipment can be rented at one of many diving centres, where boat trips to Gazirat Tiran, an island in the middle of the straits with superb corals, can also be arranged. Shipwrecks dot the shoreline, testifying to the difficulty of navigation between the reefs. *(Also see Snorkelling and Diving, pages 300–1).*

Dahab

Hotel complexes spread further and further beyond the airport, but the next major coastal settlement is **Dahab** ⓫, 90 km (56 miles) north. Sediments washed down from the mountains have created a broad sandy plain here. An Israeli-built town on a sandy cove, it has hotels, restaurants, camping and diving facilities

and a reputation as the "Ibiza of Egypt".

Across the plain 2 km (1¼ mile) to the west, the Bedu village of **Assalah** sits next to a palm-lined horseshoe bay. Here low-budget travellers stay in reed huts on the beach.

Nuwayba ⑫ is 75 km (45 miles) further north, a slightly superior resort, although the reefs here are not as good as further south. There are wide sandy beaches, a few hotels and a camp site. The coast between Nuwayba and Taba is currently being developed.

Taba ⑬ is 60 km (38 miles) north of Nuwayba and offers five-star hotel developments and an international airport. At just 200 metres/yards from the Israeli border, the resort is a popular getaway for Israelis. As a consequence, in 2004 the

Taba Hilton was bombed by terrorists.

Gezirat Fara'un, an island just offshore, is topped by a fortress built by Saladin to protect the route of the Hajj, the annual pilgrimage to Mecca. ❏

Pedaloes in Na'ama Bay, the epicentre of Sinai's tourist boom.

RESTAURANTS, CAFÉS & BARS

Andrea's
Na'ama Bay
Tel: 069-360 0972. **$–$$**
It's part of a Cairo chain but the Egyptian food, served alfresco, is pretty good.

Fish Restaurant
Next door to Fayrouz Hilton, Na'ama Bay
Tel: 069-360 0136. **$$$–$$$$**
This excellent fish restaurant is set on a terrace close to the beach, and is deservedly popular.

Abou al Sid
Na'ama Bay
Tel: 069-360 3910/012-406 1260. **$$**
Member of the atmospheric Cairo chain. Good Egyptian food served in air conditioned dining room or outside on the terrace. Above Hard Rock Café.

Cafe Picasso
Shar'i City Council (next to Go Kart), Hadaba. Tel: 010-731 2972. **$**
Quality meals and snacks.

Great Sunday roast lunch with free camel rides.

La Rustichella
Behind Na'ama Bay
Tel: 010-116 0692. **$$–$$$**
This excellent Italian restaurant away from the hubbub is a favourite with the town's many Italian residents. The pasta is superb and there is also plenty of fresh fish and seafood on the menu.

Safsafa
Na'ama Centre, Na'ama Bay
Tel: 069-360 0474/069-360 3418. **$$**
A newer version of the old Safsafa in Sharm town, this family-run restaurant became an instant success. The specialities are still fresh fish and seafood, but the place is more pleasant and upmarket than the original one.

Sala Thai
Hyatt Regency Hotel
Tel: 069-360 1234. **$$$**
If you are slightly fed up

with the Egyptian and Italian food that are the staples of Sharm al-Shaykh, you may enjoy the exotic surroundings and the menu of this stunning restaurant. The classical Thai/Asian food is first-rate and the teak interior and pleasant sea-view terrace are very calming.

TamTam
Ghazala Hotel, Na'ama Bay
Tel: 069-360 0150. **$$$$**
Excellent Egyptian dishes are served indoors in a canteen-like restaurant or outside on the pleasant terrace.

Kanzaman
Al-Zhoor mall (opposite Cataract Hotel. Tel: 064-345 6899/ 012-710 5877. **$$**
On street corner full of open-air restaurants, this place specialises in BBQ and seafood, but also offers popular Indian dishes, and and also has The Fish Market franchise next door.

Café Bedouin
Zara Sharm Panorama, Na'ama Bay.
Tel: 012-731 2972. **$**
Built into the cliffs, with stunning views, the Café Bedouin is the perfect place to catch the breeze and enjoy a cool drink on a hot evening. Good music and twinkling clay lanterns create a chilled ambience.

Pirates Bar
Fayrouz Hilton, Na'ama Bay
Tel: 069-366 0140. **$$**
An ever-popular venue for an early evening drink, the Pirates Bar is set in a romantic garden with ponds spanned by little bridges.

Prices for a three-course dinner per person with a half-bottle of house wine:
$ = under $20
$$ = $20–45
$$$ = $45–60
$$$$ = over $60

THE RED SEA AND EASTERN DESERT

The beauty of the landscape and an excellent climate are obvious reasons for this region's ever-increasing popularity, especially as a winter-sun destination

The Red Sea coast of Egypt runs for 1,600 km (1,000 miles) in a south-easterly direction from Suez. Despite the many offshore drilling wells and numerous oil depots, petrol stations are few and far between and trips by car must be planned with foresight. The rewards, however, are considerable. For most of its length, beautiful but desolate limestone and granite mountains border the coast, with range rising upon range, their shades of purple harmonising with deep-blue skies and blue-green seas.

But this once pristine coast is changing fast. Most of the coastline has been sold to developers and many large-scale tourist projects, from the basic to the luxurious, have already been built or are underway.

Desert roads

Apart from the area east of Cairo, where sprawling suburbs and industrial zones eventually join up with the pock-marked battlegrounds of past wars in the canal area, the transition from the green Nile valley is abrupt. Suddenly the lush cultivated land gives way to stony wilderness, in which rocks rise up in extraordinary formations, reminiscent of the Pyramids and Sphinx, the sand blows and spills, and there is hardly a sign of human life for hundreds of miles.

In the vicinity of Suez, the sea is liberally strewn with tankers and other ships converging on the canal, and the road along the coast has received a good

deal of wear and tear from heavy trucks. Both sea and land traffic soon thins out, however, and the beaches improve near **Ayn Sukhnah**, where up-market developments for wealthy Cairenes continues at an alarming rate.

South of Ayn Sukhnah the rocky skirts of the North Galala Plateau come right down to the edge of the sea and the drive along here is spectacular. An endless string of new resorts lines the recently renovated coastal highway. At **Al-Za'faranah**, 80 km (50 miles) south of Ayn Sukhnah, the road is joined by a

Main attractions
MONASTERY OF ST ANTHONY, P.292
MONASTERY OF ST PAUL, P.292
AL-GOUNA, P.293
HURGHADAH, P.294
EASTERN DESERT, P.295
BUR SAFAGA, P.297
MARSA 'ALAM, P.298

LEFT: the keep at St Anthony's Monastery.
BELOW: Marsa Shagra beach, near Marsa Alam.

Door detail, the monastery of St Anthony.

TIP

There are no entrance
fees to the monasteries
of St Anthony and
St Paul. However,
donations are
appreciated, and
expected. At weekends
both monasteries are
very crowded with
Coptic pilgrims. Visitors
who want to stay
overnight at either
monastery need the
permission of the Cairo
office (26 al-Kineesa al-
Moicosia, Klot Bey,
near Ramesses Station;
tel: 02-2590 0218)

good road from the Nile Valley 290 km
(180 miles) through the desert to the west.

The desert monasteries

The monasteries of St Paul and St
Anthony have lost much of their original
remoteness, but remain important centres
of Coptic Christianity.

About 25 km (15 miles) west of Al-
Za'faranah, in the rugged hills at the foot
of the South Galala Plateau and looking
out over the desolate Wadi Araba stands
the **monastery of St Anthony** ❶ (daily
9am–5pm, closed Lent and Christmas),
the 4th-century Christian hermit whose
temptations were enthusiastically illustrated by painters of the Renaissance. The
monastery was founded by Anthony's
followers after his death in AD 356, and
is often regarded as the first monastery in
the world. The oldest building in the
compound is the **church of St Anthony**,
which is adorned with murals from the
13th century onwards. A path from the
west side of the monastery leads to a
steep staircase to **St Anthony's cave**
where the saint lived as a hermit until the
age of 105. His life is considered to be
the inspiration for monasticism in Egypt,
although others credit his contemporary,
St Paul (*see below*).

When the daily visitors have gone, the
monks lead a quiet life of work and
prayer, very much as they did 15
centuries ago, when the original Desert
Fathers retired from the injustice of the
world to seek a better way of life.

Retracing the road through Al-
Za'faranah, it is an hour's drive to the
monastery of Anthony's contemporary,
St Paul, tucked into a fold of the Red
Sea Mountains. Smaller, more dilapidated and more remote, the **monastery
of St Paul the Hermit** ❷ (daily
9am–5pm, closed Lent and Christmas)
sees fewer visitors. St Paul (AD
230–342) was the earliest known hermit
but, when he was visited in his cave at
the age of 113 by St Anthony, St Paul
recognised him as being spiritually his
superior. St Paul's cave is in the **church
of St Paul**, which also contains his
remains.

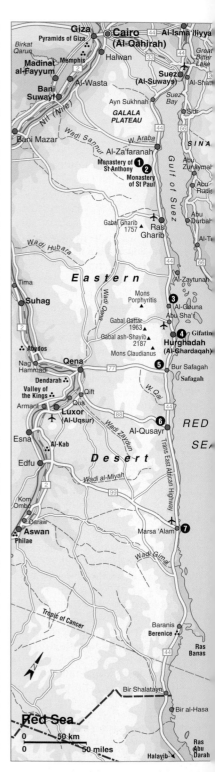

Recommended Restaurants, Cafés & Bars on page 299

Red Sea resorts

The resort of **Al-Gouna** ❸, 21 km (13 miles) north of Hurghadah, is Egypt's most luxurious purpose-built holiday village to date. A Cairene businessman, Samih Sawiris, bought the plot of land with the intention of building a few holiday homes for family and friends, but before long his business instincts got the better of him, and he seized the opportunity to create something unique in Egypt. Unlike the long stretches of often unattractive concrete structures further south in Hurghadah, Al-Gouna has been planned as a self-contained community, served by its own little airstrip. Gardens and an 18-hole golf course designed to United States Professional Golfers Association (USPGA) standards by Fred Couples and Gene Bates have been created out of the barren desert sands, and several man-made lagoons add to the impression of peacefulness.

Wealthy Egyptians, Gulf Arabs and Europeans have hurried to buy beach-front villas, while visitors can stay in one of the many attractive hotels ranging from three to five stars. The inspiration for most of the design has come from traditional Nubian architecture, revived by the late Egyptian architect Hassan Fathy, and from the Mediterranean – there's plenty of whitewash and some corners could be mistaken for old towns on the Cycladic Islands in Greece. At weekends the place is crowded with wealthy young Cairenes.

The five-star Miramar Hotel, managed by the Sheraton chain and designed by celebrity American architect Michael Graves, is a unique sight in Egypt. Blue, red and yellow buildings contrast with the bright turquoise of the lagoons and the deep purple of the mountains in the background. The village at the centre of the development is **Kafr al-Gouna**, with several restaurants and a small museum (daily 10am–2pm and 4–9pm; admission charge) displaying good replicas of many well-known examples of ancient Egyptian art.

Al-Gouna is also home to Obélisque wine and Saqqara beer. If you want everything on tap and have little interest in what lies outside, Al-Gouna is perfect; otherwise Hurghadah gives more options for activities and nightlife.

The church of St Paul, containing the cave (below), where St Paul fled to escape persecution by the Roman emperor Decius.

BELOW:
St Paul's cave.

Desert Flora and Fauna

The geological formations of the Eastern Desert are varied and strange, yielding stones and sands of amazing shapes and colours. It can look like a barren landscape, but in fact flora and fauna are plentiful, especially in the wadis, and all the more wonderful for their tenacity. There are numerous species of small migratory birds and large resident ones, including the Egyptian vulture and the sand partridge; in spring and autumn migrating cranes may be seen high above. Once in a while a gazelle or an ibex streaks across the open plain and disappears among the rocks; often a sandy picnic place is crisscrossed with bird and animal tracks. Jerboas, jackals and foxes leave dainty pad marks, while rabbits, gazelles and hyenas leave heavier prints.

TIP

Old Hurghadah is the site of an ambitious new hate-it-or-love-it marina, designed to regenerate this part of town. Shops, restaurants, cafés and nightclubs, beach volleyball, talent contests, and live music are just some of the attractions on offer.

BELOW: fishing boats in Sakala.

Hurghadah

In recent years the small fishing village of **Hurghadah** ❹ (Al-Ghardaqah), 420 km (250 miles) south of Suez, has grown into one of Egypt's most popular destinations. It has its own airport served by many European charter operators and by domestic flights from Cairo (one hour) and Sharm al-Shaykh (35 minutes). The town has a large range of accommodation, from basic hotels catering for backpackers to up-market resort hotels. A long strip of holiday villages continues to spread further south and has now reached a long way past the airport. Many of these villages, which rival each other for splendour, the size of their pools and the number of rooms, are operated by international four- and five-star chains.

The Hurghadah area can now be regarded as comprising three separate suburbs – the old downtown (known as al-Dahar), the new downtown (now called Sakala) and the developed strip running south along the coast for over 20 km (12 miles).

To the north, **al-Dahar** has some of the Red Sea's earliest hotels, built between the Gabal al-Afish hill and the sea. The hill itself is slowly being hacked away as houses and hotels push further back, and it could disappear completely within the next few years. Between al-Dahar and Sakala are the remnants of old Hurghadah – a public beach, naval dockyards and the port, from which the ferry to Sharm al-Shaykh departs.

Sakala is very much like any modern Mediterranean package resort. Shops and fast-food restaurants run along its main street, off which are side roads down to the beaches. The road rejoins the coast and climbs past the Felfela restaurant to reach the abandoned circular Sheraton Hotel. The fact that this entire stretch of Corniche from al-Dahar is still referred to by everyone as Sheraton Street shows how little was here in the early days, when the old Sheraton was a lonely outpost way south of old Hurghadah. Beyond here today are endless up-market resorts catering for everything the beach-loving tourist requires.

The modern town is not particularly attractive, the small public beaches are sometimes littered with rubbish, and the large suq area offers the usual souvenir

Map on page 292

Recommended Restaurants, Cafés & Bars on page 299

shops filled with leather, brasswork, papyrus, furry camels, statuettes and so on. That said, Hurghadah is the ideal antidote to an overdose of antiquities. The water is warm all the year round except for a few weeks in December and January; the sun is always shining and even in the hottest months there is a good breeze, which can sometimes turn into a strong wind. The beach is small, but hotel pools are large.

Holiday villages offer scuba diving, snorkelling, sailing, kite- and wind-surfing, archery and other sports. For the sport fisherman, all-day or overnight fishing trips to the offshore islands can be arranged either through the hotels, or with individual boat owners at the harbour.

The **Red Sea Aquarium** (6 Corniche Street; daily 9am–10pm; closed Fri for prayers; admission charge) offers insights into the area's rich marine life. It is an opportunity to observe the many types of fish close-up, including sharks, turtles and stone fish. Underwater trips are offered by Aquascope (tel: 065-344 3710) and the Sindbad Submarine (tel: 065-344 4688; www.sindbad-club.com); both can be booked at any of the hotel receptions.

Each of the major beach resorts has its own dive centre and offers water-sports activities and excursions. You can do everything from 4x4 and quad-bike desert safaris to meet local Bedu to one- and two-day trips to Cairo, Luxor or Aswan. Most people opt to travel by luxury coach rather than fly, but these can mean departing very early morning and getting back late at night.

Eastern Desert

In pharaonic times the **Eastern Desert**, particularly the mountains, was a source of gold and other precious metals, orna-

Once you understand how the laws of physics make it possible to spend an hour or more under-water on compressed air, you are close to taking the plunge.

BELOW: pigeon house and mosque in ad-Dahar, Hurghadhah.

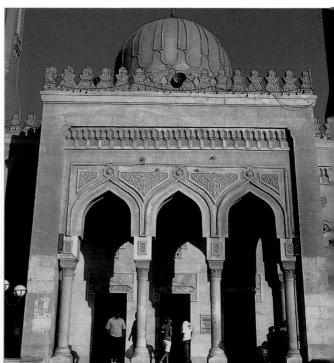

A ruined archway frames a view of the desert at Mons Porphyrites.

mental stone and other building materials, which contributed greatly to the wealth and prestige of the pharaohs and were later coveted by Assyrians, Persians, Greeks and Romans.

Thousands of prisoners in chains were used for the extraction of these riches and many died in the process. The gold was arduously mined and smelted, and both granite and limestone were quarried and transported to Thebes for the construction of temples and other monuments.

The Romans established permanent quarrying camps in the mountains, the ruins of which are visible from the road between Hurghadah and Safaga. They were particularly partial to the purple stone known as porphyry, which comes from **Mons Porphyrites** (Mountain of Porphyryr) below **Gabal Abu Dukhan** (Father of Smoke) and which is accessed along **Wadi Umm Sidri** (4x4 vehicles only, with local guide).

The stone was in great demand for the adornment of palaces and temples and was brought out of the Egyptian mountains until as late as the 5th century. Great blocks were quarried and

then dragged 180 km (112 miles) through the mountains and over the desert to Qena, where they were transported down the Nile and then across the Mediterranean to Rome. The largest columns were used to build the great temple at Baalbek in modern Lebanon, though eight of these were later moved to Constaninople to support the roof of the city's great Hagia Sophia church.

There is not much left to see at Mons Porphyrites – just toppled columns, inscribed blocks and a ruined fort – but it is worth taking a closer look if only to enjoy the landscape and peacefulness of the spot.

Another mountain nearby, **Mons Claudianus** (Mountain of Claudius), yielded a white-specked granite, also much in demand in ancient Rome; again, all that is left are the jumbled remains of a Roman town.

Ancient Egyptian ports

Further on down the coast, famous ancient ports, which continued to thrive even after the discovery of the Cape route in the 15th century, have largely fallen into disuse since the building of

Recommended Restaurants, Cafés & Bars on page 299

the Suez Canal. Some are still visible as little ghost harbours with the skeletal hulls of old wooden boats whitening in the sun; others have completely disappeared under the sand.

Bur Safagah ❺, however, which is 70 km (45 miles) south of Hurghadah, is still very much alive. A small tourist resort has developed, with a choice of hotels; almost permanently windy, the town is particularly popular with windsurfers.

But Bur Safagah has also retained its role as the nearest port to the Nile town of Qena, 177 km (110 miles) to the west, and its deep-water facilities have been expanded to meet the demands of modern trade. Truckloads of wheat and raw aluminium unloaded at Bur Safagah are transported along the old caravan trail through the mountains to the Nile valley, albeit now along an excellent paved road.

This route is also convenient for visitors wanting to travel along the Nile valley from Cairo to Luxor, cross to the Red Sea, and then return north up the coast to Suez. However, security issues make this option uncertain: at present all foreign visitors must make the journey between the Nile valley and the coast in a police convoy: if you are considering this option, you should check the current situation with the police.

In antiquity and even in Ottoman times the ports of al-Qusayr, Marsa 'Alam, Berenice and Halayib were of more importance than they are today. Like Suez and Bur Safagah they were connected to the Nile valley by caravan routes, along which laden pack animals took spices, silks, pearls and precious woods from Arabia, Persia, India and the East African coast. Muslim pilgrims from the hinterlands thousands of miles away, sometimes travelling for years, embarked at these ports for Mecca. One can still see traces of graffiti carved on the rocks, inland from the coast.

Al-Qusayr ❻ was, until the 10th century, the largest trading port on the Red Sea and the most popular port for Muslims making the pilgrimage to Mecca in Saudi Arabia. The Ottomans tried to revive the port – and the small

Quad biking is just one of many fun things to do in the desert. Most of the Red Sea resorts offer quad biking days and half days.

BELOW: Abdel Ghaffar's shrine in al-Qusayr.

The Parting of the Red Sea

The story of Moses parting the Red Sea is one of the most famous of the Biblical stories. The account of the fleeing Israelites tells how Moses led the Jewish slaves out of Egypt, pursued by Pharaoh's army (Exodus 13–15). Arriving at the Red Sea, they were trapped between the desert, mountains and sea until Moses raised his arms and parted the waves, allowing the Israelites to walk between the walls of water. Reaching the other side, Moses ordered the sea to close again, thus drowning the Egyptian Army.

With our modern understanding of natural phenomena, it is possible to find an explanation for this miracle, as well as other Biblical stories, such as the Ten Plagues of Egypt. There are three main theories for the parting of the waves: a tsunami, an earthquake (or volcanic eruption) and wind set-down. The first two are usually dismissed due to the short time which the seabed would be exposed, but a strong wind (as also described in Exodus) might force back a body of water so that it resembled a wall of water along one side.

A combination of these natural events could easily give rise to the Biblical account, especially if they occurred in quick succession. However, experts cannot even agree about the location of the crossing, whether it is the Gulf of Aqaba or the Gulf of Suez.

A few kilometres north of Al Qusayr is Al-Qusayr al-Qadim (ancient Myos Hormos), the likely departure point for Queen Hatshepsut's expedition to the Land of Punt (modern Somalia). Details of the expedition – , including the frankincense trees, giraffes and other exotica – brought back to Egypt – are inscribed on the walls of the Temple of Hatshepsut at Thebes (see pages 214–5).

BELOW: the camel market at Shelaten sells a lot more than camels.

town is still dominated by the 16th-century fort of Sultan Selim, now a good historical **museum** (9am–5pm; admission charge) – but it finally lost its importance with the opening of the Suez Canal. Excavations of the fort have revealed private letters from the 18th century relating to the provision of wheat from Upper Egypt, as well as clay pipes, dating from the very earliest days of smoking tobacco almost 500 years ago. Al-Qusayr's former prosperity is evident in the many old Ottoman houses, although these are generally in a sadly dilapidated state.

The town also has many small mosques and shrines dedicated to the various holy men from places such as Morocco, West Africa, Somalia and India who have died here en route to or from Mecca. Immediately opposite the Ottoman fort, for example, is the shrine and mosque of Abdel Ghaffar, a Yemeni shaykh.

The sleepy town is virtually untouched by tourism but developers have discovered that the surrounding coast offers excellent snorkelling and diving, and resort hotels are quickly springing up.

Marsa' Alam and further south

About 130 km (80 miles) further south, on a T-junction with the road to Edfu on the Nile, is the fishing town of **Marsa'Alam** ❼. Now overtaken by tourism, it has been the focus of some frenzied construction in recent years, with several luxury resorts and a new international airport for charter flights. The main drive behind it all is the good diving and snorkelling. The new development just outside the airport is **Port Ghalib**, slowly growing into a southerly version of al-Gouna.

The furthest south that visitors can reach is **Shelaten** where there are daily markets selling hundreds of camels freshly arrived from Sudan. The market is a popular tourist attraction, with the result that there is much on sale besides camels.

Some 54 km (33 miles) south of Marsa' Alam is the **Wadi Gibal Protectorate**, comprising the coast, the **Wadi Gimal islands**, and inland areas, which can be used only by the local Ababda tribe, and even then under strict conditions that safeguard the natural environment. ❑

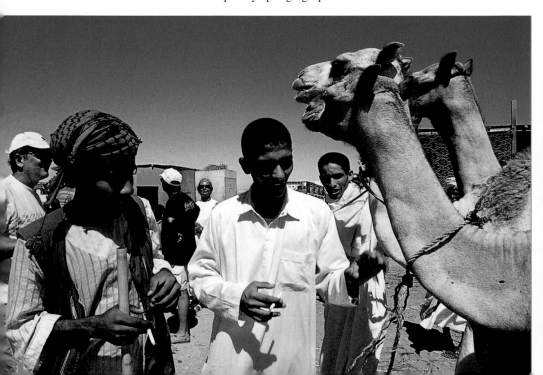

RESTAURANTS & BARS

Restaurants

Prices for a three-course dinner per person with a half-bottle of house wine:
$ = under $20
$$ = $20–45
$$$ = $45–60
$$$$ = over $60

Al Gouna

Kiki's Café
Above the museum in Kafr al-Gouna. **$$–$$$**
Fresh home-made pasta and good salads are served on two open-air terraces with great views.

Orient 1001
Sheraton Miramar
Tel: 065-354 5606, ext. 19. **$$$**
Good Lebanese/Egyptian food in a wonderful Oriental atmosphere. Sometimes there is live music.

Spagheteria Del Porto
Abu Tig Marina
Tel: 065-354 9702, ext. 77963. **$$$**
Well-prepared and authentic Italian dishes, with a fish and seafood as the specialities. Keep some space for the great desserts.

Hurghadah

Chill
Shari' Sheraton
Tel: 012-382 0694. **$$**
A relaxed beach bar with good music, which really swings on weekend nights, with lively beach parties.

Da Nanni
Resort strip, Sigala
Tel: 065-344 3743. **$$**
The Italian couple who run this cosy restaurant

serve excellent pasta and pizza.

Felfella
Tariq al-Sheraton, Sigala
Tel: 065-344 2410. **$$**
A member of the popular Cairene chain, serving reasonably good and reasonably priced Egyptian food. wonderful views.

Joker
Midan Sigala
Tel: 065-354 3146. **$$–$$$**
This is a very popular fish restaurant that serves simple but excellent fresh fish by the weight, accompanied by bread and salads. No alcohol is available.

Lo Scarabeo
Shari' Sayyed al-Qorayam
Tel: 065-354 6927. **$$**
The food is simple – pasta, pizza and salad – but it's well-cooked, the portions are large, and the setting is pleasant.

Mandarine Lebanese Restaurant
Corniche
Tel: 065-354 7007. **$$$**
Innovative Lebanese food served in an agreeable setting.

Portofino
Shari' Sayyed al-Qorayam
Tel: 065-354 6250. **$$**
The Portofino has been around for a long time and is always reliable. Mainly Italian dishes, as you would expect from the name, but some Egyptian food as well.

Red Sea I
In the suq, off Tariq an-Nasr
Tel: 065-354 9630. **$$$**
One of the best places

for seafood and fish, with a pleasant rooftop terrace. Also serves pizzas and steaks. There is a newer, sister restaurant, Red Sea II (same phone number), with a similar menu and prices.

Young Kang
5 Shari' al-Shaykh as-Sebak
Tel: 012-422 9327. **$$**
Chinese and Korean food, with seafood and Peking duck as the specialities of the house.

Cafés and Bars

Al Gouna

Barten
Abu Tig Marina
Tel: 065-354 9702, ext. 77903. **$$–$$$**
Tiny but very funky bar, popular with Cairenes and tourists alike.

Sand Bar
Kafr al-Gouna
Tel: 065-354 9702 ext. 2123. **$$$**
This lively Dutch-Italian owned bar-grill serves the coolest beers in town, as well as cocktails, tasty appetisers, as well as American-Mexican main dishes and interesting salads.

Le Tabasco
Kafr al-Gouna
Tel: 065-354 5516. **$$$**
Nisha Sursock has exported the winning formula of his popular Cairo bar and restaurant to Gouna, and it works here just as well. This is the trendiest place in Al Gouna, laid out over two floors and three terraces. A great place to come late at night.

SCUBA DIVING

Egypt's Red Sea coast has some of the best coral reefs in the world, offering spectacular diving for novices and experts alike

Egypt's Red Sea coasts are a diver's paradise, as their climate and geographical position make them ideal for the formation of coral, which grows on reefs called *shaab* or *erg*. Mounds of coral build up like islands, the tips of which are barely skimmed by the waves. Each coral accretion consists of numerous polyps, growing together in a colony. When one colony dies, a new one grows on top, attached to the calcium skeletons of its defunct ancestors.

The most common inhabitants are thousands of little orange cardinalfish, which move in great sparkling clouds. Butterfly and banner fish form a large, easily distinguishable family because of their oval shape, snub noses and deep lemon colour; they swim in pairs and stick to the same territory. Be ready for encounters with moray eel, whose size and snake-like appearance give them a vicious reputation. Simply remember an important rule: watch but don't touch. Just admire its graceful movements and leave it gasping for oxygen-rich water.

If you are diving the outer reefs, you also have a chance of seeing white tip sharks, a slim predator, feeding on small fish and crustaceans. In the deep south, sightings of hammerhead, grey reef and ocean white tip sharks are not uncommon, but don't expect to see all of them on one trip.

Nudibranchs, shellfish, shrimps and crabs living in the nooks and crannies of the coral, are also fascinating. Hawksbill turtles, a species once verging on extinction, find a habitat on the coral reefs and it seems that every reef has its own resident turtle. The odds that you'll see bottlenose or spinner dolphins while diving are remote, but the chances of meeting them on the way to your dive spot are quite high. The boat crew will let you know by blowing the horn continuously, which tends to keep the curious dolphins close to the ship.

ABOVE: corals are found in many shapes and colours: soft, undulating and bright red or yellow, solid and shaped like mushrooms, branching "elkhorns", and gorgonians – fan-shaped and perforated like Elizabethan lace collars. Be aware that corals take thousands of years to form and should never be touched or stood upon.

RIGHT: the underwater world is a peaceful environment but not, as Jacques Cousteau once said, a silent world. You'll hear boat propellers, the sound of the waves hitting the reef, and coral-crunching parrotfish; you might even hear the approach of a giant napoleon fish, well over 1.5 metres (5ft) in length.

THE BEST SPOTS FOR DIVING

For land-based diving, choose Hurghadah, Sharm al-Shaykh or Al-Gouna. They serve the northern part of the Red Sea, which is also a paradise for wreck diving.

• Al-Gouna and Hurghadah offer day trips to Shaab Abu Nuhas, where four wrecks are lined up against the reef, including the steamer *Carnatic*, which hit this infamous reef in 1869, and the more recent *Giannis D*, sunk in 1983.

• Sharm al-Shaykh serves the dive sites around the Sinai Peninsula, notably the Strait of Tiran and the wrecks of the *Dunraven* and the *Thistlegorm*. The latter was a British supply ship, sunk in 1941 by Junker bombers; it sits upright in 30 metres (90 ft) of water, with its load of motorcycles, trucks and even train wagons still on board.

• Safagah, some 60 km (36 miles) south of Hurghadah, offers dive excursions to reefs like Panorama and Abu Kefan, known for their prolific coral growth. Safagah is also a base for diving the wreck of the *Salem Express*, sunk in 1991.

• Ras Samadai, further south, is popular with those who relish the chance of snorkelling with spinner dolphins.

• Marsa Alam, in the south, the centre of live-aboard diving, is the place for die-hard divers. Live-aboards, or safari boats, allow several dives a day from a purpose-built vessel – simply jump overboard and enjoy the magnificent reefs of Elphinstone, St John's and Zabargad.

ABOVE: a green turtle drifts past. Also look out for the smaller Hawksbill turtle.

ABOVE RIGHT: it is possible to become a certified diver within a week. Simply enrol on a diving course: two days of pool training plus some theory will be followed by guided open-water dives, after which you will be ready to qualify. Some dive operators will also cater to snorkellers.

RIGHT: trained divers love the wreck *Giannis D*, sunk in 1983 against the Shaab Abu Nuhas reef, as it allows entry into the engine room, crew quarters and wheelhouse.

INSIGHT GUIDES

TRAVEL TIPS

EGYPT

TRAVEL TIPS

TRANSPORT

GETTING THERE
AND GETTING AROUND

GETTING THERE

By Air

Egypt is served by international airports at Alexandria, Marsa Matruh, Marsa Alam, Cairo, Luxor, Aswan and Hurghadah on the mainland, and at Sharm al-Shaykh on the Sinai peninsula.

Some return tickets have to be confirmed before departure; check with a travel agent or contact the airline office in Cairo. Most major airlines have offices at Cairo International Airport and around Maydan at-Tahrir in downtown Cairo. **Cairo International** airport is a first-class facility. Most planes from Europe approach it from the south, giving passengers magnificent views of the city, the Nile and the Pyramids. **Alexandria** airport is served by Lufthansa, Olympic Airlines and Egyptair. For international flights, **Luxor** airport has direct flights from various European cities via Egypt Air, Air France, Lufthansa and several charter companies. **Hurghadah** airport is served by Lufthansa while **Sharm al-Shaykh** airport receives charter flights from all over Europe and via Easyjet direct from London.

Cairo Terminals

www.cairo-airport.com
Terminal 1
Tel: 2265 5000
Terminal 2
Tel: 2265 2222
Terminal 3 is due to open in 2009, which will double the airport's capacity.

Domestic Airlines

Egypt has two national carriers for internal flights, Egyptair and Air Sinai. Egyptair flies daily from Cairo to Alexandria, Luxor, Aswan, Abu Simbel, Sharm al-Shaykh, Marsa Alam and Hurghadah, and twice a week to Al-Khargah Oasis. Air Sinai flies from Cairo to Hurghadah, Sharm al-Shaykh, St Catherine's Monastery, Al Tor and to Tel Aviv, Israel.

Egyptair Offices

www.egyptair.com.eg
Alexandria
19 Maydan Zaghlul, tel: 03-487 3357
Cairo
6 Adli Street, tel: 02-2392 7680
Cairo International, tel: 02-2265 7256
Nile Hilton Hotel, tel: 02-2577 2410
Cairo Sheraton, tel: 02-2748 9122
Midan Operax Sharia Gumhuriya, tel: 02-2391 9515
Luxor
Winter Palace Arcade, tel: 095-238 0580–1
Aswan
Corniche, tel: 02-231 5000
Hurghadah
Resort Strip, tel: 065-344 3592
Sharm al-Shaykh
Sharm al-Maya, tel: 062-366 1056

By Sea

Alexandria and Port Said on the Mediterranean Sea, and Suez and Nuwayba on the Red Sea are ports of entry. All boat services between Egypt and southern Europe are currently suspended because of the conflict with Israel. Up-to-the-minute information on the situation is available from the port authorities themselves and from the larger travel companies.

By Land

From Israel

Private or rental vehicles are not permitted to enter Egypt from Israel and the Palestinian Territories, but it is possible to enter using public transport. There are two main border crossings. Taba is the more popular of the two and is open 24 hours a day. Rafah, on the northern coast of Sinai, is, given the volatile situation in Gaza at the time of writing, mostly closed to individual travellers.

Passengers disembark from the Israeli vehicle, go through customs and take an Egyptian bus or taxi. Visas are needed; although these may be obtained in Israel, this will be evidence of your visit and may prevent entry to some other Arab and Muslim countries. However, your passport will always be stamped, thereby preventing you from visiting Lebanon, Syria and some other countries on that passport. There are no facilities for issuing visas at the border unless your visit is limited to the east coast of Sinai for which you can obtain a free Sinai-only entry permit. Visas can be obtained from the Egyptian Embassy (54 Rehov Basel, Tel Aviv, tel: 03-546 4151; Sun–Thur 9–11am) or the Egyptian Consulate in Eilat (68 Afrouni Street, tel: 972-637 6882; Sun–Thur 9–11am).

Exit fees apply to all border crossings between Israel and Egypt, and security is tight. In Eilat, Israeli buses are permitted to enter Egypt and travel as far as Sharm al-Shaykh at the southern tip of Sinai, but the situation changes often.

Mazada Tours, Tel-Aviv (tel: 03-544 4454; www.mazada.co.il) runs several air-conditioned buses between Cairo

ABOVE: buses can be crowded.

and Tel Aviv and Jerusalem via Taba (12–14 hours) and daily buses from Taba to Cairo.

From Sudan

A ferry service usually travels every Monday up the Nile from Egypt High Dam in Aswan to Wadi Halfa (Sudan) in 16–24 hours, but it is occasionally suspended. For further information contact the Nile River Valley Transport Corporation (in the shopping arcade behind the tourist office in Aswan, near the train station, tel: 097-303 348) or their office in Ramses Station, Cairo (tel: 02-2575 9058). No tickets will be issued if you do not have a Sudanese visa.

All documents must be obtained in Cairo. You must have a valid passport and a transit or tourist visa to Sudan. If you plan to pass through Sudan you must have a visa for your next destination.

From Libya

Buses and taxis make regular runs between Alexandria and Sollum. However, in spite of the thawing of relations between Libya and the US and Britain, there are some travel restrictions for Westerners and it is still not possible to get an Egyptian visa at the border. Consult the Libyan Embassy for information.

Motoring to Eygpt

All private vehicles entering Egypt must have a triptyque or *carnet de passage en douane* from an automobile club in the country of registration or pay customs duty on their vehicle, which can be as high as 250 percent. Emergency triptyques are available at the port of entry via the Automobile and Touring Club of

Egypt. This permits a car to enter Egypt for three months with one extension. The extension is available from the Automobile and Touring Club of Egypt, 10 Shari Qasr al-Nil, Cairo (tel: 02-2574 3355). All passengers must have a valid passport and the driver must have an International Driver's Licence.

GETTING AROUND

From the Airport

All airports in Egypt have a taxi service to city centres, operated on a flat-fee basis (ask airline staff for the current rate). In Cairo, transport includes limousine, taxi and bus. A curb-side limousine service at fixed fares is offered by Misr Limousine (tel: 02-2259 9381) among others.

Official taxis in Cairo are black and white; yellow taxis have begun

operating recently, and these can be taken from certain taxi stands including on Midan Tahrir, or they can be called ahead. They always use meters and are air conditioned. Alexandria taxis are black and orange. There are also Peugeot estate cars that are officially communal taxis between cities, but that when taken alone charge limousine rates.

The best bus to take from the airport and Downtown Cairo is No. 356, which runs 7am–midnight every 20 minutes from Terminal 1 via Terminal 2, Heliopolis and Abbaseya, to the Abdel Moneim Riad bus station just behind the Egyptian Museum. The bus leaves from the bus stop outside the airport car park.

Public Transport

By Rail

The government-owned Egyptian State Railway serves the Nile Valley to

By Taxi

For one of the experiences of your life, take an Egyptian taxi. Drivers seem to need to fill every empty space on the road (and sometimes the pavement). All taxis have orange licence plates and are identified by a number on the driver's door. Drivers are required to display their licence and identity numbers on the dashboard.

Official or metered prices are un-realistically low and so meters are seldom used. The fare should be agreed beforehand. The majority of taxi drivers are honest, but some try to cheat the unwary, especially between five-star hotels and such destinations as the Pyramids or the

Khan al-Khalili. Do not hesitate to ask for assistance from the tourist police. At your destination, pay in exact money. No tip is expected, but it is welcome.

Taxi drivers are usually friendly; many speak English, some are college graduates moonlighting to supplement their incomes, and most are eager to be hired by the day – ideal for seeing several scattered monuments. The fee is negotiable, but should be around LE300–400 per day.

Taxis in Luxor and Aswan are easier to find (they line up outside all the hotels), but work out more expensive than those in Cairo.

Aswan, the Red Sea cities of Suez and Port Said, the Delta and Northern Coast cities of Alexandria (two stops) and Marsa Mutrah. There are at least six through trains a day on major routes but train travel for foreigners is restricted to certain trains (check at the station). Fares are inexpensive, but unless one is travelling on an organised tour, tickets must be purchased at the main railway stations (in Cairo at Rameses Station at Maydan Ramesses).

The privately owned Abela train company runs three fast turbo trains a day from Cairo to Alexandria (two hours). You can book in advance at Ramesses Station, Cairo or at Alexandria Station. Abela also operates comfortable trains and sleepers between Cairo and Luxor (journey time 10 hours) and Aswan (15 hours).

For Abela reservations and information, opposite Ramesses Station, tel: 02-2574 9274; email: info@sleepingtrains.com; www.sleepingtrains.com.

By Bus
By Bus Around Cairo
The large red-and-white and blue-and-white buses are usually extremely overcrowded. As well as being claustrophobic, they provide ample opportunity for petty theft and unwelcome sexual encounters.

Modern blue-and-white air-conditioned buses are much more comfortable. Most buses start or pass by the Abdel Mouneem Riyad terminal, behind the Egyptian Museum on Maydan at-Tahrir.

Here are a few interesting routes for the adventurous tourist:
● No. 337 to Muhandesseen
● No. 13 to Zamalik
● Nos 346/400 airport to Downtown
● No. 755 to the Citadel
● Nos 355/357/900 to the Pyramids.

Inter-city Buses
Air-conditioned buses link most parts of Egypt to Cairo and Alexandria. Seats may be reserved up to two days in advance. There is also a fleet of cheaper non air-conditioned buses. Although bus times change without notice, departures are so frequent that this is rarely a problem.

The Cairo Gateway (Mina al-Qahira) at the Turgoman Garage on Shari' al Gisr in Bulaq, 1 km (⅔ mile) northwest of Ramesses Station, handles most of the buses travelling within Egypt and abroad. Most tickets can be bought here; tickets for air-conditioned buses should always be booked in advance.

ABOVE: a sign for Cairo's metro system.

Most buses leave from this station, but some still stop at the old bus stations too, such as the Sinai Terminal on Shari' Ramesses in Abbasiyyah, although this is increasingly rare. Buses for Al-Fayyum leave from the small el-Moneeb bus station near Maydan Giza in Giza.

To Alexandria
The fastest air-conditioned buses to Alexandria are operated by Superjet (tel: 02-2290 9017) and West Delta Bus Co. (tel: 02-2432 0049). West Delta Bus Co. also runs buses to Marsa Matruh (6 hours).

To Upper Egypt
The Upper Egypt Bus Co. (tel: 02-2576 0261) has daily departures to Luxor and Aswan. One bus a day completes the run to Aswan, departing early in the morning and arriving in the evening.

On the air-conditioned Superjets to Luxor and Aswan the services involve overnight travel with loud and uninteresting end-to-end videos.

The Upper Egypt Bus Co. also runs buses to the Western Oases.

To the Delta, the Desert, Sinai and the Red Sea
The East Delta Bus Co. (tel: 02-2574 2814) covers buses to the Canal Zone and most of the Delta. They also have services to St Catherine's, Dahab, Nuwayba, Taba and Sharm al-Shaykh in Sinai. Superjet runs faster services to Sharm al-Shaykh in Sinai and to Hurghadah on the Red Sea.

By Tram Around Alexandria
Trams are a slow but fun way to get around Alexandria. The main station is Mahattet Ramleh, called Terminus, near the Cecil Hotel. Yellow-coloured trains go west, including tram 14

going to Misr Train Station and Muharrem Bey, and tram 15, which goes to Ras at-Tin and Fort Qaytbey, past the Mosque of Abu Abbas al-Mursi. The blue trams travel east, including trams 2 and 36 to Sidi Gaber, San Stefano and Rushdy. Note that there is often a special carriage for women only on the trams.

By Metro Around Cairo
In Cairo the metro system is identified by circular signs with a big red M. The metro is clean and efficient and an easy way to get around. Trains run every few minutes from 5.30am to midnight and fares are inexpensive, usually no more than a pound to the furthest destination. Note that every train has a special carriage for women. The system runs north–south from Heliopolis to Helwan through the heart of the city. Another line runs from the northern suburb of Shubra al-Kheima to Bulaq al-Dakrour and other lines are under construction.

Useful stations include:
Mubarak Station Maydan Ramesses with access to the main train station and bus stations to Upper Egypt and the Oases.
Nasser Station Maydan Tawfiqiyyah.
Sadat Station Maydan at-Tahrir with 10 entrances and access to the Egyptian

Distances from Cairo

North
to Alexandria
225 km/140 miles (Delta road)
221 km/138 miles (desert road)
to Damietta
191 km/119 miles
to the Barrages
25 km/15 miles

South
to Al-Minya 236 km/151 miles
to Asyut 359 km/224 miles
to Luxor 664 km/415 miles
to Esna 719 km/449 miles
to Edfu 775 km/484 miles
to Kom Ombo 835 km/521 miles
to Aswan 880 km/550 miles

East
to Port Said 220 km/137 miles
to Isma'illiyyah 140 km/87 miles

West
to Fayyum 103 km/64 miles
to Bahariyyah Oasis 316 km/197 miles
to Farafrah Oasis 420 km/262 miles
to Dakhlah Oasis 690 km/413 miles
to Khargah Oasis 586 km/366 miles

Antiquities Museum, the American University in Cairo, Nile Hilton, all major airline offices and the Mugama'a (central administrative building).
Mar Girgis at Old Cairo with access to the Coptic Museum, Coptic churches and Roman fortress.
Zaghlul Station the National Assembly. Zaghlul monument.

By Tram Around Heliopolis

Cairo's tram network is slowly being phased out. Trams only operate within the Heliopolis area.

By Service Taxi

Collective service taxis are a faster alternative to buses, and will get you just about everywhere in Egypt. The fare is about the same as for the bus, and on the main routes there are several departures daily. These taxis, often estate Peugeots (hence their pet name of "Beejoo") seat six or seven and leave as soon as they are full. They are nicknamed "Flying Coffins" as the drivers are renowned for their speed and reckless driving.

The service station where you'll find these taxis is usually next to the bus or train station in a town or city.

Driving in Egypt

Car Rental

Driving in Egypt is very demanding *(see Driving Conditions, below).* The best alternative is to hire a driver and car together, thus freeing yourself to enjoy the scenery.

Car rental agencies exist at most major hotels and airports. Foreigners must have an International Driver's Licence and be at least 25 years of age to rent a car in Egypt. Some agencies offer four-wheel-drive vehicles, with or without a driver, which are a good idea for desert travel. You will need your passport, driver's licence, and a credit card.

Rental Agencies
Avis
Nile Hilton, Corniche an-Nil, Downtown
Tel: 02-2579 2400
www.avisegypt.com
Budget
22 al-Mathaf az-Zira'a, Doqqi
Tel: 02-2762 0518
www.budget.co.uk

Orientation

The Nile flows through the country from south to north. Upper Egypt is therefore the south, Lower Egypt the Delta. Upstream is south, downstream north. Many good maps are available.

Europcar
Cairo International Airport
Terminals 1 and 2
Tel: 02-2267 2439
http://car-rental.europcar.com
Also for four-wheel-drive vehicles with or without experienced desert drivers.
Hertz
Ramses Hilton, Corniche an-Nil, Bulaq
Tel: 02-2575 8914
www.hertzegypt.com

Limousines
Limousines are available for those who want to travel in more style, or at a fixed price:
All Egypt Limousine
1 Shari' Mohamed Mazhar, Zamalek
Tel: 02-2737 4422
Mobile: 012-130 5555
www.allegyptlimousine.com
Limousine Misr
Misr Travel Tower, Maydan Abbassia
13th Floor
Tel: 02-2285 6721,
at airport tel: 02-2418 9675
Smart Limousine
151 Corniche al Nile, Maadi
Tel: 02-2524 3006
www.smartlimo.com

Driving Conditions
The roads from Cairo to Upper Egypt are the longest, most congested, and most dangerous in Egypt. Most traffic moving south from Cairo has to travel a route along the western shore of the Nile.

It is not advisable for visitors to drive at night; drivers stop their vehicles dead on the road and turn out their lights; unlit donkey carts move at a snail's pace and are very difficult to see; and long-distance

taxis and overloaded trucks travel too fast, often without lights, and are frequently driven by men who use "stimulants" to keep themselves going.

There are petrol stations throughout the country. Mobil, Esso and Shell offer full service with minimarkets on the premises. Fuel, inexpensive and sold by the litre, is available in 90 octane *(tisa'iin)* which is super, or 80 *(tamaniin)*, regular. Super is better for most purposes.

Road signs are similar to those used in Europe. Driving is on the right; speed limits are enforced by radar.

Desert Travel
Use commonsense and always travel with a minimum of three cars and take a compass. Check your vehicle carefully and be sure to have a good spare tyre. Drive on loose sand as you would on snow; if your wheels get stuck, put a rug under the back tyres and move out slowly. If you spin your tyres, you will sink deeper into the sand.

If your car breaks down, don't abandon it; even in remote areas another vehicle will pass by. If you break down on a desert track (you should never leave the main road for long distances with only one vehicle), hike to the nearest road and wait. On all desert travels, have ample food, water, salt tablets, a hat and sunglasses. Cover the head and the back of the neck.

Top up your tank at every petrol station, as the next one may be hundreds of miles away. If your tank is small, carry a jerry can on long hauls like Dakhla to Farafrah (390 km/243 miles). Dehydration can sneak up on you in desert travel. In

---

BELOW: night driving is not recommended for visitors.

ABOVE: relaxing on a Nile cruise.

an emergency one teaspoon of salt and two tablespoons of sugar in a cup of water will revive you.

Desert driving can be monotonous. Remember you are still on a highway: when you wish to pass, sound your horn very deliberately, to make it clear that you are going to do something unusual. Egyptian drivers need an extra signal, since most of them over-use the horn.

Another bad habit is misusing lights at night, either leaving them off or flickering the high beams dangerously. You may find yourself blinded by oncoming vehicles; flash briefly and they may lower their beam. They may be checking to see if you are awake.

Nile Cruises

A cruise on the Nile is still a good way both to visit the temples and ancient sites and to sample the peaceful life along the river. Hundreds of ships now cruise along the Nile following more or less the same itinerary but offering a wide choice of accommodation, suitable for every budget. It is advisable to book cruises before you leave for Egypt as it is usually cheaper to buy them as part of a package. Most boats travel between Luxor and Aswan in three to four days, sometimes for six days to include Abydos and Dendarah, and only occasionally sail the whole way from Cairo to Aswan.

Differences in price reflect the standard of service, the numbers and size of the cabins and the quality of the food. More expensive boats tend to have fewer and larger cabins and will make the effort to prepare good food. All boats provide guides to accompany passengers to the sites and some have small libraries on Egyptian history and culture.

But there is no doubt that cruising is no longer as romantic as it used to be. There are often delays at Esna due to the number of boats, now about 300, passing through the lock, forcing some companies to transfer their passengers to a sister boat on the other side. For the same reason not all boats dock in the centre of Aswan or Luxor; cheaper boats are often moored further along the river bank, or are wedged between other boats and therefore without any Nile views from the inside. Your travel agent should know if you will have a Nile view.

To get a real feel of what cruising used to be like before the traffic jams on the Nile, a cruise on Lake Nasser is highly recommended. Five boats now offer the three- to four-day cruise, visiting the Nubian monuments on the shores of Lake Nasser. See Abu Simbel at dawn before breakfast (and the crowds) or take an apéritif at one of the rarely visited Nubian temples. Some more up-market tour operators in Europe and the United States offer the cruise in their brochures.

For a totally authentic experience you can sail the Nile on a historic *dahabeeyah* (literally a golden boat; *see box, page 232*). Nineteenth-century travellers like Flaubert, Amelia Edwards, Pierre Loti, Florence Nightingale and many others, sailed the Nile on wooden boats with cabins, propelled by two Latin sails. Some of these boats, which are a lot smaller than the cruise boats. have been restored and have started sailing the Nile again; others are being built in the same style. They make the journey from Luxor to Aswan slowly, usually taking six or seven days, and stopping at sites such as Gebel Silsilla and al-Kab where the bigger boats can't stop. They have a chef on board who cooks fresh food bought daily from the markets and farmers along the river.

There is no pool, no hot tubs and no nightly entertainment. However, the experience is truly unique.

There are many Nile and Lake Nasser cruise companies to choose from. Check out www.touregypt.net/egyptnilecruise.htm for specifications of a selection of boats, including size and number of cabins, and whether there is a pool or Jacuzzi.

Here we list a few that stand out from the crowd.

Nile Cruises

M/S Oberoi Zahra,
Mena House Oberoi,
Sharia al-Haram, Cairo
Tel: 02-3377 3222/3376 6644
www.oberoizahra.com

The new and most luxurious boat on the Nile, the *Zahra* offers unparalleled comfort. The 25 luxury suites have timber floors and large panoramic windows, the decor is contemporary elegance, the food is excellent and there is a spa on board with a gymnasium and four massage suites.

M/S Philae
Mena House Oberoi,
Shari' al-Haram, Cairo
Tel: 02-3377 3222/3376 6644
www.oberoiphilae.com
The award-winning *Philae* is designed as an old-fashioned paddle steamer. There are 54 comfortable wood-panelled rooms, each with bathroom and balcony, four de-luxe suites and a great library, but the very best thing about this boat is that it cannot moor alongside another cruise boat, so the views are always assured.

M/S Sudan
Seti First Travel, 16 Shari Ismail Muhammad, Zamalik, Cairo
Tel: 02-2736 9820
www.setifirst.com
The only old-fashioned steamer on the Nile, a present from Queen Victoria to King Fuad, and used as a set in the film *Death on the Nile*. It has 23 suites with private balconies; no pool but it oozes character.

M/S Sunboat IV
Tel: 02-2574 8334
www.akegypt.com
A small cruise boat offering larger than usual luxurious cabins, spacious sundecks with plunge pools, excellent food and very good mooring facilities at Luxor and Aswan. The boat has on-board internet access, satellite television connections, daily deliveries of international newspapers and excellent Egyptologists.

M/S Triton
www.capecairo.com
The M/S *Triton* is another small cruiser on the Nile, with 20 double suites and one de-luxe bridge suite, more reminiscent of cruising on a private yacht. The rooms are spacious and fully equipped, with LCD satellite TVs and luxurious bathrooms. The boat also includes in- and outdoor pools tiled with handmade mosaics, and a good spa.

Lake Nasser Cruises

Eugenie & Kasr Ibrim
Belle Epoque Travel
17 Shari' Tunis, New Maadi, Cairo
Tel: 02-2516 9653/4/6
www.kasribrim.com.eg
www.eugenie.com.eg
Two beautifully decorated and very elegant boats offering five-star luxury on Lake Nasser. The same company

Felucca Trips

A *felucca* trip is the best way to get a feel of the Nile. *Feluccas* can be hired for a few hours to watch the sunset, or for two–four day cruises with visits to temples along the way. The boatman may also cook and advise where it is safe to swim. If the wind is unreliable you are advised to sail from Aswan to Luxor, so at least the current will carry you downstream. To find a *felucca*, ask along the Corniche in Luxor or Aswan. The tourist office can recommend good captains and has a list of fixed prices. Some captains offer a trial tour to allow you to check out their abilities and boats. Agree on a price before starting out on the trip.

has also launched 12 luxury *dahabeyahs* on the Nile between Luxor and Aswan offering seven-days trips (six cabins each; www.dahabiya.com).

Lake Nasser Adventure Boats
Tel: 012-104 0255
www.lakenasseradventure.com
This company organises fishing safaris on Lake Nasser but has recently launched a small boat with four comfortable cabins to combine exploring the sites around Lake Nasser with discovering nature, the desert and the lake.

Nubian Sea
High Dam Cruises
Tel: 012-322 2065

Prince Abbas
Nile Exploration Cie
Tel: 097-314 660
www.nile-exploration.com.eg

BELOW: manning a *felucca*.

Dahabeeyahs on the Nile

Assouan
Tel: 010-657 8322/570 5341
www.nourelnil.com
Built in the style of 19th-century vessels, this boat has eight double cabins, each with a fully equipped en-suite bathroom. The same company, Nour el-Nil, now has six boats on the Nile, more or less the same, with eight or 10 cabins, the **Meroé** being the latest and most luxurious. These are by far the coolest boats on the Nile, despite there being no air conditioning in the cabins.

Dongola
Tel: 010-657 8322
Once the private yacht of Sultan Hussein, this boat has been carefully restored, with one suite and four cabins. The boat owner offers individual cruise trips, with everything arranged according to the customers' wishes.

Lazuli
Tel: 010-364 7011
www.fleuves-du-monde.com
This newly built boat in 19th-century style has a suite with a private balcony and four double cabins with private bathrooms.

Nubian Nile Cruises
1255 Post Street, Suite 506,
San Francisco, CA 94109, US
Tel: 01-415 440 1124
www.nubiannilecruises.com
This company runs various *dahabeyahs* for different budgets. The *Zarafa* is a restored boat which belonged to Sultan Kamel, while the *Royal Cleopatra* is a *sandale*, a slightly heavier boat than a *dahabeyah* which was used for transporting cargo. All these boats have good Egyptologists on board.

A CCOMMODATION

HOTELS

Where to Stay

Egypt has a long history of playing host to visitors, so it still has a few famous hotels, built in the colonial period. Egyptian hotels are rated by the Ministry of Tourism from five-star de-luxe to one-star. Then, of course, there are the fleapits. There are also a few relatively recent eco-resorts, mainly in Siwah. You should bear in mind that the number of stars does not necessarily correspond to similar ratings in Europe or the United States.

De-luxe hotels that are part of a chain are best booked through their central reservations office, while other hotels are often cheaper if booked as part of a package.

Price categories given in the listings below relate to the high season – Christmas and New Year and July to mid-September, and the two major Islamic holidays, Id al-Fitra and Id al-Adha (moveable dates in October and December respectively). Sometimes the rate includes breakfast but not always, so you should check when you book. You need to reserve in advance for the Christmas period.

For further information on hotels check the website of the Egyptian Tourist Office: www.egypthotelsdb.com, which has a comprehensive list.

ACCOMMODATION LISTINGS

CAIRO

★★★★★
Four Seasons Hotel
at The First Residence,
35 Shari' al-Giza, Giza
Tel: 02-3573 1212
www.fourseasons.com
This five-star hotel has large, sumptuous rooms that are tastefully decorated and overlook either the zoo and Pyramids or the Nile. Its spa is the perfect antidote to a day of hectic sight-seeing. The food in the restaurants is top-notch.
DoqqiNile Hilton
Maydan at-Tahrir, Downtown
Tel: 02-2578 0444/Doqqi0666
www.hilton.com
This was the first modern five-star hotel in Cairo. Located right on the Nile in the city centre, it has an authentic ancient Egyptian statue in the lobby. Abu Ali's Café serves *sheesha*,

green tea and light snacks on the covered terrace and is a popular meeting place. Jackie's is one of the most popular discos in town. The Taverne du Champs de Mars, a genuine Art Nouveau café shipped over in pieces from Brussels, is a popular jazz bar.
Nile Plaza Four Seasons
1089 Corniche al-Nil, Garden City
Tel: 02-2791 7000
www.fourseasons.com
The vast rooms are sumptuous, with marble bathrooms and sweeping views over the Nile or the old city and citadel. The service is efficient and the restaurants are exceptional. There are two pools, a spa and a wellness centre.
Semiramis InterContinental
Corniche al-Nil, Garden City
Tel: 02-2795 7171

www.ichotelsgroup.com
A central five-star hotel with rooms overlooking the Nile and some of the best bars and restaurants in town.
Cairo Marriott
16 Shari' Saray al-Gazirah
Tel: 02-2728 3000
www.marriott.com
Central hotel occupying a 19th-century palace on an island in the Nile. Vast gardens, a good spa and a casino. Worth having tea here even if you are not staying overnight. Comfortable traditionally decorated rooms.

★★★★
Golden Tulip Flamenco Hotel
2 Shari' al-Gazirah al-Wusta
Tel: 02-2735 0815/6
www.flamencohotels.com
In a quiet, tree-lined street in the residential part of

Zamalik, with rooms over-looking the Nile. Restaurant serves good paella.

★★★
Cosmopolitan
1, Shari' ibn Taalab, Downtown
Tel: 02-2393 6914
Fax: 02-2393 3531
A grand Art Nouveau hotel offering spacious, comfortable rooms. It is surprisingly quiet, given its central location.
Longchamps Hotel
21 Shari' Ismail Muhammad, Zamalik
Tel: 02-2735 2311
www.hotellongchamps.com
Spotless and airy rooms in a quiet location. A home away from home, under the management of friendly Heba Bakri.
President
22 Shari' Dr Taha Husayn, Zamalik
Tel: 02-2735 0652

ABOVE: palatial accommodation in the Cairo Marriott.

Email: preshotl@thewayout.net

This is more like a four-star hotel in its attention to detail; efficient and friendly, this hotel is a well-kept secret in a quiet street. It has a good business centre and its Cellar Bar serves good *mezze*. Represents excellent all-round value.

Talisman
39 Shari' Talaat Harb, 5th floor
Tel: 02-2393 9431
Mob: 010-125 6212
www.talisman-hotel.com

Cairo's first boutique hotel, in a lovely downtown building. Spacious rooms decorated in Oriental style, and a lovely breakfast room. The owners are serious Cairophiles, and love to share their passion with their guests.

Windsor
19 Shari' Alfi Bey, Downtown
Tel: 02-2591 5277
www.windsorcairo.com

This is a place to taste a piece of Cairo that has all but vanished. Friendly service and faded but clean rooms, albeit rather overpriced. The bar, with its old waiters and sunken sofas, is an institution.

★★
Carlton Hotel
21 Shari' 26th July (Yulyu), beside Cinema Rivoli, Downtown
Tel: 02-25/5 5181
Email: carlton@menanet.net

An atmospheric hotel with period charm. The rooms vary enormously in size and

pleasantness, so ask to have a look before checking in.

El Hussein,
Maydan al-Husayn, Al Azhar
Tel: 02-2591 8089

This is a noisy option, particularly during religious festivals, but it's a good place to stay if you want to get lost in Cairo's old city. It offers basic but clean rooms.

Happy City
92 Muhammad Farid Street, Abdin
Tel: 02-2395 9333/222
Fax: 02-2395 9777
Email: happycity@happylifehotel.com
www.happylifehotel.com (click on "other hotels")

Great-value hotel just north of Muhammad Najeeb metro station. There is a bar and restaurant, or enjoy smoking a *sheesha* on the roof terrace; 60 rooms but those on the main road can be noisy.

Lotus
7th floor, 12 Shari' Talaat Harb
Tel: 02-2575 0966
www.lotushotel.com

Good value and as central as it gets. The rooms are showing their age a little, but they are clean and airy, with balconies and air conditioning.

★
Berlin Hotel
2 Shari' al-Shawarby, off Shari' Qasr an-Nil, Downtown
Tel/Fax: 02-2395 7502
Email: berlinhotelcairo@hotmail.com

Popular budget hotel with old-style rooms and dormitories with original Art Deco fittings and polished wooden floors. There is a communal kitchen, a sauna, satellite television and internet access.

Garden City House
23, Shari' Kamal ad-Din Sale, Garden City
Tel: 02-2794 4969
www.gardencityhouse.com

A pleasant old-style *pension*, traditionally popular with scholars and archaeologists. The rooms are large and clean, and some of them overlook the Nile.

Lialy Hostel
8 Maydan Talaat Harb
Tel: 02-2575 2802
Email: lialy_hostel@yahoo.com
www.hostelworld.com

A modern hostel in a convenient, central location. Ultra-clean and spacious rooms and very friendly management, combined with reasonable prices, make this a good option.

Mayfair
9 Shari' Aziz Osman, Zamalik
Tel: 02-2735 7315
www.mayfaircairo.com

Tranquil hotel with tidy rooms and a pleasant terrace for a drink in the afternoon.

Meramees
32 Shari' Sabry Abu Alam, near Maydan Tala'at Harb, Downtown
Tel: 02-2396 2318
Email: meramees_hotel@hotmail.com

The friendly owner Mamdouh Mohamed loves

Cairo and wants to share his passion with his visitors. Rooms are clean and comfortable, and a kitchen and washing machine are available.

Osiris
49 Nobar Street, Bab al-Luq, Cairo
Tel: 02-2794 5728
Fax: 02-2794 2981
Mobile: 012 235 6082
Email: hotelosiris@yahoo.fr or osiris99fr@yahoo.fr
www.osiris.fr.fm

Small, new family-run hotel, ideally located to the east of Tahrir Square. On the 12th floor of a quiet block with rooftop terrace looking across to the Citadel. Only 15 rooms and very popular with independent travellers, so make sure for early reservation, especially if you want a room with balcony. Internet and laundry service. Highly recommended and great value. Can also arrange airport transfer.

Pension Roma
169 Shari' Muhammad Farid, 6th floor, Downtown
Tel: 02-2391 1088
Fax: 02-2579 6243

A popular hotel with travellers. All the rooms have shiny wood floors and old-style furniture. You need to book in advance.

Pension Zamalik
6 Shari' Salah ad-Din, Zamalik
Tel: 02-2735 9318

IA quiet place to stay, this is more like someone's home than a hotel. Very spacious, pleasant rooms.

Richmond Hotel
7th fl, 41 Shari' Sharif, Downtown
Tel: 02-2393 9358
Email: amarichmond@hotmail.com

Basic but clean rooms in a grand downtown apartment block. The rooms are a little on the dark side, and all have shared bathrooms, but good value nonetheless and the management is friendly.

PRICE CATEGORIES

Price ranges for double rooms with bath are:
$ $15–30
$$ $30–50
$$$ $50–75
$$$$ $75–200
$$$$$ $200–400

GIZA

★★★★★
Mena House Oberoi
End of Shari' al-Haram
(Pyramid's Road)
Tel: 02-3377 3222
www.oberoihotels.com
Mena House is an historic
landmark refurbished by
the Oberoi chain. The
rooms in the 19th-century
khedival hunting lodge are
decorated with antiques,
but most rooms are in the
modern garden wing, which
has less character. Lunch
by the pool is
recommended after visiting
the Giza Pyramids. The
Moghul Room is one of the
best Indian restaurants in
Egypt, with live music,
while the Rubayyat offers
continental and Middle-
Eastern meals and live
entertainment.

★★★★
**Mövenpick Resort
Cairo-Pyramids**
Alexandria Road, Pyramids,
PO Box 1
Tel: 3377 2555/3377 2666
Fax: 3377 5006
Email: resort.cairo-pyramids@
moevenpick.com
www.moevenpick-cairo-pyramids.com
One of several international
chains with hotels close to

the Pyramids offering pool,
health club and floodlit
tennis courts. Popular with
groups. 270 bungalow-style
rooms with cafés and
restaurants offering
glimpses of the Pyramids.
A larger Mövenpick resort
is located beyond the
Pyramids, close to the
Media City Studios and the
Magic Land amusement
park.

Pyramisa
60 Shari' Giza, Doqqi
Tel: 3336 7000/8000/9000
Fax: 3760 5347
Email: cairo@pyramisaegypt.com
www.pyramisaegypt.com
Large 11-floor building
with 377 rooms on the
west bank of the Nile,
opposite the northern end
of Roda Island. Italian,
Chinese and Egyptian
restaurants, casino, two
swimming pools,
gymnasium and piano bar.
Popular with tour groups.

★★★
Cataract Pyramids Resort
Al Haraneya, Saqqarah Road
Tel: 3771 8060/1/2
Fax: 3771 8073
Email: cpr.sales@cataracthotels.com
www.cataracthotels.com
Large complex of villas

totalling 383 rooms,
set in pleasant gardens
around a huge swimming
pool. Located south of the
Giza Pyramids along the
road to Saqqara, this is a
popular local resort in the
midst of lush countryside,
with its own health club
and disco. For a daily fee,
the pool can be used by
non-residents – useful if
visiting the other pyramids
on a hot and sweaty day.

Middle East
85 King Faisal Road, Pyramids
Tel: 3740 6061
Fax: 3740 6151
Email: middle_east_hotel@hotmail.com
www.middleeasthotel.com.eg
Large rooms spread over
five floors with coffee
shop, restaurant and
rooftop terrace. On a busy
street but good value, only
ten minutes from the
Pyramids. 80 rooms.

★★
Gawharet Alahram Hotel
103 Pyramids Road
Tel: 3771 7111
Fax: 3386 7494
Email: info@gawharetalahramhotel.com
www.gawharetalahramhotel.com
Also known as the Husa
Pyramids, this is a Spanish-
run hotel with 100 rooms

and swimming pool.
Wonderful Pyramid views
from the Panorama bar
and restaurant on the
top floor.

★
Europa
300 Pyramids Road
Tel: 3779 5940
Fax: 3584 9130
An older-style concrete
block with 240 rooms over
eight floors. Popular with
groups and great value,
considering the location.
Restaurant on the ground
floor.

Pyramid View
Nazlet al-Samman,
9 Abo al-Hool Street
Tel: 3384 5968/010-519 7669
Email: pyramidsviewhotel@yahoo.com or
rahomafayed@hotmail.com
Not to be confused with the
larger hotel of the same
name on the main
Pyramids Road. Simply
furnished in 2005 by owner
Rahoma Kamel Fayed,
there are only six small,
clean rooms in this family-
run establishment on the
doorstep of the sphinx and
Pyramids with great rooftop
views. Only breakfast
served but there are many
local restaurants nearby.

THE OASES AND THE FAYYUM

LAKE QARUN

★★★★★
Helnan Auberge
Qarun Lake, Fayyum
Tel: 084-698 1200
Fax: 084-698 1300
Email: auberge@helnan.com
www.helnan.com
Converted former
hunting lodge of King
Faruq, built in 1937 on
the banks of Lake Qarun
in the Fayyum oasis. 70
rooms set around
swimming pool with
gardens, as seen in
countless old Egyptian
movies. Ideal retreat
for those wanting to
escape the chaos of
greater Cairo.

SIWAH

★★★★★
Adrere Amellal Eco-lodge
Near the White Mountain on
Siwah Lake, 20 km (12 miles)
from Siwah
Tel: 02-736 7879
Fax: 02-736 3331
Email: info@eqi.com.eg
A little slice of paradise,
this eco-lodge is built in
local style. The pool is an
extension of the spring
that feeds the oasis.
Good food and attentive
service.

Tamazigh
Sidi Jaafar, White Mountain
Tel: 02-736 7879
Email: info@eqi.com.eg
A smaller and more

intimate version of the
Adrere Amellal eco-lodge,
with just eight very
spacious rooms, several
dining rooms and a large
spring-fed swimming pool,
surrounded by a lush
oasis garden. Some of
the rooms are made
entirely of salt crystals,
including the beds and
bedside tables.

★★★★
Siwa Shali Resort
Gebel Dakrour
Tel: 046-921 0064
Fax (Cairo): 02-383 9242
www.siwashaliresort.com
This is a new resort built
in traditional Siwan style
around a large spring-fed
swimming pool. The
rooms are equipped with

air conditioning, satellite
TV and fridge and
furnished with locally
made palm-frond
furniture. There is a good
main restaurant serving
buffet meals, as well as a
more intimate mud-brick
Egyptian restaurant
offering freshly prepared
dishes. Coffee, tea and
waterpipes are served in
a Bedouin tent.

★★★
Shali Lodge
Maydan al-Souk,
Shari' al-Seboukha, Siwah
Tel: 046 460 1299
Fax: 046-460 1799
Email: info@eqi.com.eg
Small hotel with
swimming pool, in a palm
grove near the centre of

Siwah. Under the same management as the Adrere Amellal Eco-lodge. The rooms are large and comfortable.

Tala Ranch Hotel
Gebel Dakrour
Mobile: 010-588 6003
Email: talaranch@hotmail.com
Camp-style hotel on the edge of the desert, offering an atmospheric

stay. There are six stylish and comfortable rooms, all with their own bathrooms. Sherif, the owner, organises camel safaris for guests, while his wife Siham does the excellent Egyptian cooking, which is served in a Bedouin tent.

Taziry
Sidi Jaafar

Mobile: 010-644 5881/112 2519
Email: Taziry@hotmail.com
The Alexandrian couple who run this hotel escaped from the city and found this peaceful spot, overlooking the Siwah Lake. "Taziry" means moon in Siwi, and this lovely hotel was designed and built by its friendly owners, an artist and an

engineer from Alexandria. The large rooms, with en suite bathrooms but without electricity, and the natural spring pool overlooking the lake, offer the perfect place to unwind. Bags of local atmosphere add to the experience.

MIDDLE EGYPT

ASYUT

★★★
Assiutel
146 Shari' an-Nil
Tel: 088-231 2121
Fax: 088-231 2122
This agreeable three-star hotel is the best in town but that is not saying much in a place where tourists hardly ever stay overnight, if they come at all. The rooms are comfortable, equipped with private bathroom, satellite TV and fridge, but everything thing could do with a lick of paint and some attention. The hotel also has the only bar in Asyut.

Casa Blanca Hotel
Shari Muhammad Tawfik Khashaba
Tel: 088-233 7762
The Casa Blanca is aDoqqi three-star hotel with efficient service and cleanish, comfortable rooms, but it does not have a great deal of atmosphere.

AL-MINYA

★★★★
DoqqiAton
Shari' Corniche an-Nil
Tel: 086-234 2993/4
Fax: 086-234 1517
This is still Minya's top hotel. It has well-equipped bungalow-style rooms set in a mature garden with a

swimming pool. The hotel has a bar and two restaurants.

★★★
Akhenaten
Corniche an-Nil
Tel: 086-236 5917
www.kingakhenaton.8m.com
If the Nefertiti hotel is too expensive for your budget, then this newly renovated hotel, not far away, is the next best option. The clean, comfortable rooms have air-conditioning, TV and a fridge.

★
Ibn Khassib
5 Shari' Rageb
Tel: 086-223 4535
Fax: 086-393 7828

This is a small, simple hotel, furnished in Victorian-style and with high ceilings. Some rooms have air conditioning and private baths, and breakfast is included in the price. There is a restaurant, a bar and a billiards room.

Palace Hotel
Maydan Tahrir
Tel: 086 232 4021
Beautiful hotel with high ceilings and lots of period detail, including painted pharaonic murals. Situated on the main square and therefore noisy. The hotel has seen much better days: there are very few tourists here, but the Palace is still the best budget option in town. Bathrooms are communal.

UPPER EGYPT

ABU SIMBEL

★★★★★
Seti Abu Simbel
Tel: 097-240 0720
Seti First Travel
Tel: 02-736 9820
www.setifirst.com
This is the only five-star hotel in Abu Simbel, set at the foot of the Grand Temple of Ramses; chalet-style rooms in a garden overlooking the lake. All modern amenities, and relaxing atmosphere.

★★
Eskaleh
Tel: 012-368 0521

DoqqiNubian musician Fikry Kachif runs this small but charming mud-brick hotel. It has just five rooms, which are simple and clean, and some have their own terrace overlooking the lake (request one of these when you book). There's a library with lots of books on Nubian culture, and a restaurant serving good food cooked with produce from their own organic garden. Fikry was a guide on the *Eugénie*, cruising the lake, and is an authority on all things Nubian. At night he and his friends gather to make music. Recommended.

★
Abu Simbel Village
Tel: 097-240 0092/012-363 9794
The cheapest option in town, with clean rooms around a courtyard.

ASWAN

★★★★★
Isis Island Aswan
Tel: 097-231 7400
Fax: 097-231 7405
www.pyramisaegypt.com
This huge luxurious resort hotel, set on its own island slightly upriver from the centre of Aswan, is owned by one of President Mubarak's sons. The

rooms are set in a large landscaped garden with two big swimming pools. The hotel has several restaurants and bars, and a regular launch connects the hotel with downtown Aswan. Great views over the river from most rooms.

Mövenpick Resort Aswan
Elephantine Island
Tel: 097-230 3455

PRICE CATEGORIES

Price ranges for double rooms with bath are:
$ $15–30
$$ $30–50
$$$ $50–75
$$$$ $75–200
$$$$$ $200–400

Email: resort.aswan@moevenpick.com
Recently renovated luxury spa hotel. The huge ugly tower is still there but the spacious rooms are great, with wide-ranging views over the Nile. It is a peaceful resort with a pool set in the garden, and a spa specialising in sand treatments for rheumatism. There is a free ferry that transports guests in and out of town.

Sofitel Old Cataract
Shari' Abtal at-Tahrir
Tel: 097-231 6000
www.sofitel.com
For old-style, Agatha Christie-type nostalgia and the smell of polished wood there is nowhere quite like the Old Cataract in Aswan. Rooms are cosy and tastefully furnished. North-wing, Nile-side rooms overlook the temple on Elephantine Island. Breakfast is served in the splendid former ballroom, and the terrace is still the best place in town to watch the sunset. The hotel is set to close for restoration at the time of writing.

★★★★
Basma Hotel
Shari' al-Fanadek
(past the Cataract Hotel)
Tel: 097-231 0901/2/3
Email: basma@rocketmail.com
A full-blown modern resort hotel with all the amenities you would expect, including a huge pool. Most rooms overlook the river and the Aga Khan Mausoleum. The whole place could do with some renovation, but it is still good value as prices have dropped recently. There are several restaurants but the food is pretty average. The large terrace is a good place to watch the sunset with a sundowner.

Isis Hotel
Corniche al-Nil
Tel: 097-232 4744
www.pyramisaegypt.com
Built on the riverbank in the centre of town, this resort hotel could do with some renovation but its location on the Nile is excellent. The garden has a pool and there are several restaurants,

including a reasonably good Italian on the terrace.

★★★
Cleopatra
Shari' Saad Zaghloul
Tel: 097-231 4001
Fax: 097-231 2002
Situated near the *suq*, the Cleopatra offers very clean, smart rooms, all with phones and private bathrooms. There is a small pool on the roof. The rooms are quite dark and in desperate need of updating.

DoqqiMarhaba Palace Hotel
Corniche al-Nil
Tel: 097-233 0102
www.marhaba-aswan.com
Modern hotel overlooking the Nile, with small but comfortable rooms with private bathrooms, air conditioning, satellite television and internet access. The Marhaba has a good restaurant with a view of the Nile, and a heated swimming pool in the garden. The hotel is lively and welcoming, and by far the best choice in this category.

Nile Hotel
Corniche al-Nil
Tel: 097-231 4222
www.nilehotel-aswan.com
Definitely a welcome addition to Aswan's hotel scene, the Nile Hotel is a friendly and welcoming place on the Nile, with 30 spotless rooms all with en-suite bathrooms, minibar, satellite TV and views on the Nile.

Orchida St George
Shari' Muhammad Khalid
Tel: 097-231 5997
Email: orchidahotel@hotmail.com
Friendly, clean, modern hotel; check the room before you take it, as they vary. The decor is quite kitsch, but the beds are comfortable and the bathrooms are very clean.

Sarah Hotel
Shari' al-Fanadeq, Nasr City
Tel: 097-232 7234
www.sarahotel-aswan.com
Situated on a clifftop outside the city centre, this quiet hotel commands great views over the first cataract on the Nile and

the Western Desert. The modern rooms are spacious and some have big balconies. There are several restaurants offering international cuisine, and there is a pool. This hotel is a long walk away from the city, but a shuttle bus ferries guests to and fro. The cafeteria is popular with middle-class Aswanis who come and spend the afternoon here.

★★
Keylany Hotel
25 Shari' Keylany
Tel: 097-231 7332
www.keylanyhotel.com
Very popular and friendly hotel with an internet café, the Keylany has become a favourite with travellers in recent years. The spotless rooms all have a toilet, shower, and air conditioning or fan. The management is always at hand to offer help.

Nuba Nile Hotel
Shari' Abtal at-Tahrir
Tel: 097-231 3267
Email: nubanile_hotel@hotmail.com
Good budget hotel near the train station; make sure you have a room with a window as there are a few that are windowless. Popular with backpackers who also hang out in the neighbouring *ahwa* (coffee house).

LUXOR

★★★★★
Al-Moudira
Near Haggar, Daba' iya, 5 km (3 miles) north of main sights on West Bank
Tel: 012-325 1307
Email: moudirahotel@yahoo.com
www.moudira.com
An Oriental fantasy with 54 vast rooms and beautiful bathrooms. There is a large pool in a lovely garden, right on the edge of the desert. The food is excellent, the architecture by Olivier Sednaoui stunning.

Maritim Jolie Ville Luxor
King's Island, 6 km (4 miles) south of Luxor
Tel: 095-227 4855
Fax: 095-227 4936

www.lux-maritim-jolieville.com
These 21 comfortable bungalows are scattered over an area of 24 acres (10 hectares), which includes a lush garden under the palm trees and two large swimming pools. The service is good, the food is excellent and plentiful, with a buffet-style breakfast served on the terrace beside the Nile, weather allowing. Great views from the pool over a beautiful stretch of the Nile. Free shuttle bus into town.

Old Winter Palace
Corniche al-Nil
Tel: 095-238 0422
www.sofitel.com
Built in 1886 on the banks of the Nile, the Old Winter Palace, which has received celebrities and royalties for over a century, has been restored to some of its former splendour. The hotel has a tropical garden with a large pool and a pleasant poolside restaurant. The management has recently changed and the hotel now provides good service and some great eateries. The New Winter Palace is to be bulldozed and a new all-suite hotel in the style of the Old Winter Palace will be built in its place, from June 2008.

★★★★
Iberotel
Corniche al-Nil,
near the Luxor Temple
Tel: 097-238 0925
www.iberotel-eg.com/luxor
Small, pleasant hotel near the centre of Luxor, but with views on to the Nile. The hotel has a good pool, a Jacuzzi, several restaurants and the most popular discotheque in town.

Sonesta St George Hotel
Shari' Khaled ibn al-Walid
Tel: 097-238 2575
www.sonesta.com/egypt
Very large resort hotel on the Nile with an impressive marble lounge in true Egyptian style, several good restaurants and 224 rooms. This is a lively cheerful venue, popular with Brits, with friendly and helpful staff, and in a good location.

★★★
Morris Hotel
Shari' al-Hurriyyah,
off Shari' ibn al-Walid
Tel: 097-235 9832
www.hotelmorrisluxor.com
New four-star hotel with spacious modern rooms overlooking the Nile and Luxor town. Breakfast is served on the terrace and the hotel has a bar, restaurant and swimming pool. A discotheque is planned.

New Emilio Hotel
Shari' Yousef Hasan
Tel: 095-237 3570
Fax: 095-237 0000
Email: emilio_hotel@hotmail.com
This is a very good mid-range hotel with comfort-able rooms that are equipped with all mod-cons. There is a rooftop pool and sundeck. Book in advance in winter as it is very popular with tour groups.

Philippe
Shari' Labib Habashy
Tel: Doqqi095-238 0050
Excellent three-star hotel offering spotless, air-conditioned rooms (some with balconies) with TV and fridge. The roof terrace has a small pool and bar. Recommended, but book well ahead, especially during winter.

Saint Joseph
Shari' Khaled Ibn al Waleed
Tel: 095-238 1707
Fax: 095-238 1727
Email: sjhieh2002@hotmail.com
Well-equipped budget hotel with clean, cosy rooms, pool and sauna.

★★
Al-Gezira Gardens
al-Gazirah, West Bank
Tel: 097-231 2505
www.el-gezira.com
More of a resort-style hotel than most on this side of the Nile, the Al-Gezira Gardens has 14 double hotel rooms and eight self-catering flats with two double bedrooms each. The rooms are set around a garden with a largish pool. The hotel is in a quiet location, has an internet café and two restaurants. Ideal for families.

Al-Nakhil
al-Gazirah, West Bank
Tel: 097-231 3922/012-382 1007
www.el-nakhil.com
A newcomer on the booming budget hotel scene around the ferry landing on the West Bank, al-Nakhil, or "The Palm Tree". A pleasant resort-style hotel with air-conditioned domed rooms and apartments set in a palm grove. Like the other hotels in this category, the Nakhil is very family-friendly and will provide cots for small children.

Amon Hotel
al-Gazirah, West Bank
Tel: 097-231 0912
Fax: 097-231 1353
Family-run hotel with rooms around an almost tropical garden where drinks and breakfast are served. The rooms in the annexe are more spacious and modern, with the top three rooms sharing a terrace overlooking the fields and the Nile.

Beit Sabée
Kom Lolah, near Madinat Habu, West Bank
Tel: 010-632 4926
Email: info@nourelnil.com.
Small boutique hotel in a traditional style mud-brick house, with great views across the fields of Medinet Habu temple. All eight rooms have en-suite bathrooms and fans, and are decorated tastefully with local palm-tree furnishings and woven textiles. Recommended.

Nile Valley
Al-Gazirah, West Bank
Tel: 097-231 1477/012-796 4473
www.nilevalley.nl
This Dutch/Egyptian-run family-friendly hotel offers bright and comfortable rooms with en-suite bathrooms, all of them spotless. Some rooms overlook the Nile, others the garden, and there is a heated swimming pool, several restaurants and a brilliant roof terrace.

Nour al-Gurna
Opposite the ticket office, al-Qurna, West Bank
Tel: 095-231 1430
Delightful small hotel with large, simple but stylish rooms overlooking sugar-cane fields or a pretty palm

ABOVE: the Luxor Temple in Luxor.

grove. All have fans and mosquito nets. There is also a delightful mud-brick sister hotel that is even quieter, the Nur al-Balad behind the Madinet Habu temple (tel: 095-242 6111).

★
Anglo Hotel
Maydan al-Mahatta
Tel/fax: 097-238 1679
The Anglo may have seen better days and may be quite noisy, located as it is near the train station, but the location is convenient and it offers very good value for its immaculate well-kept rooms.

Habu Hotel
Opposite Madinat Habu, Nag Lolah, West Bank
Tel: 095-237 2477
The Habu offers basic and somewhat shabby rooms, but they come at a low price, and the local atmosphere and spectacular views over the temple are great.

**Marsam Hotel
(also known as Shaykh Ali's Hotel)**
Opposite the Tombs of the Nobles, al-Qurna, West Bank
Tel: 095-237 2403
www.luxor-westbank.com/
marsam_e_az.htm
This simple, clean hotel with 30 rooms, some with private bathrooms, is run by a charming Australian woman. The tranquil garden has views over green fields.

Oasis Hotel
Shari' Muhammad Farid, East Bank
Tel: 097-496 1848/010-300 5882
www.luxoroasis.com
Popular budget hotel painted in bright blues with

spotless rooms. Air-conditioning and private spic and span bathrooms. Wi-fi and afternoon tea are included in the room price, and the owner can pick you up from the train station.

Saint Mina
Off Shari' Ramesses
Tel: 095-237 5409
Fax: 095-237 6568
This is a family-run hotel, quiet and very friendly. There are 20 spotlessly clean rooms with air conditioning or fans, and some have private bathrooms.

Senmut B&B
Ar-Ramlah, south of the ferry landing on the West Bank
Tel: 097-231 3077/012-736 9159
www.senmut-luxor.com
The first bed and breakfast accommodation in Luxor offers a home from home with 10 very clean and comfortable rooms, including the most attractive room with a rooftop terrace and great views. The Senmut is run by a Dutch-Egyptian couple – he is an official tour guide – who are willing to help guests at all times. Guest can use the communal kitchen to prepare their own meals or order a delicious home-cooked meal for the evening.

PRICE CATEGORIES
Price ranges for double rooms with bath are:

★	$15–30
★★	$30–50
★★★	$50–75
★★★★	$75–200
★★★★★	$200–400

ALEXANDRIA

★★★★★
As-Salamlek Palace
Muntazah Palace grounds
Tel: 03-547 7999
www.sangiovanni.com
The old *salamlek*, or
guesthouse of the palace,
offers luxurious, comfortable rooms in the quiet
surroundings of the
Muntazah gardens, and
has its own beach and
Alexandria's only casino.
A real treat
**Green Plaza Hilton
Alexandria**
Green Plaza Shopping Mall,
14th of May Bridge, Smouha
Tel: 03-420 9120
www.hilton.com
This is at present the most
sumptuous hotel in town.
The large rooms are
equipped with all mod
cons, the hotel has a good
business centre and it is
close to Nozha Airport. The
Green Plaza Mall has
abundant shopping, eating
and drinking facilities,
cinemas, etc. The hotel is

quite a distance (a 20-
minute taxi ride) from the
city centre.
Helnan Palestine Hotel
Muntazah Palace grounds
Tel: 03-547 4033
www.helnan.com
An Alexandrian institution,
very popular with ex-
patriate residents and local
families, who come here at
weekends to enjoy the
peaceful bay and to swim
in the sea. The 230 rooms
and suites are comfortable
and the views make a stay
here worthwhile.

★★★★
Paradise Inn Metropole
52 Shari' Saad Zaghlul, Downtown
Tel: 03-486 1465
www.paradiseinnegypt.com
Ornate period hotel with
lots of atmosphere,
mouldings and antiques in
the reception area, all mod
cons in the 66 rooms, and
comfortable beds. Cheaper
than the Cecil Hotel; be
sure to book in advance.

**Sofitel Alexandria Cecil
Hotel**
16 Maydan Saad Zaghlul
Tel: 03-483 7173
Fax: 03-483 6401
www.sofitel.com
The Cecil is haunted by the
ghosts of Noel Coward,
Somerset Maugham and by
Lawrence Durrell – the
latter immortalised it in
The Alexandria Quartet. The
glamour has long gone, but
the charm of the place and
the views over the bay still
pull in the romantics. The
coffee shop is a popular
meeting point. 83 rooms
and six suites.
Windsor Palace
17 Shari' Shohada, Corniche
Tel: 03-480 8123/8256
www.sigmahotels.com
Built in 1907, the Windsor
was bought by Paradise
Inns in the late 1990s and
given a total make-over; it
now belongs to the Sigma
chain. The make-over was
sensitively done and most
of the period details,

including the grand lobby
and ancient elevators, have
been kept in all their glory,
and the rooms remain
comfortable and cosy. The
more expensive ones have
glorious sweeping views
over the Mediterranean.

★
Nile Excelsior Hotel
16 Shari' al-Bursa al-Qadima
Tel: 03-480 0799/1369
Email: nilehotel@gmail.com
Centrally located in the
same street as the well-
known Spitfire Bar, this
hotel offers clean and
comfortable rooms.
Union
164 Shari' 26th of July
Tel: 03-480 7312
The Union is the best
budget option in Alexandria,
offering clean, if rather
small rooms and it is
staffed by friendly, helpful
people. It's a favourite
among those who come to
Alexandria regularly, so
book well ahead.

SINAI

DAHAB

★★★★★
Hilton Dahab
Tel: 069-364 0310
www.hilton.com
A resort-style hotel that,
like most places in Dahab,
caters mainly for package
tours. On-site diving school,
two pools and restaurants.
Lacking in atmosphere.

★★★
Nesima
Mashraba, Dahab
Tel: 069-364 0320
www.nesima-resort.com
A wonderful hotel and
diving centre, inspired by
traditional architecture with
lots of domes and a great
outdoor pool. Child care is
available.

★
Canyon Dive Resort
9 km (6 miles) north of Dahab
Tel/Fax: 069-364 0219/7

Isolated, but ideal for those
who only want to dive.
Christina Residence
Mashraba, Dahab
Tel: 069-364 0352
Fax: 069-364 0351
Email: christina_residence@yahoo.com
The Christina is a small but
pleasant hotel on
the beach, with clean,
adequate rooms.

Unclassified
Bedouin Village (Dahab)
Most travellers head for the
so-called Bedu Village
Assalah – Bedu-run camps
with huts of either concrete
(which are hot) or reed
(less secure), some with
electricity and fans. Two of
the best are:
Mirage Village
Tel: 069-364 0341
Fax: 069-364 0332
Provides accommodation
either in huts or in more
expensive proper rooms.
7Heaven Hotel
Assalah, Dahab
Tel: 069-364 0080

www.7heavenhotel.com
Simple but wonderful camp
with huts, as well as a two-
storey building which has
whitewashed rooms with
private bathrooms. Very
friendly and relaxed
atmosphere. There is a
restaurant, a dive centre
and an internet café.

NUWAYBA

★★
Habiba Village
Tel: 069-350 0770/0565
Fax: 069-350 0339
www.sinai4you.com/habiba
Simple but pleasant camp
with 10 comfortable rooms,
equipped with air
conditioning and private
bathrooms, plus 10
wooden simple and clean
cabins equipped with fans.
Sultana Village
Tel: 069-350 0490
Fax: 069-350 0491
www.sinai4you.com/sultana

Simple but comfortable
beach resort with laid-back
atmosphere and stone
huts, on a beautiful beach.

★
Basata Camp
23 km (14 miles) north of Nuwayba
Tel/Fax: 069-350 0481
(or 02-350-1829 in Cairo)
www.basata.com
Clean and extremely
relaxed eco-lodge with
simple bamboo huts, a
bakery and a communal
kitchen. Book well ahead.

ST CATHERINE'S

**St Catherine's Monastery
Hostel**
Tel: 069-347 0353
Email: moussaboules@yahoo.com
Monastic but comfortable
rooms, some with private
bathrooms, overlooking a
courtyard. This is the best
place to stay if you want to

make an early ascent of the mountain. Meals are included. You must book ahead.

Ecolodge Al-Karm
Wadi Garba (turn off at Garba), St Catherine
Tel: 069-347 0032/33
Beautiful eco-lodge in the St Catherine Protectorate, which is run by the local Bedu tribe. It is built in the stone of the surrounding mountains. Simple, clean rooms offer shared facilities. No electricity, but solar powered hot water.

SHARM AL-SHAYKH

★★★★★
Four Seasons Sharm
9 km (5 miles) north of Na'ama Bay
Tel: 069-360 3555
Fax: 069-360 3550
www.fourseasons.com
The five-star classification does not really do justice to the excellent service and the facilities at this new

Four Seasons hotel. With the possible exception of the Ritz-Carlton, this is as good as it gets.

Mövenpick Jolie Ville
Na'ama Bay
Tel: 069-360 0100
Fax: 069-360 0111
www.movenpick-hotels.com
Good but very large resort hotel with bungalows set in a beautiful garden and with several restaurants. In the heart of Na'ama Bay.

Ritz-Carlton
Ras Umm Sid
Tel: 069-366 1919
Fax: 069-366 1920
www.ritzcarlton.com
All rooms are equipped with the latest hotel gadgets, including internet via the television. There are several top-quality restaurants, a cigar lounge, a waterfall, two big pools and a fitness centre.

★★★★
Hilton Sharm El Sheikh Fayrouz Resort
Na'ama Bay
Tel: 069-360 0137
www.hilton.com

One of the first up-market hotels in the bay, the Hilton Fayrouz continues to offer an efficient service. The bungalows are set in a lovely garden. Four outdoor pools and two dedicated children's pools. Horse riding and watersports are available, as is a diving centre.

★★★
Sanafir
Na'ama Bay
Tel: 069-360 0197
www.sanafirhotel.com
One of the liveliest hotels in the bay. Not on the beach, but with an interior courtyard and pool. Comfortable rooms furnished in an attractive Moorish style. Guests get a free pass to use the beach at the nearby Aquanaute Diving Club. Has several restaurants and the Pacha nightclub, a popular hang-out.

Sharks Bay Bedouin Home
10 km (6 miles) from Na'ama Bay on Sharm Al-Shaykh/Dahab Road
Tel: 069-360 0947
www.sharksbay.com
A relaxing atmosphere, with

bamboo beach huts or wooden cabins on a private beach with a beautiful coral reef. Excellent fish restaurant.

★
The Pigeon House
Northern edge of Na'ama Bay
Tel: 069-360 0996
Fax: 069-360 0995
Email: pigeon@access.com.eg
Budget hotel with basic but clean bamboo huts with fans, some smaller rooms and communal bathrooms. Fills up quickly.

TABA

★★★★★
Hyatt Regency
Taba Heights
Tel: 069-358 0234
www.taba.hyatt.com
One of several large hotel chains that has opened at Taba Heights, just south of Taba. More than 420 rooms, plus a wealth of facilities, i ncluding children's club and a casino.

THE RED SEA

AL-GOUNA

Al-Gouna is a smaller resort than Hurghadah and in many ways preferable for a sand and sun holiday: the architecture is more attractive, the beaches are nicer and the nightlife is good. Al-Gouna lagoon has a wide variety of modern resort hotels of all categories. For more information, see www.elgouna.com.

★★★★★
Al-Gouna Mövenpick
Tel: 065-354 4501
Email: resort.elgouna@moevenpick.com
www.moevenpick-elgouna.com
Huge resort hotel (554 rooms) where you could easily get lost. Despite its large number of rooms, there is plenty of space for everyone around the four swimming pools, the

lagoons, or on the large stretch of beach. Good selection of bars and restaurants and plenty of sporting options.

Miramar (Sheraton)
Tel: 065-354 5606
www.sheraton.com/elgouna
This hotel offers world-class architecture by celebrity American architect Michael Graves, who was inspired by the work of the late Egyptian architect, Hassan Fathy. The 338 rooms are painted in muted primary colours and the hotel is built in a low simple style. The Miramar is surrounded by lagoons. Three restaurants and three bars.

Steigenberger Golf Resort
Tel: 065 358 0140
Fax: 065 358 0149
www.steigenberger.com
This luxurious golf resort, also designed by Michael Graves, won a prestigious

award from the American Institute for Architects. Surrounded by Gouna's blue lagoons and 18-hole USPGA championship golf course, it caters for both golfers and up-market holidaymakers. Excellent food in its three restaurants, and impeccable service.

★★★★
Club Med Al-Gouna
Tel: 065-354 7934
Fax: 065-354 7933
www.clubmed.co.uk
A pleasant resort hotel overlooking the sea, with three swimming pools and several good restaurants, as well as all water sports facilities.

Dawar al Omda
Kafr al-Gouna
Tel: 065-354 5600
Fax: 065-354 5601
Email: res@dawarelomda-elgouna.com
Built in the traditional style of a "House of the Mayor"

(the English translation for *Dawar al Omdar*), the rooms are in domed bungalows around a pool and lagoon, elegantly decorated with new and period furniture, antiques, tiles and local crafts.

Sultan Bey
Tel: 065-354 5600
Fax: 065-354 5601
Email: resa.sultanbey@optima-hotels.com
This is a labyrinth of alleyways, courtyards and domes surrounded by lagoons. Stylishly deco-rated rooms with balconies overlook the lagoon or the

PRICE CATEGORIES

Price ranges for double rooms with bath are:

★	$15–30
★★	$30–50
★★★	$50–75
★★★★	$75–200
★★★★★	$200–400

TRANSPORT

ACCOMMODATION

ACTIVITIES

A – Z

LANGUAGE

ABOVE: poolside lounging.

pretty central courtyard. Three restaurants, a couple of bars and a children's club.

★★★
Ali Pasha Hotel
Abu Tig Marina
Tel/Fax: 065-358 0088
Email: marinapasha@orascom.net
This 34-room boutique hotel, built in contemporary Oriental style around a pool and garden, is in one of El Gouna's liveliest areas, full of shops, bars and restaurants.
Captain's Inn
Abu Tig Marina
Tel/Fax: 065-358 0170
Email: captainsinn@elgouna.com
A stylish boutique guesthouse with 41 rooms overlooking the marina. Centrally located near the shopping outlets, restaurants and nightlife at Abu Tig Marina. Residents can use the pools at the nearby Ocean View.

HURGHADAH

★★★★★
Sahl Hasheesh Oberoi
On the Sahl Hasheesh coast, 25 minutes' drive from Hurghadah centre, 20 minutes from the airport
Tel: 065-344 0777
Fax: 065-344 0788
www.oberoihotel.com

This is the most exclusive all-suite luxury hotel on this coast, set in 20 hectares (48 acres) of palm-filled grounds, with 850 metres/yds of private sandy beach. The environmentally friendly resort is sumptuous, with domed pavilions and traditionally inspired, contemporary Arabic architecture.

★★★★
Hilton Hurghadah Resort
Shari' Safaga, 17 km (10 miles) south of Hurghadah
Tel: 065-344 2116
www.hilton.com
Rooms overlook the bay; all have internet access. There are extensive leisure and water sports facilities, including a special programme for children, and a choice of 11 bars and restaurants.

★★★
Al-Arousa
ad-Dahar, Hurghadah
Tel: 065-354 8434
Fax: 354 9190
One of the best mid-range hotels in Hurghadah. Impeccable rooms with balconies and sea views. Indoor pool and free access to beach of Geisum Village across the road.
Giftun Village
11 km (7 miles) from downtown Hurghadah

Tel: 065-344 2665
Fax: 065-344 2666
www.giftunbeachresort.com
Large resort hotel (522 rooms) with a diving and windsurfing centre and bright rooms with tiled floors.
Jasmin Village
21 km (13 miles) from Downtown Hurghadah
Tel: 065-344 6443
Fax: 065-344 6441
Email: info@jasmin-diving.com
www.jasmin-diving.com
Resort-style hotel with bungalows built in a Moorish style with large rooms, ideal for families. Good water sports facilities, swimming pool, private beach and a children's playground.
Le Pacha Cataract
Shari' Sheraton, Sigala
Tel: 065-344 4150
Email: shrouk5@hotmail.com
One of the better mid-range hotels in this area, built in Moorish style around a swimming pool, and with its own private beach.

★
Four Seasons
Just off Shari' Sayyed al-Qurayem, ad-Dahar
Tel: 065-354 9882
Fax: 065-354 5456
The Four Seasons is a popular budget hotel with clean, functional rooms, all with private bathrooms. Guests can use the swimming pool

belonging to the Geisum Hotel next door.

AL-QUSAYR

★★★★
Mövenpick Sirena Beach
Al-Qadim Bay
Tel: 065-333 2100
Fax: 065-333 2128
www.moevenpick-hotels.com
A beautifully designed hotel with dome-ceilinged rooms built and decorated in traditional style, and with excellent service and facilities. Highly recommended if you want a few days of peace and quiet.

★★★
Mangrove Bay
30 km (18 miles) south of al-Qusayr
Tel: 065-325 2821/02-748 6748
Fax: 02-760 5458
Email: mangrove@egypt-online.com
Very peaceful hotel on a great beach, excellent for reef diving.

MARSA ALAM

Red Sea Diving Safari
Marsa Shagra, 20 km (12 miles) north of Marsa Alam
Tel: 02-337 1833
www.redsea-divingsafari.com
For those who would like to get away from the sprawl in Hurghadah, this is ideal: a great eco lodge where you can still dive in the way you like. The owner, Hossam Helmi, is a committed environmentalist who deliberately keeps the place small so that he can retain the personal touch and share with his guests his knowledge and enthusiasm for diving.

PRICE CATEGORIES

Price ranges for double rooms with bath are:

★	$15–30
★★	$30–50
★★★	$50–75
★★★★	$75–200
★★★★★	$200–400

ACTIVITIES

THE ARTS, NIGHTLIFE, CINEMAS, SHOPPING AND SPORTS

THE ARTS

Art Galleries

There has always been a small number of serious art galleries in downtown Cairo, but over the past few years the art scene has really taken off. The Townhouse Gallery has expanded, and many of the trendy café-bars have a gallery attached, or at least display local art.

Akhenaten Centre of Arts
1 Shari' Maahad al-Swissry, Zamalik
Tel: 02-2735 8211
Grand villa on the Nile with several galleries. The official exhibition halls of the Ministry of Culture.

Atelier du Caire
2 Shari' Karim ad-Dawla, off Shari' Mahmoud Bassiouni, Downtown
Tel: 02-2574 6730
Exhibition space for Egyptian contemporary artists.

El-Sawy Cultural Centre
End of Shari' 26th July, at Shari' Abul-Feda, under 15 May Bridge, Zamalik
Tel: 02-2736 6178
Excellent gallery in this well-run cultural centre.

Seattle Coffee/Karim Francis
20 Shari' Muhammad Mahmoud, Downtown
A space for younger Egyptian artists.

Mashrabia
8 Shari' Champollion, just off Maydan at-Tahrir, Downtown
Tel: 02-2578 4494
Beautiful gallery space with a good crowd of artists.

Picasso
30 Shari' Hasan Assem, Zamalik
Tel: 02-2736 7544
Interesting gallery displaying work by international and local artists.

Sony Gallery
American University in Cairo, Shari' Shaykh Rihan, Downtown
Tel: 02-2797 5422
Excellent photographic exhibitions.

Townhouse Gallery
Shari' Hussein Pasha, off Shari' Mahmoud Bassiouni
Tel: 02-2575 8600
By far Cairo's most exciting and most active gallery, spread over three floors of an old town house, with two annexes. It stages the best exhibitions in town, as well as films and book readings, and has a good art bookshop in one of the annexes.

Zamalik Art Gallery
11 Shari' Brazil, Zamalik
Tel: 02-2735 1240
Very good exhibitions of contemporary Egyptian works.

Ballet and Dance

Ballet

Egyptian ballet dancers are trained at the National Ballet Institute in the City of Art complex on the Pyramids road. The Institute was founded with Russian help in 1960, staffed with Russian experts. In 1966 the first graduating class premiered with *The Fountain of Bakhchiserai* in the old Cairo Opera House. The Cairo Opera Ballet Company performs in the new Opera House on Gazirah Island in Zamalik.

Traditional Dance

Folk dance is very popular in Egypt and there are more than 150 troupes. The most prominent are the National Troupe and Reda Troupe which perform in Cairo and Alexandria.

At-Tannoura Egyptian Heritage Dance Troupe performs every Wednesday and Saturday at around 8.30pm at the **Gabal Theater** up in the Wikalat al-Ghuri on Al Azhar Road (tel: 02-2512 1735). They perform *raqs sharqi* (Oriental dance) and sufi dance, a form of ecstatic mystical dance.

Theatre in Cairo

The theatre season in Cairo is September–May. There is a summer season in Alexandria. Curtain is at 9.30pm (10.30pm during Ramadan). Theatres are dark on Tuesday or Wednesday. Except at the American University and the British Council, all performances are in Arabic.

Al Genina Theatre
In the al-Azhar Park, Shari' Salah Salem, Darassa
Tel: 010-575 5191/510 7378

American University in Cairo
AUC Campus Maydan at-Tahrir, Downtown
Tel: 02-2797 5020
Regular music recitals and English-language plays of varying quality at the three auditoriums: Ewart Hall, Wallace Theatre and Falaki Theatre.

Cairo Opera House
Gazirah Island
Tel: 02-2737 0601
Box office tel: 02-2739 8114
www.cairooperahouse.org
In 1971 the Cairo Opera House, built to celebrate the opening of the Suez Canal in 1869, burned down along with the scenery, costumes and props. In 1988 a new facility opened at the Gazirah Exhibition Grounds, and the performing arts are enjoying seasons of first-class entertainment. Built with Japanese co-operation, the facility includes three theatres, an art gallery and a library. Stalls and boxes require a

jacket and tie for men, but there is no dress code for the balcony.

Cairo Puppet Theatre
Azbakiyyah Gardens
Tel: 02-2591 0954
Dialogue is in Arabic, but the meaanings are not difficult to follow.
Thursday and Friday at 6.30pm.

El-Sawy Cultural Centre
End of Shari' 26th July, at Shari' Abul-Feda, under 15th May Bridge, Zamalik
Tel: 02-2736 6178
Plays by local or visiting groups.

Gumhuria Theatre
12 Shari' Gumhuriyyah
Tel: 02-2390 7707
A flourishing venue.

Hilton Ramses Theatre
Hilton Ramses Annex
Tel: 02-2574 7435
Regular performances of good Egyptian plays.

Cultural Centres

Foreign cultural centres are very active in Cairo. For non-Arabic speakers they are good places to soak up some culture and meet fellow nationals. For programmes check with the daily *Egyptian Gazette*, *Al-Ahram Weekly* or *Cairo Times*.

American Cultural Center
US Embassy, 5 Shari' Latin Amerika, Garden City
Tel: 02-2797 3529/337 8277

American Research Center in Egypt
2nd floor, 2 Maydan Símon Bolívar, Garden City
Tel: 02-2794 8239
Excellent library for researchers. Also holds lectures and films.

British Council
192 Shari' an-Nil, Agouza
Tel: 02-2303 1514/300 1666

Centre Français de Culture et de Cooperation
1 Shari' Madrasset al-Huquq al-Faransiya, Mounira
Tel: 02-2794 4059

Egyptian Center for International Cooperation
11 Shari' Shagaret ad-Dorr, Zamalik
Tel: 02-2736 5410

Goethe Institut
5 Shari' al-Bustan, Downtown
Tel: 02-2574 8261
Good films and concerts.

Netherlands Institute
1 Shari' Mahmoud Azmi, Zamalik
Tel: 02-2738 2522
Interesting lectures on Egyptian history and archaeology every Thursday evening.

ABOVE: the At-Tannoura Heritage Dance Troupe.

National Theatre (Qawmi)
Maydan Attaba
Tel: 02-2591 7783
Arabic and Western plays in translation.

Sayyid Darwish Concert Hall
Gamal al Din al Afghani, Giza
Tel: 02-2560 2473
There are two Sayyid Darwish concert halls, one in Cairo, another in the old Alexandria Opera House. This one is a showcase for performers of traditional Arabic music and composers working to develop new music with classical themes. There are classical Arabic concerts most Thursdays at 9.30pm.

NIGHTLIFE

Music

After Eight
6 Shari' Qasr al-Nil, Downtown
Tel: 02-2574 0855

Al-Gumhuriyah Theatre
12 Shari' Gumhuriyyah, Downtown
Tel: 02-2390 7707/391 9956
Regular concerts by local musicians, and performances of classical Arabic songs by the National Arabic Music Ensemble.

Al Manisterli Palace
2 Shari' Malik al-Saleh, near the Nilometer, Manyal, Roda Island
Tel: 02-2363 1537
Regular Arab music concerts.

Al Mastaba Centre For Egyptian Folk Music
4 Shari' Seweqat al-Saba'een, off Shari' Maglis as-Sha'ab, Sayyida Zeinab
Tel: 02-2392 6768/010-585 6671

Al-Sawy Cultural Centre

Shari' 26th of July, Zamalik, under the bridge to Aguza
Tel: 02-2736 6178
www.culturewheel.com
Very active cultural centre with nightly performances of experimental theatre, Arabic music or jazz, lectures and screenings of films and documentaries.

The Arab Music Institute
22 Shari' Ramesses, Downtown
Tel: 02-2574 3373
Regular concerts by the Arab Music Heritage Ensemble, with a repertoire of classical Arabic songs.

Bayt al Harrawi
Behind Al Azhar Mosque, Islamic Cairo
Tel: 02-2510 4174
On the first Thursday of every month there is a free concert of classical Arab music, as well as other performances (check local listings), in a restored 18th-century house. Story-telling and performances take place every night in Ramadan.

Cairo Jazz Club
197 Shari' 26th July, al-Agouza
Tel: 02-2345 9939;
www.cairojazzclub.com
Daily live jazz performances.

Cairo Opera House
Gazirah
Tel: 02-2737 0601 (info);
02-2739 8114/8132 (box office)
www.cairooperahouse.org
The main venue for dance, music and theatre.

Casinos

Gambling is only available for foreigners and only in five-star hotels. Most casinos are in Cairo, but there is also one at the Hilton International in Luxor. They offer roulette, black jack, chemin de fer and slot machines until the early hours.

(Note: in Cairo *casino* can also mean "teahouse on the Nile".)

CINEMAS

Some cinemas downtown are old with poor acoustics, but several new venues have opened in recent years, most featuring North American and European films. As these are usually subtitled, the audience often talks through them.

Films are listed in the *Egyptian Gazette*, *Al Ahram* and *Cairo Times*.

Bandar Mall
1 Shari' Falastine, Maadi
Tel: 02-2519 0455
This is one of the better cinemas in Cairo.

City Centre
City Centre Shopping Mall,
3 Shari' Makram Ebeid,
Madinat Nasr
Tel: 010-667 5096

Concorde al-Salam Hotel
65 Shari' Abdel-Hamid Badawi,
Heliopolis
Tel: 02-2622 6376
Mainly foreign films.

Cosmos (5 screens)
12 Shari' Emad ad-din, Downtown
Tel: 02-2574 2177

Galaxy
67 Shari' Abd al-Aziz al-Seoud,
Manyal, Roda Island
Tel: 02-2532 5742
Multiscreen complex.

Good News Grand Hyatt (3 screens)
Grand Hyatt Annexe, Nile Corniche,
Garden City
Tel: 02-2365 4448/368 1515

Odeon
4 Shari' Abdel Hamid Said,
Downtown, off Shari' Talaat Harb
Three good screens with a wide selection of movies.

Renaissance
World Trade Center Annexe, Corniche en Nil, Bulaq
Tel: 02-2578 4915

SHOPPING

Amber

Pale yellow, honey-coloured, brown, red, white and almost-black amber can all be found in shops in the Khan al-Khalili in the form of beads, necklaces, pipe parts and cane handles. The most famous shop is **Mohammed R. al-Kady**, in Khan al-Khalili bazaar.

Sound and Light Shows

For information on all shows, tel: 02-2385 2880/7861, or see online: www.soundandlight.com.eg

The Pyramids
Every evening three performances of a one-hour sound-and-light show are held on the Giza Plateau, in front of the Sphinx. English-language shows are held every night apart from Sunday (consult the tourist office or your hotel for a timetable). Photography is permitted but no video cameras are allowed.

Luxor
The Karnak sound and light show is recommended. It is held three or four times a night, with a daily

Antiquities and Antiques

Pharaonic and Islamic antiquities can only be exported though a few shops. Each sale should be accompanied by a letter of authenticity and permission to export the item.

Street vendors selling antiquities are selling fakes: these are worth purchasing for their own merit, but not as authentic articles. In fact, the best buys in Cairo are European antiques.

There are many little antiques shops in Cairo around Shari' Huda Shaarawi and on Shari' 26th July in Zamalik, and in Maadi. In Alexandria, the Attarin district around the street of the same name is popular with antique-hunters.

Appliqué

The **Tentmakers' Bazaar** (Suq al-Khiyamiyyah), the only covered bazaar left in Cairo, is the place to buy appliqué tenting. This craft, probably traceable to ancient Egypt, when appliqué banners billowed from the tops of temple gates, comes in pharaonic and Islamic designs in the form of pillowcases, tablecloths and wall hangings.

Senouhi on the 5th floor, 54 Shari' Abd al-Khaleb Sarwat, Downtown (tel: 391 0955) has a good selection of appliqué work and hand-woven carpets from the Wissa Wasef school in Haraniyya.

Baskets

Every region has its own style of basketry. In Aswan, flat Nubian baskets are still available. The oases crafts shops have an abundance of baskets.

English-language performance. It lasts around 90 minutes and some walking through the temple is involved. To get to Karnak in the evening, hire a taxi: the driver will wait while you watch the show.

The Temple of Isis, Philae
This rescued temple, rebuilt on Aqilqiyyah Island near Aswan, has an excellent sound-and-light show relating the temple's history. English-language shows are held every evening except Sunday and Thursday.

Abu Simbel
The latest technology is used to spectacular effect in the show at the two temples.

Bookshops

For rare books try **L'Orientale**, Shop 757, Nile Hilton Shopping Mall. Among other good bookshops are:
American University in Cairo Bookshop, 113 Shari' Qasr al-Ayni, Hill House, tel: 02-2797 5377. Also at 16 Shari' Muhammad Ibn Thaleb, Zamalik, tel: 02-2739 7045. The best collection of English-language books on Egypt.
The Anglo-Egyptian Bookshop, 165 Shari' Muhammad Farid, tel: 02-2391 4337. Good selection of English and Arabic books on Egypt and the Middle East in general.
Diwan, 159 Shari' 26th July, Zamalik, tel: 02-2736 2578; www.diwanegypt.com. Sumptuous bookstore and multimedia centre, with books, tapes and videos in English, Arabic and German. Good selection on Egypt and of Egyptian fiction translated into English. Also has a great café.
Lehnert and Landrock Bookshop, 44 Shari' Sharif, tel: 02-2392 7606. German and English books, maps and old postcards.
Zamalik Bookshop, 19 Shari' Shagaret al-Dorr, Zamalik, tel: 02-2736 9197. Very good selection of English books on Egypt and the wider region.

Brass and Copper

The **Suq an-Nahhasin** on Shari' Mu'izz li-Din Allah near Khan al-Khalili bazaar is the best place to buy brass and copper, both antique and modern.

Clothing

The world's finest cotton is Egypt's major export product, but it can be

ABOVE: Suq an-Nahhasin, Cairo.

difficult to find good-quality cotton inside the country. Imported designer wear and casual wear are available in the cities. **On Safari** (branches in major resorts) sells good, locally produced cotton holiday wear. The malls at the **Nile Plaza Four Seasons**, on the Corniche in Garden City, and the **First Mall** on Shari' al-Nil in Giza both have a large selection of boutiques selling local and imported clothing. The largest shopping mall in Egypt is the recently opened **City Stars Mall** in Medinet Nasr.

For lounging around there is nothing like an Egyptian *gallabiyya*. A good place to buy a basic one as well as cheap cotton fabrics is **Ouf** in the alley beside the Madrasah of Sultan Barsbay off Shari' al-Muizz Li-Din Allah, Islamic Cairo.

Bedu dresses are handmade. Those from northern Sinai are cross-stitched in reds, oranges and yellows, or blues and pinks. They can be bargained for in villages on the way to Al Arish, or in Khan al-Khalili bazaar, or at Kirdassah, or bought in the more up-market shops such as **Nomad** in the Cairo Mariott Hotel (tel: 02-2736 2132) or their shop on 14 Shari' Saray al-Gazirah (tel: 02-2736 1917), or at the Nile Hilton (tel: 02-2578 0666).

Craft Shops

Al-Ain Gallery, 73 Shari' al-Hussayn, Doqqi, tel: 02-2349 3940. Randa Fahmy produces and sells intricate Oriental-style metalwork lamps, while her sister Azza creates fabulous silver jewellery *(see box, right)*. **Al Khatoun**, 3 Shari' Muhammad Abdu, behind al-Azhar Mosque, next

to Bayt al-Harrawi, tel: 02-2514 7164. A great shop with modern weavings, paintings, lights and furniture inspired by traditional motifs. **Egypt Crafts Center**, 29 Shari' Yehia Ibrahim, Apt 8, Zamalik, tel: 02-2736 5123; www.egyptcrafts.com. Fair-trade crafts shop with products from income-generating projects throughout Egypt, including embroidery, recycled handmade Bedouin rugs and woven fabrics. **Khan Misr Tulun**, 17 Maydan Ahmed Ibn Tulun, opposite the Ibn Tulun Mosque, tel: 02-2365 2227 (closed Sat and Sun). The owners support various craft cooperatives throughout the country and stock

Jewellery

From modern pharaonic cartouches to antique Turkish, Art Deco and Art Nouveau, jewellery is one of the best buys in Egypt. Gold is sold up to 21 carat for traditional jewellery, and 18 carat for modern chains and charms. One of the best places to shop is the **Suq al Sagha** in Cairo's Khan al-Khalili. Here you will find traditional designs in the form of necklaces, earrings and bracelets. Special shops sell 21-carat hand-tooled or stamped Nubian designs.

Shops that sell gold plate are identified by a gilded camel in the window. Modern designs are found in jewellery stores throughout the city, many on Shari' Abdel Khalek Sarwat, west of Opera Square. In Luxor the jewellery bazaar is just behind Luxor Temple to the north of the Luxor Hotel. In Aswan look for jewellery shops in the *suq*.

Bedouin embroidery from Sinai, recycled glass products, weavings, pottery and other original items. **Nourzen**, 17 Shari' Muhammad Mazhar, Zamalik, tel: 02-2735 2449. Beautifully made and very sculptural Egyptian candles. **Suq al-Fustat**, located between the mosque of Amr Ibn al-As and Coptic Cairo. Modern *suq* with some of Cairo's best craft workshops. **Umm el-Dounia**, on the first floor at 3 Shari' Talaat Harb, Downtown, tel: 02-2393 8273 (daily 10am–7pm), has a great selection of the best of Egyptian crafts at reasonable prices and includes a great bookshop.

Muski Glass

Muski glass is recycled hand-blown glass. It comes in six main colours: navy blue, brown, turquoise, green, aqua and purple and has distinctive air bubbles. A good selection of glasses, lamps and amulets is available from **New Agaat Bazaar**, 6 Haret al-Salhia in the Khan al-Khalili market.

Papyrus

The cultivation of papyrus has been revived at **Dr Ragab's Papyrus Institute** at Shari' an-Nil, between Cairo Sheraton and University Bridge, Doqqi, tel: 02-2748 8177. The Arabic word for papyrus is "bardi" or "warak bardi". Shops all over Egypt now sell hand-painted papyrus sheets.

Hanafi Bazaar on Corniche al-Nil (tel: 097-231 4083) in Aswan has a great selection of Nubian and African beads and jewellery.

If you are interested in silver Bedu ware, ask, as these items are often hidden away under the counter. **Hareem Kahn** at 6 Shari' al-Saramatia in Khan al-Khalili, tel: 02-2593 1581, sells only Bedouin jewellery. **Nomad** *(see under Clothing)* also has a good selection.

Modern jewellery inspired by traditional designs by Azza Fahmy is on sale at the **Al-Ain Gallery**, 73 Shari' Al-Husayn, Doqqi, tel: 02-2338 1737, or at the First Mall in Giza. **Sheba Gallery**, 6 Shari' Sri Lanka, Zamalik, near the Marriott Hotel, tel: 02-2735 9192; www.shebagallery.com, has amazing original designs in silver and gold.

Perfume

Perfume shops, with their beautifully decorated bottles, are easy to spot. Egypt grows and exports jasmine, geranium, rose, violet, camomile and orange for perfumiers in France, from whom essence is then re-imported.

Nefertari products, available from the better craft shops, are locally made, 100 percent natural beauty products, made with extra virgin olive oil, aloe vera in place of water, and milk, honey and beeswax. They are hand-milled and perfumed with essential oils.

Weaving and Textiles

Kirdassah, on the western fringes of greater Cairo, has a large market where Bedouin weaving is available. Bedu rugs, made on small looms in the desert, vary according to the tribe.

The village of Harraniyyah near the Giza Pyramids is famous for its tapestries, woven by villagers using naturally dyed wools. There are several carpet weavers, but the **Wissa Wassef Art Centre**, situated just off Saqqarah Road, in Harraniyyah, tel: 02-2385 0403; www.wissa-wassef-arts.com, specialises in distinctive woollen rugs and wall hangings depicting rural and folkloric scenes. Their fine and colourful rugs

are now widely sold but here they have the best and largest selection.

Nagada, at 13 Shari' Refa'a in Dokki, tel: 02-2748 6663/012-391 5011; www.nagada.net, sells fabulous weavings from Naqada, as well as one-off fashion items inspired by Egyptian traditions, plus good jewellery and hand-made pottery.

Woodwork

Mashrabiyyah, traditional latticed screens of turned wood joined together using polygonal blocks, covered the windows of old Cairene houses and shielded the sanctuaries of mosques.

Alif, 14 Shari' Muhammad Anis, Zamalik, tel: 02-2737 0848, sells an eclectic, and often inspired mixture of old and new furniture and amazing textiles.

Loft, 12 Shari' Sayyed al Bakri, Zamalik, tel: 02-2736 6931; www.loftegypt.com, is a great store full of Oriental-style furniture, textiles and gifts.

Makan, 4 Shari' Ismail Muhammad, Zamalik, tel: 02-2738 2632; www.makanegypt.com, is another wonderful and stylish shop that sells a mix of furniture and lighting made by contemporay designers, including many recycled items. Particularly unusual are lights made out of musical instruments.

Football

Football is the national pastime of Egypt. Three leagues compete at 3pm each Friday and Sunday afternoon from September to May, at various stadiums throughout Egypt. Among the top teams are Ahly, Zamalik and the Arab Contractors.

If you fancy seeing a match, just ask at your hotel: tickets can usually be procured.

SPORT

Participant

Fishing

The Nile, Lake Nasser and the lakes along the northern coast support commercial and sport fishing. Fishing is forbidden off Sinai, but is a thriving sport elsewhere in the Red Sea and in the Mediterranean.

For information about international fishing tournaments contact the **Egyptian Federation for Fishing**, tel: 02-2395 3953.

For fishing trips on Lake Nasser, contact **The African Angler** in Aswan, tel: 097-230 9748, www.african-angler.co.uk, or **Lake Nasser Adventure**, tel: 012-104 0255, www.lakenasseradventure.com.

BELOW: there are plenty of opportunities to play golf in Egypt.

ABOVE: there are plenty of water sports on and under the Red Sea.

Golf (Cairo Area)

Dreamland Golf and Tennis Resort
6th of October City Road, Dreamland
City, south of Cairo
Tel: 011-400 577; www.dreamgolf.com
Exceptional 18-hole course.
Gazirah Club
Zamalik
Tel: 02-2736 0434/735 6000
A nine-hole course.
JW Marriott Golf Club at Mirage City
Tel: 02-2408 5041
**Katameya Heights Golf and Tennis
Resort**
New Cairo City 5th District,
Ring Road, West Heliopolis, Cairo
Tel: 02-2758 0512/17
www.katameya.com/indexnet.htm
Eighteen-hole and nine-hole golf
courses.
Mena House Oberoi Hotel
Tel: 02-2383 3222/383 3444
www.oberoihotels.com/mena.htm
Nine-hole course with the Pyramids
as a backdrop.
Pyramids Golf and Country Club
Tel: 049-600 953
The largest resort in Cairo, with 99
holes in total.

On and under Water

Diving and snorkelling in the Red Sea
are among the best sports offered in
Egypt. On good days, the sea is calm,
the visibility near perfect and the currents mild. However, swells may develop and it is easy to lose sight of
the boat after swimming below the
surface. All diving should be done in
the company of experts after suitable
instruction, which is available at many
hotels. More information can be
obtained from the **British Sub Aqua
Club**, tel: 02-2291 7892 or the Cairo
Divers Group, tel: 02-2570 3242.
Most of the resorts on the Red Sea
provide windsurfing lessons.

Pharaoh's Rally

The Pharaoh's Rally has earned a
niche in the rally world and is second
in endurance and difficulty only to the
Paris–Dakkar Rally. It takes place in
October and is an 11-day, 4,500-km
(2,790-mile) endurance race through
the deserts of Egypt, for dirt bikes,
cars and trucks. Information from
Emeco Travel, tel: 02-2574 9360;
www.emeco.com.

Horse Riding (Cairo Area)

The Bedu at the Giza Pyramids have
been catering for riders for generations and there are several stables in
the area; day trips to Saqqarah can
be arranged.
    Good stables include **MG**, tel: 02-
2385 3823 and **AA**, tel: 02-2385
0531. The **Saqqarah Country Club** in
Giza offers more up-market horse
riding in the desert, tel: 02-2384
6115; or try the excellent
International Equestrian Club (at the
end of al-Mounib ring road), tel:
0105-001 103/02-2385 5016/02-
2742 7654. On the West Bank in
Luxor you can go for a ride through
the fields with horses from the
Pharaoh's Stables, located near the
Mobil station, tel: 02-2231 0015.

Rowing

There are several rowing clubs in
Cairo, and almost all are located on
the west bank of the Nile from Giza
to Imbaba. It is possible to join a
crew at the al-Nil Sporting Club,
near Kubri Abbas on the Corniche at
Giza, tel: 02-2393 4350. For those
who just want to watch, Friday is the
big day.

Running

The Cairo Hash House Harriers meet
every weekend to run in the

surroundings of Maadi. For
information, check www.cairohash.com.

Swimming

All four- and five-star hotels have a
pool, but people staying in budget
accommodation may fancy a swim
too. The following hotels in the Cairo
area are open for non-residents upon
payment of a fee.
Marriott Hotel, Zamalik, tel: 02-2735
8888.
Mena House Oberoi, at the Pyramids,
tel: 02-2383 3222.
Nile Hilton, Maydan Tahrir,
Downtown, tel: 02-2578 0444
Saqqarah Palm Club, Saqqarah,
tel: 02-2381 1282.
Semiramis InterContinental, tel: 02-
2795 7171.
Spa and Wellness Centre, at the
Four Seasons Hotel First Mall in Giza,
tel: 02-2567 2040.

Yachting

Docking facilities exist at major ports
in Egypt and along the Nile at major
cities. Yachts may enter the country
through the various ports if they have
the proper documents.
    Egyptian tourist information cen-
tres throughout the world can provide
a booklet for yachting enthusiasts
entitled *Egypt for Yachtsmen*, which
gives entry information and maps.
See *Useful Addresses, page 343* for
listings.

Spectator

Cycling

The Cairo Cyclists (tel: 02-2352
6310) have regular Friday- and
Saturday-morning cycle rides in and
around Cairo, starting from outside
the Cairo American College, Midan
Digla in Maadi, at 8am.

Horse Racing

Horse racing takes place from
October/November to May at the
Heliopolis Hippodrome (tel: 02-2241
7086/7134), the **Gazirah Sporting
Club** (tel: 02-2736 0434/735 6000)
and the **Smouha Race Course** in
Alexandria on Saturday and Sunday
from 1.30pm. *The Egyptian Gazette*
lists details of events.
    Arab horses are known for their
beauty, stamina and intelligence.
There are many stud farms in
Egypt but the biggest, with 300
horses, is the government-owned
Egyptian Agricultural Organisation
(EAO),az-Zahraa Station, Shari'
Ahmad Esmat, tel: 02-2243 1733.
This farm has only pure-bred
bloodlines and was the home of
the most famous Arabian stallion
of the 20th century, Nazeer.

A – Z

A HANDY SUMMARY OF PRACTICAL INFORMATION, ARRANGED ALPHABETICALLY

ACCOMMODATION

ACTIVITIES

A dmission Charges

Two levels of charges operate at most of the major sights: one for Egyptians and a much higher one for non-Egyptians, which is fair enough considering the disparity in incomes in most cases and the high cost of maintaining the sights.

B usiness Hours

Banks: 8.30am–1.30pm, closed Friday, Saturday and most holidays.
Businesses: business hours are flexible. Few businesses function before 8am; many are open until 5pm, but some close in the afternoon and then re-open at 5pm.
Clinics: customarily open from 5pm to 8pm.
Government offices: 8am–2pm , closed Friday, Saturday and most holidays.
Shops: shop opening hours vary according to demand. In central Cairo, many shops, including those owned by Muslims and Jews, are closed on Sunday.
Khan al-Khalili bazaar: open daily 10am–6pm or 7pm (later in summer and during Ramadan); most shops in the bazaar close on Sunday.

C alendars

The business and secular community in Egypt operates under the Western (Gregorian) calendar. But other calendars also have official status.

The Islamic calendar is used to fix religious observances, and is based on a lunar cycle of 12 months of 29 or 30 days. The Muslim year is thus 11 days shorter than the year in the Gregorian calendar and months move forward accordingly. In the Gregorian calendar, for example, April is in the spring, but in the Muslim calendar all months move through all seasons in a 33-year cycle.

The Coptic calendar follows the Julian calendar, which was replaced in the West by the Gregorian calendar between 1582 and 1752, but the months carry their current Egyptian names.

The Coptic year consists of 12 months of 30 days and one month of 5 days. Every four years a sixth day is added to the shorter month. An adaptation of the Coptic calendar is often used for planting and harvesting crops. It is used by the authorities of the Coptic Orthodox Church.

Muslim Calendar	Coptic Calendar
Muharram	Toot (begins 11 or Sept)
Safar	Baaba
Rabi' il-awal	Hatour
Rabi' it-tani	Kiyaak
Gamada-l-uula	Tuuba (mid-Jan)
Gamada-l-ukhra	Amshir
Ragab	Baramhat
Sha'aban	Barmuda
Ramadan	Bashans
Shawal	Bauna
Dhu'l	Abiib
Dhu'l	Misra
	Nasi (5–6 days)

Climate

Summers are hot and dry in Upper Egypt, humid in the Delta and along the Mediterranean coast. In recent years humidity has spread to Cairo and the city swelters in August. Winters are mild with some rain, but usually there are bright, sunny days and cold nights. Spring and autumn are short; during the 50 days *(khamseen)* between the end of March and mid-May, dust storms may occur. The creation of Lake Nasser has affected the climate of the whole Nile Valley.

A – Z

LANGUAGE

What to Wear

Be modest, be sensible and travel light. Egypt is a conservative country, and it is an affront to your hosts to appear in a mosque or even on the street in clothing that is considered immodest. Women should keep their shoulders and upper arms covered, and skirts should not be too short. Neither men nor women should wear shorts except at resorts or on the tennis court. No topless or nude bathing is permitted.

On the practical side, leave your synthetics at home as they will prove too hot in the summer and not warm enough in winter. Cotton is suitable for all seasons, but bring a woollen jumper or cardigan or light jacket for winter and to cover up on cool summer nights.

Loose and flowing garments are appropriately modest and extremely practical in a hot climate. Hats are vital to protect against heat stroke, and so are sunglasses to defend the eyes against the glare.

Bring stout, comfortable shoes: you will be doing a lot of walking and neither the streets nor the temple floors are friendly to feet.

CLIMATE CHART

Aswan

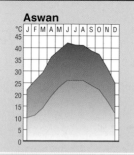

Cairo

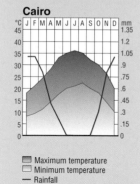

◼ Maximum temperature
◻ Minimum temperature
— Rainfall

Temperatures

Average Year-round Temperatures
(max/min, in Celsius)

	winter	summer
Alexandria	21/11	30/21
Cairo	21/11	36/20
Luxor	26/6	42/22
Aswan	26/9	42/25

Average Year-round Temperatures
(max/min, in Farenheit)

	winter	summer
Alexandria	69/51	86/70
Cairo	70/52	97/68
Luxor	79/43	108/72
Aswan	79/48	108/77

Crime and Safety

Like several other countries, in recent years Egypt has been troubled by radical Islamic terrorists. In 1997 two attacks specifically targeting tourists – one outside the Egyptian Museum in Cairo and another at Hatshepsut's Temple, Luxor – significantly raised the overall death toll. More recently, in October 2004, 34 people died when bombs exploded in the Taba; in the summer of 2005 a bomb killed more than 80 people in Sharm al-Shaykh; and in April 2006 three bombs killed 23 people in the Red Sea resort of Dahab. A heavy military response from the government, designed to protect tourists and deter further terrorist activities, seems to have calmed the situation at the time of writing. Visitors should nevertheless be warned that there are restrictions on travel into or through Middle Egypt – the zone along the Nile between Al-Minya and Luxor as well as in Upper Egypt. Middle Egypt is beautiful and contains some very interesting and least-spoiled ancient sites, but it is also a poorer rural area that is historically given to violence. Travel along the Nile, south of Cairo, is possible only in armed convoy (contact the tourist office for information on times of departure).

Elsewhere, common caution is advised. Social restrictions on women in Egypt can make foreign women seem particularly enticing to young Egyptian men. Also, as Egypt's economic reforms have created great hardship, the number of petty thefts has increased, although you are still more likely to have a lost wallet returned intact in Egypt than in the majority of Western countries. If you do experience problems, you should report to the nearest tourist police post or police station.

Culture and Customs

Whether Muslim or Copt, the Egyptians as a whole tend to be religious, and piety is important in their daily lives. So is commitment to the extended family. Each family member is responsible for the integrity of the family and for the behaviour of other members. Certainly, one result of these concerns is that the city of Cairo is safer than any Western metropolis.

Yet when Westerners visit Egypt they are often apprehensive. Their views of Egyptians and Arabs, fomented by alarmist and exaggerated media stories, often bear no relation to reality at all. Travellers normally receive friendly, hospitable treatment and take home with them good feelings about the warmth and goodwill of the Egyptian people.

The average Egyptian is also extremely honest. If you leave a bag, wallet or other personal belongings in a restaurant or other public building the chances are it will be kept safe and sound until you can retrieve it.

Customs Regulations

Entry

A visitor is permitted to enter Egypt with 200 cigarettes or 25 cigars, one litre of alcohol, one litre of perfume and personal effects. Animals must have a veterinary certificate confirming their good health and also a valid rabies certificate, as rabies is a problem in the country.

Duty-free purchases of liquor (three bottles per person) and other items may be made within 24 hours of arrival at ports of entry or at the special tax-free shops in Cairo, Luxor, Hurghadah or Alexandria.

People travelling with expensive electronic equipment may be required to list these items in their passports so that authorities can check that they are exported upon departure and have not been sold to locals.

Departure

Although travellers are free to buy and export reasonable quantities of Egyptian goods for personal use, the export of large quantities of items will require an export licence. Egyptian-made items that are more than 20 years old are not permitted to leave the country, nor are foreign-made items deemed to have "historic value".

The export of carpets, Egyptian-made or not, is restricted. Travellers may be requested to show bank receipts as proof of payment for

other valuable items. Excess
Egyptian pounds may be changed
back at the airport on presentation of
valid bank receipts.

Disabled Travellers

Few hotels or cruise boats and no
public buildings, restaurants,
theatres or historical sites provide
facilities for people with disabilities.
Major airlines provide services for
those with disabilities upon entering
and leaving the country.

Egypt for All, 334 Shari' Sudan,
Muhandesseen, tel: 012-311 3975;
email: sales@egyptforall.com; www.egypt
forall.com, is a Cairo-based company
offering specialised programmes
for people with disabilities.
Programmes include river cruises,
as well as hot-air ballooning,
desert safaris and diving and
snorkelling holidays on the Red Sea.
Also bear in mind that Egyptians are
very friendly and will readily lend a
hand.

E mbassies in Cairo

Australia
World Trade Centre, 1638, 11th floor,
1191 Corniche al-Nil, Bulaq
Tel: 02-2575 0444
www.dfat.gov.au/missions
Canada
26 Shari' Kamel ash-Shenawy,
Garden City
Tel: 02-2794 3110
Ireland
7th floor, 3 Shari' Abu a-Feda,
Zamalik
Tel: 02-2735 8547
www.dfa.ie
UK
7 Shari' Ahmed Ragheb, Garden City
Tel: 02-2794 0852
www.britishembassy.gov.uk
US
8 Kamal El Din Salah St, Garden City
Tel: 02-2797 3300
cairo.usembassy.gov

Entry Regulations
Visas and Passports

All travellers entering Egypt must
have a passport valid for at least six
months and a valid visa. For most
visitors, including nationals of the
European Union and the United
States, it is easiest and cheapest to

Emergency Numbers

Fire: **180**
Ambulance: **123**
Police: **122**
Tourist Police: **02-2390 6028**

Type of Visa

Single entry tourist visa: usually
valid for a period not exceeding
three months; allows you to stay
maximum of one month in Egypt.
Multiple entry tourist visa: valid for
up to three months; should be
requested if you plan to exit and re-
enter Egypt during your stay,
maximum three visits.
Entry visa: required for any
foreigner arriving in Egypt for
purposes other than tourism,
e.g. work, study, etc. A valid entry
visa is needed to complete the
residence procedure in Egypt.

For those wishing to stay longer
than one month, there is a short
period of grace up to 14 days after
your visa has expired. If you fail to
apply for an extension after that you
will need a letter from your embassy
and pay a fine of about £100. It is
now easy to obtain a six-month or
one-year extension of the visa for
tourism purposes from passport

get a tourist visa at the point of
arrival. They can be obtained from
Cairo International Airport, Luxor
Airport, Aswan Airport, Hurghadah
Airport, Sharm al-Shaykh and
Alexandria Port. It is more time-
consuming and costly to acquire it in
advance at an Egyptian consulate
abroad *(see page 332, Useful
Addresses)*.

Lost or stolen passports must be
reported to the police immediately.
It is a good idea to keep a
photocopy of your passport
somewhere safe. New passports
can be issued in a matter of hours
at the consular office of your
embassy in Egypt but you will require
a copy of the police report verifying
the loss.

Extension of Stay

Visas can be renewed at the
Mugama'a (Cairo's massive central
administrative building on Maydan at-
Tahrir), generally after a long wait.
Visas are considered valid for 15
days after their expiry date, but if
they are not renewed by then you will
need a letter of apology from your
embassy before an extension will be
granted.

H ealth and Medical Care

Evidence of yellow fever and cholera
immunisation may be required from
travellers who have been in an
infected area up to six days prior to
their arrival in Egypt.

offices in Egypt. Take a photograph
and copy of the photograph and
visa page in your passport, and a
few dollars.

If you have a single entry visa
and want to leave and re-enter the
country, you can apply for a multiple
entry visa at the passport offices.
Cairo: Mogamma Maydan Tahrir,
Downtown
Luxor: Shari Khaled Ibn al-Walid
(tel: 095-3237 0259)
Aswan: Corniche al-Nil (tel: 097-
231 2238)
Alexandria: 25 Shari' Talaat Harb
(tel: 03-482 7873)
Hurghada: Shari an-Nasr, Ad-Dahar
Sinai permits: If you enter from
Taba (on the Israeli border),
Nuwayba (port) or Sharm al-Shaykh
(port or airport) and are just
travelling in Sinai, including to
St Catherine's Monastery, you
will be issued with a free entry
stamp allowing a 14-day stay.

Hospitals

There are good hospitals in Cairo and
Alexandria. However, they operate on
a cash upfront basis and will not
provide treatment on the production
of foreign medical insurance plans.
Hospitals in Cairo include:
Anglo-American Hospital Zohoreya
next to the Cairo Tower, Zamalik
Tel: 02-2735 6162/Doqqi5
As Salam International Hospital
Corniche al-Nil, Maadi
Tel: 02-2524 0250/0077
Al Salam Hospital
3 Shari' Syria, Muhandesseen
Tel: 02-2302 9091/9095

Pharmacies

Pharmacies are usually open
10am–10pm and are staffed by
competent professionals.
Both locally made and imported
medication is subsidised by the
government and is inexpensive.
Some medication requiring
prescriptions abroad is sold over the
counter in Egypt. Pharmacies that
open 24 hours in Cairo include:
Al-Ezaby
Arcadia Mall, Corniche an-Nil, Bulaq;
tel: 02-2575 5235
1 Shari' Ahmed Taysir, Kulliyet
al-Banat, Heliopolis, tel: 02-2418
0838.
Ali & Ali
Shari' Qasr al-Ayni, Downtown;
tel: 02-2365 3880.
Al-Isaaf
Corner Shari' Ramesses and Shari'
26 Yulyu, Downtown; tel: 02-2574
3369.

ABOVE: no shortage of reading matter in Alexandria.

Delmar
Corner of Shari' 26 July and Shari'
Muhammad Farid, Downtown;
tel: 02-2575 1052.

I nternet

Internet facilities are widely available
through both commercial offices and
educational institutions. There is an
increasing number of internet cafés
in all the main cities.

In Cairo, the followi ng ones are
central:
Cyber Café, Nile Hilton Food Court,
Corniche al-Nil, Downtown
Tel: 02-2578 0444
4U Internet Café, 8 Maydan Tala'at
Harb, 1st floor, Downtown
Tel: 02-2575 9304
Internet @Café de Paris,
al-Bustan Centre, basement,
Shari' al-Bustan, Downtown
Tel: 02-2392 0892
Internet Egypt,
2 Maydan Simón Bolívar, Garden City
Tel: 02-2796 2882
Onyx Internet Café,
26 Shari' Mahmoud Bassiouni,
Downtown
Tel: 02-2578 9180

M edia
Radio

European Radio Cairo, 557 AM and
95 FM, 7am–midnight, plays
European classical music, pop and
jazz. News in English is at 7.30am,
2.30pm, and 8pm; in French at 8am,
2pm and 9pm; in Greek at 3pm; in
Armenian at 4pm; in German at 6pm.
The **BBC** World Service broadcasts
to Egypt on various radio frequencies
including 639 and 1323 AM (see
www.bbc.co.uk/worldservice for details).
The higher metre band provides
better reception between sunrise and

sunset. There are also shortwave
alternatives. News is on the hour.
VOA (Voice of America) broadcasts
on a variety of wavelengths including
on 1290kHz.

Television

The arrival of satellite and cable
television has revolutionised viewing
in Egypt. Most hotels, even quite
modest ones, offer satellite TV, and
satellite dishes now top many of
Cairo's apartment blocks as well as
rural houses. Local television is
rarely exciting.

Check the listings in the *Egyptian
Gazette* for daily schedules.
Schedules vary during Ramadan and
in the summer.
Channel 1: on the air daily
8am–2am, mainly in Arabic.
Channel 2: broadcasts 11am–2am
daily, with many foreign-language
programmes.
Channel 3: a Cairo-only station in
Arabic daily 1pm–midnight.
CNN: arrived in Egypt in 1991. It
broadcasts to subscribers 24 hours
a day, with an uncensored
programme, as does BBC World and
al-Jazeera.
Nile TV: tourism promotion station.

Newspapers

In Cairo, all the major English,
French, German and Italian daily
newspapers are available at larger
hotels and at newsstands in Zamalik
and Maadi.

The two most important local daily
newspapers are *Al-Ahram* and
Al-Akhbar. *Al-Ahram*, "The Pyramids",
was established in 1875, making it
the oldest newspaper in Egypt. Published daily, it also has a UK edition,
an excellent weekly English-language
edition, *Al-Ahram Weekly* and a
weekly French-language edition, *Al-*

Ahram Hébdo. *The Daily Star*
(www.dailystaregypt.com) is a recent
arrival that has daily news and good
listings. Other English-language
weeklies include the *Middle East
Times* (online at www.metimes.com), the
Cairo Magazine and the *Arab Times*.
The Egyptian Gazette, established in
1880, is the oldest foreign-language
daily newspaper still in operation in
Egypt.

English-language magazines
include the *Arab Press Review*, a
bi-weekly political magazine,
Business Monthly, featuring business
news, and *Cairo's*, a monthly "what's
on" publication that can be very
useful for visitors. *Egypt Today* and
Egypt's Insight are monthly general-
interest magazines designed to
appeal to tourists and foreign
residents.

Money
Airport Exchange

There are banks at the airports for
currency exchange. The currency is
the Egyptian pound (EGP OR LE);
currently there are just under 11 EGP
to £1 sterling and just over 5 EGP TO
US$1. The Egyptian pound consists
of the following:
•pound notes in denominations of
200, 100, 50, 20, 10, 5, 1.
•piaster notes in denominations of
50, 25, 10.
•coins in denominations of 25 and
10.

Credit cards are accepted in most
major hotels, but not always in
shops. It is advisable to bring some
traveller's cheques or use the ATM
machines, which are widespread in
the cities.

P hotography

Egypt is a photographer's paradise.
The best film speeds for daylight

shots outdoors are low (100 and under), but fast film (400, 1,000) is necessary for interior photography, high-powered lenses and night shots. Photography is forbidden in security zones, and a variety of rules pertain to pharaonic monuments. In other areas photography is permitted for a fee. Charges for cameras run as high as EGP50, for video cameras up to EGP200. There are no restrictions on photography anywhere in Cairo. Flash photography is not allowed inside tombs and in museums.

Scholars and professional photographers working on projects may apply to the Supreme Council for Antiquities for a special permit. Passes are not given out freely.

Photographing people requires a bit of consideration. Egyptians are constantly having cameras pushed in their faces, so be courteous, ask first and be prepared to pay if necessary.

Postal and Courier Services

The Central Post Office at Maydan al-Atabah in Cairo is open Saturday– Thursday 7am–7pm, Friday and public holidays 7am–noon. All other post offices are open 8.30am–3pm daily, except Friday. Postboxes, found on street corners and in front of post offices, are red for regular Egyptian mail, blue for overseas airmail letters and green for Cairo and express mail within Cairo.

Allow five days for airmail to Europe, 10 days to America. Mail sent from hotels seems to arrive quickest.

Express Mail Services (EMS)
The major post offices, marked with the EMS sign, offer an Express Mail Service (EMS), which is more expensive but much faster. Express Mail Service (EMS), Maydan al-Atabah, tel: 02-390 5874. In addition to this there are various international courier services:

DHL
Shari' Gawad Hasri, Garden City
Tel: 02-2792 1145
38 Abdel Khalek Sarwat
Tel: 02-2393 8988
El Mona Towers 16, Shari' Lubnan, Mohandesseen
Tel: 02-2302 9801
www.dhl.com

Porter Service

For a charge of around 10 EGP, baggage trolleys are available at Cairo International Airport. There are also porters available with larger trolleys to service individuals and groups.

Federal Express
General enquiries:
Tel: 02-2268 7888
15 Shari' Shehab, Muhandesseen
Tel: 02-2760 7922
17 Wadi al-Nil, Maadi
Tel: 02-2358 3284
www.fedex.com
TNT Skypak
33 Shari' Doqqi, Doqqi
Tel: 02-2760 3695
www.tnt.com

Mail can be received at American Express offices, and you don't need to be a cardholder to use the service. Letters can also be sent *poste restante* to post offices in most Egyptian cities or to 15 Shari' Qasr al-Nil, Cairo, A.R.Egypt. You will need to produce your passport to pick up your mail.

Some embassies may also offer a mail holding service for their nationals, but you should check this in advance.

R eligious Services

Islam is the official religion of Egypt, but there is a large Coptic community and other Christian sects represented in the country. There is also a small Jewish community. Islam is part of the Judaeo-Christian family of religions and was revealed to the Prophet Muhammad in what is now Saudi Arabia.

Islam

Islam has five major principles, known as "pillars", which form the foundation of the religion. The first principle is the belief that there is only one God and that the Prophet Muhammad is the messenger of God. The second is prayer, which should be performed five times every day. The third is almsgiving, and Muslims often donate a percentage of their earnings to others. The fourth pillar is fasting during daylight hours throughout the holy month of Ramadan. The fifth pillar is the pilgrimage to Mecca, *haj*, which all Muslims hope to perform at least once. The pilgrimage is performed during the month of Dhu'l-Higga, which begins 70 days after the end of the Ramadan fast.

Public Holidays

There are six official government holidays a year. Banks, government offices, many businesses and schools are closed on these days. In addition, there are Islamic and Coptic holidays spread throughout the year.
New Year's Day. Public holiday.
Liberation of Sinai Day, 25 April. Public holiday.
Labour Day, 1 May. Public holiday.
Anniversary of the 1952 Revolution, 23 July. Businesses are closed.
Armed Forces Day, 6 October. Public holiday.

Muslim Holidays
These are governed by the Muslim lunar calendar *(see Calendars, page 327)*.
Feast of Breaking the Fast, 'Id al-Fitr, celebrates the end of Ramadan, the month of day-time fasting. During Ramadan, Muslims abstain from food, drink and sex during daylight hours. Business and social life, centring on the meal eaten after sunset, called *iftar*, becomes nocturnal and intense. 'Id al-Fitr, which is signalled by the appearance of the new moon, is a happy celebration with new clothes, gifts and a feast. It usually lasts for three days.
Feast of the Sacrifice, 'Id al-Adha, begins about 70 days after the end of Ramadan and commemorates Abraham's sacrifice of a sheep in place of his son. It is traditional to kill a sheep and share the meat with the extended family, neighbours and the poor. The festivities last for four days.
Islamic New Year, Ras al-Sana al-Higriya. Public holiday.
Prophet's Birthday, Mawlid al-Nabi, is celebrated in honour of the Prophet Muhammad. A parade with drums and banners is held in the historic zone of Cairo. Public holiday.

Coptic Holidays
Coptic Christmas, 7 January. Copts observe the birth of Christ on the same date as all other Orthodox churches except the Armenian. Prior to the feast they abstain from animal flesh and products for 43 days.
Coptic Easter ends the Coptic Lenten season. It is usually celebrated one week after Western Easter, Coptic businesses are closed.
Sham an-Nissim, "Sniffing the Breeze". This is celebrated on the Monday after Coptic Easter and is a real spring festival. Dating from pharaonic times, it is marked by all Egyptians regardless of their religion. The tradition is for everyone to take a picnic out to the countryside or to an urban green space for the day. All businesses close.

Coptic Orthodox

The Copts, who account for about 10 percent of the population, are a Christian sect which separated from the Byzantine and Latin churches in AD 451 over a disagreement in religious doctrine. Copts founded the world's first monasteries, and the monastic tradition is an important part of the faith.

Religious Observances

Non-Muslims should not enter mosques while prayers are in progress, and in mosques listed as antiquities they will not be asked an entrance fee, but the custodian will expect a tip. Muslims may enter any mosque free of charge. Non-Muslims should remove their shoes before entering a mosque, and women should cover their hair.

Services

Visitors can attend any church service, and there are numerous services held all over Cairo, with times listed in the monthly *Egypt Today* magazine or in the weekend newspapers. The church of St Sergius and the Hanging Church in Coptic Cairo have the holy liturgy in Coptic and Arabic on Sunday from 6–8am. Even though you may not understand the words, the chanting is something quite special.

T elephones

Most five-star hotels offer a direct-dial service. The Central Telephone and Telegraph offices (8 Shari' Adli, 13 Maydan at-Tahrir, 26 Shari' Ramesses) are open 24 hours a day. Others are open from 7am–10pm daily. Telex and fax services are also available.

Menatel card phones are found all over the city; cards can be bought from the telephone offices.

Calls booked at telephone offices must be paid for in advance, with a three-minute minimum. Between 8pm and 8am the cost of phone calls is greatly reduced.

If your have an AT&T calling card it is possible to charge a call to the United States to a US account. You may place a call with a New York operator by dialling 356-0200 or 510-0200. You must supply both the American number and the number of your AT&T account.

It is cheap to buy a SIM-card in Egypt, which can be used if your mobile phone is unblocked. It is perhaps the cheapest way to call abroad as a traveller. There are mobile phone shops everywhere in all cities.

Travel Agents

Abercrombie and Kent
10th floor, Bustan Commercial Centre 18 Shari' Youssef al-Guindi, Downtown, tel: 02-2393 6255
www.abercrombiekent.com
American Express
Nile Hilton, Maydan at-Tahrir, tel: 02-2578 5001; 15 Shari' Qasr an-Nil, Downtown, tel: 02-2574 7991
www.americanexpress.com.eg
Egypt Panorama Tours
4 Road 79, opposite Ma'adi Metro, tel: 02-2359 0200; www.eptours.com
Hamis Travel
Annexe south of Ramesses Station, First floor, Maydan Ramesses, tel: 02-2574 9257; www.hamis.com.eg
Misr Travel
1 Talaat Harb, Downtown, tel: 02-2393 0010; www.misrtravel.org
Soliman Travel
95 Shari' Farid Semika, Maydan Higaz, Heliopolis, tel: 02-2635 0350; email: Cairo@solimantravel.com; www.solimantravel.co.uk
Thomas Cook
17 Shari' Mahmoud Bassiouni, Downtown, tel: 02-2574 3776; www.thomascook.com

U seful Addresses

Tourist Offices and Information Centres Abroad

New York
Suite 1706, 630 Fifth Ave, New York, NY 10111, tel: 212-332 2570; email: egyptours@aol.com.
Los Angeles
Suite 215, 8383 Wilshire Boulevard, Beverly Hills, CA 90211, tel: 323-653 8815; email: egypt@etala.com.
London
3rd floor, Egyptian House, 170 Picadilly, W1V 9DD, tel: 020-7493 5283; email: eqypt@freename.co.uk.

Egyptian Consulates Abroad

For a complete list of Egyptian embassies consult:
www.egypt.embassyhomepage.com

Telephone codes

Alexandria	03
Aswan	097
Asyut	088
Cairo	02
Hurghada	065
Ismailia	064
Luxor	095
Port Said	066
Sharm al-Shaykh	069
Suez	062
Directory enquiries:	
in Cairo	140
outside Cairo	10

Canada
454 Laurier Avenue, East Ottawa, Ontario K1N 6R3; tel: 613-234 4931;
http://egypt.embassyincanada.com
1 Place Sainte Marie, Suite 2617, Montreal, Quebec H3B 4S3; tel: 514-866 8455;
www.egyptianconsulatemontreal.org
UK
2 Lowndes Street, London SW1X 9ET (Visa Section); tel: 020-7235 9719; www.egyptianconsulate.co.uk
US
www.egyptembassy.net
3521 International Court NW, Washington DC 20008; tel: 202-895 5400
500 N Michigan Avenue, Suite 1900, Chicago IL60611; tel: 312-828 9162/64
1110 2nd Avenue, Suite 201, New York, NY 10022; tel: 212-759 7120

W ebsites

www.touregypt.net
Official site of Ministry of Tourism.
www.sis.gov.eg
Information on Egypt from the Egyptian State Information Service.
www.egypthotelsdb.com
Hotel information.
www.redsea-diving.info
Good information about the Red Sea and diving.
www.yallabina.com
Cairo nightlife, with listings, new openings, restaurant and bar reviews.
www.egy.com
Modern history and architecture by Samir Raafat.
www.guardians.net
Egyptology site run by the director of the Supreme Council of Antiquities, Zahi Hawass.
www.horus.ics.org.eg
Egypt and Egyptology, specially designed for children.
www.cairotimes.com
Cairo Times online.
www.animalmummies.com
Animal mummies in the Egyptian Museum in Cairo.
www.cairotourist.com
Virtual travel guide and listings.
www.egyptair.com.eg
www.thebanmappingproject.com

What to Bring

Almost everything you are likely to need can be bought in Cairo, but may be cheaper at home. Bring medications with you. A supply of plasters, antibiotics and remedies for diarrhoea may well come in handy. If you have a favourite sun lotion, toothpaste or shampoo, bring it with you.

L ANGUAGE

UNDERSTANDING THE LANGUAGE

Pronunciation

Vowels

' = glottal stop
a = a as in cat
aa = a as in RP English castle
e = e as in very
i = i as in if, stiff
ii = ee as in between
o = o as in boss
u = u as in RP put
uu = o as in fool

Consonants

(all emphatic consonants omitted):
All consonants are pronounced
individually and as they normally are
in English, with these exceptions:
kh = ch as in Scottish loch
sh = sh as in shut
gh = Arabic ghayn, usually described
as resembling a (guttural) Parisian r
q = Arabic qaf, frequently pronounced
in Cairo as a k or a glottal stop

Vocabulary

airport matár
boat mérkeb
car arabiyya, sayára
embassy sefára
hospital mustáshfa
hotel fúnduq
post office bosta
restaurant matáam
square maydan/midáan
street shaaria
right yemiin
left shemáal
and/or wa/walla
yes/no aywa/laa'
please/thank you minfadlak/shukran
big/little kibiir/sughayyar
good/bad kwáyyis/mish kwáyyis
here/there hena/henáak
hot/cold sukhn/baarid
many/few kitiir/olayyel
up/down fo' (foq)/taht

more/enough kamáan/kefáya
breakfast íftar
dinner asha
today innahárda
tomorrow bokra
yesterday embáareh
morning is-sobh
afternoon bad id-dohr
at night belayl
I/you ana/enta
he/she huwwa/hiyya
they/we humma/ehna

Common Expressions

Hello, welcome ahlan wa sahlan
Good morning sabáh-il-kheyr
Good evening masáal-kheyr
Goodbye mas-saláama
What is your name? íssmak eh?
(to a male); íssmik eh? **(to a
female)**
How are you? izzáyak **(to a male)**;
izzáyik **(to a female)**
I am fine kwayiss (M), kwayíssa (F)
Thank God il-hamdo li-lah (standard
reply)
   Often heard is "insha'Allah", which
means "God willing". The standard
reply to a casual "see you tomorrow",
for instance, is "insha'Allah".

Numerals

1 wáhid
2 itnéyn
3 taláatah
4 arbá
5 khamsa
6 sitta
7 séba
8 tamánya
9 tíssah
10 áshara
11 hedásher
12 itnásher
13 talatásher
14 arbatasher

15 khamastásher
16 sitásher
17 sabatásher
18 tamantásher
19 tissatásher
20 ashríin
30 talatíin
40 arbaíin
50 khamsíin
60 sittíin
70 sabaíin
80 tamaníin
90 tissaíin
100 miiya, miit

Money

money filúus
50 piastres khamsíin 'ersh (qersh)
1 pound wáhid guineh masri
change/no change fakka/mafiish
fakka
the bill al hesáb
this/that di/da
how much? bekáam?

Days/Months

Sunday yowm al had
Monday yowm al-itnéyn
Tuesday yowm it-taláat
Wednesday yowm al-árba
Thursday yowm al-khamíis
Friday yowm ig-góma
Saturday yowm is-sabt
January yanáyer
February febráyer
March máris
April abreel
May mayuu
June yuunyuu
July yiilyuu
August aghustus
September sibtímbir
October októbir
November nofímbir
December disímbir

FURTHER READING

General

Arnold, Dieter *The Encyclopaedia of Ancient Egyptian Architecture.* New York, 2003.
Biegman, Nicolas *Egypt: Moulids, Saints, Sufis.* London, 1990.
Bloom, Jonathan and Blair, Sheila *Islamic Arts.* London, 1997.
DoqqiDanielson, Virginia, *The Voice of Egypt: Umm Kulthum, Arabic Song and Egyptian Society in the Twentieth Century.* Chicago, 1997.
Egypt Almanac *The Encyclopedia of Modern Egypt.* Cairo, 2003. Excellent collection of articles by resident and local journalists and experts on all aspects of Egypt today.
Hassan, Fathy *Architecture for the Poor,* Cairo, 1989
Herodotus *The Histories.* London, 1996.
Hoath, Richard *Natural Selections: a Year of Egypt's Wildlife.* Cairo, 1992.
Livingstone, Marco *David Hockney Egyptian Journeys.* Cairo, 2001
Moorehead, Alan *The White Nile* London, 1973. *The Blue Nile.* London, 1984.
Roden, Claudia *A New Book of Middle Eastern Food.* London, 1986. **Rossant, Colette** *Apricots on the Nile, A Memoir with Recipes.* London, 2001.
Sanders, Sarite and Arnold, Dorothea *The Eternal Light of Egypt: A Photographic Journey.* London, 2008.
Sattin, Anthony *Lifting the Veil.* London, 1988; *The Pharaoh's Shadow – Travels in Modern and Ancient Egypt.* London, 2000; *The Gates of Africa.* London, 2003.
Shaw, Ian *The Oxford History of Ancient Egypt.* London, 2003.

Cairo

Antoniou, Jim *A Walk Through the Islamic City.* Cairo, 1998; *Museum with No Frontiers, Mamluk Art, The Splendour and Magic of the Sultans.* Cairo, 2001.
DoqqiBehrens-Abouseif, Doris *Islamic Architecture in Cairo.* Cairo, 1996.
DoqqiCooper, Artemis *Cairo in the War, 1939–45.* London, 1989.
Golia, Maria *Cairo City of Sand.* London, 2004.

DoqqiLane, Edward William *Manners and Customs of the Modern Egyptians.* London, 1833–5.
Miles, Hugh *Playing Cards In Cairo: Mint Tea, Tarneeb and Tales of the City.* London, 2008. A story about falling in love in and with Cairo.
Muntti, Cynthia *Paris along the Nile – Architecture in Cairo from the Belle Epoque.* Cairo, 1999.
Raymond, André *Cairo.* New York, 2002.
Rodenbeck, Max *Cairo, The City Victorious.* London, 1998.
Shaath, Randa *Under the Same Sky: Cairo.* Rotterdam/Barcelona, 2004. Cairo seen by this talented young Cairene photographer.
DoqqiWilliams, Caroline *Islamic Monuments in Cairo: a Practical Guide.* Cairo, 2002.

Alexandria

Bowman, Alan K. *Egypt After the Pharaohs: 332BC–AD642, from Alexander to the Arab Conquest.* London, 1986.
Empereur, Jean-Yves *Alexandria Rediscovered.* London, 1998
Forster, E.M. *Alexandria, a History and Guide.* London, 1986.
Grant, Michael *Cleopatra: a Biography.* London 1992.
Haag, Michael *Alexandria, City of Durrell, Forster and Cavafy.* London, 1998.
Haag, Michael *Alexandria, City of Memory.* London, 2004.
Pinchin, Jane Lagudis *Alexandria Still: Forster, Durrell and Cavafy.* Cairo, 1989.
Smart, Alan *Alexandria Lost, Three Stories.* Alexandria, 2008.
Woodsworth, Nicholas *The Liquid Continent. A Mediterranean Trilogy Volume I: Alexandria.* London, 2008.

The Oases

Abed, Wael *The Other Egypt, Travels in No-Man's Land.* Cairo, 1998.
Bagnold, R.A. *Libyan Sands.* London, 1987.
Fakhry, Ahmed *The Oases of Egypt.* Cairo.
Vivian, Cassandra *The Western Desert of Egypt: An Explorer's Handbook.* Cairo, 2004.

Sinai

Buckles, Guy *Dive Sites of the Red Sea.* Cairo, 1995.
Carletti, Alessandro and Andrea Ghisotti *Red Sea: Diving Guide.* Cairo, 1994.
Jahn, Wolfgang and Rosel *Sinai and the Red Sea.* Cairo, 1997.**Doqqi**

Ancient Egypt

Andreu, G. *Egypt in the Age of the Pyramids.* London, 1997.
Baines, John and Jaromir Malek *Atlas of Ancient Egypt.* Oxford, 1980.
Champollion, Jean-François *Egyptian Diaries, How One Man Solved the Mysteries of the Nile.* London, 2001.
Clayton, Peter *The Rediscovery of Ancient Egypt.* London, 1990; *Chronicle of the Pharaohs.* London, 1994.
Dodson, Aidan and Ikram, Salima *The Tomb in Ancient Egypt: Royal and Private Sepulchres from the Early Dynastic Period to the Romans.* London, 2008.
Lehner, Mark *The Complete Pyramids.* London, 2008.
Reeves, Nicholas and Wilkinson, Richard *The Complete Valley of the Kings.* London/Cairo 1996. *The Complete Valley of the Kings: Tombs and Treasures of Egypt's Greatest Pharaohs.* London, 2008.
Shaw, Ian *The Oxford History of Ancient Egypt.* London, 2003.
Tyldesley, Joyce *Pyramids, The Real Story Behind Egypt's Most Ancient Monuments.* London, 2003.
Verner, Miroslav *The Pyramids, Their Archaeology and History.* London, 2002.
Weeks, Kent *The Illustrated Guide to Luxor Tombs, Temples and Museums.* Cairo, 2005.
Wilkinson, Toby *Dictionary of Ancient Egypt.* London, 2005.

Travellers

Duff Gordon, Lucy *Letters from Egypt, 1862–69.* London, 1986.
Edwards, Amelia *A Thousand Miles Up the Nile.* London, 1982.
Flaubert, Gustave *Flaubert in Egypt.* London, 1983.
Frank, Katherine *Lucie Duff Gordon, a Passage to Egypt.* London, 1994.

ABOVE: a tea man on the corniche in Alexandria.

Ghosh, Amitav *In an Antique Land.* London, 1992.
Manley, Deborah *A Traveller's Anthology.* London, 1991.
Manley, Deborah and Abdel-Hakim, Sahar *Egypt Through Writers' Eyes.* London, 2007.
Stewart, Stanley *Old Serpent Nile: A Journey to the Source,* London, 1990.

Fiction

Abdullah, Yahya Taher *The Mountain of Green Tea and Other Stories.* Cairo, 1991.
Al Aswany, Alaa *The Yacoubian Building.* London, 2007. Superb evocative novel about the lives of several families sharing one apartment building in downtown Cairo.
Al-Khamissi, *Khaled Taxi.* London, 2008. Wonderful short stories based on conversations with taxi drivers in Cairo.
Al-Sharqawi, Abdel Rahman *Egyptian Earth.* London, 1990.
Belben, Rosalind *Our Horses in Egypt.* London, 2007. A novel set in wartime Cairo.
Cavafy, Constantine *Collected Poems.* London, 1994.
Chatham, Maxim *The Cairo Diary.* London, 2007.
Durrell, Lawrence *The Alexandria Quartet.* London, 1968.
Ghali, Waguih *Beer in the Snooker Club.* London, 1987.
DoqqiMahfouz, Naguib *The Cairo Trilogy, Miramar* and many others. Cairo/London.
Nassib, Selim *I Loved You for Your Voice.* London, 2007.
el Saadawi, Nawal *Woman at Point Zero.* London, 1983.

Serageldin, Samia *The Cairo House.* London, 2004.
Soueif, Ahdaf *In the Eye of the Sun,* London, 1992; *Aisha,* London, 1996; *The Map of Love,* London, 2001.Doqqi

Other Insight Guides

Other **Insight Guides** in this region include *The Nile, Cairo, Jordan,*

Send Us Your Thoughts

We do our best to ensure the information in our books is as accurate and up-to-date as possible. The books are updated on a regular basis using local contacts, who painstakingly add, amend and correct as required. However, some details (such as telephone numbers and opening times) are liable to change, and we are ultimately reliant on our readers to put us in the picture.

We welcome your feedback, especiallly on your experience of using the book on the road. Maybe we recommended a hotel that you liked (or another that you didn't), or you came across a great bar or new attraction that we missed.

We will acknowledge all contributions, and we'll offer an Insight Guide to the best letters received.

Please write to us at:
Insight Guides
PO Box 7910
London SE1 1WE
Or email us at:
insight@apaguide.co.uk

Israel, Jerusalem, Syria & Lebanon and *Oman & the UAE.* Each contains the same standard of insightful text and lavish photography as this book.

In addition, Insight publishes a series of **Step By Step** guides, itinerary-based guidebooks, whose authors are usually resident in the destination. Their aim is to help visitors make the most of a place in a limited amount of time, and they include a large fold-out map with plotted routes. Step By Step guides to destinations in North Africa and the Middle East include Marrakesh and Dubai.

New in the Insight range of guidebooks, **Smart Guides** is a listings-based series. Among the titles published so far are London, Paris, New York, Copenhagen, Las Vegas, Sydney, Venice and Hong Kong.

Insight also publishes **Fleximaps**, a series of hard-wearing laminated maps, including ones on Egypt and Cairo.

ART & PHOTO CREDITS

ABACA/PA Photos 33BR, 91
AFP/Getty Images 28, 99
AISA 53
akg-images 49, 50, 81, 200, 222T, 228, 244R, 245
Stefano Amantini/4Corners Images 225
Ancient Art & Architecture Collection 44
Ancient Egypt Picture Library 36L&R, 39
Apa Photo Agency 8TR, 31T, 34, 38, 42L, 43, 48, 65, 72L&R, 73, 75, 79, 82, 83, 85, 86, 88L, 96R, 130L
AP/PA Photos 89, 90R, 94
Arco Images GmbH/Alamy 212
Jon Arnold Images Ltd/Alamy 228T
The Art Archive 10L, 30TR, 32B, 35, 54, 58, 67, 68, 70, 71, 76, 77
Pete Bennett/APA 43B, 145T
Bettmann/Corbis 33BL, 87, 90L
Gary Blake/Alamy 205
Chris Bradley/APA 1, 2/3, 3B, 6L&B, 6/7T, 7CTL, CBL, CR&BL, 19C, 20, 22R, 24, 25, 29, 30TL, 32T, 64, 69, 78, 102, 104R, 109, 110, 120, 121L, 124, 125, 127, 128, 129B, 130R, 131T&B, 132, 133(all), 134T&B, 136T&B, 137, 138L&R, 139, 140, 141, 143, 145, 146, 147, 148, 149R, 150L&R, 151T&B, 152L&R, 153T&B, 155T&B, 162, 163, 164, 165, 166, 167, 168L&R, 169T&B, 170T&B, 171, 173, 174, 175, 180, 181, 183T&B, 189, 192L, 195, 229T, 255T, 257, 258T&B, 259, 260, 272, 274T, 275T, 276T&B, 277T&B, 278/279, 280, 281, 283, 284T&B, 285, 287, 288, 289, 290, 291, 292, 293T&B, 294, 295(all), 296T&B, 297T&B, 298, 299, 302, 320, 322
The Bridgeman Art Library 59, 60
John Carr/The Travel Library 239, 245T
Christie's Colour Library 52R
Gary Cook/Alamy 217T
Corbis 7TR, 9TL
Danita Delimont/Alamy 213
Colin Dutton/SIME-4Corners Images 224T
Egyptian Tourist Board/Hemis.fr 4T, 6CR, 12/13, 18, 30B,

118/119, 202/203, 204, 207, 216, 217, 227, 231, 234, 242, 244L
Mary Evans Picture Library 40, 84
Eye Ubiquitous/Julia Waterlow 191
Werner Forman Archive 212T
Fotógrafos Oronoz 61
Gamma/Eyedea/Camerapress 97L
Patrick Godeau 107
Albano Guati 14/15, 16/17, 22L, 26, 41, 45, 56/57, 62, 63R, 108, 111, 114/115, 116/117, 142, 144, 230T, 238, 248/249, 255, 286T
Thomas Hartwell 103, 104L, 105
Jim Henderson/Alamy 194T, 198R
Johanna Huber/SIME-4Corners Images 210, 246
iStockphoto.com 4B, 5B, 11B, 199T, 200C, 211T, 214T, 215, 218, 232T, 241
The Kobal Collection 92/93
Axel Krause/Apa cover, flaps and spine(all), 7BR, 8TL, 9TR&B, 10T, 11T, 19T&B, 27, 31BR, 51R, 55, 62B, 66, 106, 121R, 128T, 129T, 135, 139T, 140T, 149L, 154, 156, 165T, 178, 179, 182, 184, 185T&B, 186T&B, 187T&B, 188, 192R, 193, 195T, 196T, 199, 208, 211, 219, 221, 223T, 225T, 230, 232B, 233, 252, 253, 256, 260T, 261, 262, 263, 265, 266, 267(all), 268, 273, 274B, 286, 308, 313, 324, 325, 326, 330
Lehnart & Landrock Succ. 63L
The London Art Archive/Alamy 196, 220
James Morris/Axiom 229
Richard Nowitz 275
Werner Otto/Alamy 198L
Photolibrary 224
Picture Contact/Alamy 197
Pictures Colour Library 222, 223BL&BR, 243
Polaris/eyevine 23
Aline Princet/StockFood UK 227T
Sarah Louise Ramsay 8B, 21, 42R, 50B, 129CR, 168T, 172, 209, 214, 215T, 233T, 240T, 247T&B, 307, 309, 310, 311, 317, 335
Reimer/laif/Camerapress 10BR
Rex Features 96L
Sipa Press/Rex Features 98
Strand/Everett/Rex Features 97R
Topfoto 52L, 201

Sandro Vannini/Corbis 194
Cassandra Vivian 240B
David White/Alamy 213T
Justin Williams/Rex Features 95
World Illustrated/Photoshot 31BL
Joseph Yogerst 51L, 264

PICTURE SPREADS

46/47: Ancient Art & Architecture Collection 46BR, 47TR&B; **The Ancient Egypt Picture Library** 46BL, 47CL; **The Art Archive** 46/47T; **Axiom** 46CR
100/101: **Gamma/Eyedea/Camerapress** 100BR; imagebroker/Alamy 101B; iStockphoto.com 100BL; **Peter Mumford/Alamy** 100/101T; **Starstock/Photoshot** 101CL; **WpN/Photoshot** 101TR
112/113: akg-images 112BL&BR, 113TR, BL&BR; **The Print Collector/Alamy** 112/113T; Topfoto 113CL
158/159: The Art Archive 158BR, 159TR; Chris Bradley/APA 158/159T, 159BR; **Mike Nelson/epa/Corbis** 159CL
160/161: all Chris Bradley/APA
176/177: Chris Bradley/APA 176/177T, 176BL&BR, 177CL; **Mary Evans Picture Library** 177TR; iStockphoto.com 177B; **Tony Stone Worldwide** 176CR
242/243: The Ancient Egypt Picture Library 236BR; **The Gallery Collection/Corbis** 242/243T; iStockphoto.com 237BL&BR; **Planet Earth Pictures** 236CR&CB, 237TR
280/281: all Stephane Compoint/Sygma
300/301: Dan Burton/drr.net 301CL; **Emmler/laif/Camerapress** 301TR; iStockphoto.com 300BR; **Photolibrary** 300/301T, 301BR; Reimer/laif/Camerapress 300C

Map Production Colourmap Scanning

© 2009 Apa Publications GmbH & Co. Verlag KG (Singapore branch)

Production: Linton Donaldson

INDEX

Numbers in italics refer to photographs